CASPIC SEA

MITANNI

ASSYRIA

NAHARIN

hemish

Haran

Ninive

Keilah

Arrapkha

Ashur   Nuzi

Terqa

Hamath

Qatna

adesh   Tadmor

Mari

bo-hamath

Eshnunna

Euphrates   · Sippar

s

BABYLONIA SUMER

Babylon   Kish

Tigris

Shushan (Susa)

ELAM

roth

Nippur

h

Isin   Lagash

Uruk   Larsa

ath-ammon

Ur

Eridu

Tema

THE ANCIENT EAST
IN THE SECOND MILLENIUM B.C.E.

Locality mentioned in the Bible................Hazor

Ancient locality mentioned in other sources.........Isin

Modern name ....[Beni Ḥasan]

A jug of the Israelite Period with a tall neck, trefoil rim, red-slipped and burnished
(Photo No. 281 in the book).

ANCIENT POTTERY

MASSADA PRESS LTD. JERUSALEM - RAMAT GAN

OF THE HOLY LAND

FROM ITS BEGINNINGS IN THE NEOLITHIC PERIOD
TO THE END OF THE IRON AGE

BY

RUTH AMIRAN

WITH THE ASSISTANCE OF

PIRHIYA BECK

AND

UZZA ZEVULUN

THE HEBREW EDITION OF
ANCIENT POTTERY OF THE HOLY LAND
WAS PUBLISHED BY
THE BIYALIK INSTITUTE
AND THE ISRAEL EXPLORATION SOCIETY

Designed by: ARYE BEN-DAVID

TABLE OF CONTENTS

LIST OF ACKNOWLEDGEMENTS

We are indebted to various institutions and persons for their kindness in providing photographs, or for kind permission to reproduce vessels in their possession.

Since the majority of the illustrations are of vessels in the possession of the Israel Department of Antiquities (IDA), some of which of recent excavations, we wish to express our thanks to its director and the following excavators:

Mr. P. Bar Adon: Nos. 52, 53, 64, 66, 67, 68, 69, 70, 71.

Dr. I. Ben Dor: Nos. 115, 116, 117, 118, 124.

Dr. M. Dothan: Nos. 24, 25, 27, 38, 94.

Mr. A. Drunks: No. 106.

Mr. R. Gofna: No. 99.

Dr. O. Negbi: Nos. 110, 111.

Institute of Archaeology, Hebrew University, Jerusalem (HU): Nos. 19, 21, 35, 39, 40, 41, 42, 43, 48, 49, 50, 65, 76, 77, 78, 96, 109, 162, 167, 180, 191, 224, 228, 244, 250, 258, 260, 262, 263, 264, 265, 266, 282, 285 (photographed·by A. Volk).

The Hazor Expedition — of which the three authors were members — and its director Prof. Y. Yadin: Nos. 113, 208, 215, 217, 220, 221, 222, 225, 236, 245, 246, 255, 256, 280, 300, 341.

Ecole Biblique et Archéologique Française de Jérusalem.

Tell Farach (N) Expedition, and its director Père R. de Vaux: Nos. 12, 22, 23, 26, 28, 33, 37, 104, 154, 278.

Mission Archéologique Française en Israel and its director M.J. Perrot: Nos. 11, 14, 15, 17.

Israel Museum, Archaeological Section (IMA): Nos. 81, 281.

Oriental Institute, University of Chicago: Nos. 92, 95, 108, 127, 138, 146, 147, 148, 149, 150, 153, 342, 350.

Prof. P. Delougaz: No. 36, from the yet unpublished excavation at Nahal Tavor.

Pontifical Biblical Institute, Jerusalem: Nos. 123, 155, 156.

Welcome Marston Expedition to Lachish, and Miss O. Tufnell: Nos. 130, 247.

Metropolitan Museum of Art, New York: Nos. 131, 172, 205, 206, 207, 283.

Institute of Archaeology, University of London: Nos. 3, 226, and 165.

Petrie Collection of the Department of Egyptology — University College, London: No. 59.

Ashmolean Museum, Oxford: No. 58.

Musée du Louvre, Paris: Nos. 29, 30, 31, 32, 122, 151.

Agora Museum, Athens: No. 132.

Dagon Collection and Dr. R. Recht, Haifa: No. 80.

Mr. M. Dayan: Nos. 170, 171.

Photographers: Mr. S. J. Schweig, Mrs. Bieberkraut, Mr. A. Volk, Mr. M. Pan, Mr. H. Burger, Mr. Rothenberg and Miss P. Dorn.

ABBREVIATIONS

AAA	*Annnals of Archaeology and Anthropology.* Liverpool.
AASOR	*Annual of the American Schools of Oriental Research.*
ABSA	*Annual of the British School at Athens.*
Abydos	Petrie, W.M.F., *Abydos*, I–II. London, 1902–1903.
ADAJ	*Annual of the Department of Antiquities of Jordan.*
Ade	Stekelis, M., *Les monuments megalithiques de Palestine* (les fouilles d'el-Adeimeh). Paris, 1935.
AG I–IV	Petrie, W.F., *Ancient Gaza*, I–IV. London, 1931–1934.
AG V	Petrie, W.F., *City of Shepherd Kings* and Murray, M.A., *Ancient Gaza*, V. London, 1952.
AJA	*American Journal of Archaeology.*
Anat. St.	*Anatolian Studies.*
APEF	*Annual of the Palestine Exploration Fund.*
AS	Grant, E., and Wright, G.E., *Rumeileh, Ain Shems Excavations*, I–V. Haverford, 1931–1939.
Astrom	Astrom, P., *The Middle Cypriote Bronze Age.* Lund, 1957.
Ay	Marquet-Krause, J., *Les fouilles de ʿAy* (*Et-Tell*). Paris, 1949.
BASOR	*Bulletin of the American Schools of Oriental Research.*
BBSAJ	*Bulletin of the British School of Archaeology in Jerusalem.*
Beth Shemesh	Grant, E., *Beth Shemesh.* Haverford, 1929.
Beth Yerah	Bar-Adon, P., *Report on the Excavations at Beth Yerah* (unpublished ms.).
BMB	*Bulletin du Musée de Byrouth.*
BS	*Beth-Shan Excavations*, I, II, 1, and III by A. Rowe; II, 2, and IV by G.M. Fitzgerald. Philadelphia, 1930–1940.
Byblos et l'Egypte	P. Montet. *Byblos et l'Egypte*, Cairo, 1928.
CoA	*The City of Akhenaten, Excavations at Tell el-Amarna.*
COWA	Ehrich, R.W. (ed.), *Chronologies in Old World Archaeology*, Chicago, 1965.
CPP	Duncan, J.G., *Corpus of Palestinian Pottery.* London 1930.
EEP	Glueck, N., *Explorations in Eastern Palestine*, I–IV. In: *AASOR* XIV, XV, XVIII–XIX, XXV–XXVIII (1934, 1935, 1939, 1951).
EI	*Eretz-Israel, Archaeological, Historical and Geographical Studies*, published by the Israel Exploration Society (Hebrew).
Gerar	Petrie, W.M.F., *Gerar.* London, 1928.
Gezer	Macalister, R.A.S., *The Excavation of Gezer*, I–III. London, 1911–1912.
Gh.	*Teleilat Ghassul*, I–II. A. Mallon, R. Koeppel, R. Neuvill. Rome 1934, 1940.
Gibeon	Pritchard, J.B., *Hebrew Inscriptions and Stamps from Gibeon.* Philadelphia, 1959.
Grace	Grace, V.R., "The Canaanite Jar," in *The Aegean and the Near East* (*Studies Presented to Hetty Goldman*), S.S. Weinberg (ed.), New York, 1956.
Graeberfeld	H. Bonnet, *Graeberfeld bei Abusir*, Leipzig, 1928.
Hazor	*Hazor*, I, II, III–IV Plates by Y. Yadin, Y. Aharoni, R. Amiran, M. Dothan, T. Dothan, I. Dunayevsky, J. Perrot. Jerusalem, 1958–1961.
HIC	Petrie, W.M.F., *Hyksos and Israelite Cities*, London 1906.
HU	Hebrew University, Jerusalem.
IDA	Israel Department of Antiquities.
IEJ	*Israel Exploration Journal.*
ILN	*Illustrated London News.*
IMA	The Israel Museum, Jerusalem, Archaeological Section.
JEA	*Journal of Egyptian Archaeology.*
Jer.	Kenyon, K.M., *Excavations at Jericho*, I: *The Tombs Excavated in 1952–4.* London 1960.
JNES	*Journal of Near Eastern Studies.*
JPOS	*Journal of the Palestine Oriental Society.*
Kerma	Reisner, G.A., *Excavations at Kerma*, Parts IV–V. Cambridge, Mass., 1923.
La.	Tufnell, O.C. Inge. L. Harding, *Lachish* (*Tell ed-Duweir*), II, III, IV. Oxford, 1940, 1953, 1958.
Lahun	W.M. Flinders Petrie, *Lahuh II*, London, 1923.

Meg. I	Lamon, S., and Shipton, G.M., *Megiddo I.* Chicago, 1939.
Meg. II	Loud, G., *Megiddo II.* Chicago, 1948.
Meg. Cult	May, H.G., *Material Remains of the Megiddo Cult.* Chicago, 1935.
Meg. T.	Guy, P.L.O., *Megiddo Tombs.* Chicago, 1938.
Meg. Mut.	Schumacher, G., *Tell el-Mutesellim*, I. (Leipzig, 913.)
MJ (BS)	*The Museum Journal*, University of Pennsylvania, 1935: G.M. FitzGerald, Beth-Shan: Earliest Pottery.
Nagel	Nagel, G., *La ceramique du Nouvel Empire à Deir el Medineh*, I. Le Caire, 1938.
Olivet	Saller, S.J., *The Excavations at Dominus Flevit (Mount Olivet, Jerusalem), Part II: The Jebusite Burial Place*, Jerusalem, 1964.
PBI	Pontifical Biblical Institute, Jerusalem.
PEQ	*Palestine Exploration Quarterly.*
PMB	*Palestine Museum, Jerusalem, Bulletin.*
PPEB	Wright, G.E., *The Pottery of Palestine to the End of the Bronze Age.* New Haven, 1937.
Qasile	Maisler (Mazar), B., The Excavations at Tell Qasile, Preliminary Report, in *IEJ* I (1950–51), pp. 61 ff., 125., 194 ff.
QDAP	*Quarterly of the Department of Antiquities in Palestine.*
RB	*Revue Biblique.*
Sediment	Petrie, W.M.F., and Brunton, G., *Sediment*, I–II. London, 1924.
Sellin-Watzinger	Sellin, E., and Watzinger, C., *Jericho.* Leipzig, 1913.
SS I–III	Crowfoot, J.M., K.M., Kenyon, E.L. Sukenik, *Samaria-Sebaste*, I–III. London, 1938, 1942, 1957.
Stra. Comp.	Schaeffer ,C.F.A., *Stratigraphie comparée et chronologie de l'Asie Occidentale.* London, 1948.
Stubbings	F.H. Stubbings, *Mycenaean Pottery from the Levant*, Cambridge, 1951.
Ta'annek	Sellin, E., *Tell Ta'annek*, Wien, 1904.
TAH	Hamilton, R.W., Excavations at Tell Abu Hawam, in *QDAP* IV (1953),
TBM I–III	Albright, W.F., *The Excavation of Tell Beit Mirsim*, I, I A, II, III, in *AASOR* XII, XIII (pp. 55–127), XVII, XXI–XXII (1932, 1933, 1938, 1943).
TN I–II	*Tell en-Nasbeh*, I, by C.C. McCown; II, J.C. Wampler, Berkeley and New Haven, 1947.
Up. Gal.	Aharoni, Y., *The Settlement of the Israelite Tribes in Upper Galilee.* Jerusalem, 1957 (Hebrew).

CHRONOLOGICAL TABLE

The Neolithic Period (Pottery Neolithic)	6th and 5th mill, B.C.
The Chalcolithic Period	4th mill. B.C.
The Early Bronze I (EB I) Period	3100–2900
The Early Bronze II (EB II) Period	2900–2650
The Early Bronze III (EB II) Period	2650–2350
The Early Bronze IV (EB IV) Period	2350–2250/2200
The Middle Bronze I (MB I) Period	2250/2200–2000/1950
The Middle Bronze II A (MB IIA) Period	2000/1950–1730
The Middle Bronze II B–C (MB II B–C) Period	1730–1550
The Late Bronze I (LB I) Period	1550–1400
The Late Bronze II A (LB IIA) Period	1400–1300
The Late Bronze II B (LB IIB) Period	1300–1200
The Iron I Period	1200–1000
The Iron II A Period	1000–900
The Iron II B Period	900–800
The Iron II C Period	800–586

INTRODUCTION

In 1890 Petrie conducted the first excavation of a tell in this country, after accumulating much knowledge and experience in ten years of digging in Egypt. While working at Tell el-Hesy,[1] Petrie recognized the chronological value of potsherds in stratigraphical excavation and established a basic scale of dated sherds. Every field or desk-work undertaken since then has contributed to a continuous progress in the study of pottery, and other aspects of archaeology as well.

Following a general trend of the 19th century,[2] still lingering on in the current one, several 'Corpora' of ancient pottery have been published. However, the designation of 'corpus' includes two basically different kinds of works: a true corpus, and another group of works that can be more accurately named 'type-corpora.' The *Corpus vasorum antiquorum*,[3] is true to its definition. It was planned to present all the pottery of the classical age existing in collections throughout the world, hence, the very nature of the work prevents its ever being completed, since all the additional acquisitions made by museums or collections require the publication of new suppliments. All the other corpora of pottery: Petrie's two corpora of Egyptian pottery (the *Corpus of Prehistoric Pottery of Egypt*[4] and the *Corpus of Proto-Dynastic Pottery*[5]), the *Corpus of Palestinian Pottery*[6] by Petrie-Duncan, Fisher's[7] unfinished corpus of Palestinian pottery, as well as the system devised by Delougaz[8] for the pottery excavated in the Diyala region, belong to the second, type-corpus group.

The main purpose of this latter kind of corpus, the idea of which seems to have originated with Petrie, was to classify pottery into a series of main types. Naturally such an analysis can be effected only if satisfactory quantities of material have become available. Moreover, since the simple determination of the criteria lying at the basis of type-corpora was a

---

1. W. M. Flinders Petrie, *Tell el Hesy* (*Lachish*), London, 1891.
2. Cf. e.g. CIG = *Corpus inscriptionum graecarum*, the first volume of which appeared in 1877, and the last in 1928 (having been changed into *Inscriptiones Graecae*).
   CIL = *Corpus inscriptionum latinarum*, the first volume of which appeared in 1869, and it still goes on.
   CIS = *Corpus inscriptionum semiticarum*, the first volume appeared in 1881, and is still going on.
3. For the history of this Corpus cf. Jan W. Crous, *Konkordanz zum CVA*, Roma, 1942. It started to appear in 1921, and until 1942 there appered 74 volumes. It is still going on.
4. W. M. Flinders Petrie, *Corpus of Prehistoric Pottery and Palettes*, London, 1921, being the conclusive form of Petrie's idea of the relative sequence of the prehistoric cultures of Egypt, which he started in: W. M. Flinders Petrie and J. E. Quibell, *Naqada and Ballas* 1895, London, 1896; and W. M. Flinders Petrie and A. C. Mace, *Diospolis Parva*, the *Cemeteries of Abadiyeh and Hu*, London, 1901.
5. W. M. Flinders Petrie, *Ceremonial Slate Palettes and Corpus of Proto-Dynastic Pottery*, London, 1953, which was ready for publication in 1914.
6. J. G. Duncan, *Corpus of Dated Palestinian Pottery*, London, 1930. It is based both on the material excavated by Petrie at Tell Jemmeh, and on his classification.
7. Cf. S. Fisher, *A Corpus of Palestinian Pottery*, has never been published owing to the death of the author. The MS is kept in the archives of the Oriental Institute of the University of Chicago. Disregarding chronology, the whole pottery is classified into groups according to the function of the vessels.
8. P. Delougaz, *Pottery of the Diyala Region*, Chicago, 1952.

matter of subjective appreciation, these works reflected the different views of various scholars. Only Fisher's uncompleted corpus and Delougaz's system display any efforts to reduce, if not eliminate, the subjective factor in the classification of ancient pottery, and their attempts to adopt an objective, strictly impersonal mathematic-geometrical line of approach. Personally we consider that the day when non-subjective data about pottery will be fed to computers is at hand, or has already come.

The present book is to be assigned to the second, type-corpora group, in the light of the distinction discussed. We would like however, to emphasize one important feature which makes it basically different from the works reflecting the Petrie–Duncan–Fisher conception of the study of ancient pottery. The whole conception and structure of this book is axed upon the chronological factor — considered by us of primary importance — but which is totally and intentionally left aside by the latter scholars. The result of the fact that Petrie-Duncan based their classification on pure(?!) morphological criteria,[9] cutting through all the archeological periods, was that they distinguished only 100 main types in the total range of Palestinian pottery. The importance we accorded to the chronological factor has dictated the division of the book into chapters covering archaeological periods, without insisting, nevertheless, upon an exaggerated rigidity of that framework. Thus, in some chapters two or three periods are discussed simultaneously, while paying due consideration to the specific character of each period's pottery.

Our decision to classify pottery within the chronological framework of the chapters according to such subtle distinctions as both form and use, style and cultural affinity, has been the fruit of much reflection. This interplay of individual character and features specific of each period has permitted the further division of the chapters into their principal components. According to these criteria the 101, or more accurately 102 plates (since the Mycenaean pottery illustrated here by photographs instead of drawings is to be considered a plate) do not present types, but 102 subjects of this country's pottery. The majority of these subjects (goups or families), are determined by their fundamental aspect, namely form-use. However, a certain number of them has been gauged by other criteria, such as decorative style, geographical units or commercial function. We experience a certain satisfaction at having been able to "establish" such stylistic groups as 'chocolate and white' or 'palm-tree and ibex.' Moreover, it is for the first time that geographical subdivisions such as North (Israel) South (Judah) have been adopted in the classification of the whole Iron Age pottery. This experiment was undertaken under the impression of the report about Iron Age material found at Hazor which the authors had been preparing during the years immediately preceding the writing of this work. Thus historically significant factors, like international relations,

---

9. A minute critical study of this corpus is of course out of place here. The following questions, however, will clarify that our main criticism is concerned with the principles and logic of its classification system: a) Why are the bowls divided into the classes 2–16 and 18–29? b) On what principle are the jars divided into the classes 31, 41–48? c) Why a certain detail is assigned to class 22 J and not to class 22 L? d) What is the distinguishing element between 22 B and 22 N? e) Why are the bowls with horizontal handles (a feature clearly of Mycenaean-Phylistine origin) divided into many classes?

14

have prompted us to establish such groups as the 'Abydos ware' or the 'Canaanite Jar.' Whatever the satisfaction, we are nevertheless perfectly aware that the classification according to subjects (or groups, or families) attempted in this book is not final, but subject to further deep reflection.

Our main effort, which concentrated upon sifting all the archaeological reports on the search for the main types within every group (or subject, or family) and the gradation of the numerous variants encountered according to their internal importance, proved itself a most rewarding toil. However, it would be pretentious to hope that *every* plate in this book illustrates what we consider an ideal presentation of the subject, and all the main types with their most important variations. The achievement of any degree of perfection in this matter would require much more research work. Although the present corpus deals only with daily use vessels, we considered it suitable and interesting to conclude the description of this long series of household utensils with the mention that other objects — instrumental in different realms of human life — were also made of clay. To illustrate this point a number of photographs and drawings of vessels and stands, apparently instrumental in the cultic life of ancient people throughout the periods discussed, have been included in this book. No figurines or zoomorphic vessels are presented, although they also seem to have played some part in the cultic aspect of man's daily life. Neither have we presented clay made ossuaries, specimens of jewelry, nor pottery writting utensils, etc.

The order of presentation adopted within every period chapter follows the same line: Bowl, Chalice, Goblet, Krater, Cooking-pot, Pithos, Jar, Amphoriskos, Jug, Juglet, Pilgrim-flask, Pyxis, and lamp. Here is the place to point out that Mrs. Piri Yarden, who did all the graphic work from copying drawings to the execution of all the plates in this book, had to overcome one great difficulty: the lack of uniformity in the scales used by the various pulications. We have solved that problem by adopting the scale system used by the Megiddo expedition: all drawings are 1:5, 1:10 (or 1:2, for very small objects). Nevertheless, we consider that a uniformization of that technical detail would be very useful. We also followed the convention of the Megiddo publications in designating red slip or painting by diagonal hatching.

The origin of the present book is the booklet bearing the same title, published in Hebrew and English in 1958 under the auspices of the Department of Antiquities, at the suggestion of Prof. S. Yeivin, then its Director, and Mrs. Ina Pommeranz, the Scientific Secretary. The idea of turning that booklet into a full book belongs to my friend, Mr. Y. Aviram, Honorary Secretary of the Israel Exploration Society. The Hebrew original of the present book, published by the Biyalik Institute and the Israel Exploration Society in 1963, was conceived and written in the years 1959–61, and was intended to reflect the state reached by the knowledge of Palestinian pottery in the late fifties. The design of this Hebrew version of the book was the work of Mr. S. Y. Schweig, a distinguished archaeological photographer. Since the preparation of the English version began as early as 1964, it is perforce almost identical with the Hebrew original, except the emendations or changes brought to several plates and the corresponding adjustment of the text.

To conclude we would like to express our deep gratitude to Mrs. Ina

Pommeranz whose work the English translation of this book is. Further we would like to express our gratitude to Mrs. Miriam Man who translated and checked all the descriptive lists accompanying the plates. The authors consider themselves infinitely indebted to all the excavators who kindly granted permission to draw from their publications the material for the plates and the photographs without which such a book cannot be written. We feel equally indebted to our colleagues Mrs. Miriam Tadmor, Mrs. Miriam Man, Prof. Y. Aharoni, Mr. A. Eitan and Mr. J. Perrot who helped us greatly during numerous discussions. The final result of our work, this book, is dedicated to Prof. W. F. Albright whose impact as teacher of Palestinian archaeology and history, and whose impulse toward a greater and deeper understanding of the ancient Near East, permeates every quarter of this book.

Personally, I wish to express my appreciation to my friends Dr. Pirhiya Beck, Mrs. Uzza Zevulun and Mrs. Piri Yarden, for their inspiring and fruitful cooperation during the many days we worked at this book.

To my husband, David Amiran, who carried much of our daily burden, I am ever thankful.

Ruth Amiran

Jerusalem, May 1969.

CHAPTER ONE

THE NEOLITHIC PERIOD

The phase of civilization in which pottery first makes its appearance is preceded by a long history of settled life. The last stage of this history, the Pre-Pottery Neolithic B period (abbreviated PPNB), has been found in village-farming communities all over Palestine. "Well-built houses with large rectangular rooms" characterize the Jericho[1] settlement of this period. Of intrinsic interest to the subject is the fact that "Walls and floors are covered by a continuous coat of fine plaster, cream or pinkish in color, and burnished to a high finish." Mud-brick walls and plastered mud floors with basin-like plaster-lined hollows, as well as floors, clay figurines, plastered human skulls, and colored and burnished floors — all these are manifestations of man's dawning awareness of the usefulness and handiness of clay, a natural material available at everyone's doorstep.

There are two main theories concerning the appearance of pottery and the character of its first manifestations in Palestine. Both are as yet only working hypotheses:

a) The ability to make vessels of clay developed locally, and grew out of the PPNB features mentioned above. This theory assumes that, like the cultivation of cereals and the domestication of animals a few thousand years earlier, the 'invention' or 'discovery' that clay can be made into pottery, that is, hardened by firing it, developed independently over a long period in various regions or sites of Western Asia.

b) This knowledge was introduced — fully developed — from outside.

Two points have to be explained away if we are to accept the second theory: First, there began to develop locally something which might have led to the knowledge of the full use of clay; many links are still missing in this chain of development, and they may perhaps prove untraceable. Second, the nearest center showing a sequence of phenomena parallel to the one known in Palestine has come to light in southwestern Anatolia (Hacilar — Chatal Hüyük).[2]

In our opinion, the PPNB incipient awareness of clay and the PNA (Pottery Neolithic A) clay vessels show clear affinities, and the links between them should be sought locally.[3] Of course, such a theory does not exclude outside connections and influences, some of which will be suggested presently in relation to one of the decorative styles of this period.

---

1. K. M. Kenyon, "Some Observations on the Beginnings of Settlement in the Near East," *Journal of the Royal Anthropological Institute*, 89 (1959), 35–43.
2. J. Mellaart, *Earliest Civilizations in the Near East*, London, 1965.
3. An interesting phenomenon is the 'vaisselle blanche' uncovered in the late pre-pottery layers at Tell Ramad (*Annales archéologiques de Syrie*, XIV [1964], 116), Ras Shamra (*Ugaritica IV*, pp. 261 & 318), and Tell Soukas (*AAS* XI–XII [1961–2], 135–6). Most difficult to understand is that these vessels are formed in a mould!

Our knowledge of the Neolithic repertoire is derived mainly from the excavations at Jericho[4] (Garstang's Strata IX and VIII, Kenyon's Strata PNA and PNB), Sha'ar ha-Golan,[5] Batashi,[6] and Munhata (Stratum 2).[7] Fragmentary but significant remains have also been uncovered at Megiddo (Stratum XX).[8] Tell el-Far'ah (N)[9] Tel Aviv, Tell Eli,[10] in the Caves of Murabba'at in the Judean Desert,[11] and at other sites. Ghrubba (a site situated on the further side of the Jordan opposite Jericho, about 13 km. to the east),[12] has been included here, although it may belong to the Chalcolithic period.

The repertoire of the Pottery Neolithic A period is one of primeval simplicity in its forms and techniques, though not in its decoration. We have attempted to show the main features of this repertoire on Plate 1. As far as possible, only complete vessels are represented. A fairly clear picture of the simple and primitive forms of the period is obtained. Essentially, there are six kinds of vessels: small bowls, rather like cups (No. 4); medium-sized deep bowls with sloping or rounded sides (Nos. 5–7); a krater-like large deep bowl (No. 8); a chalice, or footed bowl (No. 9); two kinds of jars of small and medium size, one with neck (Nos. 1–3, 12, and Photo 1), and the other without (Nos. 11, 13).

The handles in this period are simple loop-handles or small pierced lug-handles, sufficient for suspending the vessel. What may be the beginnings of the ledge-handle, which is encountered in the Early Bronze Age, appear in this remote period in the shape of an enlarged knob found in pottery of the Yarmukian culture (No. 11) and on fragments from Batashi. In this latter ensemble this enlarged knob (or small ledge-handle) may occur also on the inside of the neck, or vertically on the rim.[13] The largest vessel of this period known up to the present does not exceed 0.35 to 0.40 m. in height. The vessels are built up of coils or bands (or perhaps increments). Among the nonplastic elements added to the clay (degraissants or tempering materials), straw has been noted, mainly at Jericho. Not enough attention has been devoted to the study of the composition and technology of this early pottery.

The neolithic pottery of Palestine can be divided according to methods of decoration into at least six groups:

Photo 1. Jar, Sha'ar ha-Golan, IDA 49–154.

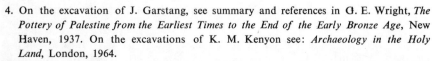

4. On the excavation of J. Garstang, see summary and references in G. E. Wright, *The Pottery of Palestine from the Earliest Times to the End of the Early Bronze Age*, New Haven, 1937. On the excavations of K. M. Kenyon see: *Archaeology in the Holy Land*, London, 1964.

5. M. Stekelis, "A New Neolithic Industry: The Yarmukian of Palestine," *IEJ*, 1 (1951), 1–19.

6. J. Kaplan, "Excavations at Teluliot Batashi in the Vale of Sorek," *Eretz Israel*, 5 (1958), 9-24 (Hebrew).

7. J. Perrot, "Les deux premières campagnes de fouilles à Munhatta (1962–1963), Premiers resultats," *Syria*, XLI (1964), 323–345. *Id.* "La troisième campagne de fouilles à Munhatta (1964)," *Syria*, XLIII (1966), 49–63.

8. *Meg. II*, pl. 2 : 30–42.

9. R. de Vaux, *RB* (1947), p. 407, fig. 1 : 34 & pl. XIV : 7, et al.

10. M. Prausnitz, "The First Agricultural Settlement in Galilee," *IEJ*, 9 (1959), 166–174.

11. P. Benoit, J. T. Milik and R. de Vaux, *Les Grottes de Muraba'at*, Oxford, 1961 p. 16, fig. 2 : 35, 37–39, 44.

12. J. Mellaart, "The Neolithic Site of Ghrubba," *ADAJ*, III (1956), 24–33.

13. J. Kaplan, "Excavations at Teluliot Batashi in the Vale of Sorek," *Eretz Israel*, 5 (1958), fig. 8 : 8, 11.

1) Plain (Nos. 3, 11). Most of the forms found among the decorated vessels are also present in the plain pottery.

2) Dark-faced burnished ware (a name coined by the excavators of the Amuq and the Cilician sites). Fragments of this slipped ware are known from various sites, especially Batashi.

3) Bands and rows of incisions made with a point or a fingernail. This type of decoration is known at Batashi, Tell Eli, and other sites.

4) Red-burnished slip (Nos. 6, 9) This ware, known from Jericho, Munhata, and other sites, appears to belong mainly to the first part of the period (Jericho IX–PNA) and is less frequent in the second part (Jericho VIII–PNB).

5) Painting applied with a brush. We include in this group every decoration made with a brush, which covers with paint only part of the surface of the vessel. The same red, reddish-brown, or yellowish-brown paint was used both for painting designs on the vessel and for covering the entire surface with slip. Two kinds of painted decoration should be noted: the paint is applied to the vessel so as to produce the design of the potter's choice, or the design is obtained by leaving the pattern free of paint and painting the rest of the vessel, a technique called 'reversed slip' (No. 7). The predominant design in both kinds of decoration is the zig-zag line, which permits many variations, such as a number of zig-zags forming a chevron, or paint-filled triangles on one side of the zig-zag line, etc. This painted style is known from Jericho, Batashi, Munhata, and other sites, and from Ghrubba, where the assemblage is especially rich in painted wares (Nos. 10, 13).

6) A combination of incised and painted decoration (Nos. 1, 2, 4, 5, 8, 12, Photos 1–2). This style is abundant at Sha'ar ha-Golan (it is called Yarmukian, as Sha'ar ha-Golan is situated on the Yarmuk River), Munhata, and in Jericho Stratum VIII (–PNB). Sherds occur at Megiddo, Stratum XX, Tell el-Far'ah (N), and Tel Aviv; a single sherd was found at Hazor and some sherds in the Murabba'at Caves in the Judaean Desert.[11]

On closer examination, the technique of decorating the vessels of this group becomes apparent: both incision and painting were carried out before firing. For the first operation the potter used a point to incise the basic pattern, composed of bands of herringbone or parallel incisions delineated by grooves. These bands encircle the body of the vessel once or twice in zig-zag fashion, and a straight band of the same kind runs around the base of the neck. For the second stage, the potter used a brush to fill the areas between the bands with red, yellow, or light brown paint. The incised band was left free of paint, with the natural colour of the clay remaining visible. The difference between groups 5 and 6 is mainly a matter of technique, for the decorative concept is the same — the zig-zag line. In the one case the potter used a fine brush to paint groups of zig-zag lines, or a thicker brush for a broad zig-zag line, while in the other he used a fine point to incise his zig-zag patterns. No specimens of the pottery found at Tell Eli have been shown on Plate 1, because the material is still being studied by the excavator. From the point of view of decorative technique, this pottery represents an additional group (7). Here too, the predominant decoration is produced by two techniques: part of the wall near the rim is covered with red paint and

Photo 2. Decorated sherds, Sha'ar ha- Golan, IDA.

Photo 3. Three sherds from Hassuna (upper row), Institute of Archaeology, London, and one sherd from Sha'ar ha-Golan, IDA.

often burnished, while the rest of the vessel is covered with wavy combing, both outside and inside. Sometimes the entire vessel is closely covered with small notches instead of the combing. Apparently both combing and notching were intended to strengthen the texture of the vessel, rather than furnish a decorative pattern.

Photo 3, made at the Institute of Archaeology in London, shows side by side a decorated sherd of group 6 from Sha'ar ha-Golan and three sherds from Hassuna, of the type there called painted-and-incised ware.[14] The resemblance between these sherds is striking, and seems to demonstrate a relationship between the Yarmukian culture of Palestine and the Hassuna culture of Northern Mesopotamia.

PLATE 1

1. Jar, buff, incised-and-painted red decoration	1 : 5	Sha'ar ha-Golan		IDA 49–154
2. Amphoriskos, buff, incised decoration	1 : 5	Munhata	II	Syria, 1964, Fig. 4 : 11
3. Bowl, buff, incised-and-painted red decoration	2 : 5	Megiddo		Meg. II, pl. 2 : 37
4. Krater, buff, incised-and-painted reddish decoration	1 : 5	Munhata	II	Syria, 1964, Fig. 4 : 13
5. Bowl, buff, incised-and-painted red decoration	1 : 5	Munhata	II	Syria, 1964, Fig. 4 : 2
6. Chalice (?), buff, red decoration	1 : 5	Munhata	II	Syria, 1964, Fig. 4 : 9
7. Bowl, brown, cream slip, brown decoration	1 : 4	Jericho	IX	AAA, XXIII, pl. XXXI : 19
8. Bowl, buff, red slip	1 : 2	Batashi		EI, V, p. 17, Fig. 7 : 6
9. Jar, brown, incised-and-painted red decoration	1 : 8	Jericho	VIII	AAA, XXIII, pl. XXXIII : 18
10. Jar, buff	1 : 4	Jericho	IX	AAA, XXIII, pl. XXIX : 11
11. Jar, brown-grey	1 : 5	Sha'ar ha-Golan		IDA 49–152
12. Bowl, buff, red decoration	1 : 5	Ghrubba		ADAJ, III, Fig. 5 : 65
13. Jar, buff, red decoration	1 : 5	Ghrubba		ADAJ, III, Fig. 6 : 122

14. S. Lloyd and F. Safar, "Tell Hassuna," *JNES*, IV (1945), 255–289.

PLATE | 1

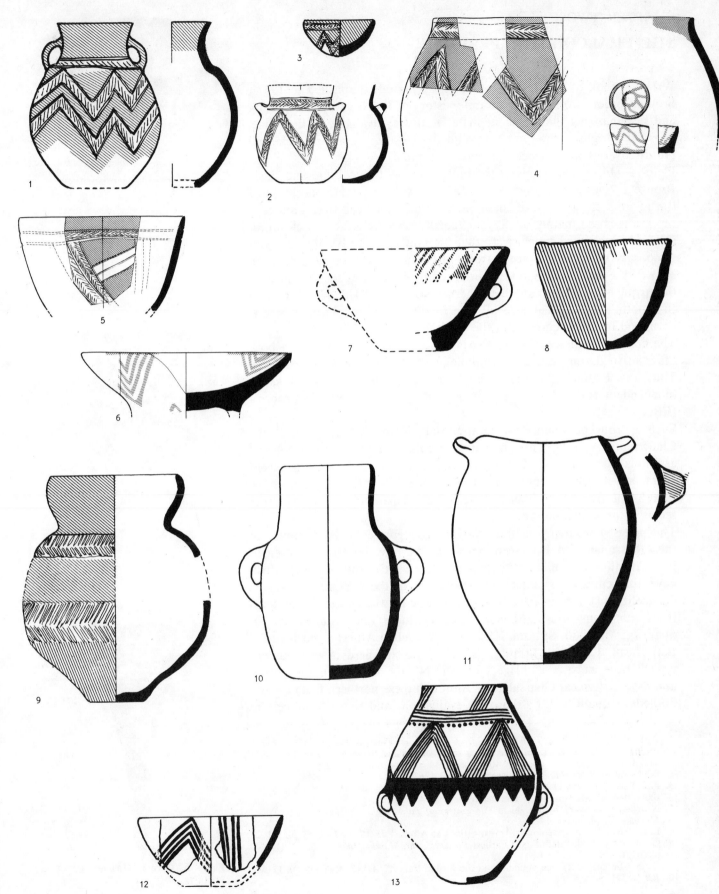

CHAPTER TWO

THE CHALCOLITHIC PERIOD

Wright's book on the pottery of the early periods, published in 1937[1], brought order into the early ceramic history of Palestine by interpreting and systematizing the abundant material already available at that time. Most of Wright's views are still valid despite the passage of time and the discoveries made since the book was published.

Plates 2—14, which represent the pottery of the Chalcolithic and Early Bronze I Ages are arranged in accordance with a certain conception of the relative chronology of these early periods and cultures. This conception is based mainly on R. de Vaux's excavations at Tell el-Far'ah (N)[2], which showed conclusively that the grey-burnished ware was contemporary with the painted ware of the South (see detailed discussion below). Further confirmation is furnished by discoveries such as those of the Arqub edh-Dhahar cave in northern Transjordan,[3] where P. Parr noted that both wares appear side by side in the early group found in this cave, and in the assemblage in the tomb near Tell el-Ásawir.[4]

The contemporaneity of these two wares is a key factor affecting both the relative dating and the terminology of a whole range of subjects. Thus, the 'Esdraelon' culture[5] should no longer be considered as an independent entity, but as part of the early phase of the Early Bronze I (EB I).

Such a concept requires a re-appraisal of the interrelation of the Chalcolithic cultures. The Ghassulian is undoubtedly the major cultural assemblage in this period. The Beer-sheba culture, as revealed in recent years, has added an important element. Essentially, this culture is the same as the Ghassulian. Thus a designation as Ghassul-Beer-sheba culture seems at present more appropriate.

The plates accompanying this chapter give representative examples of the Ghassulian and Beer-sheba cultures. We have purposely chosen to illustrate the Ghassulian with material taken only from the site which gave this culture its name. The existence of the Ghassul-Beer-sheba Chalcolithic culture in the north of Palestine as well is attested by finds from numerous sites, although some of these finds are limited in quantity: Megiddo, Stratum XIX: some cornets;[6] Afula: a 'bird-vase';[7] Beth-shean Pits and Stratum XVIII: painted sherds;[8] esh-Shuneh: typical Beer-sheba assemblage;[9] Far'ah (N), the Chalcolithique moyen and cave U: typical Ghassulian.[10] Although these northern finds are too limited in quantity for a thorough evaluation, and in spite of certain

Photo 4. V-shaped bowl, Ghassul, IDA 36.94.

Photo 5. Bowl-chalice, Ghassul, IDA 36.90.

Photo 6. Cornet, Ghassul, *Gh.* I, Pl. 48:78.

---

1. G. E. Wright, *The Pottery of Palestine from the Earliest Times to the End of the Early Bronze Age*. R. de Vaux *Palestine during the Neolithic and Chalcolithic Periods, CAH*, Vol. I, Ch. IX (6) 1966, appeared too recently to have been consulted.
2. Published in *Revue Biblique*, between 1947 and 1962.
3. P. J. Parr, "A Cave at Arqub el Dhahar," *ADAJ*, III (1956), 61–63.
4. Excavated by M. Dothan of the Department of Antiquities.
5. A detailed summary by Wright in *The Pottery of Palestine*.
6. *Megiddo* II, pl. 96:11–17.
7. E. L. Sukenik, "Archaeological Investigations at Affula," *JPOS*, XXI (1948), pl. 1:1–2.
8. G. M. FitzGerald, "Beth-Shan: Earliest Pottery," *The Museum Journal*, XXIV (1935), pl. III:16–19.
9. H. de Contenson, "Three Soundings in the Jordan Valley," *ADAJ* IV–V (1960), 12–30.
10. *RB* (1957), p. 554, fig. 1.

Photo 7. Cornet, Ghassul, IDA 36.66.

Photo 8. Goblet, Adeimeh, IDA 36.97.

Photo 9. Goblet, Adeimeh, IDA 36.1798.

Ghassulian features, some differences are evident: the frequent use of the small, thick loop-handle with broad attachments, the more general use of the rope decoration, and certain other elements. In the present state of investigation the understanding of these regional differences is still not complete.

A survey of the Chalcolithic pottery must perforce include clay objects, such as ossuaries, outside the range of domestic utensils. Cemeteries or burial caves containing ossuaries have been excavated at a number of coastal sites, such as Hadera, Bene Beraq, Azor, Giv'atayim, Yavne, and others. While most of the ossuaries were shaped like houses or animals, jars were used as well. The potter transformed the jar into an ossuary by pinching together the neck and mouth of the vessel, when it was 'leatherhard,' into the characteristic knob found at the top of an ossuary, and by cutting an opening into the wall of the jar for introducing the bones.

The Ghassulian Culture (Plates 2—3).

The term 'Ghassulian' refers mainly to the material culture of the two upper strata at Teleilat Ghassul (IV—III), since very little of Stratum II and practically nothing of Stratum I has been excavated.

Ghassulian pottery comprises a varied repertory of types and a wide range of wares. A glance at the plates immediately raises an important question: Did this variety of forms develop from the Neolithic pottery with a yet undiscovered intermediate stage, or was this culture introduced from outside by an intrusive ethnic element?

The nature of Ghassulian pottery has been briefly defined by the excavator, Father Mallon, as "une céramique à oreillettes et à empreintes."[11] To these, he might have added two more elements — plastic and painted decoration. The combination of these four elements, three of which are decorative and the fourth functional, determines the character of Ghassulian pottery.

Bowls: The predominant type is the V-shaped bowl (Plate 2:1—2, Photo 4), with a red painted band ornamenting the rim. This type is also very common at Beer-sheba. Other bowls have gently rounded sides (Plate 2:3—4). A special type, which resembles a cup and is related to the chalices with trumpet bases, is shown on Plate 2:10—11 (Photo 5).

Cornets: This vessel has become almost a hallmark of the Ghassulian pottery, not so much because of its quality or its frequent appearance, but mainly because of its distinctive shape. The commonest type (Nos. 5—7, Photos 6—7) somewhat resembles a horn, and is often flattened at the tip. Some cornets are painted, others are plain; some are without handles, others have two pairs of tiny lug handles. Another type of cornet is shorter, with the pointed tip cut off to form a flat base (Nos. 8—9).

Goblets: The goblets (also called egg-cups) in Photos 8-9 show a certain affinity with the cornets and appear to be cornets set on a foot of varying height. These goblets often have a tiny lug handle.

---

11. A. Mallon, R. Koeppel, R. Neuville, *Teleilat Ghassul* I, Rome, 1934, p. 128.

Chalices or incense-burners: These vessels (Nos. 14-15), which vary in height, are bowls with sloping sides, set on solid, hollow, or fenestrated feet. They are generally called incense-burners and are thought to have been used for cult purposes. Some basalt incense-burners have been found at Ghassul, and many more at Beer-sheba; pottery vessels of the same shape are among the finds from the ossuary caves at Hadera, Azor, etc. Photos 10–12 show three such vessels: the basalt specimen comes from Beer-sheba (No. 10), the pottery example from Hadera (No. 11), while the third, from Tell el-Far'ah (N), belongs to the grey-burnished ware of EB I.

Photo 10. Basalt fenestrated-pedestalled bowl, Abu Matar, *IEJ*, V, Pl. 18.

Jars: The jars can be divided, according to size and decoration, into three groups. It is interesting to note that the Ghassulian potters gave each size of vessel its own particular kind of decoration.

S m a l l   j a r s : The three specimens shown here (Nos. 16—18) represent a varied group of small jars characterized by painted decoration and especially by numerous lug-handles. Often there are two rows of at least four handles each, which seem to have served a purely decorative purpose.

M e d i u m .- s i z e d   j a r s : Some jars, such as Nos. 21–22, recall in their simplicity Neolithic forms. No. 21 is one of the few examples where the lug-handle has "grown" into a loop-handle. These jars are usually painted.

H o l e m o u t h   j a r s : The holemouth rim (No. 20), which later enjoyed widespread popularity, especially in the Early Bronze Age, begins to appear in the Ghassulian culture.

The vessels have large, pierced, usually longitudinal lug-handles, with a triangular profile.

Photo 11. Fenestrated-pedestalled bowl, Azor, *Atiqot*, III, Pl. 17.

Photo 12. Fenestrated-pedestalled bowl, Far'ah(N), RB, 1949, Pl. VI.

Pithoi: These very large containers (Plate 3) are of course hand-made, being built up of coils or bands; the difficulties encountered by the potter in making these vessels are evident. Most characteristic is the elaborate plastic decoration, produced by applying rope-like clay bands to the wall of the vessel and decorating the ridge thus produced with a row of finger indentations or with crescentic nail or reed impressions. The explanation for the widespread use of the applied rope-decoration may be fairly simple: during the manufacture of these large jars, which are 0.50 to 1.50 meter high, the potter had to use real ropes to help build up the jar of rings or bands of clay. These rope fastenings were intended for strengthening rather than for transporting the vessel, although there is no doubt that ropes were also required for carrying these jars. The utilitarian function of these ropes is echoed in the plastic ornamentation as a decorative element. The isolated knob is another plastic element frequently found in this period. The development of the ledge-handle (see Plate 8) can be inferred from this trend of plastic decoration.

A short-handled spoon of coarse clay, which is peculiar to the Ghassulian, is shown on Plate 2:19.

A distinctive form in the varied repertoire of the period is a vessel called at Teleilat Ghassul a 'bird-vase' (vase-oiseau), and now more frequently called a churn. A separate section (Plate 7) has been devoted to this vessel because of its chronological and cultural significance.

PLATE | **2**

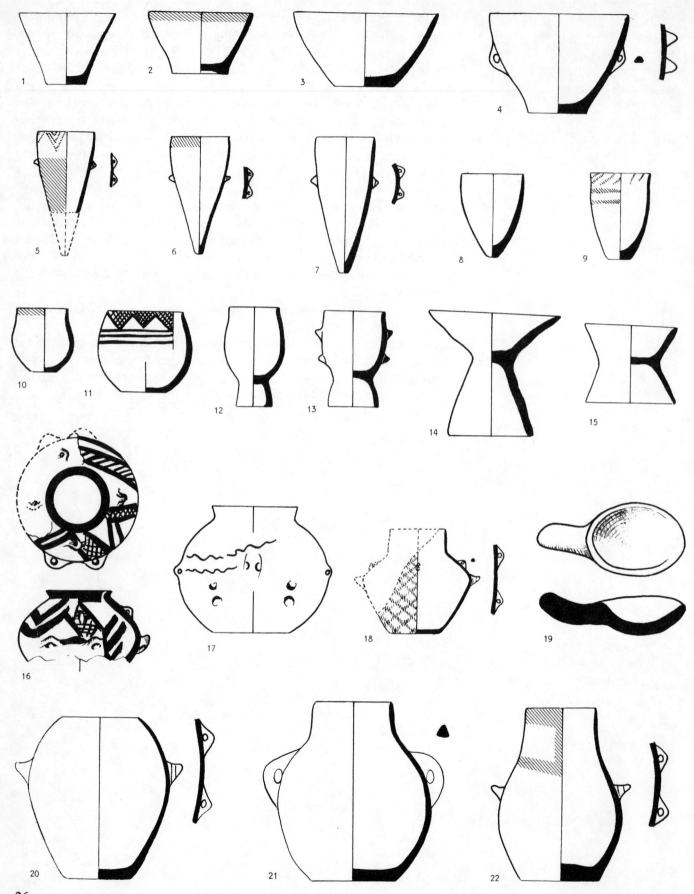

PLATE | 3

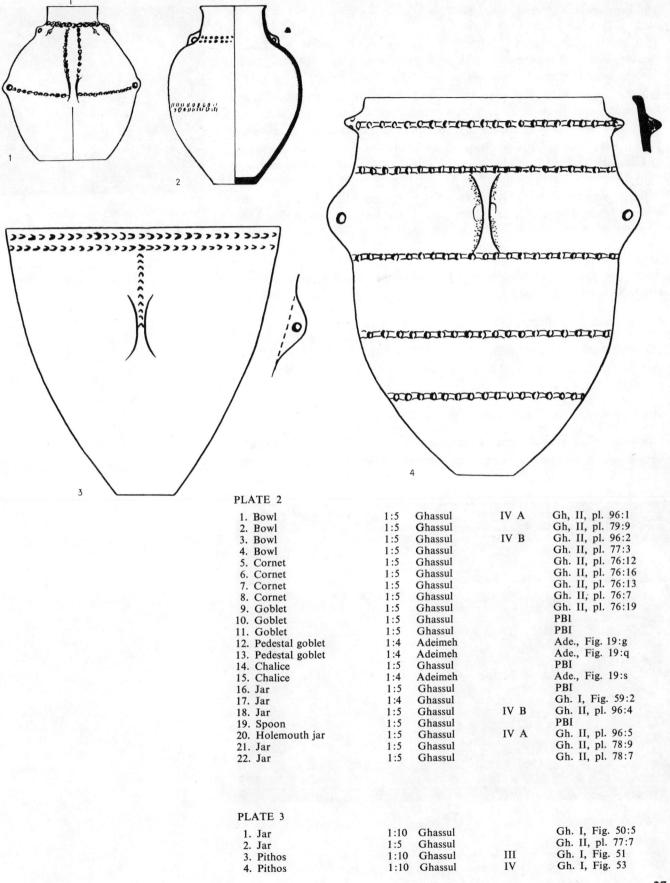

PLATE 2

1. Bowl	1:5	Ghassul	IV A	Gh, II, pl. 96:1
2. Bowl	1:5	Ghassul		Gh, II, pl. 79:9
3. Bowl	1:5	Ghassul	IV B	Gh. II, pl. 96:2
4. Bowl	1:5	Ghassul		Gh. II, pl. 77:3
5. Cornet	1:5	Ghassul		Gh. II, pl. 76:12
6. Cornet	1:5	Ghassul		Gh. II, pl. 76:16
7. Cornet	1:5	Ghassul		Gh. II, pl. 76:13
8. Cornet	1:5	Ghassul		Gh. II; pl. 76:7
9. Goblet	1:5	Ghassul		Gh. II, pl. 76:19
10. Goblet	1:5	Ghassul		PBl
11. Goblet	1:5	Ghassul		PBl
12. Pedestal goblet	1:4	Adeimeh		Ade., Fig. 19:g
13. Pedestal goblet	1:4	Adeimeh		Ade., Fig. 19:q
14. Chalice	1:5	Ghassul		PBl
15. Chalice	1:4	Adeimeh		Ade., Fig. 19:s
16. Jar	1:5	Ghassul		PBl
17. Jar	1:4	Ghassul		Gh. I, Fig. 59:2
18. Jar	1:5	Ghassul	IV B	Gh. II, pl. 96:4
19. Spoon	1:5	Ghassul		PBl
20. Holemouth jar	1:5	Ghassul	IV A	Gh. II, pl. 96:5
21. Jar	1:5	Ghassul		Gh. II, pl. 78:9
22. Jar	1:5	Ghassul		Gh. II, pl. 78:7

PLATE 3

1. Jar	1:10	Ghassul		Gh. I, Fig. 50:5
2. Jar	1:5	Ghassul		Gh. II, pl. 77:7
3. Pithos	1:10	Ghassul	III	Gh. I, Fig. 51
4. Pithos	1:10	Ghassul	IV	Gh. I, Fig. 53

The Beer-sheba Culture (Plates 4—6).

This recently discovered culture,[12] which has proved to be a veritable treasure-house of information concerning various aspects of Chalcolithic civilization in Palestine, belongs, as we have already mentioned, to the Ghassulian horizon. However, there are certain differences between the assemblages at Beer-sheba and at Ghassul proper, of which three are mentioned here: a) the cornet, which is so characteristic of Ghassul, is rare at Beer-sheba; b) rope-decoration of various kinds is very popular at Ghassul, while at Beer-sheba few vessels are decorated in this manner; c) the so-called 'cream-ware' (Plate 5:7—9) appears only in the Beer-sheba culture, where it is a highly characteristic feature. The offshoots of this culture reached up to Gezer, where Macalister first discovered this ware. The range of types at Beer-sheba includes:

Photo 13. V-shaped bowl, Beter, IDA 53–955.

Small bowls:
These are usually V-shaped, with a red painted band around the rim (Plate 4:1–4, Photo 13).

Large bowls: The deep bowls have profiled rims.

Goblets or closed bowls (Plate 5:1–2, Photo 14): Similar vessels were shown on Plate 2:10–11. An interesting variant is the spindle-shaped vessel on Plate 5:3.

Open cooking pots: Sometimes with spouts (Plate 4:9).

Small jars: This very characteristic form (Plate 5:4—6, Photo 15) is found in several small and medium sizes. The handleless vessel is decorated

Photo 14. Bowl-chalice, Abu Matar, *IEJ*, V, Pl. 14.

Photo 15. Jar, Abu Matar, *IEJ*, V, Pl. 17.

---

12. J. Perrot, *IEJ*, 5, (1955); H. de Contenson, *IEJ*, 6 (1956); M. Dothan, *Atiqot*, II (1958).

in a manner typical of the Ghassul-Beer-sheba culture with broad, carelessly painted reddish bands on the body or on the rim. Sometimes such jars have spouts (No. 6).

Large jars: These (Plate 6) are almost as large as the pithoi. They have either small loop-handles, or elongated lug-handles which are not pierced, or ordinary pierced lug-handles. Often the jars are decorated with red paint. In Nos. 2–3, the decoration, using the handle as a nose, imitates a human face, showing imagination and a sense of humor.

Photo 16. 'Cream Ware' jar, Gezer, Archaeological Museum, Istambul.

Photo 17. 'Cream-Ware' jar, Safadi, *IEJ* V, p. 231, Fig. 11:1.

Cream-ware: (Plate 5:7–9, Photos 16–17) Macalister coined this term,[13] apparently because of the light, creamy color of the ware. We believe that this effect was achieved by using kaolin, a clay found in the Negev, and that the absence of the cream-ware at Ghassul can be explained by the fact that kaolin is not found in the Jordan Valley.

The characteristic shapes of this ware are easily recognized even when only fragments are found. The unusual vessel in Plate 5:9, from Gezer, is painted, an uncommon feature in the cream-ware found at Beer-sheba. There, the cream-ware is distinguished by a special way of cutting off the base of the vessel from the slab on which it had been fashioned, and by the emphasis on handles — whether these be numerous tiny pierced lug-handles or tubular handles. It appears likely that Negev kaolin was also used in the manufacture of other vessels, perhaps mixed with other clays and temper.

We have now several Carbon 14 datings for Beer-sheba,[14] which indicate 3500/3400–3200/3100 B.C. as the upper and lower limits for this culture.

---

13. R. A. S. Macalister, The *Excavation of Gezer*, II, London, 1912, 137.
14. *Atiqot*, II, p. 38–9.

PLATE | 4

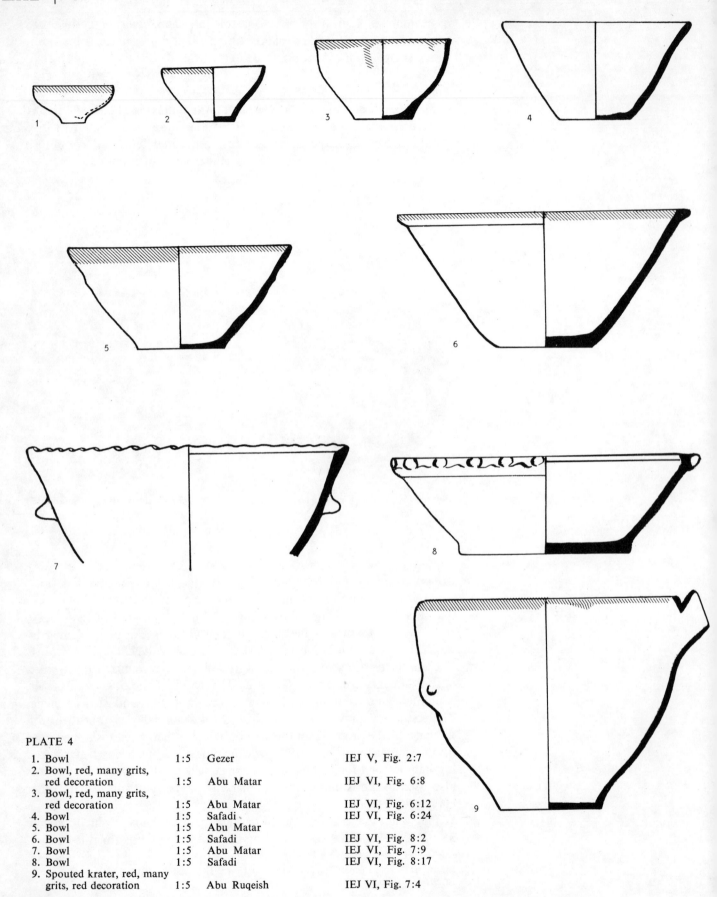

PLATE 4

1. Bowl	1:5	Gezer	IEJ V, Fig. 2:7
2. Bowl, red, many grits, red decoration	1:5	Abu Matar	IEJ VI, Fig. 6:8
3. Bowl, red, many grits, red decoration	1:5	Abu Matar	IEJ VI, Fig. 6:12
4. Bowl	1:5	Safadi	IEJ VI, Fig. 6:24
5. Bowl	1:5	Abu Matar	
6. Bowl	1:5	Safadi	IEJ VI, Fig. 8:2
7. Bowl	1:5	Abu Matar	IEJ VI, Fig. 7:9
8. Bowl	1:5	Safadi	IEJ VI, Fig. 8:17
9. Spouted krater, red, many grits, red decoration	1:5	Abu Ruqeish	IEJ VI, Fig. 7:4

PLATE | 5

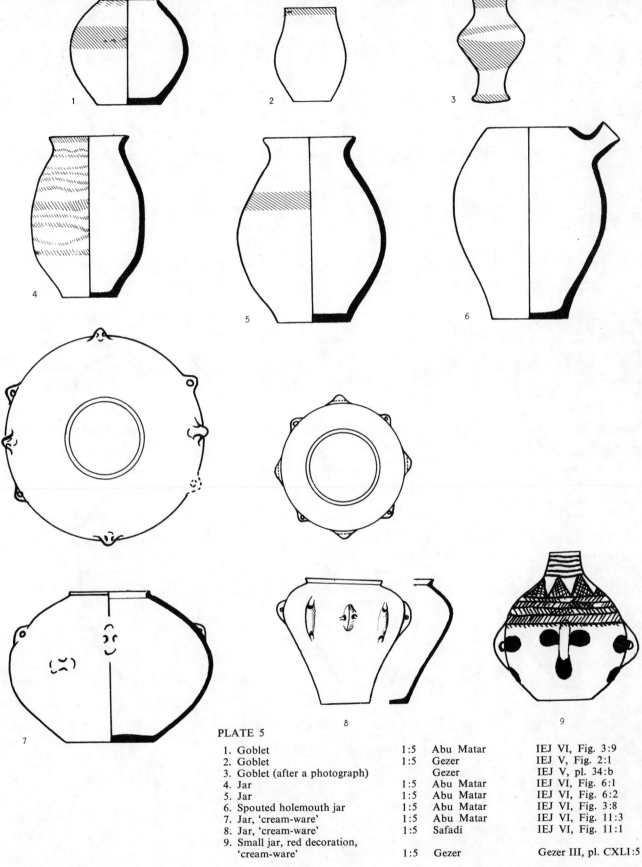

PLATE 5

1. Goblet   1:5   Abu Matar   IEJ VI, Fig. 3:9
2. Goblet   1:5   Gezer   IEJ V, Fig. 2:1
3. Goblet (after a photograph)   Gezer   IEJ V, pl. 34:b
4. Jar   1:5   Abu Matar   IEJ VI, Fig. 6:1
5. Jar   1:5   Abu Matar   IEJ VI, Fig. 6:2
6. Spouted holemouth jar   1:5   Abu Matar   IEJ VI, Fig. 3:8
7. Jar, 'cream-ware'   1:5   Abu Matar   IEJ VI, Fig. 11:3
8. Jar, 'cream-ware'   1:5   Safadi   IEJ VI, Fig. 11:1
9. Small jar, red decoration,
   'cream-ware'   1:5   Gezer   Gezer III, pl. CXLI:5

PLATE | **6**

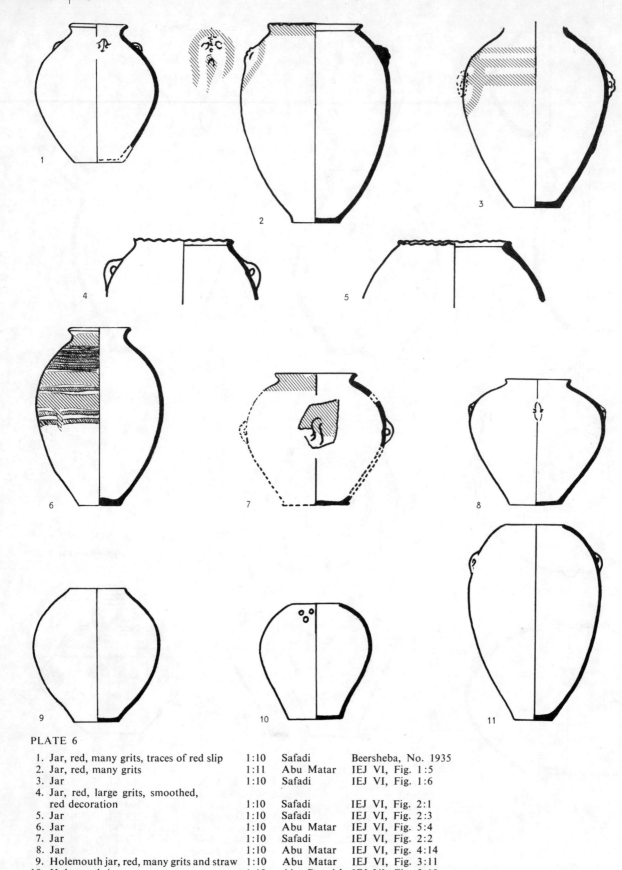

PLATE 6

1.	Jar, red, many grits, traces of red slip	1:10	Safadi	Beersheba, No. 1935
2.	Jar, red, many grits	1:11	Abu Matar	IEJ VI, Fig. 1:5
3.	Jar	1:10	Safadi	IEJ VI, Fig. 1:6
4.	Jar, red, large grits, smoothed, red decoration	1:10	Safadi	IEJ VI, Fig. 2:1
5.	Jar	1:10	Safadi	IEJ VI, Fig. 2:3
6.	Jar	1:10	Abu Matar	IEJ VI, Fig. 5:4
7.	Jar	1:10	Safadi	IEJ VI, Fig. 2:2
8.	Jar	1:10	Abu Matar	IEJ VI, Fig. 4:14
9.	Holemouth jar, red, many grits and straw	1:10	Abu Matar	IEJ VI, Fig. 3:11
10.	Holemouth jar	1:10	Abu Ruqeish	IEJ VI, Fig. 2:10
11.	Holemouth jar, red, many grits	1:10	Abu Matar	IEJ VI, Fig. 2:11

The Churn (Plate 7).

We have devoted a special plate to this vessel for a number of reasons: its frequency in the Chalcolithic cultures, its peculiar shape and its still enigmatic (or rather only incompletely understood) function. The barrel-shaped body of this horizontal vessel appears to imitate a goat-skin in clay. The neck rising in the middle of the body often swells markedly, and a strainer is set in the neck of the smaller specimens. In these, both ends are tapered, and are surmounted by a small loop-handle. In the larger churns the ends are different — one end is tapered, while the other is flat (Photo 18). The large specimens are decorated with red painted bands, imitating ropes.

The small variety (Nos. 1–2) was first discovered at Ghassul, and named there a 'bird-vase.' This name was later assigned also to the specimens found at Afula (No. 2) and at other sites. Of the large variety, most frequent in the Beer-sheba sites, only a few specimens were found at Ghassul.[15] Kaplan [16] has suggested that this vessel served as a churn, supporting his idea with convincing arguments. It appears likely that it should be assigned some function in the dairy industry of a community of farmers and herdsmen, rather than in water transport.

Fragments of churns have been found in the Umm Qatafa cave in the Judaean Desert.[17] Tiny, to some extent degenerate specimens are known, for instance, at Gezer (No. 4), which belongs to the Beer-sheba horizon. Small, highly stylized churns were uncovered in the ossuary cave at Azor (No. 6). A fragment found at Tell Delhamiya (near Ashdot Ya'aqov in the Jordan Valley)[18] has two small loop-handles instead of the single handle. The Stratum V assemblage at Arad contains fragments of churns,[19] and also Level I at esh-Shuneh appears to contain some fragments of churns.[20]

Photo 18, 'Churn', Beter, *Atiqot*, II, Pl. 4.

15. *Ghassul I*, p. 111, fig. 59:3; Ruth Amiran, *BASOR*, 130 (1953), 11–14; M. Dothan, *PEQ* (1953), pp. 132–7.
16. *PEQ*, (1954), pp. 97–100.
17. R. Neuville and A. Mallon, "Les débuts de l'âge des métaux dans les grottes du Désert de Judée," *Syria* (1931), pl. XVIII.
18. In the collections of the Qibbutz Ashdot Ya'aqov.
19. To be published shortly.
20. Unrecognized by the excavator as such, H. de Contenson, *ADAJ*, fig. 5:3.

PLATE | 7

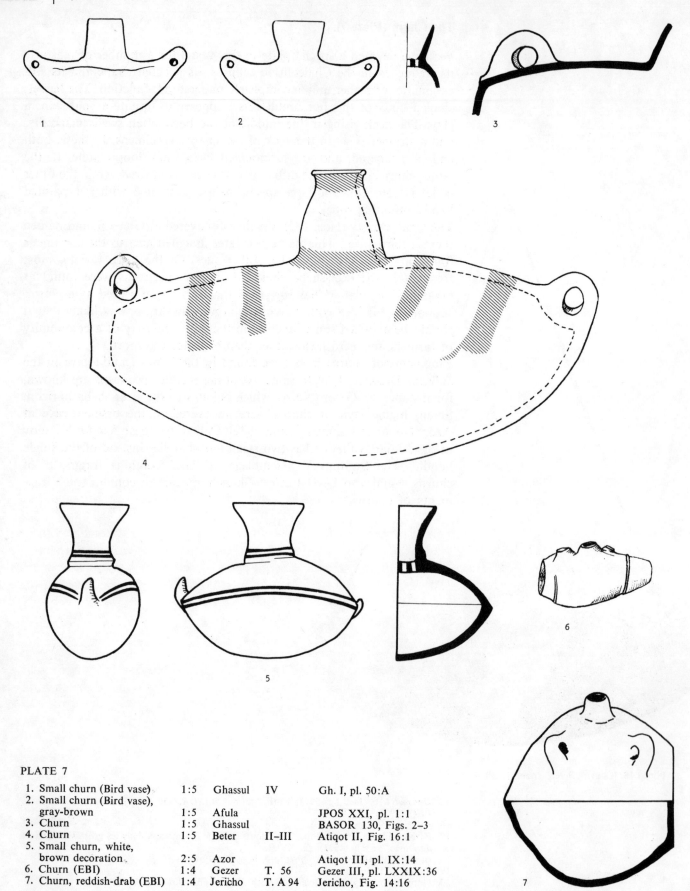

PLATE 7

1. Small churn (Bird vase)	1:5	Ghassul	IV	Gh. I, pl. 50:A
2. Small churn (Bird vase), gray-brown	1:5	Afula		JPOS XXI, pl. 1:1
3. Churn	1:5	Ghassul		BASOR 130, Figs. 2–3
4. Churn	1:5	Beter	II–III	Atiqot II, Fig. 16:1
5. Small churn, white, brown decoration	2:5	Azor		Atiqot III, pl. IX:14
6. Churn (EBI)	1:4	Gezer	T. 56	Gezer III, pl. LXXIX:36
7. Churn, reddish-drab (EBI)	1:4	Jericho	T. A 94	Jericho, Fig. 14:16

CHAPTER THREE

THE EARLY BRONZE PERIOD

The chronology of this period — an entire millennium — is pegged to a few reliable dates, and these are only relative and not absolute. The most important is the correlation between Early Bronze II and the First Dynasty of Egypt, based on the presence of Canaanite vessels among the funerary offerings in the royal tombs of the First Dynasty.[1] These vessels (Plate 17) have become one of the corner-stones in the chronology of the Near East in the Early Bronze period. However, it should be remembered that the date of the First Dynasty of Egypt is still disputed, with a difference of about 200 years between the two chronological systems. In this book we have followed Albright, and adopted the lower chronology, in which the First Dynasty is dated to about 2900 B.C., rather than the higher chronology (about 3100 B.C.). Here, an attempt has been made to give somewhat more weight than usual to the evidence of recent archaeological work in Palestine: a) The first synchronological correlation with Egypt antedated the First Dynasty and the unification of that country; contacts between Gerzean (-Naqada II) Egypt and Early Bronze I Canaan are evident in a whole series of Canaanite pottery vessels found in Egypt and Egyptian objects found in Palestine.[2] b) Carbon 14 tests carried out on material from Chalcolithic sites at Beer-sheba have furnished a date of ca. 3200/3100 B.C. for the end of the Chalcolithic period and the beginning of EB I. An estimate of 200 years seems reasonable for the duration of EB I. Thus the archaeological evidence in Palestine supports a date of about 2900 B.C. for the beginning of EB II and of the First Dynasty.

The Early Bronze period extended over a very long span of time, during which there were contacts between various regions of the Near East. In the absence of historical records, the nature of these contacts can be understood only in so far as they were reflected in the material culture and especially in the pottery. The following chapters describe both the trends of development of the pottery from one period to the other during this millennium, and the contacts or connections with neighboring regions.

We have arranged the ceramic material according to the accepted sub-periods. At the same time we have endeavored to present the special subjects which determine the character of each period. After much consideration, and for the reasons specified below (cf. Chapter VII), the authors have decided not to include the pottery of the Early Bronze IV in this volume.

The Ledge-handle (Plate 8).

We have devoted a special plate to the ledge-handle and its development

1. As in the previous two chapters also for the chapters on the Early Bronze periods, the main work of reference remains G. E. Wright, *The Pottery of Palestine from the Earliest Times to the End of the Early Bronze Age*. R. de Vaux, *Palestine in the Early Bronze Age*, in: *CAH*, Vol. I, Ch. XV(6), 1966, appeared too recently to have been consulted. Fresh evidence is now turning up in the excavations in the EB city of Arad, corroborating, generally, the accepted conception of this synchronology ,and adding some new aspects (cf. Ruth Amiran, *BASOR*, 179, [1965], 30–33).
2. Petrie's ideas have been followed by works of Scharff, Frankfort, Kantor, Baumgaertel, and others; cf. H. J. Kantor in *Relative Chronologies*.

(Photos 19–20) because of its prevalence throughout the Early Bronze period, and because of the important role it played in the history of Palestinian archaeology, and in the comparative archaeology of Palestine, Syria, and Egypt.

We shall discuss here three main aspects of the ledge-handle: a) origin; b) form and development; c) regional variations.

a) Origin.

This has long occupied the attention of scholars. The controversy as to whether it originated in Palestine or in the Delta of Egypt belongs to the past, and is mentioned here only for the sake of completeness.[3] The ledge-handle is a feature quite foreign to the general spirit of pre-Dynastic Egyptian pottery, and its appearance in the Gerzean complex is indisputable evidence of contacts with Canaan, where the ledge-handle belongs organically to the complex of ceramic forms and ideas. It is one of the most conspicuous elements of Palestinian pottery to have migrated to Gerzean Egypt,[4] and its role in the chronology of pre-Dynastic Egypt is of foremost importance.[5] As we have seen above, the first rudiments of the ledge-handle appear already in the Neolithic period. Its beginnings are undoubtedly bound up with the development of applied rope decoration in its various forms, both scalloped and finger-indented. The application of a clay rope or of a horizontal strip of clay to the side of the vessel and their decoration with finger indentations derive both from the same idea or from the same ceramic invention. The few instances found in the Ghassulian of a broad knob-handle resembling a ledge-handle decorated with finger indentations on the outer edge are sufficient to confirm this view. The same broad knob-handles, often finger-indented, also appear at Beer-sheba, although, as we have already noted, applied rope decoration is not particularly popular in the Beer-sheba branch of the Ghassulian culture.[6]

b) Form and Development.

Another important question relating to the ledge-handle is whether its typological variations (Photo 19) have a clear-cut chronological significance. Ever since 1891, when Petrie named such handles discovered at Tell el-Hesi *ledge-handles*[7] and recognized them also in Egyptian pottery, where he named them *wavy handles*, various ledge-handle forms have been described. However, a typological analysis of the ledge-handle was undertaken only when the material from the excavations on the east slope of Megiddo was studied.[8] At Megiddo, Engberg and Shipton distinguished eight kinds of ledge-handles, which they arranged in a typological chart according to the seven layers observed in that excavation

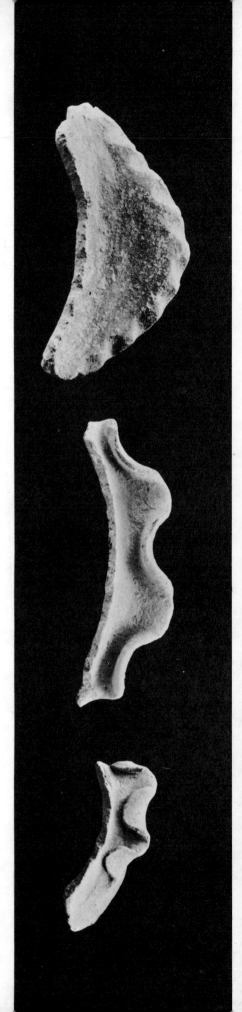

3. W. F. Albright, *The Excavations of Tell Beit Mirsim*, I, pp. 1–4.
4. The migration of the ledge-handle to Egypt may be considered as one of the arguments against Frankfort's conception of the route by which Sumerian influences reached Egypt during the Gerzean period. The land road through Syria-Palestine is thus at least one of the possible alternative routes. The ledge-handle in Egypt lived through a long development, or rather, degeneration, which constitutes an interesting example of a cultural trait undergoing transformations in a foreign milieu.
5. It is one of the main types in the Sequence-Dating system (S.D.) devised by Petrie.
6. *Ghassul*, I, pl. 40:3. *IEJ*, 6 (1956), p. 234, fig. 12:18, 29, 30.
7. F. Petrie, *Tell el-Hesy* (*Lachish*), London, 1891, p. 42, pl. V:42–47.
8. R. M. Engberg and G. M. Shipton, *Notes on the Chalcolithic and Early Bronze Age Pottery of Megiddo*, Chicago, 1934.

Photo 19. Series of ledge-handles, Afula, Ai and Ras el-Ain.

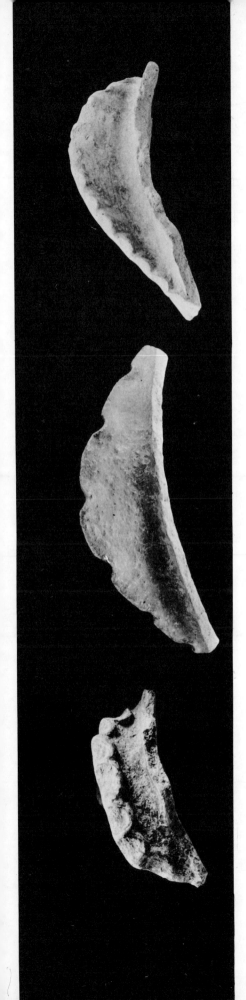

Wright,[9] in his detailed discussion of the ledge-handle, accepts this typological division, though with a number of changes. Recently, Olga Tufnell[10] proposed a slightly different division, which is both clearer and better suited to the nature of the material than the other systems. We have attempted to simplify matters in Plate 8. There are five main types of ledge-handle, with numerous variants within each type: 1) the plain ledge-handle (Nos. 1—6, Photo 20); 2) the thumb-indented ledge-handle (Nos. 7—15); we have included under this name all the examples in which the edge of the handle has been treated decoratively, although some of the ornamentation was certainly not produced by the thumb, but by a small stick, a bone, or a reed; for convenience we have subdivided this type into two groups — fine and coarse indentations; 3) the pushed-up ledge-handle (Nos. 16–19); 4) the folded ledge-handle (Nos. 20–22);

Photo 20. Jar, ledge-handles and spout, Ai.

5) the degenerated or vestigial ledge-handle (No. 23), which no longer had any practical function. Shown in the right-hand column are ledge-handles from Glueck's survey of Transjordan.[11]

The table below shows side by side the typological division and terminology of Engberg-Shipton, Wright, and Tufnell, and the division proposed by the authors.

	Engberg-Shipton	Wright	Tufnell
Type 1 Plain	14 D — Plain narrow 14 E — Plain broad	I c — Plain	Form 7
Type 2 Indented	14 C — Small thumb-indented 14 F — Oblique wavy 14 G — Thumb-indented 14 H — Wavy	I b — Wavy I a — Scalloped	Forms 1, 2, 3, 4, 5
Type 3 Pushed-up	14 B — Pushed-up	I d — Pinched-lapped I e — Pushed-up	Form 8
Type 4 Folded	14 A — Folded	I g — Pushed-up scalloped I f — Folded	Form 6 Forms 10, 10a, 11
Type 5 Vestigial			Form 12

9. Wright, *The Pottery of Palestine*, passim and Appendix.
10. O. Tufnell, *Lachish, IV, The Bronze Age*, London, 1958, pp. 148–155, fig. 7.
11. N. Glueck, *Explorations in Eastern Palestine*, IV, New Haven, 1951.

PLATE | 8

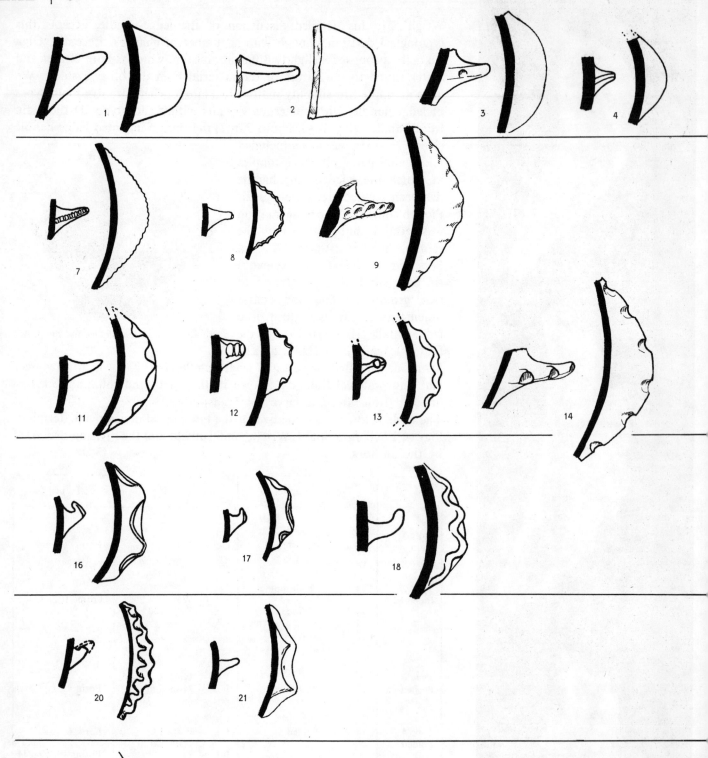

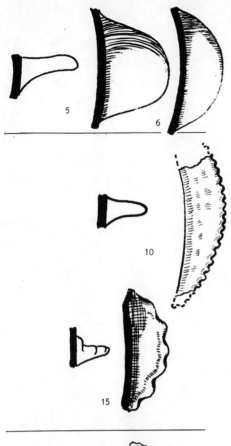

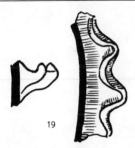

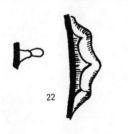

PLATE 8

1.	Plain ledge-handle	Jericho	AAA XXII:15
2.	Plain ledge-handle	Afula	JPOS XXI, pl. VII:17
3.	Plain ledge-handle	Afula	JPOS XXI, pl, VII:15
4.	Plain ledge-handle	Jericho	AAA XXII, pl. XXXV:12
5.	Plain ledge-handle	Deir Sa'aneh Mahladieh	EEP IV:II, pl. 135:2
6.	Plain ledge-handle	Ras Abu Lofeh	
7.	Thumb-indented ledge-handle	Ai	Ay, pl. LXXXVII:1228
8.	Thumb-indented ledge-handle	Beth-shan	MJ (BS), pl. II:3
9.	Thumb-indented ledge-handle	Afula	JPOS XXI, pl. VII:6
10.	Thumb-indented ledge-handle	es-Saidiyeh	EEP IV:II, pl. 161:3
11.	Thumb-indented ledge-handle	Ai	Ay, pl. XXXVII:1432
12.	Thumb-indented ledge-handle	Beth Shan	MJ (BS), pl. II:5
13.	Thumb-indented ledge-handle	Jericho	AAA, XXII, pl. XXXV:5
14.	Thumb-indented ledge-handle	Afula	JPOS XXI, pl. VII:3
15.	Thumb-indented ledge-handle	es-Saidiyeh	EEP IV:II, pl. 148:12
16.	Pushed-up ledge-handle	Jericho	AAA XXII, pl. XXXV:2
17.	Pushed-up ledge-handle	Ai	Ay, 380 (pl. LXXXVI)
18.	Pushed-up ledge-handle	Megiddo	Meg. Notes, Chart 14 B
19.	Pushed-up ledge-handle	es-Saidiyeh	EEP IV:II, pl. 148:7
20.	Thumb-indented-enveloped ledge-handle	Lachish	La. IV, Fig. 7:8
21.	Enveloped ledge-handle	Megiddo	Meg. T., pl. 12:6
22.	Enveloped ledge-handle	Umm Hamad Gharbi	EEP IV:II, pl. 153:3
23.	Vestigial ledge-handle	Lachish	La. IV, Fig. 7:12

c) Regional Variations.

What are the boundaries of the area in which the ledge-handle is found, and especially what is its northern boundary? Albright, who first approached this subject, proposed, on the basis of a surface survey, to regard the Jezreel Valley as the northern boundary.[12] Since then, excavations carried out in sites north of the Jezreel Valley, such as Beth Yerah, Tell Quneitira, Rosh Hanniqra, and Hazor, have extended the range of the ledge-handle northwards. Can regional differences be distinguished within the area of diffusion of the ledge-handle? Such differences indeed appear to exist, and perhaps both questions can be answered together: the home of the ledge-handle is most probably in the south of Palestine, and, from the very beginning, it seems to have had more than one form. It is likely that the plain ledge-handle and certain variants of the indented ledge-handle originated at the same time and were used side by side already in EB I, at the beginning of the ledge-handle's long period of popularity. The further north we move from its original home, the less frequent it becomes. The fact that it is absent from the E-G assemblages of the Amuq excavations,[13] and from the K strata at Hama,[14] suggests that the northernmost limit of its expansion may have been Upper Galilee.

12. Albright, *TBM*, I, pp. 3–4.
13. R. J. Braidwood and L. S. Braidwood, *Excavations in the Plain of Antioch*, I, *The Earliest Assemblages*, Phases A–J, Chicago, 1960.
14. E. Fugmann, *Hama, L'Architecture des périodes pré-Hellénistiques*, Copenhagen, 1958, pp. 24–48.

CHAPTER FOUR

THE EARLY BRONZE I PERIOD

Included here in the chapter on EB I are those wares and phases which used to be termed Late Chalcolithic (see introduction to Chapter II), in addition, of course, to the wares and strata traditionally designated as EB I. It is not a mere change of nomenclature, but a change of conception. The contemporaneity, or partial contemporaneity, of wares formerly considered to be consecutive, and the occurrence in one context of two such wares formerly considered to be consecutive, and regionally apart, make this change in nomenclature much more conceptual. In view of the fact that in this period, along with small villages, larger and walled settlements are already known, the designation[1] Proto-Urban, coined by Kathleen M. Kenyon, seems appropriate. However, since the occurrences of larger and walled settlements are as yet very few, we decided to adhere to the long-accepted terminology, in order to avoid confusion. Furthermore, although Southern and Northern elements have recently been found together in the same context (see above), we follow here for convenience's sake the accepted regional division into Northern and Southern Cultures.

The Northern Culture (Plates 9—10).

The ceramic ensemble on Plate 9, which represents a variety of types,

Photo 21. Sherds of jars, band-slip painting, Afula, *JPOS*, XXI, Pl. XVIII.

1. Cf. e.g. the walled site of Tell el-Far'ah (N), in Strata 1 and 2 of Ancient Bronze I. We have followed the excavator in using the material from these strata in our EB I plates. However, there seems to be some possibility that these strata and the walled city should be attributed to the beginning of EB II and not to EB I — a suggestion which must await the publication of the full report of the excavations.

shows that painted decoration was uncommon. Only four vessels in this group bear such decoration (no statistical precision is, of course, intended). However, it should be mentioned that the picture presented by Plates 9 and 14 is incomplete, since neither shows the band-slip or grain-wash technique of painting, which was very popular in the north during EB I. In this style (sherds shown on Photo 21), the surface of the vessels, usually holemouth jars, is entirely covered with diagonally intersecting bands of paint in many nuances of brown, red, and yellow, made by a multiple brush, to judge from the partly thick and partly thin striations. In contrast to the rarity of painted decoration (besides the band-slip or grain-wash style), this period is characterized by red burnished and grey burnished wares.

Photo 22. Bowls with conical omphalos, Farah(N), RB, 1951, Pl. XXI.

Red Burnished Ware (Plate 9).

This clearly distinguishable ware comprises in the main various types of bowls, one with omphalos; various types of teapots; amphoriskoi, of which one medium-sized type has diagonal handles; large jars; small wide-mouthed jars; jugs and juglets with high loop-handles. This group has many common family features, both in details of form, as well as in texture and finish: the pinkish fat clay is well levigated (without large grits), the walls are relatively thick, and the all-over red slip is evenly burnished. This ware is known from Megiddo,[2] Tell el-Far'ah (N), the Asawir tomb, Tell Ayadiya,[3] and other sites. We bring in here a group

2. No complete vessel has been found at Megiddo, but the spout presented in *Megiddo*, II, pl. 96:27 belongs to a teapot made of this red-slipped ware.
3. A. Bentor, *Atiqot*, 3 (1963) (Hebrew).
4. I am grateful to Professor A. Parrot, Conservateur-en-chef des Antiquités au Musée du Louvre, for his kind permission to publish these vessels.

Photo 23. Bowl with ledge-handles, Farah(N), *RB*, 1951, Pl. XXII.

42

Photo 26. Spouted vessel, Farah(N), *RB*, 1951, Pl. XXII.

Photo 24. Spouted vessel, Assawir, IDA 53–746.

Photo 25. Spouted vessel, Assawir, IDA 53–747.

Photo 27. Small jar with diagonal handles, Assawir, IDA 53–541.

Photo 28. Juglet with high loop-handle, Farah(N), RB, 1951, Pl. XXII.

of four vessels from Aktanit in Lebanon[4] which we noticed in the collection of the Louvre, including two vessels (Photos 29–30) similar to our No. 17, (Photo 27, though with different handles); one juglet with a high loop-handle (Photo 31); and one bowl with four knob-handles (Photo 32), described below with the Grey Burnished Ware.

Bowls: The bowl with a relatively high conical omphalos (No. 2 and Photo 22) is a type yet to be explained. Somewhat related types are Nos. 3–6. Some of these bowls have ledge-handles (No. 6 and Photo 23). One type of a large deep bowl (not reproduced here) has two loop-handles, and is distinctive for its craquelé brown burnished slip, similar to Plate 10:10. V-shaped bowls like those of the preceding period are still found (No. 1), although they disappear gradually. The most common form is the hemispherical bowl (Nos. 2–6, 8–9); the low omphalos in the base seems well suited to the spherical shape. No. 7 is one of the earliest forms of the platter, a common form in the Early Bronze period. No. 8 is a spherical bowl with an omphalos and a spout. Spouts are characteristic of this group as we shall see when describing the teapot. No. 9 is a bowl painted in the Southern style, and No. 10 is a large and relatively deep bowl.

Teapots: The teapots from various sites shown in Nos. 11—16, together with the three specimens from Jericho on Plate 12:15–17, make up an interesting family, which can be divided into two main types: 1) teapot with narrow neck, usually with a ridge at the base of the neck (Plates 9:14–15, 12:15, 17, and Photos 24–25). 2) teapot with wide necks (Plates 9:11–13, 12:16, and Photo 26). Plate 9:16 is an entirely different form. Its typological history and stratigraphic attribution are as yet unknown. The teapot has been the subject of a number of comparative studies, dealing with relations between Mesopotamia and Egypt in the late pre-Ðynastic period.[5]

5. Cf. J. H. Kantor, in *COWA*.[2]

43

PLATE 9

1. Bowl, pink   1:5   Far'ah (N)   T.14   RB, 1952, p. 581, Fig. 12:11
2. Bowl, pink   1:5   Far'ah (N)   T.14   RB, 1952, p. 851, Fig. 12:9
3. Bowl, pink, traces of red slip   1:5   Far'ah (N)   T.16   RB, 1955, p. 543, Fig.   1:12
4. Bowl, grey, brown burnished slip   1:5   Far'ah (N)   T.14   RB, 1952, p. 581, Fig. 12:10
5. Bowl, grey, brown burnished slip   1:5   Far'ah (N)   T.12   RB, 1951, p. 582, Fig. 11:1
6. Bowl, buff, red burnished slip   1:5   Far'ah (N)   T.12   RB, 1951, p. 582, Fig. 11:11
7. Bowl, pink, red burnished slip   1:5   Far'ah (N)   T.14   RB, 1952, p. 581, Fig. 12:13
8. Bowl, buff, red burnished slip   1:5   Far'ah (N)   T.17   RB, 1955, p. 547 Fig.   3:1
9. Bowl, pink, red decoration   1:5   Far'ah (N)   T.14   RB, 1952, p. 581, Fig. 12:7
10. Bowl, buff, red burnished slip   1:5   Far'ah (N)   T.14   RB, 1952, p. 581, Fig. 12:14
11. Teapot, red, brown vertically burnished slip 1:6   Ras el-Ain   QDAP V 4, p. 121, 63
12. Teapot, pink, pink slip   1:5   Far'ah (N)   T.12   RB, 1951, p. 584, Fig. 12:1
13. Teapot, red slip   1:5   Far'ah (N)   T.12   RB, 1951, p. 584, Fig. 12:2
14. Teapot, cream, red burnished slip   1:5   Far'ah (N)   T.8   RB, 1949, p. 135, Fig. 13:8
15. Teapot, yellow, brown-red burnished slip   1:5   Asawir   Tomb   IDA, No. 53–537
16. Teapot, yellow, red slip   1:5   Beth-shan   PMB 3, pl. I:13
17. Amphoriskos, white-yellow, red slip   1:5   Megiddo   Meg. T., pl. 3:7
18. Jar, brown-ocher, red burnished slip   1:5   Megiddo   T.910D   Meg. T., pl. 4:22
19. Amphoriskos, buff, red burnished slip   1:5   Fara'h (N)   T.5   RB, 1949, p. 127, Fig. 8:28
20. Amphoriskos, buff, brown-red decoration   1:5   Fara'h (N)   T.2   RB, 1949, p. 120, Fig. 6:3
21. Bottle, buff, red decoration   1:5   Asawir   Tomb   IDA, No. 53–549
22. Juglet, buff, red burnished slip   1:5   Asawir   Tomb   IDA, No. 53–540
23. Juglet, buff, red burnished slip   1:5   Asawir   Tomb   IDA, No. 53–542
24. Juglet, buff, red burnished slip   1:5   Far'ah (N)   Tomb 14   RB, 1952, p. 579, Fig. 11:1
25. Holemouth jar, pink, red burnished   1:5   Far'ah (N)   T.5   RB, 1949, p. 127, Fig. 8:16
26. Jar, red, burnished   1:5   Far'ah (N)   T.3   RB, 1949, p. 113, Fig. 1:21
27. Jug, pink, burnished   1:5   Far'ah (N)   T.14   RB, 1952, p. 579, Fig. 11:20
28. Spouted jar, buff, red decoration   1:5   Far'ah (N)   T.5   RB, 1949, p. 127, Fig. 8:31
29. Jar, buff, red burnished slip   1:5   Far'ah (N)   T.11   RB, 1951, p. 575, Fig. 6:12
30. Jar, pink, red burnished slip   1:5   Far'ah (N)   T.13   RB, 1952, p. 575, Fig. 10:15
31. Jar, pink, made in two parts   1:5   Far'ah (N)   T.3   RB, 1949, p. 113, Fig. 1:26

44

PLATE | 9

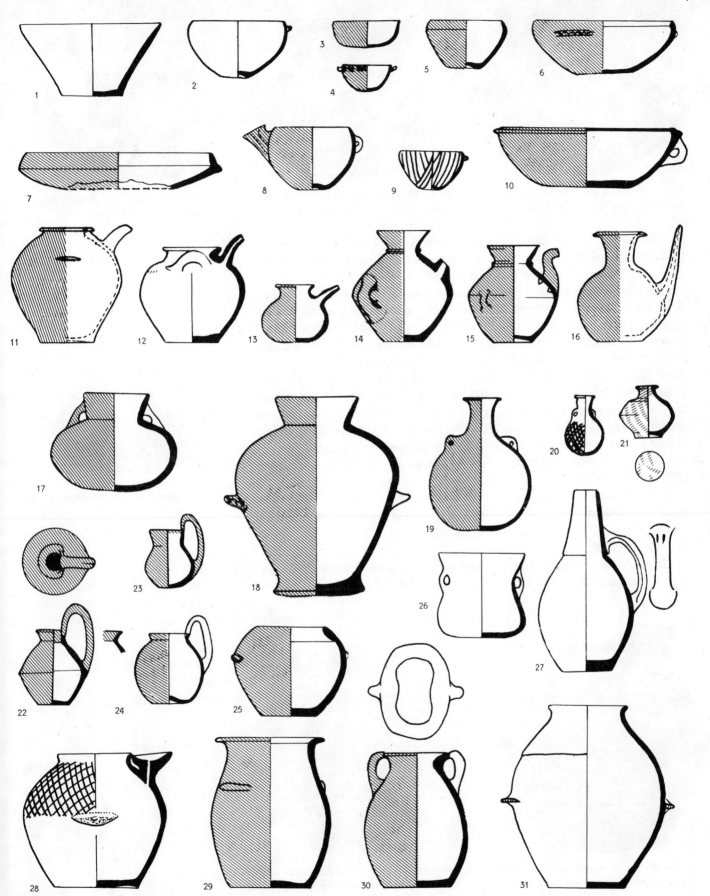

Photo 29. Small jar, Aktanit (Lebanon), Musée du Louvre, No. AO 10987.

Photo 30. Small jar, Aktanit (Lebanon), Musée du Louvre, No. AO 11022.

Photo 31. Cup, Aktanit (Lebanon), Musée du Louvre, No. AO 10989.

Amphoriskoi: The amphoriskos is an important vessel for the characterization of this period. It is more at home in the Southern than in the Northern culture. We show two variants: one (No. 20), resembles closely the painted amphoriskos common in the Southern culture (see below); the other (No. 19), is much larger in size, red-slipped and burnished. A related type is No. 17 (Photo 27) characterized by its bag-shaped body, everted neck, and the development of the two lug-handles into larger ones, diagonally connecting the neck with the shoulder.

Jars: Nos. 25–26 and 28–31 are representative of various types and sizes of jars: No. 25 is a small holemouth jar; No. 26 has been included here for lack of a more accurate designation, it resembles in many features the amphoriskos just mentioned (No. 17); No. 28 is painted in the southern style and has a spout with a bowl-like top pierced by a narrow hole. It has been suggested that such spouts served as stands for dipper-juglets (Photos 33–34). This type of jar continues to be made in EB II; Nos. 29 and 30 are unusual in having an oval cross-section. Until now such jars have been found only in the Tell el-Far'ah (N) assemblage. No. 31 is a common type of jar with two ledge-handles.

Photo 32. Bowl, Aktanit (Lebanon), Musée du Louvre, No. AO 11046.

Jugs and juglets: Jug No. 27 is most probably one of the predecessors of the jug which will become the hallmark of EB II. Juglets 22–23 are typical of the period, and have a high loop-handle (Photo 28).

Photo 33. Jar with slip and net paiting, and a spout, Farah(N), *RB*, 1949, Pl. X.

Photo 34. Spouted-jar, Ai (the juglet has been placed in the bowl of the spout).

Photo 37. Fenestrated-pedestalled bowl, Grey-burnished, Farah(N), *RB*, 1951, Pl. XXII.

Photo 36. Fenestrated-pedestalled bowl Grey-burnished, Nahal Tavor, (Published for the first time, courtesy Prof. P. Delougaz).

Grey Burnished Ware (Plate 10).

This ware used to be considered as the main component of the culture designated as 'The Esdraelon Culture'. Both clay and slip are grey, giving this ware its name. The 'grey' may vary from light to dark, including many shades of yellowish-grey. The high burnish of the slip gives the ware a lustrous and distinctive appearance. There is a certain resemblance between this ware and the Khirbet Kerak Ware (to be discussed in EB III, Chapter Six), both in the quality of the burnish and in some details of manufacture, such as the way the rims are fashioned.

Three main types can be distinguished, a division which may have chronological implications:[6]

1) Nos. 1–2 are two varieties of a wide bowl with sloping, softly carinated sides, with a sinuous ridge or a series of broad knobs (Photo 35) placed on the line of carination. This type has been found at Beth-shan, Afula, Megiddo, Beth Yerah, on Tell Bagura, Tell esh-Shuneh, and Arqule el-Dholy[7] and elsewhere. This type appears also on a fenestrated pedestal, like No. 6 (Photo 36).

2) The second type (No. 3), found up to now only at Tell el-Far'ah (N), has a deeper bowl, no carination, and has a twisted clay rope applied to the upper part of the bowl wall. Sometimes a row of broad knobs is reminiscent of the previous type, as in No. 5. Such bowls sometimes also have a fenestrated pedestal (Nos. 7–8, Photo 37). These pedestals have, of course, an affinity to the pedestalled bowls (sometimes called incense burners or chalices) of the Chalcolithic period.

3) In this type (No. 4), much of the striking appearance of the ware has disappeared. The carination has become rigid, there is no applied moulded decoration, the slip is much poorer in quality and is less burnished. This type has been made on the wheel, in contrast to the first two which are hand made. Most of the examples come from tombs at Megiddo and Asawir (Photo 38).

Photo 35. Bowl, Grey-burnished, Afula, HU 4411.

Photo 38. Bowl, Grey-burnished, Assawir, IDA 53–546.

6. G. E. Wright, "The Problem of the Transition between the Chalcolithic and the Bronze Ages," *Eretz Israel*, V (1958), 37–45.

7. H. de Contenson, ADAJ IV–V, 1960, Fig. 9. P.J. Parr, ADAJ III, 1956, Fig. 13.

PLATE | 10

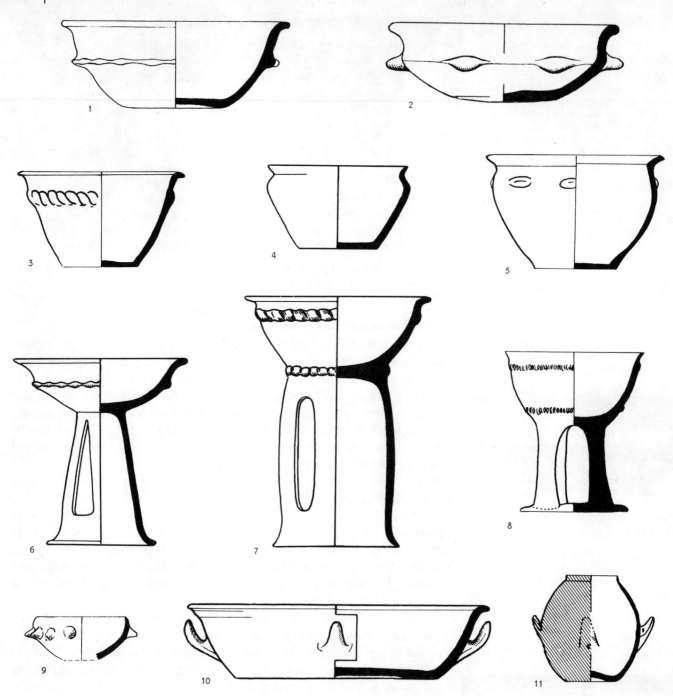

PLATE 10

1.	Bowl, grey, burnished	1:5	Beth-shan	XVI	MJ (BS), pl. III:4	
2.	Bowl, grey, burnished	1:5	Afula		JPOS XXI, pl. II:1	
3.	Bowl, grey, burnished	1:5	Far'ah (N)	T.11	RB, 1951, p. 575, Fig. 6:3
4.	Bowl, grey, burnished	1:5	Far'ah (N)		RB, 1949, p. 114, Fig. 2:8
5.	Bowl, grey, burnished	1:5	Far'ah (N)	T.14	RB, 1952, p. 58!, Fig. 12:20
6.	Incense-burner, grey, burnished	1:5	Far'ah (N)		RB, 1949, p. 114, Fig. 2:4
7.	Incense-burner, grey, burnished	1:5	Far'ah (N)	T.8	RB, 1949, p. 114, Fig. 2:10
8.	Incense-burner, grey, burnished	1:5	Far'ah (N)		RB, 1949, p. 127, Fig. 8:32
9.	Bowl, light brown, brown slip	1:5	Afula		JPOS XXI, pl. XII:2
10.	Bowl, brown-grey	1:5	Beth Yerah	XVI	IDA, No. 50–4082
11.	Holemouth jar, buff, red slip	1:5	Far'ah (N)	T.5	RB, 1949, p. 127, Fig. 8:23

Photo 41. Small jar, line group-painting, Ai, HU 5163.

Photo 42. Amphoriskos, net-painting, Ai, HU 5249/1.

Photo 43. Amphoriskos, net-painting, Ai, HU 5246/1

Photo 45. Net-painted amphoriskos Ghor es-Safi IDA 46.39.

Photo 44. Net-painted jar, Ghor es-Safi, IDA 46.38.

A few sherds of these three types have been found at Tulul Abu-Alayiq near Jericho,[8] a discovery important both for the regional and the chronological aspects of the period under consideration. Grey Burnished sherds found as far south as Jericho weaken the view of the strictly northern diffusion of this ware.

We have purposely included in Plate 10 three vessels which have projecting knobs but do not belong to the Grey Burnished Ware in the strict sense (Nos. 9–11). However, their general relationship with this ware is apparent. The brown slip of the large bowl with four upright knobs (No. 10) looks as if it were crackled. The same kind of brown burnished slip has been noted in the bowls of the Burnished Red-slipped Ware (see above). A similar bowl from Aktanit (Lebanon) is reproduced in Photo 32.

Photo 39. Bowl, line group-painting, Yabrud, HU 2173.

Photo 40. Amphoriskos, line group-painting, Yabrud, HU 2174.

The Southern Culture (Plates 11—12).

Plate 11 and Photos 39–45 show clearly that the painted style is dominant in the pottery of southern Palestine[9]. This style of painting, which we shall designate as 'line-group,' consists of straight or wavy lines, mostly composed in groups, with the pattern formed by the diagonal intersection of these groups. The pattern covers the entire body, reaching to just above the base. Bowls are often painted on the inside only. The color of the paint ranges between red and reddish-brown. Small vessels are mostly painted directly on the bare clay. Large vessels are painted less carefully: no real pattern emerges from the lines, painted with a broad brush, mostly on a white slip of lime.

A comparison between the repertoires of the Northern and the Southern cultures shows that most of the types are present in both. This fact alone should be considered as a point against a clear-cut regionalism. However, the following summary brings out the intrinsic differences:

Bowls: Very common are the hemispherical bowls (No. 2), also with a shallow omphalos (No. 1, Photo 48). Platters are common in the South as well as in the North (Nos. 3–4). Most typical is No. 6, in the tradition of the V-shaped bowl, which is painted all over.

Teapots (Pl. 12): These have been discussed above; they occur in both regions, but specimens with red burnished slip are restricted to the North.

Amphoriskoi: The amphoriskos shows many more variations in the South (Nos. 5, 8–9, 12–15, Photos 40, 42, 43, 44, 49).

---

8. J. B. Pritchard, *The Excavations at Herodian Jericho*, New Haven, 1951, pp. 17–19.
9. Specimens of this ware are turning up in the North, as e.g. at Arqule al-Dhabr (ADAJ. III) and now at Nahal Tavor (unpublished — courtesy Prof. P. Delougaz).

PLATE 11

1.	Bowl, pink	1:5	Ai	T.C	Ay, pl. LXXI:731
2.	Bowl, pink	1:5	Ai	T.G	Ay pl. LXXIII:987
3.	Bowl, pink, red burnished slip	1:5	Ai	T.G	Ay pl. LXXV:1315
4.	Bowl, buff, brown slip	1:5	Ai	T.B	Ay pl. LXVII:14.24
5.	Spouted jug, buff, red slip	1:5	Ai	T.C	Ay pl. LXVII:7.587
6.	Bowl, pink, red decoration	1:5	Ai	T.G	Ay pl. LXXII:828
7.	Bowl, pink	1:5	Ai	T.C	Ay, pl. LXVII:39.135
8.	Amphoriskos, buff, red decoration	1:5	Ophel	T.3	PMB 3, pl. IV:3
9.	Bottle, red, dark red decoration	1:5	Ophel	T.3	PMB 3, pl. IV:4
10.	Spouted jug, light brown, brown-red decoration	1:5	Ai	T.G	Ay, pl. LXVII:10.922
11.	Spouted bowl, pink, red decoration	1:5	Ai	T.G	Ay, pl. LXXII:825
12.	Twin-bottles, yellow, brown decoration	1:5	Ophel	T.3	PMB 3, pl. IV:10
13.	Amphoriskos, pink, red decoration	1:5	Ai	T.G	Ay, pl. LXXII:870
14.	Amphoriskos, buff, dark brown decoration	1:5	Ai	T.C	Ay, pl. LXX:552
15.	Juglet, buff, dark red decoration	1:5	Ai	T.	Ay, pl. LXVII:50.91
16.	Amphoriskos, grey	1:5	Ai	T.C	Ay, pl. LXXIX:561
17.	Jug, grey	1:5	Ai	T.C	Ay, pl. LXVII:37.554
18.	Jar, buff	1:5	Ai	T.C	Ay, pl. LXVIII:145
19.	Jug, buff, red burnished slip, red decoration	1:5	Ai	T.G	Ay, pl. LXXV:1313
20.	Juglet, pink	1:5	Ai	T.G	Ay, pl. LXXII:826
21.	Juglet, brown-pink	1:5	Ai	T.G	Ay, pl. LXXIII:928
22.	Jar, brown-pink	1:5	Ai	T.G	Ay, pl. LXXIII:927
23.	Spouted jug, light brown	1:5	Ai	T.G	Ay, pl. LXVII:1.912
24.	Jar, brown-pink, white slip, red decoration	1:5	Ai	T.G	Ay, pl. LXXIII:933
25.	Spouted jar, light brown, traces of red decoration	1:5	Ai	T.G	Ay, pl. LXXIII:931

PLATE | 11

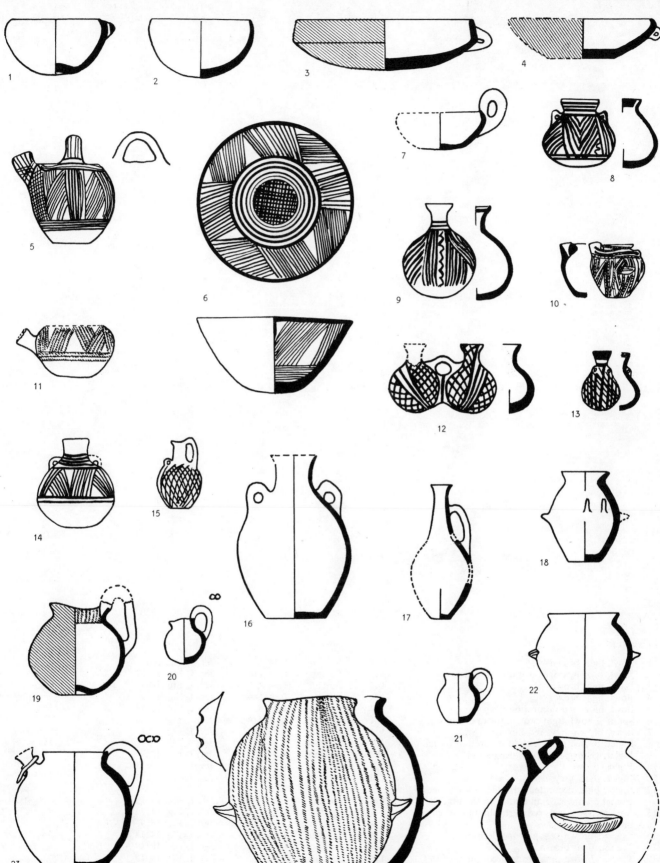

PLATE | 12

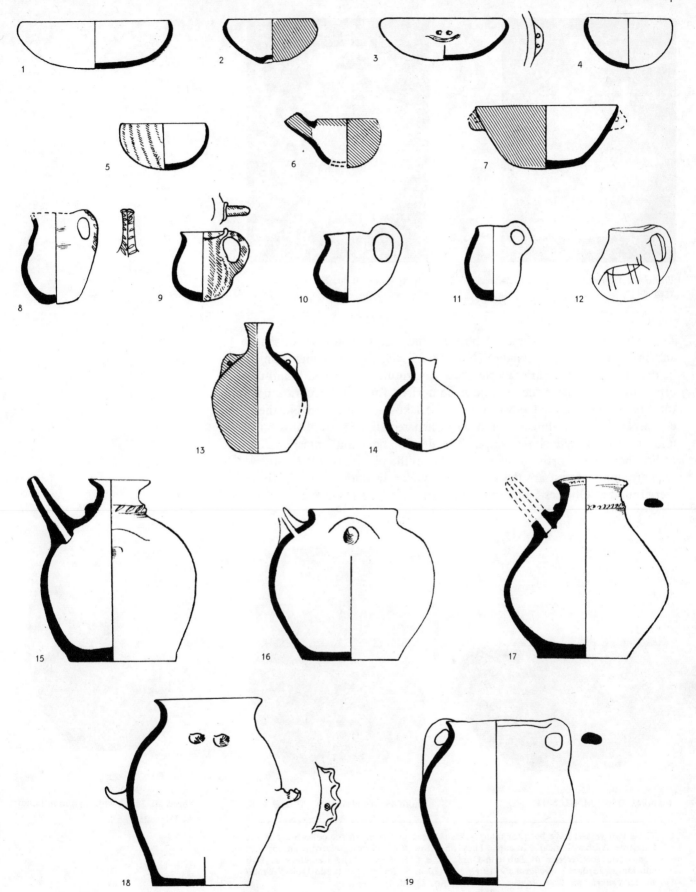

Photo 46. Amphoriskos, Kh. Masada,
IDA V. 1785.

Photo 47. Small jar, Kh. Masada,
IDA V. 1790.

Jars, jugs, and juglets: These, of both regions, are very similar in shape
and in their spouts and handles (Nos. 18–25). The logical conclusion to
be drawn is that there are two elements, one rooted in the South and the
other in the North: the Southern comprises form-and-decoration —
the 'line-group' painted bowl and amphoriskos — while the Northern
comprises form-and-finish — the burnished red-slipped omphalos-bowl
and the bag-shaped closed vessel. The development and intermingling
of Southern and Northern elements make up the picture of EB I pottery.
Of particular interest are the two vessels shown in Photos 44–45, which
were found at Ghor es-Safi, at the southern end of the Dead Sea.[10]

Photo 48. Bowl, Ai, HU 5011.

Photo 49. Amphoriskos, Ai, HU 5142.

Photo 50. Juglet with high loop-handle,
Ai HU 5251.

10. These two vessels have been for many years isolated specimens in the collections of the
Palestine Archaeological Museum. They find now their closest relatives among the
tremendous discoveries of Bab edh-Dhra: cf. e.g. P. Lapp, "The Cemetery at Bab
edh-Dhra, Jordan," *Archaeology*, 19 (1966), 110 ff. S. Saller, "Bab edh-Dhra," *Studii
Biblici Franciscani liber Annuus*, XV, 1966, pp. 137 ff.

Material from Stratified Deposits (Plates 13—14).

Most of the pottery shown in Plates 9-12 comes from tomb-deposits. Such a selection, though rich and varied enough, has its shortcomings, since it lacks many vessels of daily use. This is especially true in the Early Bronze, when there is a noticeable difference between funeral and stratified deposits. Were special types of pottery made for use in the cult of the dead, or rather, did the cult of the dead require special types of vessels?

Platters and bowls: Platters Nos. 2–5 represent variations of this most characteristic form of the EB. They have low, inverted or sometimes everted walls, a broad, flattish, often slightly rounded base, and a characteristic inverted rim (No. 4); sometimes a single pierced lug-handle is attached (No. 3). They are red-slipped and burnished mainly on the inside. Pattern- or net-burnishing begins in the EB I, but becomes more common in EB II. No. 1 is a rather large tray. Nos. 6–8 are the typical hemispherical bowls, common in stratified deposits as well as in tombs.

Amphoriskoi: These are less common than in tombs. Plain examples (No. 10) and unusually large painted specimens (No. 9) are also known.

Jugs and juglets: No. 11 is a very large juglet which is really a hybrid juglet-amphoriscos painted in the Southern style. The dominant type is, of course, the juglet with the high loop-handle (No. 12). The twin-vessel (No. 13) also appears in such deposits.

Cooking-pots: This is one of the vessels least to be expected in tomb-deposits. The cooking-pot throughout the EB period is a holemouth vessel. At Arad we have been able to differentiate between holemouth cooking-pots and holemouth storage-jars: the first has a globular body and a rounded base, while the second has a pear-shaped elongated body and a flat base. However, sometimes a smaller version of the flat-based holemouth jar shows the same covering of soot as the globular holemouth cooking-pots, in contradiction of clear-cut distinction. Much more work is needed to elucidate this culturally important question. Nos. 6–7 (Plate 14) seem to be cooking-pots of this last-mentioned kind.

Jars: These continue the tradition of the Chalcolithic period, both in the use of rope decoration, and in the forms: jars with and without neck. Jars with neck show several types: short everted necks (Nos. 1, 4, 5, 8) and rail-rims (Nos. 2–3). Many are decorated with painting. As will be remembered, the Northern style of painting differs from the Southern. Jars without neck, that is, with holemouth rims (Nos. 9–10) show minor variations in the thickening of these rims. These rims may be decorated with a sort of rope-decoration, a thin band of clay applied immediately below the rim, sometimes with slight finger-indentation, or twisting. Ledge-handles are the main feature in jars of EB I, but loop-handles also occur. No. 10 (which contained a child-burial), has a small loop-handle in an unexpected location.

PLATE | 13

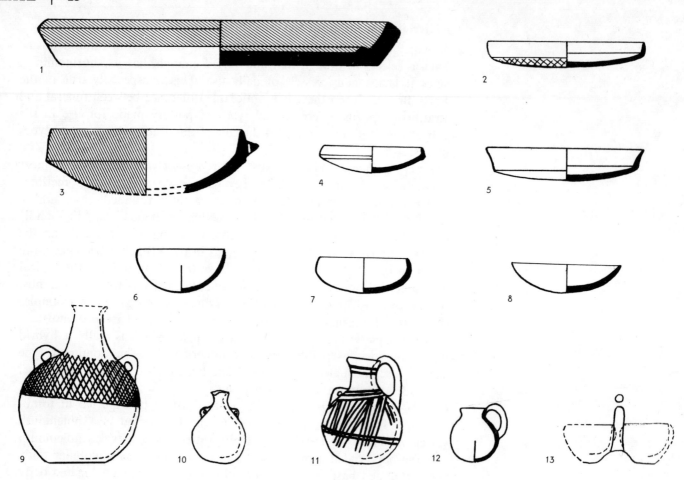

PLATE 13

1.	Platter, buff, red slip	1:5	Megiddo	XVIII	Meg. II, pl. 4:10
2.	Platter, grey, brown-red burnished slip	1:5	Far'ah (N)		RB, 1947, p. 413, Fig. 4:8
3.	Platter, buff, red burnished slip	1:5	Far'ah (N)		RB, 1948, p. 561, Fig. 6:15
4.	Bowl	1:4	Beth-shan	XIV	MJ (BS), pl. V:21
5.	Bowl, grey, red slip	1:5	Far'ah (N)		RB, 1947, p. 413, Fig. 4:14
6.	Bowl, brown	1:5	Jericho	VI	XXIII, pl. XXXVI:8
7.	Bowl, buff	1:5	Far'ah (N)		RB, 1948, p. 559, Fig. 5:28
8.	Bowl, pink	1:5	Far'ah (N)		RB, 1948, p. 559, Fig. 5:22
9.	Amphoriskos, grey, red decoration	1:5	Jericho	VI	AAA XXIII, pl. XXXVI:1
10.	Amphoriskos, grey	1:5	Jericho	VI	AAA XXIII, pl. XXXVI:3
11.	Juglet, brown, red decoration	1:5	Jericho	VI	AAA XXIII, pl. XXXVI:4
12.	Juglet, brown-grey	1:5	Jericho	VII	AAA XXIII, pl. XXXVI:21
13.	Twin-bowls, light brown	1:5	Jericho	VII	AAA XXIII, pl. XXXVI:23

PLATE 14

1.	Pithos, pink	1:10	Ras el-Ain		QDAP V, p. 121:73
2.	Pithos, reddish-brown	1:8	Jericho	VII	AAA XXIII, pl. XXXIV:19
3.	Jar	1:10	Beth-shan	XIV	MJ (BS), pl. IV:17
4.	Jar, light brown, brown slip	1:8	Afula		JPOS XXI, pl. V:1
5.	Jar, pink	1:10	Far'ah (N)		RB, 1947, p. 411, Fig. 3:11
6.	Spouted krater, yellow-brown	1:10	Far'ah (N)		RB, 1947, p. 411, Fig. 3:6
7.	Holemouth jar, yellow	1:10	Far'ah (N)		RB, 1947, p. 411, Fig. 3:1
8.	Jar, pink	1:10	Far'ah (N)		RB, 1947, p. 411, Fig. 3:10
9.	Holemouth jar	1:10	Beth-shan	XIV	MJ (BS), pl. IV:1
10.	Holemouth jar	1:10	Beth Yerah	XVI	IDA

PLATE | 14

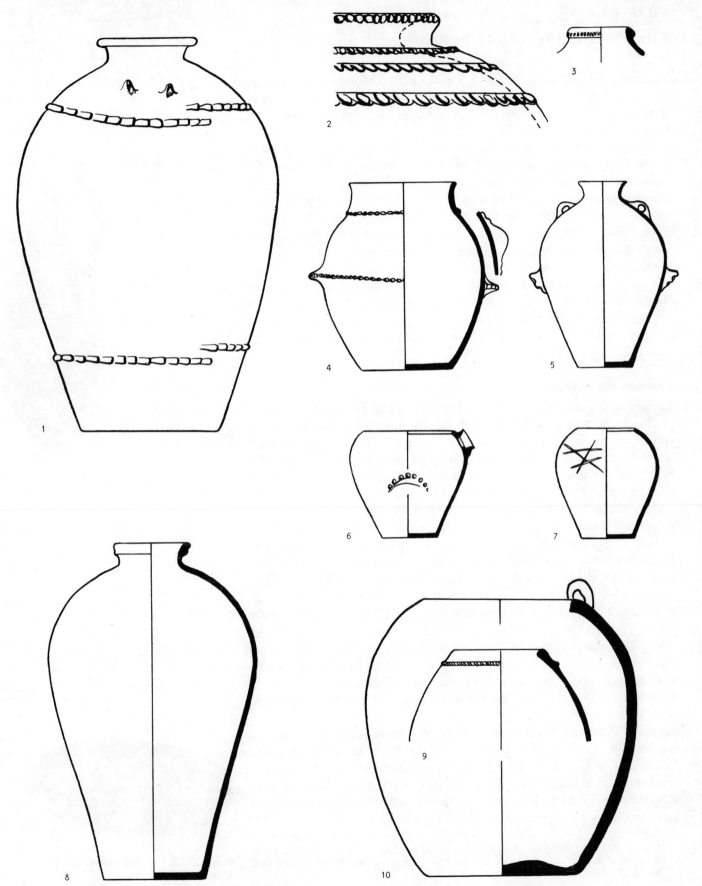

CHAPTER FIVE

THE EARLY BRONZE II PERIOD

This period is justifiably designated as the period of urbanization. Large sites and walled cities have been discovered and some partly excavated, throughout Palestine, from the forested hills of Upper Galilee to the Negev of Arad.

The pottery of EB II is the main anchor of Palestinian chronology in the entire Early Bronze Period, and indirectly it bears on the history and chronology of Egypt in the Proto-Dynastic period and in the Old Kingdom. The synchronization of EB II with the First Dynasty of Egypt is based on the foreign pottery found in the First Dynasty tombs of Pharaos, nobles, and commoners at Abydos, Saqqara, Abusir el-Melek, and other sites.[1] This foreign pottery was undoubtedly imported into Egypt from the Canaanite area. As we shall see below, new evidence from Arad may perhaps narrow down the region where the homeland of this pottery should be sought from the extensive area between the Amuq and Jericho to the area of southern Palestine.

We have arranged the material in three Plates, and placed the types which also occur in Egypt in the last Plate.

Common Wares (Plates 15—16).

Platters and bowls: (Plate 15:1–9, Photo 51). The platter is one of the predominant forms in EB II, and usually has a red burnished slip, sometimes burnished in a net or trellis pattern. A characteristic feature is the roughly finished base, often bearing an incised mark, considered to be a potter's mark, such as the star in Photo 51. Another type of platter, or rather tray, has a flat base (Nos. 7–8), while the deep large bowl with sloping sides (No. 9), is also quite common.

Chalices: (Plate 15:10). This is an uncommon type, and may be the earliest example of this form of chalice. Alternatively, it should perhaps be considered as an echo of the Chalcolithic tradition, which, as we saw above, is also evident in the Grey Burnished Ware of EB I.

Amphoriskoi: (Plate 15:14–17). Vessels like No. 14, painted in the Southern 'line-group' style, continue to appear, but to a much lesser extent than in the preceding period. Three variants of this style, all diverging considerably from the EB I prototype, and from No. 14, are shown in Nos. 15–17. The neck has grown, the location of the lug-handles has changed, and other traits have undergone degeneration.

Twin-vessels: (Plate 15:11). We met this type earlier in EB I. The present form is much larger in size.

Juglets: (Plate 15:12–13). The commonest type of juglet of the period is a diminutive version of the typical jug. Photo 57 shows that degenerated handles, as on the jug in Photo 51, also occur on juglets, which are sometimes actual miniatures. No. 12 is a variant of the common juglet. No. 13 is a combination of juglet and amphoriskos, and shows that this hybrid type continues to appear (cf. above, Plate 13:11).

Photo 51. Platter, Star incised on base, Kefar-Ata, IDA 45.204.

---

1. Various aspects of the subject have been treated by Frankfort, Albright, Wright, Braidwood, and Kantor. Cf. H. J. Kantor, in *Chronologies in Old World Archaeology*, (ed. R. W. Ehrich), Chicago, 1965.

Jars: (Plate 16). The tradition of the previous period continues, though with a number of significant changes. The applied rope ornamentation has almost gone out of use, and combing, a new method of decoration, makes its appearance (No. 1, Photo 52). The entire surface of the jar is combed in two directions so as to form an over-all pattern. This combing seems to be primarily a technique for improving the quality of the ware rather than an ornament. And indeed the new combed ware is better levigated, better fired, and gives off a metallic sound. The painted net-pattern continues to be popular (No. 2, Photo 53). The jars can again be divided into those with neck (Nos. 1, 7–9), and those without (holemouth jars, No. 6). An intermediate type has a very short neck (Nos. 2–3) with a thick rail-like rim, or only such a rim without any neck at all (Nos. 4–5). The holemouth jars are very common, mostly with rims thickened on the inside, as if the rim had been folded over during the manufacturing. No. 3 is of particular interest: the thin-walled jar is made of fine, well-levigated ware, well-baked to a metallic quality, and has an unusual delicately profiled rim. The jar has a burnished rose-red slip. Tubular handles, encountered since the Chalcolithic period, continue to be made (No. 4, Photo 53).

The 'Abydos' Ware (Plate 17).

The importance of the Canaanite pottery found in the royal tombs of the First Dynasty in Egypt has already been mentioned. Plate 17 attempts to show the full range of this class of pottery — jugs, bottles, and jars — side by side with similar vessels found in Palestinian excavations. The designation 'Abydos', after the site in Upper Egypt where it was first found, is not a happy one.

Jugs: The jug is the most typical shape of the period and the commonest form among the foreign vessels found at Abydos, and at other sites in Egypt. The shape of its body is oval, with an almost perfect symmetry

Photos 54–56. Jug and two juglets, Kefar-Ata, IDA 45.205–7.

Photo 52. Jar, combed, Beth-Yerah, IDA 51-802.

Photo 53. Jar, net-painted, Beth-Yerah, IDA 69-7013.

PLATE 15

1.	Platter	1:5	Beth-shan	XIII	MJ (BS), pl. V:22
2.	Platter, grey-buff, red burnished slip	1:5	Far'ah (N)		RB, 1948, p. 565, Fig. 8:8
3.	Bowl, buff, red burnished slip	1:5	Far'ah (N)		RB, 1948, p. 565, Fig. 8:6
4.	Platter, pink		Beth Yerah	XIII B	IDA
5.	Platter, buff, red pattern burnished slip	1:5	Megiddo	XVII	Meg. II, pl. 5:17
6.	Platter, buff	1:5	Megiddo	XVII	Meg. II, pl. 5:16
7.	Deep platter, white-buff	1:5	Megiddo	XVII	Meg. II, pl. 5:19
8.	Platter, buff	1:5	Megiddo	XVII	Meg. II, pl. 5:18
9.	Bowl, pink-buff, white slip	1:5	Megiddo	XVIII	Meg. II, pl. 4:8
10.	Chalice, brown-red, red decoration	1:4	Jericho	V–IV	AAA XXIII, pl. XXXIX:7
11.	Twin-vessels, buff, brown-red decoration	1:5	Megiddo	XVII	Meg. II, pl. 5:5
12.	Juglet	1:5	Far'ah (N)		RB, 1948, p. 565, Fig. 8:2
13.	Jug, light brown	1:4	Jericho	V	AAA XXIII, pl. XXXIX:13
14.	Amphoriskos, light brown, red decoration	1:4	Jericho	IV	AAA XXIII, pl. XXXIX:6
15.	Amphoriskos	1:5	Beth-shan		MJ (BS), pl. V:9
16.	Amphoriskos, buff, pink slip	1:5	Far'ah (N)		RB, 1948, p. 565, Fig. I:11
17.	Amphoriskos, buff, red slip	1:5	Far'ah (N)		RB, 1948, p. 565, Fig. 8:10

PLATE | 15

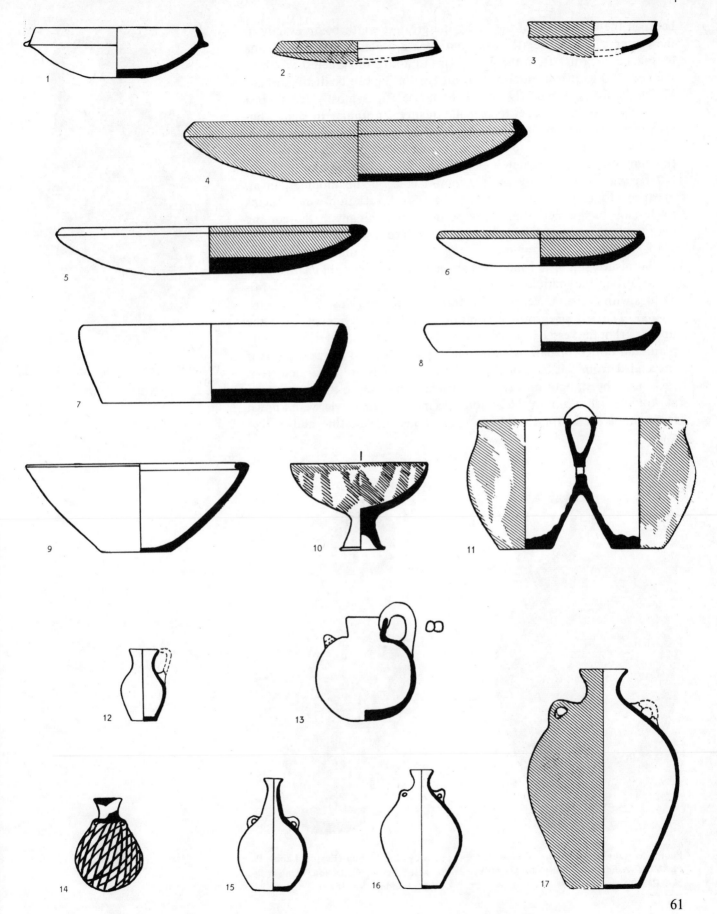

between the two halves of the body, the greatest width being exactly in the center; the diameters of base and neck are almost equal, and one loop-handle springs from the flaring rim to above the greatest width of the body. At least five variations of this type of jug can be distinguished: 1) The typical specimen (Nos. 1–2, Photo 55); it is mostly red-slipped and sometimes hard-baked to metallic quality. 2) Similar in shape, but provided with two small, mostly degenerated loop-handles on the body of the vessel, in addition to the usual handle (Nos. 3–4, Photos 54, 59); the same shape comes also in juglets (Photo 57). 3) Also similar in shape, but having one small degenerated loop-handle on the shoulder, in an unexpected location (No. 5 and Photo 58). 4) A variation which begins to develop in this period and will become predominant in the coming one: the lower part of the jug has developed into a somewhat cylindrical shape, designated as a stump-base. This jug is also commonly finished in red burnished slip. The handle has also undergone a certain change: it is drawn from the middle of the neck to the shoulder (Nos. 13–14). 5) Jugs with a distinctive style of painted decoration (Nos. 6–10, Photos 60–61). The red or brown decoration, which covers mostly only the upper part of the vessel, consists of bands divided into triangles, alternately plain and dotted or hatched, with the uppermost band of triangles as if suspended from the base of the neck. These bands are separated from each other by straight or wavy lines or chevrons. Before the excavations at Arad (which began in 1962) more specimens of this style were known from tombs in Egypt than from excavations in Palestine and Syria–

Photo 57. Juglet, Arad, Excavation No. 5009.

Photo 58. Juglet, Abydos, Abydos I, Pl. VIII, Ashmolean Museum, Oxford No. E3240.

Photo 59. Jug, Lahun (Egypt), Lahun II, Pl. LIII, Petrie Collection, University College, London, No. 16250.

PLATE | 16

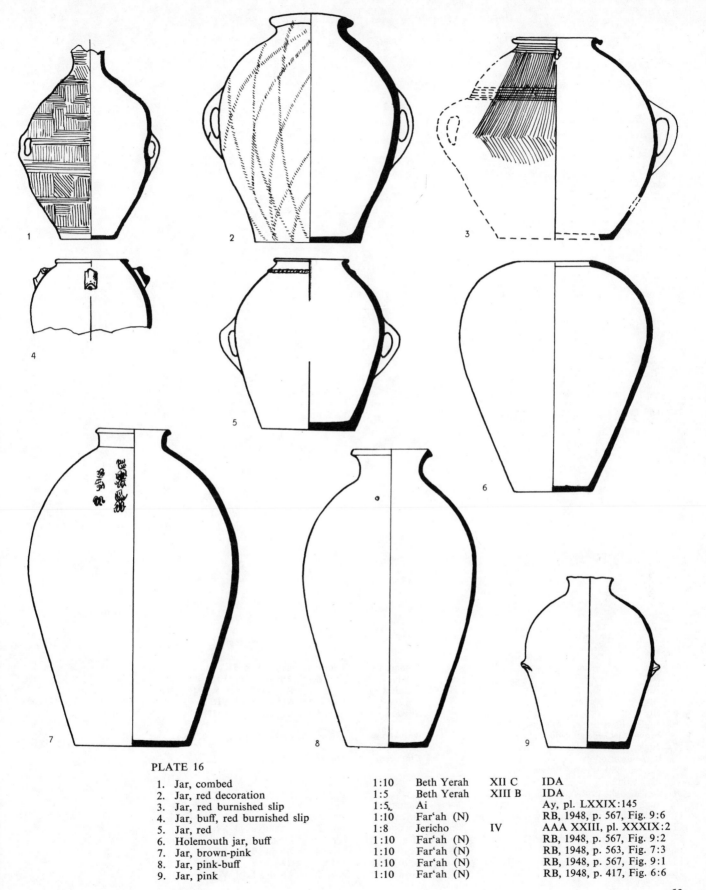

PLATE 16

1.	Jar, combed	1:10	Beth Yerah	XII C	IDA
2.	Jar, red decoration	1:5	Beth Yerah	XIII B	IDA
3.	Jar, red burnished slip	1:5	Ai		Ay, pl. LXXIX:145
4.	Jar, buff, red burnished slip	1:10	Far'ah (N)		RB, 1948, p. 567, Fig. 9:6
5.	Jar, red	1:8	Jericho	IV	AAA XXIII, pl. XXXIX:2
6.	Holemouth jar, buff	1:10	Far'ah (N)		RB, 1948, p. 567, Fig. 9:2
7.	Jar, brown-pink	1:10	Far'ah (N)		RB, 1948, p. 563, Fig. 7:3
8.	Jar, pink-buff	1:10	Far'ah (N)		RB, 1948, p. 567, Fig. 9:1
9.	Jar, pink	1:10	Far'ah (N)		RB, 1948, p. 417, Fig. 6:6

PLATE 17

1.	Jug	1:5	Kinnereth	Tomb	Unpublished
2.	Jug	1:6	Abydos	T. of Zer	Abydos I, pl. VIII:4
3.	Jug	1:5	Far'ah (N)		RB, 1948, p. 555, Fig. 4
4.	Jug	1:6	Abydos	T. of Zer	Abydos I, pl. VIII:8
5.	Jug	1:6	Abydos	T. of Zer	Abydos I, pl. VIII:5
6.	Juglet, light brown, brown-black brown-black decoration	1:2	Beth-shan		Beth-Shan III, pl. XXX:1
7.	Juglet, light brown, brown-black decoration	1:3	Kinnereth	Tomb	BJPES X, pl. I:44
8.	Juglet, light brown, brown-black decoration	1:3	Kinnereth	Tomb	BJPES X, pl. I:45
9.	Juglet, light brown, black decoration	1:4	Jericho	T. 127 A	Jer. I, Fig. 25:34
10.	Jug		Saqqara		Kantor, COWA, Fig. 3:4
11.	Bottle, light grey, brown burnished slip	1:5	Jericho		AAA XXII, pl. XXVII:24
12.	Bottle	1:6	Abydos	T. of Zer	Abydos I pl. VIII:2
13.	Jug, buff red burnished slip	1:5	Megiddo	XVII	Meg. II pl. 5:1
14.	Jug	1:6	Abydos		Abydos I pl. VI:17
15.	Jar, combed	1:10	Beth Yerah	XII C	IDA
16.	Jar, combed	1:6	Abydos	T. of Zer	Abydos I pl. VIII:6

PLATE | 17

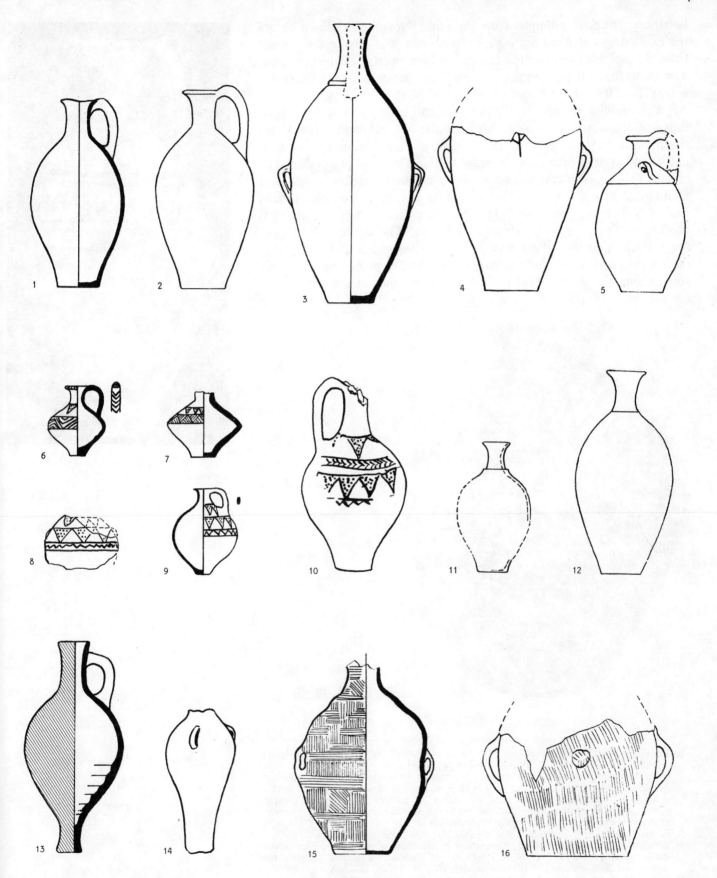

Lebanon. The four examples from Palestine (Nos. 6–9)[2] known before the excavations at Arad are juglets rather than jugs. Up to the present time, no jugs with this painted decoration have been unearthed at Arad. The forms found there are various types of jars, much as that in Photo 61: a small jar, with degenerated handles, somewhat resembling a jar from Abydos[3] published years ago. Sherds of this painted style have been found in other excavations, e.g., Megiddo, Beth Yerah, and in the Amuq sites, Phase H.[4] The preponderant quantity of specimens of this style now found at Arad permits us to suggest that its home of origin should be sought in southern Canaan, and not in its northern reaches, as has been maintained before. Plate 17:15–16 are two jars with comb-decoration, one of which was found in Egypt. Net-burnished vessels, mostly jars, are known from the same deposits in Egypt.[5] The bottles Nos. 11–12 are variations of the jug. It may perhaps be suggested that most types of the closed vessel have 'wandered' down to Egypt as containers for some Canaanite goods, most probably various kinds of oil.

Photo 60. Painted jug, Abusir (Egypt), *Graeberfeld bei Abusir*, Pl. 27.

Photo 61. Painted jar, Arad, Excavation No. 4163.

2. The tiny juglet from Beth-shan (*No.* 6); I hesitated between the possibility of assigning it to the 'Chocolate-on-White' Ware (see below, Plate 49) and the 'Abydos' style. After examining the specimen in the University Museum at Philadelphia, I incline rather to the second possibility. As for No. 7 — since it was found completely covered with a greenish-white incrustation — it was not drawn as painted in Maisler's (Mazar) publication. The two small juglets from the Tomb at Kinnereth date most probably to the very end of the EB II, on the border of EB III.
3. E. Amélineau, *Les nouvelles fouilles d'Abydos*, 1895–1896 (Paris, 1899) pl. 13.
4. R. W. and Linda S. Braidwood, *Excavations in the Plain of Antioch*, I, *The Earliest Assemblages, Phases A–J* Chicago, 1960. Miriam Tadmor, "Contacts between the 'Amuq and Syria-Palestine'" (Review-article), *IEJ*, 14 (1964), 253–269.
5. H. Frankfort, *Studies in the Early Pottery of the Near East*, I, London, 1924, pl. X.

CHAPTER SIX

THE EARLY BRONZE III PERIOD

Chronologically this period corresponds to the duration of the Old Kingdom in Egypt, that is, Dynasties III–VI. Interconnections between Canaan and Egypt — for which there is now more varied evidence than mere pottery — continued to flourish. Besides large quantities of Canaanite pottery found in many Egyptian tomb deposits,[1] and Egyptian imports into Canaan, such as the group of Egyptian alabaster vessels from Sanctuary A at Ai,[2] there is evidence of trade relations and raids into Palestine from Egyptian wall-reliefs and records.[3]

The outstanding ceramic feature of the period is the Khirbet Kerak Ware, which opens up interesting speculations concerning connections with remote regions to the north of Canaan. Plate 19 has been devoted to this ware.

Plate 18 shows a selection of the common forms of the period as well as some special types. We have followed here the accepted date for Sanctuary A at Ai,[4] using some of the material from there to illustrate the common EB III forms.

Common Wares (Plate 18).

Platters and bowls: Nos. 1–5 are derived from the large platters current since EB I, with changes evident in the profiling of the rim and in the finish of the base. The deep bowl (No. 6), usually equipped with ledge-handles, is a characteristic feature of the period.

Chalices: The chalice (No. 7) is uncommon in this period.

Cups: The cup with flaring wall (Nos. 8–9, Photo 62) is also an uncommon form. The suggestion has been made that these cups are imitations in pottery of Egyptian stone prototypes. This suggestion seems plausible, in view of the alabaster vases found at Ai.

Photo 62. Goblet, Ai, IDA 36.584.

Cooking-pots: No. 11 represents one of the types of holemouth cooking-pots. This specimen is furnished with two ledge-handles and a spout very near the rim.

Jars: No. 10 has four small elongated knobs, reminiscent of the tubular lug-handles of the preceding periods (Photo 63). No. 12 has ledge-handles and is the commonest type current. No. 13, a large jar, is furnished with two of the most distinctive features of the period: pattern-combing and rope-decoration at the base of the neck.

Photo 63. Jar, Lachish, La. IV, Pl. 15.

1. G. A. Reisner and W. S. Smith, *A History of Giza Necropolis*, II, *The Tomb of Hetep Heres, the Mother of Cheops* Cambridge, Mass., 1955.
2. J. Marquet-Krause, *Les fouilles de 'Ay (Et-Tell) 1933–1935*, Paris, 1949.
3. *ANET*, pp. 227–228.
4. Cf. e.g. Wright, "The Archaeology of Palestine," *The Bible and the Ancient Near East*, London, 1961.

Photo 65. Pot, Afula, IDA 37.666.

The Khirbet Kerak Ware (Plate 19).

With the Khirbet Kerak Ware an element entirely foreign to the Palestinian pottery of the Early Bronze period appears on the scene. Forms and techniques differ in many respects from those current in local pottery: 1) quality of the clay; 2) methods of manufacture; 3) surface finishing; 4) firing; 5) conception of form and details; 6) decoration.

1) The quality of the clay, especially in the larger vessels, is poor; the ware is brittle, perhaps due to imperfect mixing of the clay with the temper.

2) The methods of manufacture differ radically. In vessels of the Khirbet Kerak Ware — whether large or small — there is no sign of the knowledge of the potter's wheel.

3) The vessel is covered both inside and out with a heavy slip, which is burnished to a high gloss. Perhaps the heavy slip and the well burnished finish of the surface were meant to compensate for the poor quality of the clay.

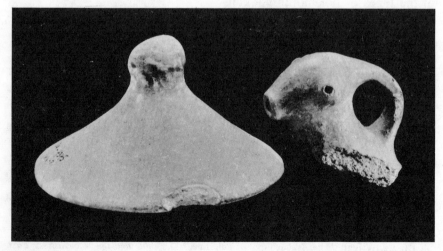

Photo 66. Lid, Beth-Yerah, IDA 51–1554.   Photo 67. Lid, Beth-Yerah, IDA 50–4345.

68

Photo 64. Large bowl, Beth-Yerah, IDA 51–3418.

Photo 68. Sherds of bowls and stand, Beth Yerah, IDA.

4) The method of firing, which produced partly black and partly red vessels, is otherwise unknown in the Palestinian pottery repertoire. Any vessel whose surface is partly black and partly red bears witness to the technical knowledge of smoke-blackening during firing. It should be emphasized that this red-and-black color scheme is not accidental — it reflects a definite aesthetic conception and requires a high standard of specialized technical knowledge.[5] Besides the Khirbet Kerak Ware, two other pottery cultures in the Eastern Mediterranean show the same combination of colors: 1) The Egyptian Pre-Dynastic 'Black-Topped' ware;[6] 2) The Red-Polished Ware of the early Cypriot period. At present it seems impossible to recognize any relationship between the Khirbet Kerak Ware and the 'Black-Topped' ware of Egypt. The Red-Polished Cypriot Ware, on the other hand, may prove to be a distant relative of our ware.

5) We are confronted with a radically different conception of form. The most striking difference is found in the proportions of the vessel. In the Early Canaanite world of forms we feel the proportions to be 'normal' (if such an evaluation may be considered as descriptive): the base is always either larger than the mouth or of the same diameter, and the vessel is never top-heavy. In the Khirbet Kerak Ware the base is small in proportion to the body and the mouth in vessels of all sizes. Another point of difference is the outline of the body: the Early Canaanite vessel grows from the base with one curve only until it draws in to the rim. In the Khirbet Kerak Ware a complicated S-line marks the outline. It is beyond the scope of this book to attempt an explanation of these differences.

The range of forms of the Khirbet Kerak Ware includes: a) small delicate bowls with omphalos base and straight wall (No. 1 and Photo 68:2); b) small deep bowls, with small omphalos base and S-line wall (Nos. 2–4, Photo 68:5); c) large bowls (Nos. 9, 12, and Photos 64, 68:1, 3); d) pots of small and medium size, with S-line profile and usually one handle (Nos. 5–8, Photo 65); it is difficult to describe this form by means of the usual Palestinian terminology; e) the large jugs Nos. 13 and 16 are Canaanite in form, but Khirbet Kerak in their ware and their deco-

5. Y. Yadin, *BASOR*, 106 (1947), pp. 9–17.
6. F. Petrie, *Diospolis Parva* London, 1901.

Photo 72. Cylindrical Jar, Beth Yerah, IDA 69.7012.

Photo 71. Horseshoe-shaped stand fragment, Beth Yerah, IDA 50–3773.

Photo 70. Horseshoe-shaped stand fragment, Beth Yerah, IDA 51–1540.

Photo 69. Horseshoe-shaped stand, Beth Yerah, IDA 53–1019.

ration; f) the stands (Nos. 10, 14, 15 and Photo 68:4) are common vessels in this culture and appear in several variants. Sometimes such stands are fenestrated or have a small internal ledge-handle; g) lids are very common in this assemblage (No. 11, Photos 66–67), and sometimes the top of the lid is shaped like an animal head; h) a horseshoe-shaped hearth or stand (Photos 69, 70, 71), with three knobs on the inner side and decorated with stylized human heads, is a very characteristic vessel. Photo 72 shows a unique cylindrical vessel which was found at Beth Yerah (Khirbet Kerak), many of whose features indicate a relationship to the Khirbet Kerak Ware.

There are many new details of form, such as the thin, ribbon-like loop-handle which stands off from the body of the vessel. The rim, too, has a special character — it is flaring and "squared off", as if the potter had finished it with a smoothing finger. In the discussion of the Grey Burnished Ware (above, p. 47) we noted that the rims are a point of resemblance between these two wares.

PLATE | 18

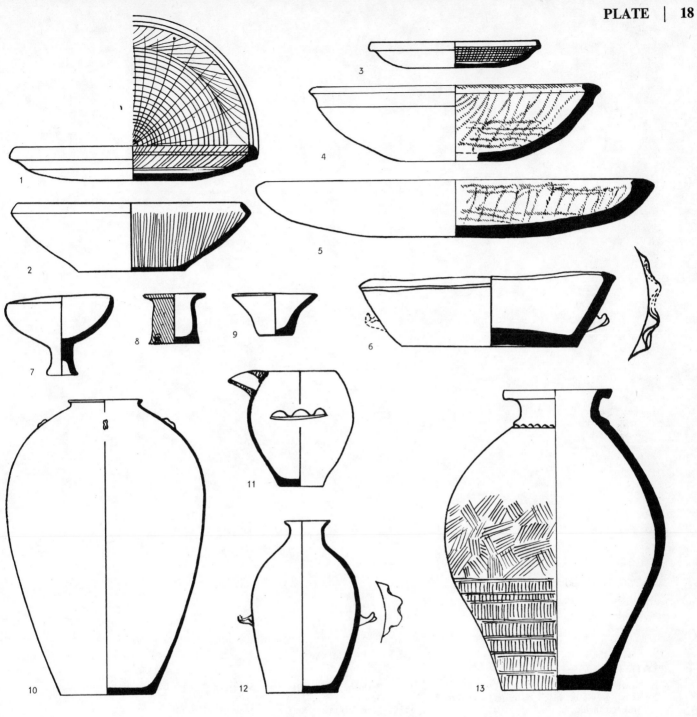

PLATE 18

1.	Platter	1:5	Beth-shan	XII	MJ (BS) pl. VIII:25
2.	Bowl	1:5	Beth-shan	XI	MJ (BS) pl. VIII:2
3.	Platter, brown, red pattern, burnished slip	1:5	Ai	Temple A	Ay pl. LXXVII:2023
4.	Bowl	1:5	Beth Yerah	X B	IDA
5.	Platter	1:5	Beth Yerah	X B	IDA
6.	Bowl	1:5	Ai	Temple A	Ay pl. LXV:1562
7.	Chalice	1:5	Ai	Temple A	Ay pl. LXXVII:2014
8.	Goblet, brown-pink	1:5	Ai	Temple A	Ay pl. LXV:24.1519
9.	Goblet, pink, red burnished slip	1:5	Ai	Temple A	Ay pl. LXV:18.1536
10.	Jar, pink-buff	1:10	Megiddo	XVl	Meg. II pl. 6:7
11.	Spouted holemouth jar	1:6	Ai	Temple A	Ay pl. LXV:23.1510
12.	Jar	1:6	Ai	Temple A	Ay pl. LXV:26.1503
13.	Jar	1:10	Beth Yerah	X B	IDA

PLATE 19

1.	Bowl	1:5	Beth-shan	XII	MJ (BS) pl. VIII:9
2.	Bowl, grey-buff, black burnished slip outside and red inside	1:5	Megiddo	XVII	Meg. II pl. 5:14
3.	Bowl	1:5	Beth-shan	XII	MJ (BS) pl. VIII:4
4.	Bowl	1:5	Beth-shan	XI	MJ (BS) pl. VIII:7
5.	Pot	1:5	Beth-shan	XII	MJ (BS) pl. VII:6
6.	Pot, grey, red burnished slip inside and black outside	1:5	Jericho	T.A	AAA XIX pl. VI:11
7.	Pot, grey, black burnished slip outside and red inside and over rim	1:5	Afula		JPOS XXI pl. X:2
8.	Pot, dark brown, burnished	1:5	Afula		JPOS XXI pl. II:28
9.	Krater	1:5	Beth Yerah	X B	IDA
10.	Pot-stand	1:5	Beth-shan	XI	MJ (BS) pl. VIII:6
11.	Lid	1:5	Beth-shan	XII	MJ (BS) pl. X:4
12.	Krater	1:5	Beth-shan	XII	MJ (BS) pl. VII:4
13.	Jug	1:5	Beth-shan	XII	MJ (BS) pl. VII:17
14.	Pot-stand, grey, brown burnished slip outside and red inside	1:5	Afula		JPOS XXI pl. XI:1
15.	Pot-stand	1:5	Beth-shan	XII	MJ (BS) pl. VIII:2
16.	Jug	1:5	Beth-shan	XII	MJ (BS) pl. VII:6

PLATE | 19

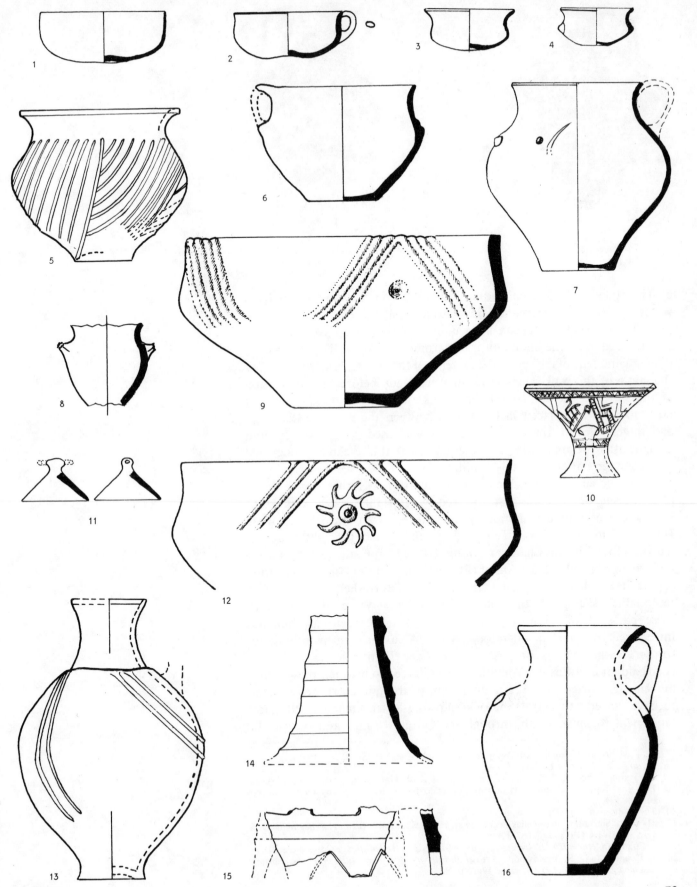

Photo 73. Juglet, painted white, Jericho, IDA 32.1791.

Photo 74. Jug, Jericho, IDA I.10039.

6) The style of decoration is quite different from any known in local wares: painted ornamentation is conspicuously absent; the grooved, incised, and relief decoration is so unlike anything we have previously encountered that the similarity is in terminology only. The decoration is an integral part of the vessel, the patterns of furrows and ridges following the curve of the wall. These patterns were made before the application of the slip and are sometimes shaped like a thistle (No. 12); isolated button-knobs are placed in the spaces between the groups of furrows and ridges (No. 9). Incised decoration is also used, as on No. 10, and is made after the application of the slip. A stylized bird can be recognized among other patterns on this stand.

The ceramic culture designated in this country as Khirbet Kerak Ware, after the site where it was first observed by Albright,[7] is not confined to Palestine, where its distribution is fairly dense, from Hazor[8] and Rosh Hanniqra[9] in the north to Tell Nagila[10] and Jericho[11] in the south. It has been found in Ras Shamra (Stratum III A),[12] in Hama (Stratum K),[13] and in various tells of the Amuq (Phase H-I).[14] In the Amuq excavation report it has been designated as Red-Black Burnished Ware. It is a reasonable assumption that the Khirbet Kerak Ware did not reach these parts of the Near East by means of trade relations, but was introduced by waves of migratory people. As a working hypothesis for further research, it is proposed to consider Transcaucasia, Armenia, Azarbaidjan and Eastern Anatolia as the home from which these ethnic movements started out. The main stream of the migratory waves seems to have flowed to Central Anatolia, allowing lesser streams of the same movement to move south, through the Orontes Valley and the coastal

---

7. W. F. Albright, "The Jordan Valley in the Bronze Age," *AASOR*, VI (1926).
8. *Hazor*, III–IV, pls. CLIV–CLV.
9. M. Tadmor and M. Prausnitz, "Excavations at Rosh Hanniqra," *Atiqot*, II (1959), 88.
10. The final report including this information is to be published shortly by R. Amiran and A. Eitan.
11. To be discussed in the following chapter.
12. Cl. F. A. Schaeffer, "Nouvelles découvertes á Ras Shamra," *Annales archéologiques de Syrie*, VIII–IX (1958–59), 167–178.
13. E. Fugmann, *Hama II* 1: *L'Architecture des périodes pre-Hellénistiques* Copenhagen, 1958.
14. R. J. and Linda S. Braidwood, *Excavations in the Plain of Antioch*, I, *The Earliest Assemblages, Phases A–J* Chicago, 1960, p. 82.

plains, as far as Jericho in the southern Jordan Valley.[15] These immigrant-settlers continued to make pottery in their native tradition although they found local traditions in their new homeland.

Tomb A at Jericho (Plates 20—21).

In view of the rich and varied deposits in this tomb, we have thought it useful to show here its main types, which illustrate in many forms and variations the pottery assemblage of EB III. To a great extent this pottery repertoire continues that of the previous period. At the same time it contains germs of elements which will develop in the coming period. On the one hand, jugs like Nos. 9, 12, and 15 manifest in many respects 'Abydos Ware' traditions, including the degenerated handles, and No. 13 (Photos 74–75) is derived from the stump-based jug of the previous period. On the other hand, jug No. 11 will find its continuation in a certain family in the coming MB I period. Juglets Nos. 18–20 are the precursors of the piriform juglet, which will be the dominant form in MB II A and B-C periods, and indicate the lines along which the juglet will develop. It is difficult to decide whether the black juglet No. 18 and Photo 73, both decorated with white dots, should be considered a prototype of the Tell el-Yahudiyeh juglets. Still more difficult to explain is the obvious typological relationship between EB III and MB II, which appears to skip one or perhaps two periods. The assumption that there exist regional cultures with chronological overlapping may be a useful stepping stone towards the understanding of such problems. Bowls Nos. 1–2 show traces of the spherical form so popular in preceding periods. The large shallow platters have evolved, and the base has become wide and flat instead of slightly rounded. No. 3 is a cup which recalls those found in the sanctuary at Ai, and possibly imitates stone prototypes. The Khirbet Kerak Ware is also represented in this tomb: No. 7 is a typical bowl, and No. 8 is a jug with many characteristics of the Khirbet Kerak Ware, such as the form and the knob-decoration. The same plastic decoration also appears in this group on other vessels, such as jugs Nos. 15–16, which do not belong to the Khirbet Kerak Ware. Decoration with pairs of knobs is, of course, not restricted to the Khirbet Kerak Ware. The storage jars in Tomb A shown on Plate 21 are the usual types current in the period. No. 1 is similar to jars found in the Megiddo tombs, discussed below in Chapter Seven. No. 3 has a small loop-handle on the holemouth rim, encountered before in Plate 14:10. Additional tombs of this period have been excavated more recently at Jericho (like Tomb F 4),[16] supplementing the information gained from Tomb A.

Photo 75. Jug, Jericho, IDA I.10032.

15. M. Tadmor, "Contacts Between the Amuq and Syria–Palestine" (Review-article), *IEJ*, 14, 1964, pp. 253 ff. Miss W. Lamb incorporated all the literature preceding her article in *Anatolian Studies*, IV (1954) ("the Culture of North East Anatolia and its Neighbors"). Some main items in literature after that article: C. A. Burney, "Eastern Anatolia in the Chalcolithic and Early Bronze Age," *AS*, VIII (1958). M. Mellink, in *Bibliotheca Orientalis*, XIX (1962), 223–24. P. Piotrovsky, "The Aeneolithic Culture in Transcaucasia in the Third Millennium," *VI International Congress of Prehistoric and Protohistoric Sciences* (Moscow, 1962). O. M. Dzhaparidze, "The Culture of Early Agricultural Tribes in the Territory of Georgia," *VII International Congress of Anthropological and Ethnological Sciences* (Moscow, 1964). H. Z. Kosay and H. Yary, *Pulur Kazisi*, Ankara, 1964. T. Ozguc, "Early Anatolian Archaeology in the Light of Recent Research," *Anatolia*, VII (1964). R. Amiran, "Yanik Tepe, Shengavit and the Khirbet Kerak Ware," *Anatolian Studies*, XV (1965).
16. K. M. Kenyon, *Excavations at Jericho* I, London, 1960, 126–146.

PLATE | 20

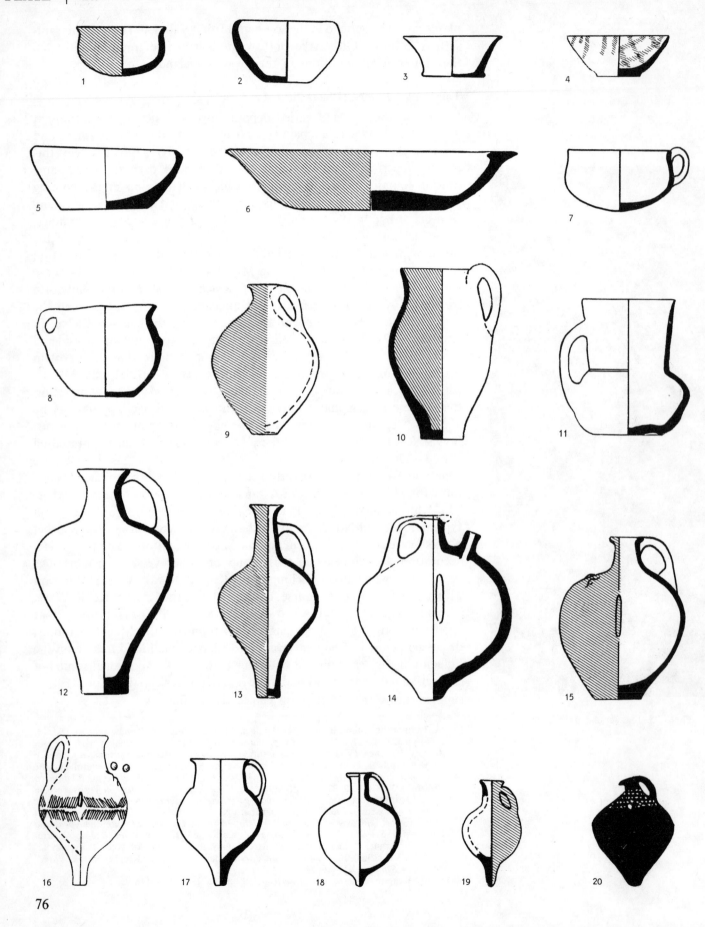

PLATE | 21

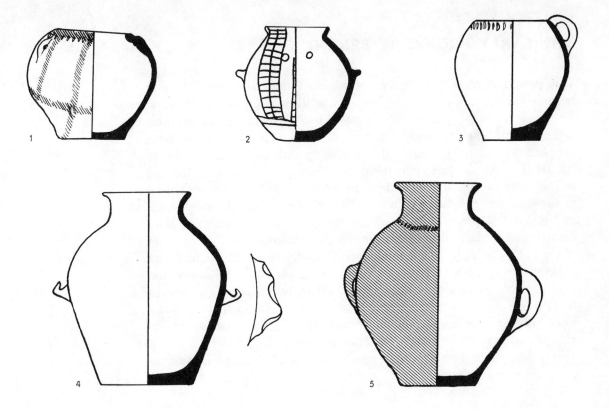

PLATE 20

1.	Bowl, light red, red slip	1:4	Jericho	T.A	AAA XIX pl. III:12
2.	Bowl, brown, black inside	1:4	Jericho	T.A	AAA XIX pl. IV:10
3.	Bow, grey, brown burnished slip	1:4	Jericho	T.A	AAA XIX pl. III:4
4.	Bowl, light red, red decoration	1:4	Jericho	T.A	AAA XIX pl. VIII:14
5.	Bowl, red	1:4	Jericho	T.A	AAA XIX pl. IV:17
6.	Bowl, buff, red burnished slip	1:4	Jericho	T.A	AAA XIX pl. IV:23
7.	Bowl, light red, red slip	1:4	Jericho	T.A	AAA XIX pl. VI:3
8.	Pot, cream, red slip	1:4	Jericho	T.A	AAA XIX, pl. VI:9
9.	Jug, yellowish-red, red burnished slip	1:4	Jericho	T.A	AAA XIX, pl. XXVII:7
10.	Jug, light red, red burnished slip	1:4	Jericho	T.A	AAA XIX, pl. V:9
11.	Jug, light brown	1:4	Jericho	T.A	AAA XIX, pl. VII:8
12.	Jug, light red	1:4	Jericho	T.A	AAA XIX, pl. III:21
13.	Jug, light brown, red slip	1:4	Jericho	T.A	AAA XIX, pl. III:20
14.	Spouted jug, grey-black, burnished	1:4	Jericho	T.A	AAA XIX, pl. VII:1
15.	Jug, light red, red burnished slip	1:4	Jericho	T.A	AAA XIX, pl. VII:7
16.	Jug, brown-grey, burnished, incised decoration	1:4	Jericho	T.A	AAA XIX, pl. VIII:6
17.	Jug, grey-black, burnished	1:4	Jericho	T.A	AAA XIX, pl. II:25
18.	Juglet, grey, black burnished slip	1:4	Jericho	T.A	AAA XIX, pl. II:20
19.	Juglet, light red, red slip	1:4	Jericho	T.A	AAA XIX, pl. II:17
20.	Juglet, black, white decoration	1:4	Jericho	T.A	AAA XIX, pl. XXVIII:12

PLATE 21

1.	Holemouth jar, light red painting and incised decoration	1:4	Jericho	T.A	AAA XIX, pl. VIII:3
2.	Jar, light red	1:4	Jericho	T.A	AAA XIX, pl. VIII:9
3.	Holemouth jar, grey, incised decoration	1:4	Jericho	T.A	AAA XIX, pl. VI:12
4.	Jar, light red	1:4	Jericho	T.A	AAA XIX, pl. VII:12
5.	Jar, light red, red slip, incised decoration	1:4	Jericho	T.A	AAA XIX, pl. VI:15

THE EARLY BRONZE IV PERIOD

This period is to a great extent problematic, and we have therefore refrained from trying to assemble a plate illustrating typical pottery. The existence of this phase was recognized by Albright in his excavations at Tell Beth Mirsim. The initial settlement of that site, Level J, has been assigned to this phase, later designated by Albright and Wright as EB III B.[1] Similar clues concerning the existence of a phase at the end of the Early Bronze, and preceding the beginning MB I, have turned up in various other excavations, such as Beth-shemesh, Bethel, Beth Yerah, and others. However, all these discoveries are at present no more than scanty hints, and are insufficient for any clear definition of the character of the EB IV pottery. As for tomb-deposits, three tombs at Megiddo are generally assigned to this period: 1101 A Lower, 1101 B Lower and 1102 Lower,[2] reproduced here in full. Part of the material in some of the EB-MB tombs at Jericho may also prove to belong to this phase, since typologically there is much affinity between the Megiddo tomb-groups and part of the Jericho material, e.g., from Tomb F 4.[3]

This period, more than any other, needs further study before a summarizing picture can be attempted.

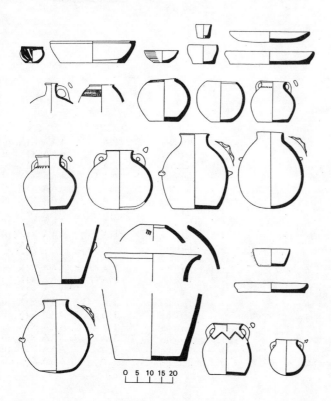

POTTERY FROM ASSOCIATED TOMBS 1101–2 LOWER AT MEGIDDO.

1. W.F. Albright, *The Archaeology of Palestine*, 1956, p. 77; G.E. Wright, in *The Bible and the Ancient Near East, Essays in Honour of W.F. Albright*, London, 1961, p. 86.
2. R. M. Engberg and G. M. Shipton, *Notes on the Chalcolithic and Early Bronze Age Pottery of Megiddo*, Chicago, 1934, p. 53, fig. 14.
3. K. M. Kenyon, *Excavations at Jericho*, I London, 1960, p. 144, fig. 47.

CHAPTER EIGHT

THE MIDDLE BRONZE I PERIOD

The MB I period is known to archaeology so far mainly through its tombs, rather than through occupational strata of excavated sites, a situation which reflects clearly the archaeological-historical character of the age. Remains of this period, rather than strata in the usual sense of the word, have been uncovered in various sites, such as Tell Beth Mirsim, Lachish, Megiddo, Jericho, Hazor, Beth Yerah, and others. The information supplied by these remains is not of the kind which regularly emerges from excavations, but rather evidence of a negative nature: there are no city walls, there are hardly any building remains, there are some cave-dwellings. Stratum H at Tell Beth Mirsim[1] and the corresponding strata at Jericho[2] supply a picture of semi-sedentary life existing on these sites and in their vicinity (in the case of Jericho, upon the site of a large destroyed city of the EB). This conception of the semi-nomadic character of the population in this period is somewhat impaired by the excavation at Mt. Yeroham[3] in the Negev, which produced a well-preserved small settlement about one acre in size, with architecture, pottery, and artifacts, including copper ingots. This culture is usually thought to be connected with the arrival of the Amorites in Canaan.

Division into Three Groups (Plates 22—24).

The numerous and rich tombs of this period furnish a solid basis for the knowledge of the pottery repertoire of the MB I, and permit an attempt at typological analysis.[4] This analysis shows that the pottery of the MB I has a general character strikingly new to Palestinian pottery. Within this general framework it can be divided into three sub-groups, mainly according to decorative elements. The two main groups seem to follow the regional division of the country into a southern and a northern group, while the third is chiefly represented in the rich tombs at Megiddo and neighboring sites. This division into three groups, each with its own characteristic features, will be of some help in trying to understand the nature of the MB I culture.

In examining the general character of the MB I assemblage,[5] stress must be placed first and foremost on the break between this pottery and that of the Early Bronze Age. There is hardly a doubt that the new MB I civilization was instrumental in destroying the old. Although some reminiscences survive and remain embedded in the MB I repertoire, the new is much stronger than the traditional element.

1. TBM, II, pp. 15–16.
2. K. M. Kenyon, *Archaeology in the Holy Land*, 1964, p. 137.
3. M. Kochavi, "The Excavations at Har Yeroham, Preliminary Communication," *BIES*, 27 (1964), 284–292 (Hebrew).
4. G. E. Wright, "The Chronology of Palestinian Pottery in Middle Bronze I," *BASOR*, 71 (1938), K. M. Kenyon, "Tombs of the Intermediate Early Bronze — Middle Bronze Age at Tell Ajjul," *ADAJ*, III (1956). R. Amiran, "The Pottery of the Middle Bronze Age I in Palestine," *IEJ*, 10 (1960).
5. This period and its pottery are variously termed in archaeological literature: The Palestine Archaeological Museum Card-Index termed it "Early Bronze-Middle Bronze." Albright termed the period "MB I," and the pottery sometimes as "Caliciform Ware." Kenyon has coined the term, "Intermediate Early Bronze-Middle Bronze Age."

General Characteristics:

Form: The vessels are spherical or barrel-shaped, without pronounced shoulders, and have either a large flat base, or none (i.e., the lower part is rounded in continuation of the spherical form of the body). Very characteristic is the absence of handles. One type of handle is, however, common in this period: a pair of small loop-handles connecting the middle of the neck and the shoulder. The degenerated ledge-handles, which sometimes occur on jars, are one of the few vestiges of the EB.

Ware: The clay is light greenish-grey, in contrast to the predominantly red or pinkish-brown colors of the Early Bronze wares. This may be due to different methods of preparing the clay and firing the vessels, indicating different pottery-making traditions.

Methods of manufacture: Observation of the vessels by an expert eye reveals an interesting combination technique: the body of the vessel is made by hand, while the neck and rim seem to be wheel made. The potter's fingerprints are clearly visible on the uneven surface of the vessel, and his handiwork is evident in their irregular shapes. When both parts of the vessel were 'leather-hard', the potter joined them and smoothed over the join. Traces of his smoothing finger are still visible on the inside of the vessels.

Decoration: Incisions of various kinds are generally used in MB I. These are made either with a point or with a three-to-five-pronged comb or fork. The patterns consist of groups of straight or wavy lines, or groups of shallow stabs or notches, or groups of diagonal incisions made by a single point. The decoration is always placed at the base of the neck, and may have been intended to cover the join between the separately made body and neck.

Description of the Groups:

The above brief outline of the main features of MB I pottery refers mainly to the Southern Group, A, and the Northern Group, B. These two groups, represented in Plates 22 and 23, differ from each other chiefly in decoration; in the Southern Group fine incisions made with a comb are popular (Photos 76–80), while the Northern Group appears to prefer incisions made with a single point (Photos 83, 85). The Southern Group has as an additional decorative element — small conical or elongated knobs placed singly and somewhat strangely on the shoulders of jars. On one jar of the Northern Group three conical knobs are placed on the neck, pointing downwards (Plate 23:5). The barrel-shaped jar with a large flat base predominates among Southern forms (Photo 78),

Photo 76. Bowl, Menahat, HU 5186.

Photo 77. Goblet-chalice, Benaya, HU 5562.

Photo 78. Jar, Halhul, HU 2190.

80

Photo 81. Mug, Tel Aviv, IMA 69.9–1.

while the Northern Group shows a preference for the spherical form (Photos 84–86). However, even the barrel-shaped jars of the Southern Group show something of the fondness of the period for the rounded form.

The third group, C (Plate 24), which can also be termed the Megiddo Group, differs from the two others in many respects, such as methods of manufacture, repertoire of forms, and decoration. (These differences might perhaps raise the question as to whether the C Group should be included within the MB I at all. However, its general character appears to outweigh the differences, and compels us to see it as part of the MB I culture.) Although some of the vessels are produced by the combined hand-and-wheel method, the vessels look much less irregular, and are more neatly made. Part of the pottery in this group is altogether wheel-made. Among the new forms, mention should be made of a strikingly interesting shape, the hybrid teapot-amphoriskos (Plate 24:11, Photo 88). This form, which adds a spout to an amphoriskos, is a distinctive feature of this group. Significantly, the Megiddo tombs in which this form has been found are of a more developed type than those which yielded pottery of the Southern and Northern groups. These are four-chambered tombs, which occur only very rarely in the tombs of the other two groups. The decoration of the Megiddo Group shows something like a 'return' to the red slip (Plate 24:7–9, Photo 89) and even to painted decoration (Plate 24:17–19, Photo 90). It may well be that this 'return' is due to some surviving traditions of earlier periods.

A special feature within the Megiddo Group is the 'grey teapot' style (Plate 24:1–6, Photos 91–92), which includes four forms. Together these make up a pronounced style, in technique as well as in decoration. There are two types of teapot and two types of goblet: the tall teapot with a narrow neck (24:1) and the low teapot with a wide neck (24:2–4); the low goblet (24:5), and the tall goblet (24:6). All these are wheel-made, including the spouts; the clay is dark, either black, grey, or dark red-brown, baked to give off a metallic sound when struck. The decoration mostly consists of line-painting in yellowish-white thick paint. No. 6 has a zig-zag line incised on the painted band, exposing the dark surface of the

Photo 79. Amphoriskos, Lachish, IDA 34.2922.

Photo 80. Jar, Azor, Dagon Museum, Haifa.

Photo 82. Lamp, Azor, *QDAP*, X, Pl. XIV.

Photo 83. Amphoriskos, Ma'ayan-Barukh.
IDA 55–42.

Photo 84. Amphoriskos, Ma'ayan-Barukh.
IDA 55–41.

Photo 85. Jar, Ma'ayan-Barukh.
IDA 53–6.

Photo 86. Jar, El-Uusn, *APEF*, VI, Pl. I.

clay. In the present state of our knowledge, there is nothing we can add to the discussion of this style in the Megiddo publication.[6]

The lamps associated with all three groups are of the four-spouted type (Plates 22:11, 23:9, 24:13 and Photo 82). Its should, however, be emphasised that the single-spouted lamp makes its first appearance in this period (Plates 22:16, 24:14).

Chronological Evaluation:

Although the above analysis is typological in nature, some chronological value can be derived from it, based mainly on Albright's observations at Tell Beth Mirsim, Strata I and H.[7]

Two conclusions emerge from this typological analysis:

a) Groups A and B are closely related to each other, a kind of relationship which is probably more "horizontal" than "vertical", i.e. a relationship that may point to pottery traditions of kindred tribes which came from the same general cultural area, rather than generic relationship.

---

6. *Megiddo Tombs*, p. 148.
7. Albright's recent discussion of these problems appears in *Chronologies in Old World Archaeology*, (ed. R. W. Ehrich), Chicago, 1965, pp. 53–54. This discussion illuminated many points of the problem and led to the thoughts expressed here.

Photo 87. Jar, Ma'ayan-Barukh.
IDA 55–50.

Photo 88. Amphoriskos-Teapot, Megiddo, *Mrg. T.*, Pl. 101.

Photo 89. Jug, Megiddo, IDA 34. 1578.

Photo 90. Amphoriskos, painted, Megiddo, *Meg. T.*, Pl. 101.

Photo 91. Teapot, painted white, Megiddo, IDA, I.3345.

Photo 92. Teapot, painted white, Megiddo, *Meg. T.*, Pl. 92.

b) Group C is preponderantly close to the pottery of the following period, the MB II A; this kind of affinity is more "vertical" than "horizontal". Group C should be considered the direct predecessor of the MB II A, and a link between MB I and MB II.[8] Another fact with some chronological bearing is the affinity of the special family within the C Group, the Grey Teapot style, with some material of Stratum J at Hama (compare our goblet No. 6 with Goblet Type IV of Hama[9]).

The chronological correlations emerging from these conclusions are as follows: The C Group, representing, in Palestine, the bridge to the MB II A, seems to be contemporaneous with Hama J 5–1 (or only J 4–1), while the A and B Groups are contemporaneous with the middle phases of Hama J, i.e. with Hama J, 6–5. Such a suggestion would entail raising the beginning of MB II A to somewhere around the beginning of the second millennium, that is, the early Twelfth Dynasty of Egypt. One point of caution has to be emphasized: all 8 strata of Hama J represent sedentary settlements, with houses and streets and other urban characteristics.[10]

---

8. Contrary to Kenyon's conception, who recognizes a break also at the end of the MB I period.
9. H. Ingholt, *Rapport préliminaire sur sept campagnes de fouilles à Hama en Syrie* Copenhagen, 1940, p. 35, pl. XI:2; E. Fugmann, *Hama, l'architecture des periodes préhellenistiques*, Copenhagen, 1958, p. 74, fig. 93:2 H 352, 3 H 353.
10. C 14 tests made on Hama samples produced a date in the 21st century for the later part of Stratum J, and the 22nd century for the early part of that stratum. Cf. E. Fugmann, *Hama*, pp. 281–282.

PLATE 22

1.	Goblet, pink, ribbed	1:5	Lachish		La. IV, pl. 66:396
2.	Goblet, orange, ribbed	1:5	Lachish		La. IV, pl. 66:409
3.	Goblet, light brown	1:5	Benaya		IDA, No. 57:544
4.	Goblet, light brown, combed decoration	1:5	El-Metaba		PBI
5.	Goblet, orange, combed decoration	1:5	Lachish	T.2030	La. IV, pl. 66:397
6.	Teapot, red, incised decoration	1:5	Lachish		La. IV, pl. 67:455
7.	Teapot, light brown, combed decoration	1:5	Ras Tawil		YMCA coll. Jerusalem, No. 2675
8.	Teapot, light brown, combed and incised decoration	1:5	Unknown		YMCA coll. Jerusalem, No. 2628
9.	Bowl, light brown	1:5	Benaya		IDA, No. 57:541
10.	Bowl, light brown	1:5	Benaya		IDA, No. 57:542
11.	Lamp, pink	1:5	Lachish	T.2018	La. IV, pl. 66:448
12.	Amphoriskos, light brown	1:5	Beth Mirsim	H	TBM I A, pl. 3:10
13.	Amphoriskos, light brown, combed and punctured decoration	1:5	Unknown		YMCA coll. Jerusalem
14.	Amphoriskos, light brown, combed and punctured decoration	1:5	Unknown		YMCA coll. Jerusalem
15.	Goblet, light brown	1:5	Kh. Samiya		YMCA coll. Jerusalem ,No. 2680
16.	Lamp, brown	1:5	Lachish	1529	La. IV, pl.66:399
17.	Mug, light brown, incised decoration	1:5	Unknown		Dayan coll.
18.	Jar, brown-green, incised decoration	1:10	Lachish	T.2092	La. IV, pl. 67:459
19.	Jar, light brown, combed and punctured decoration	1:10	Benaya		Dayan coll.
20.	Jar, light brown, punctured decoration	1:10	Azor		Kollek coll.
21.	Jar, brown-green, combed decoration	1:10	Beth Mirsim	H	TBM IA pl. 2:1
22.	Jar, brown-green, combed decoration	1:10	Beth Mirsim	H	TBM IA pl. 2:7
23.	Jar, red, combed decoration	1:10	Lachish	T.2045	La. IV pl. 67:469
24.	Jar, pink, combed and punctured decoration	1:10	Lachish	T.2059	La. IV pl. 67:482

PLATE | 22

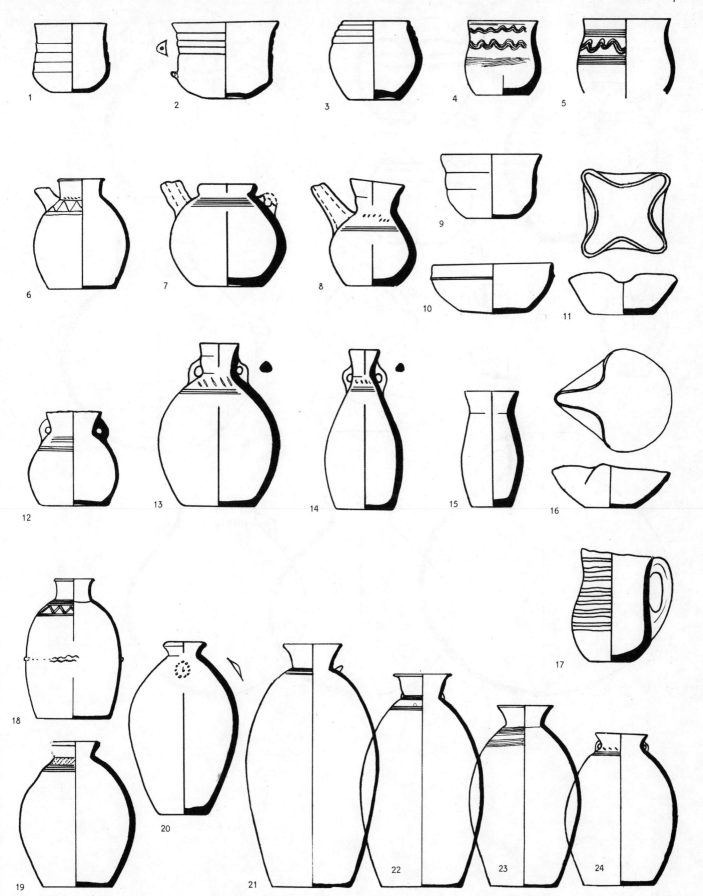

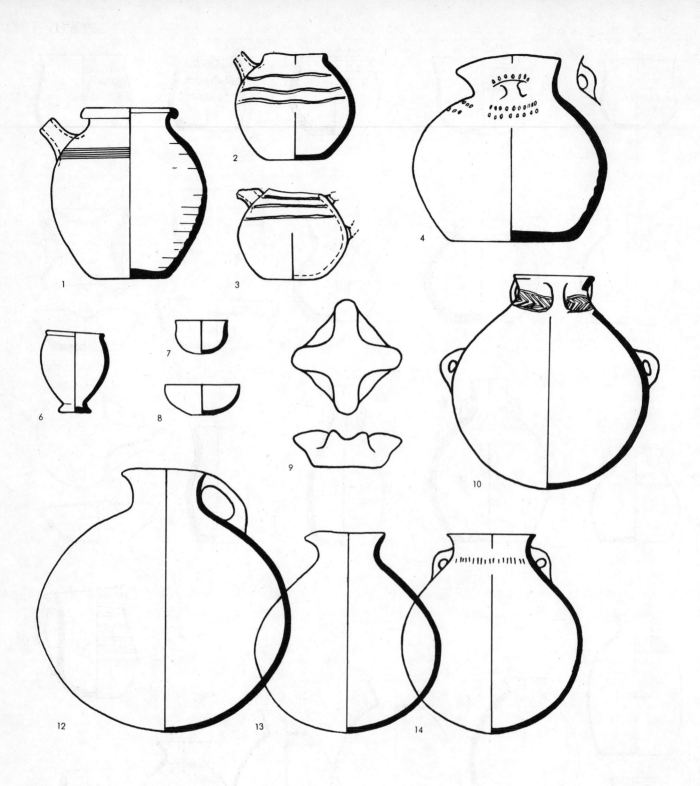

PLATE | **23**

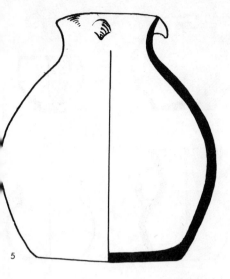

PLATE 23

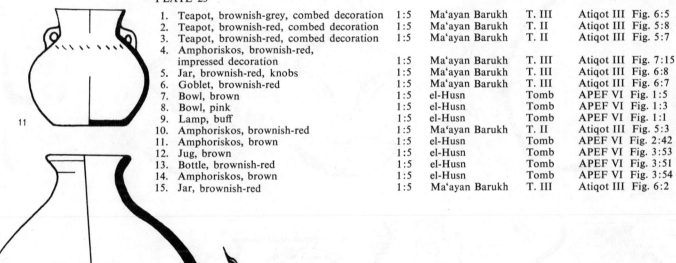

1.	Teapot, brownish-grey, combed decoration	1:5	Ma'ayan Barukh	T. III	Atiqot III Fig. 6:5
2.	Teapot, brownish-red, combed decoration	1:5	Ma'ayan Barukh	T. II	Atiqot III Fig. 5:8
3.	Teapot, brownish-red, combed decoration	1:5	Ma'ayan Barukh	T. II	Atiqot III Fig. 5:7
4.	Amphoriskos, brownish-red, impressed decoration	1:5	Ma'ayan Barukh	T. III	Atiqot III Fig. 7:15
5.	Jar, brownish-red, knobs	1:5	Ma'ayan Barukh	T. III	Atiqot III Fig. 6:8
6.	Goblet, brownish-red	1:5	Ma'ayan Barukh	T. III	Atiqot III Fig. 6:7
7.	Bowl, brown	1:5	el-Husn	Tomb	APEF VI Fig. 1:5
8.	Bowl, pink	1:5	el-Husn	Tomb	APEF VI Fig. 1:3
9.	Lamp, buff	1:5	el-Husn	Tomb	APEF VI Fig. 1:1
10.	Amphoriskos, brownish-red	1:5	Ma'ayan Barukh	T. II	Atiqot III Fig. 5:3
11.	Amphoriskos, brown	1:5	el-Husn	Tomb	APEF VI Fig. 2:42
12.	Jug, brown	1:5	el-Husn	Tomb	APEF VI Fig. 3:53
13.	Bottle, brownish-red	1:5	el-Husn	Tomb	APEF VI Fig. 3:51
14.	Amphoriskos, brown	1:5	el-Husn	Tomb	APEF VI Fig. 3:54
15.	Jar, brownish-red	1:5	Ma'ayan Barukh	T. III	Atiqot III Fig. 6:2

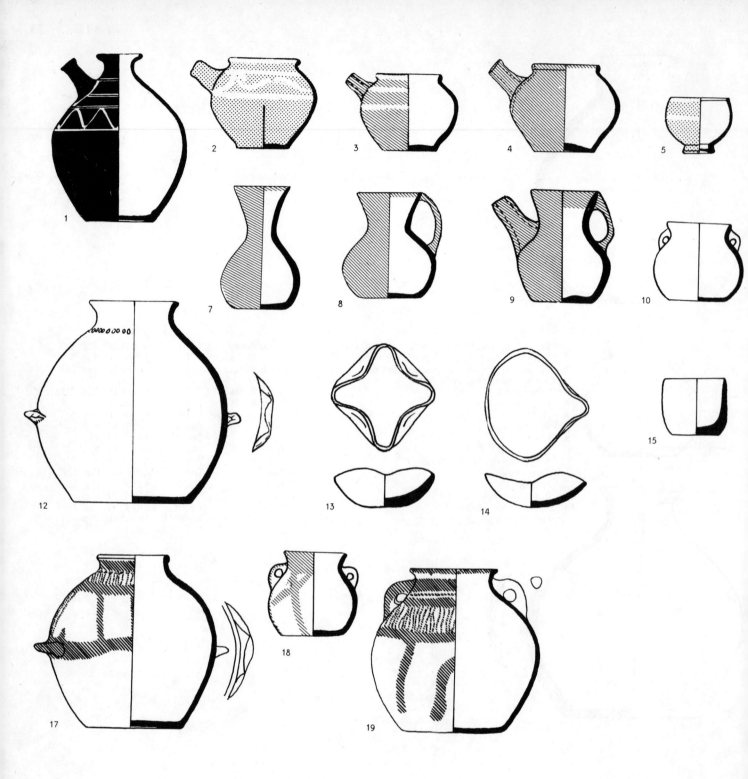

PLATE | **24**

PLATE 24

1.	Teapot, blue-black outside, white-yellow decoration	1:5	Megiddo	T.41	Meg. T. pl. 10:5
2.	Teapot, blue-black, white-yellow decoration	1:5	Megiddo	T.877 A 2	Meg. T. pl. 11:30
3.	Teapot, red, white-yellow decoration	1:5	Megiddo	T.877 B 2	Meg. T. pl. 12:7
4.	Teapot, red	1:5	Megiddo	T.41	Meg. T. pl. 10:4
5.	Cup, black-reddish, white-yellow decoration	1:5	Megiddo	T.877 A 2	Meg. T. pl. 11:27
6.	Goblet, blue-black outside, white-yellow decoration, incised zig-zag	1:5	Megiddo	T.1120 B	Meg. T. pl. 22:19
7.	Bottle, yellow-brown light red slip	1:5	Megiddo	T.1014 A	Meg. T. pl. 22:7
8.	Jug, brown ocher, red slip	1:5	Megiddo	T.1120 A	Meg. T. pl. 22:17
9.	Spouted jug, brown, red burnished slip	1:5	Megiddo		IDA 55–14
10.	Amphoriskos, brown ocher	1:5	Megiddo	T.922 A	Meg. T. pl. 22:2
11.	Teapot-amphoriskos, white-yellow	1:5	Megiddo	T.877 A 2	Meg. T. pl. 12:2
12.	Jar, yellow, incised decoration	1:5	Megiddo	T.41	Meg. T. pl. 10:9
13.	Lamp, brown	1:5	Megiddo	T.217 B	Meg. T., pl. 10:28
14.	Lamp, burnt umber	1:5	Megiddo	T.217 B	Meg. T., pl. 10:27
15.	Bowl, white-yellow	1:5	Megiddo	T.1120 A	Meg. T., pl. 22:12
16.	Bowl, white-yellow	1:5	Megiddo	T.1120 A	Meg. T., pl. 22:10
17.	Jar, white-yellow, red and incised decoration	1:5	Megiddo	T.1098 A	Meg. T., pl. 21:10
18.	Amphoriskos, red decoration	1:5	Megiddo	T.1098 A	Meg. T., pl. 21:8
19.	Amphoriskos, red decoration	1:5	Megiddo	T.1098 A	Meg. T., pl. 21:9
20.	Jar	1:5	Megiddo	T.41	Meg. T., pl. 10:10
21.	Bottle	1:5	Megiddo	T.1098 A	Meg. T., pl. 21:11

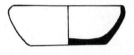

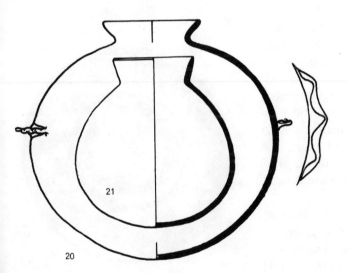

CHAPTER NINE

THE MIDDLE BRONZE II A AND II B–C PERIODS

The correspondence of MB II A in Palestine to the Twelfth and Thirteenth Dynasties in Egypt is based mainly on the evidence from Byblos (see below, Plate 35 and the comparative analysis of MB II pottery and Khabur ware). A date for MB II A between about 1950 and 1730 B.C. accords well with the historical and archaeological evidence. The correspondence of MB II B to the Hyksos Dynasties in Egypt is also established with a fair measure of certainty and is generally accepted.

As we have already mentioned above, the Megiddo pottery group is a link between MB I and MB II A. Many features of the Megiddo group — such as form, decoration, and technical improvements in pottery making — continue to appear in MB II A, thus indicating a steady development of the local material culture. Some of these features are: the absence of handles, the carination of the bowls, the development of the lamp, the increasing popularity of the red slip. The widespread use of the potter's wheel is mainly responsible for the technical advances in pottery making and for the greater refinement of forms. We have already noted the use of the wheel at the end of MB I, especially in the Megiddo group. Now, in MB II A, pottery making attains new artistic and technical levels. The wheel gives the potter a greater mastery of his craft and enables him, for instance, to shape rims and bases with greater delicacy and precision.

A close analysis of MB II A and B–C pottery shows many differences between the two periods, but a definite continuity of form and decoration can undoubtedly be observed. In this chapter, the discussion of each pottery form includes both periods, in order to bring out clearly the differences as well as the continuity.

This analysis offers one of the most striking examples of the development of pottery forms. New types emerge, catch the popular fancy, and proliferate in many variations into a whole group of related forms, whose influence is echoed in the following periods. The carinated bowl, for instance (Plate 27), first appears in MB II A, develops into a wide range of variants in MB II B–C, and continues to be produced in the Late Bronze Period (Plate 39).

Each of the two periods has its own aesthetic approach to decoration: the deep red burnished slip (which goes back to the Megiddo group of MB I) predominates in MB II A, together with painted decoration. In MB II B the red slip loses some of its popularity and many vessels are plain. Highly stylized rope decoration appears, painted wares are few, and the Tell el-Yahudiyeh Ware (the dark burnished surface is decorated with white-filled punctures) is a characteristic feature of the period.

Of special interest is the comparison between the silver bowl from a foundation deposit in a temple at Byblos (Photo 93)[1] and the pottery bowl from a tomb near Tell Asawir (Photo 94). The photographs of these vessels are shown side by side in order to suggest that MB II A and B pottery forms are influenced by metal prototypes. However, such resemblances are never the result of a one-way traffic, but are instead the

---

1. P. Montet, *Byblos et l'Egypte*, Paris, 1929, Pl. LXXI:605.

Photo 93. Silver bowl, Byblos (Lebanon), *Byblos et l'Egypte*, Pl. LXXI.

Photo 95. Bowl, Megiddo, The Oriental Institute, Chicago No. A16524.

result of an interplay of influences between techniques in different materials.

Open Rounded Bowls (Plates 25—26).

MB II A (Plate 25): Some general characteristics of the open bowls in this period can be distinguished: the sides are always gently rounded; the rims are profiled; the bases, the outstanding feature of all the vessels of this period, are flat or low discs (Photo 95), sharply separated from the body. Sometimes a shallow ring base begins to appear.

A number of groups are shown in Plate 25:

a) Nos, 1, 4, 5, 6: bowls with wide profiled rims, often painted red. This is the predominant form.

b) Nos. 2, 3, 7, 9: bowls with turned-in rims.

c) No. 2: the bowl is decorated on the inside with a red painted cross, an ornament which continues to be popular also in the following period.

d) Nos. 1, 7: bowls with plastic decoration on the rim. Forms resembling two ornamental ledge or bar-handles are added to the rim of the bowls, most of which are burnished. Photo 96 shows such a bowl, found at Gibeon.

MB II B–C (Plate 26): Generally speaking, the forms described in the preceding section continue to be produced, but the walls of the bowls are less rounded and at times even almost straight. A still greater change is evident in the bases, which are now higher; ring bases predominate and the convex disc base makes its appearance.

The following groups can be distinguished in Plate 26:

a) Nos. 3, 4, 7: bowls with inverted rims triangular in section. This is the commonest bowl of the period.

b) Nos. 5, 8: plain rounded rims.

c) Nos. 2, 6: flattened rims.

d) No. 1: the projections on the rims of such bowls continue the fashion of **MB II A**, but only horns or spiral-shaped curlicues remain of the bars and ledges of that period.

Photo 94. Bowl, Asawir, IDA 53–532.

Photo 96. Bowl, Gibeon, HU 1988.

PLATE | 25

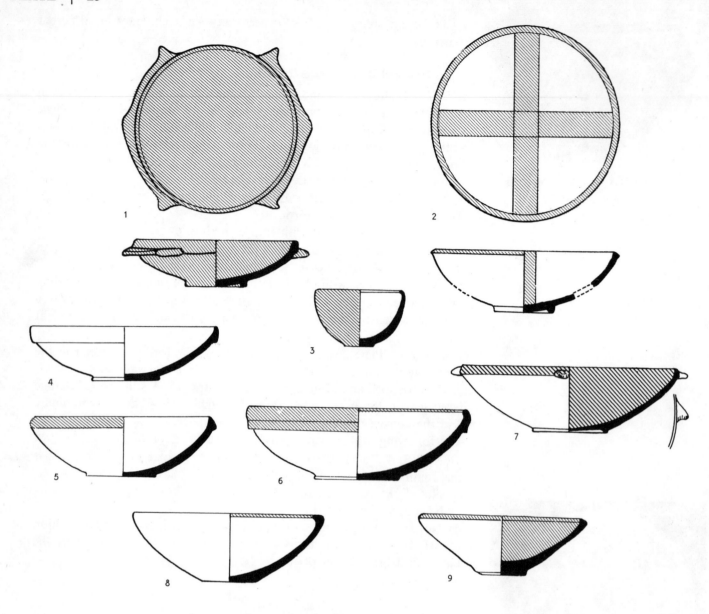

PLATE 25

1.	Bowl, cream-buff, red wheel-burnished slip	1:5	Megiddo	XIV (T.3162)	Meg. II, pl. 15:15
2.	Bowl, buff, red decoration, burnished	1:5	Beth Mirsim F		TBM IA, pl. 5:5
3.	Bowl, cream-buff, brown-red vertically burnished slip	1:5	Megiddo	XIV (T.4016)	Meg. II, pl. 14:36
4.	Bowl, pink-buff, smoothed, wheel-burnished inside	1:5	Megiddo	XIV (T.4046)	Meg. II, pl. 14:7
5.	Bowl, pink-buff, smoothed, red decoration	1:5	Megiddo	XIV (T.3143)	Meg. II, pl. 14:6
6.	Bowl, buff, smoothed, red decoration	1:5	Megiddo	XV (T.5167)	Meg. II, pl. 9:3
7.	Bowl, brown-ocher, red vertically burnished slip	1:5	Megiddo	T.911 D	Meg. T., pl. 31:13
8.	Bowl, pink-buff, wheel-burnished inside, red decoration	1:5	Megiddo	XIV (T.3148)	Meg. II, pl. 14:17
9.	Bowl, pink-buff, smoothed red burnished slip	1:5	Megiddo	XIII A (T.5094)	Meg. II, pl. 19:10

PLATE | **26**

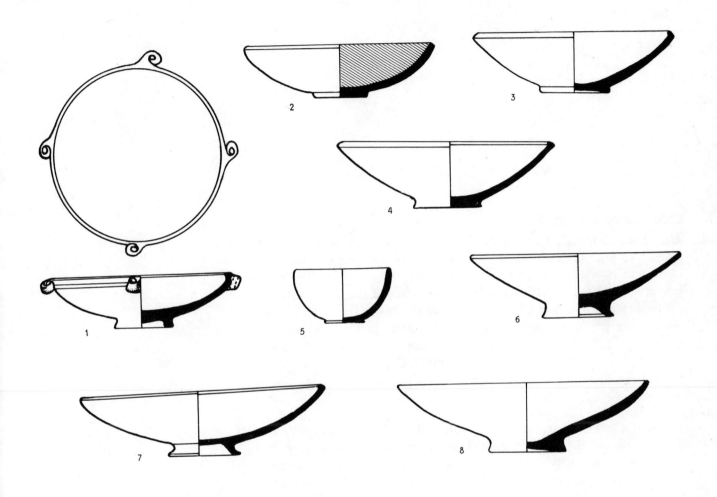

PLATE 26

1.	Bowl, buff	1:5	Megiddo	XI (T.3081)	Meg. II, pl. 38:10
2.	Bowl, buff, red spirally burnished slip inside	1:5	Megiddo	XI (T.3071)	Meg. II, pl. 37:27
3.	Bowl, buff, spirally burnished inside	1:5	Megiddo	XI (T.3080)	Meg. II, pl. 37:26
4.	Bowl, buff	1:5	Megiddo	X (T.3167)	Meg. II, pl. 44:39
5.	Bowl, buff	1:5	Megiddo	XII	Meg. II, pl. 28:4
6.	Bowl, buff, burnished inside	1:5	Megiddo	XII (T.3095)	Meg. II, pl. 29:25
7.	Bowl, pink-buff	1:5	Megiddo	XII (T.3087)	Meg. II, pl. 29:26
8.	Bowl, buff	1:5	Megiddo	XI (T.4055)	Meg. II, pl. 37:23

Photo 97. Bowl, Far'ah(S), IDA I. 7036.

Carinated Bowls (Plate 27).

MB II A: Although the carinated bowl is common in this period, it appears to have been produced in a few variants only. All the bowls are small and closed; they are wheel made, and the wheel marks, which resemble combing, are visible on the entire surface of the bowl, including the base (Photo 95). A red, highly burnished slip covers the vessel without obliterating the 'combing.' As in the open bowls, the low disc base and the sharply set off flat base are common, but the shallow ring base is also.found. The rims often have a gutter lip on the inside. The carination is of two kinds: the most common is the sharp carination suggesting metallic prototypes (Plate 27: 1–2), but a gentler carination is also found (Nos. 3–4).

MB II B–C: The carinated bowl of MB II B–C in all its variants (Nos. 7–24) is one of the most characteristic features of the pottery of that period and is, properly speaking, an innovation. We shall not attempt to trace here the origin of this bowl, but it is not derived from the carinated bowl of MB II A, which continues to be made also in MB II B–C (Nos. 5–6). The new bowl-form shows a tendency to vary the place and the angle of the carination, and has better formed bases.

This type of bowl appears in many variants:

a) Nos. 7, 8, 10, 11, 13, and Photo 97 represent the predominant type of the flaring carinated bowls, with an S-shaped carination.

b) No. 12 is a similar bowl, but with a quatrefoil mouth.

c) Nos. 9, 14, and 15 are deep, gently carinated, fairly narrow-mouthed bowls, with short necks. Sometimes handles are attached (No. 9).

d) Nos. 16 and 17 are deep, closed bowls, with a fairly high neck and a trumpet base.

e) Nos. 18–24 could be classified either as bowls or as chalices. This type has a wide and varied range and is distinguished by its thin, white, well-baked ware. The same technique is also found in jugs (Plate 34:7). Trumpet bases and a wide range of carinations are characterisitic of many vessels of this group (Photo 99).

94

Photo 98. Goblet-Chalice, Ras el-Ain, IDA 35.3439.

Photo 99. High-footed goblet-chalice, Barqay, IDA 57-130.

Goblets and Chalices (Plate 28).

These terms require explanation: Nos. 1–4 of MB II A and No. 6 of MB II B–C are derived from MB I goblets (Plate 22:1–5, 16). Accordingly, the term 'goblet' has been retained also for these MB II A and B–C forms. In LB, vessels similar in form are classified as jugs or mugs. In MB II B–C and later, we have used the term 'goblet' for a high, closed chalice.

MB II A: Nos. 1–4 represent the dominant form, which sometimes has one handle and sometimes none. The handle may be a double one. No. 5 is unusual: it has a barrel-shaped body, a flat base, and a large loop handle attached to the widest part of the vessel.

The decoration of the goblets follows the style of the period: a red slip applied over the fine combing (wheelmarks) or black and red painted bands. The chalice appears to have been unknown in MB II A.

MB II B–C: No. 6 is still in the tradition of the preceding period. Together with the chalice, which, as we shall see below, develops in this period in various forms, appear closed goblets on pedestals, which should also be considered as part of the chalice class (Nos. 7 and 8).

Generally speaking, the chalice-types correspond to the bowl-types:

Nos. 10 and 12 and Photo No. 99 are in effect part of the carinated bowl class, and we have purposely shown here a chalice (No. 10).

No. 11 (Photo 338) is a lavishly decorated specimen with an unusual feature — a tube or goblet rising from inside the chalice and connected with it by holes at the bottom of the inner goblet. This beautiful chalice may be a cult vessel.

Nos. 14–16 represent the second type. The chalice-bowl is wide and shallow with slightly rounded walls, and resembles the open, rounded bowls of the period (Plate 26). The variants of this type differ from each other mainly in the height and shape of the foot. No. 13 is uncommon, but the shape of its foot and the quality of the thin ware indicate that it belongs to this type.

PLATE 27

1.	Bowl, pink-buff, red burnished slip	1:5	Megiddo	XIV (T.5252)	Meg. II, pl. 19:3
2.	Bowl, buff, red burnished slip	1:5	Megiddo	XIV (T.5178)	Meg. II, pl. 15:2
3.	Bowl, red, wheel combed outside	1:6	Ras el-Ain		QDAP V, 4, p. 124:52
4.	Bowl, pink-buff, red burnished slip	1:5	Megiddo	XIV (T.5178)	Meg. II, pl. 14:34
5.	Bowl, pink-buff, dark red vertically burnished slip	1:5	Megiddo	XII (T.3104)	Meg. II, pl. 28:9
6.	Bowl, brown	1:5	Hazor	BA 12	H. III–IV, pl. CCXXXVI:6
7.	Bowl, pink-buff	1:5	Megiddo	XXI (T.2138)	Meg. II, pl. 28:13
8.	Bowl, pink, red slip	1:5	Lachish	T.129	La. IV, pl. 68:518
9.	Bowl, brown	1:5	Megiddo	T.43	Meg. T., pl. 24:8
10.	Bowl, pink-buff	1:5	Megiddo	XI	Meg. II, pl. 36:22
11.	Bowl, pink-buff	1:5	Megiddo	XII (T.4102)	Meg. II, pl. 28:17
12.	Bowl, pinkish, well-fired	1:5	Hazor	Pit 9024	H. I, pl. CXIV:18
13.	Bowl, red-brown	1:5	Hazor	T.3314	H. III–IV, pl. CXCVIII:1
14.	Bowl, cream, horizontally burnished outside	1:5	Megiddo	XII (T.3137)	Meg. II, pl. 28:10
15.	Bowl, buff, cream burnished slip outside	1:5	Megiddo	XI (T.2143)	Meg. II, pl. 36:11
16.	Bowl, buff, red burnished slip	1:5	Beth Mirsim	E	TBM IA, pl. 7:13
17.	Bowl, buff, red burnished slip	1:5	Beth Mirsim	E	TBM IA, pl. 7:12
18.	Bowl, green-buff	1:5	Megiddo	XII (T.2135)	Meg. II, pl. 29:1
19.	Bowl, pink-buff	1:5	Megiddo	X (T.4054)	Meg. II, pl. 44:19
20.	Bowl, brown	1:5	Megiddo	T.24	Meg. T., pl. 23:2
21.	Chalice, buff	1:5	Megiddo	XII (T.3095)	Meg. II, pl. 29:3
22.	Chalice, yellow, white burnished slip	1:5	Beth Mirsim	D	TBM I, pl. 43:6
23.	Chalice, pink-buff	1:5	Megiddo	XI	Meg. II, pl. 37:9
24.	Chalice, green-buff, vertically burnished outside	1:15	Megiddo	XII (T.3095)	Meg. II, pl. 29:5

96

PLATE | **27**

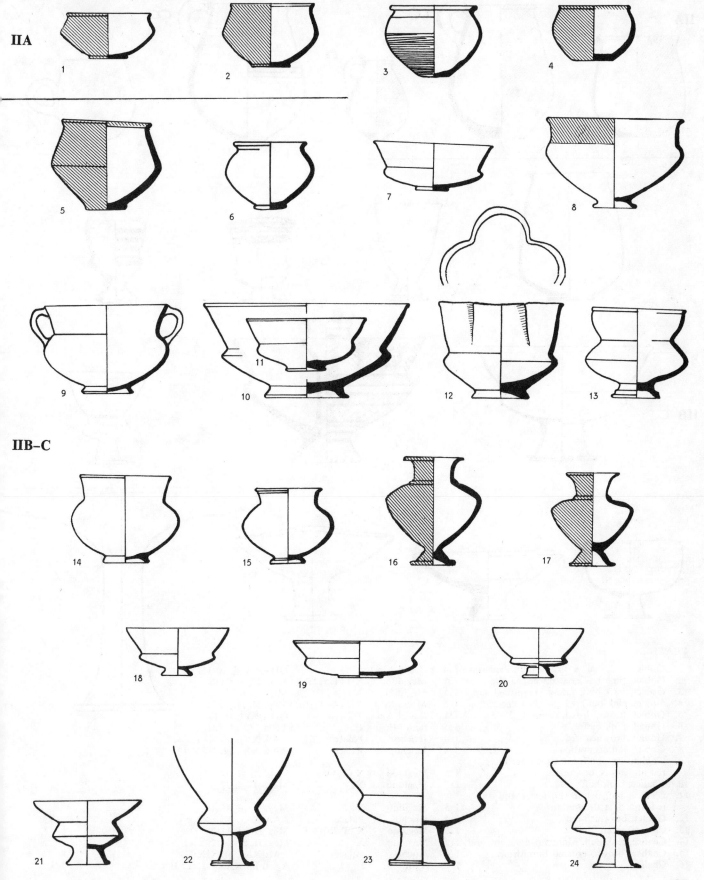

IIA

IIB–C

PLATE | 28

IIA

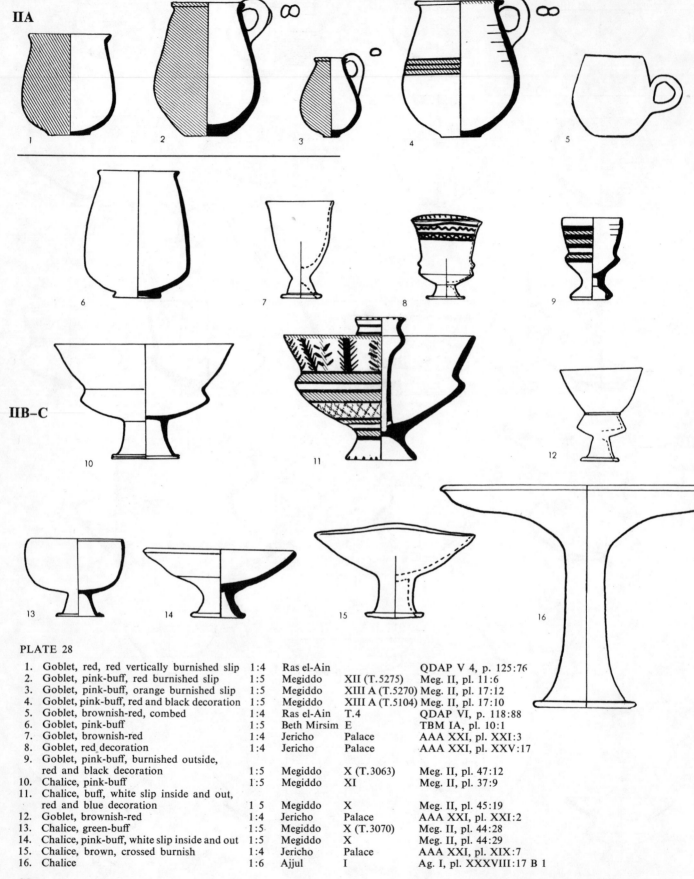

IIB–C

PLATE 28

1. Goblet, red, red vertically burnished slip   1:4   Ras el-Ain   QDAP V 4, p. 125:76
2. Goblet, pink-buff, red burnished slip   1:5   Megiddo   XII (T.5275)   Meg. II, pl. 11:6
3. Goblet, pink-buff, orange burnished slip   1:5   Megiddo   XIII A (T.5270) Meg. II, pl. 17:12
4. Goblet, pink-buff, red and black decoration   1:5   Megiddo   XIII A (T.5104) Meg. II, pl. 17:10
5. Goblet, brownish-red, combed   1:4   Ras el-Ain   T.4   QDAP VI, p. 118:88
6. Goblet, pink-buff   1:5   Beth Mirsim E   TBM IA, pl. 10:1
7. Goblet, brownish-red   1:4   Jericho   Palace   AAA XXI, pl. XXI:3
8. Goblet, red decoration   1:4   Jericho   Palace   AAA XXI, pl. XXV:17
9. Goblet, pink-buff, burnished outside,
     red and black decoration   1:5   Megiddo   X (T.3063)   Meg. II, pl. 47:12
10. Chalice, pink-buff   1:5   Megiddo   XI   Meg. II, pl. 37:9
11. Chalice, buff, white slip inside and out,
     red and blue decoration   1 5   Megiddo   X   Meg. II, pl. 45:19
12. Goblet, brownish-red   1:4   Jericho   Palace   AAA XXI, pl. XXI:2
13. Chalice, green-buff   1:5   Megiddo   X (T.3070)   Meg. II, pl. 44:28
14. Chalice, pink-buff, white slip inside and out   1:5   Megiddo   X   Meg. II, pl. 44:29
15. Chalice, brown, crossed burnish   1:4   Jericho   Palace   AAA XXI, pl. XIX:7
16. Chalice   1:6   Ajjul   I   Ag. I, pl. XXXVIII:17 B 1

Photo 100. Krater, Ginosar, IDA 56–847.

Kraters (Plate 29).

MB II A: Since most of the pottery available from this period comes from tombs, it includes few kraters and cooking vessels, and not many variants are known.

Four types of krater can be distinguished:

No. 1 resembles a deep rounded bowl and has four elongated knobs placed at right angles to the rim.

No. 2 is a decorated krater fragment, which shows all the features characteristic of the period — red and black painted triangle pattern, stylized rope decoration, and a profiled rim.

No. 3 is a krater fragment displaying some features related to a group of jugs discussed below (Plate 33:6 and 7); globular body, burnished red slip, and especially the rims and well-made triple handles. Another point of resemblance is the attachment of the handle to the shoulder without touching the rim.

No. 4 recalls MB I teapots.

MB II B–C: Several types of krater can be distinguished:

No. 5 is a large vessel, whose height is about equal to its diameter, with a well-defined neck, and handles joining the rim to the shoulder. This type of krater continues to be produced throughout MB II, LB and the entire Iron Age, without much change in form (see below). The decoration consists of an applied stylized rope, and an incised wavy line, an unusual feature in this period. No. 7 resembles a deep bowl.

Nos. 8 and 11 are two versions of a krater standing on three loop handles. No. 8 has in addition a spout and a loop handle. No. 11 has an upright neck.

No. 9 is very like No. 8, but is smaller and has a ring base.

No. 6 (Photo 100) could be classified either as a krater or as a deep bowl. It has a straight neck, a folded rim, and thin walls. Although their bases are different, Nos. 6 and 11 are similar in style and finish.

No. 10 has the body of a krater with the handles placed low as on a jar. Photo 101 shows a large handleless krater from a tomb at Tell Nagila, with rope decorations and incisions.

Photo 101. Krater, Nagila, Tomb DT 2, IDA 66.906.

99

PLATE | 29

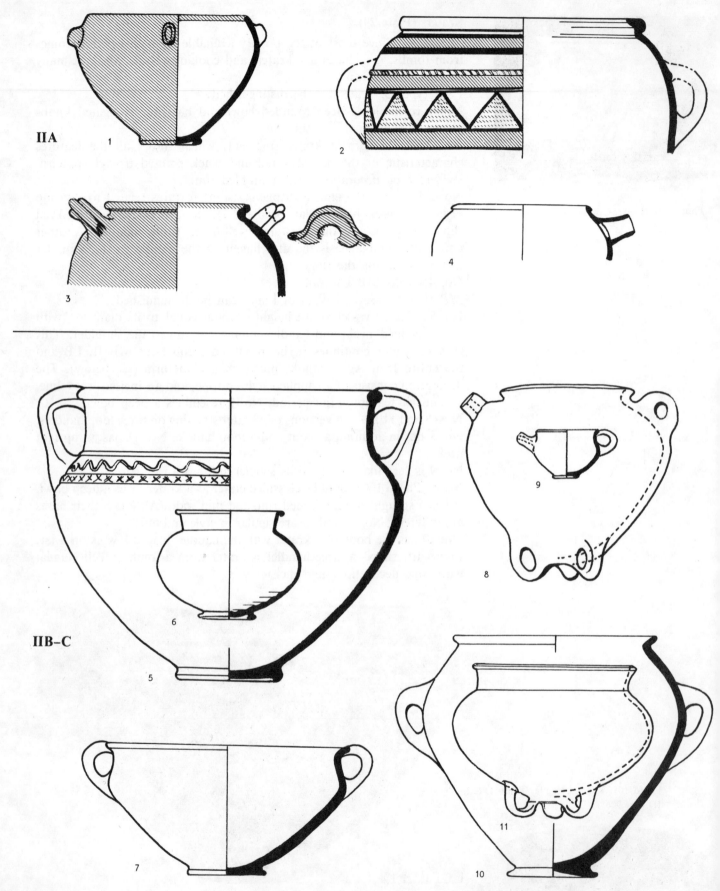

IIA

1

2

3

4

IIB–C

5

6

7

8

9

10

11

PLATE | 30

IIA

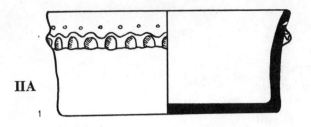

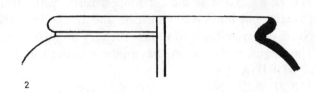

IIB–C

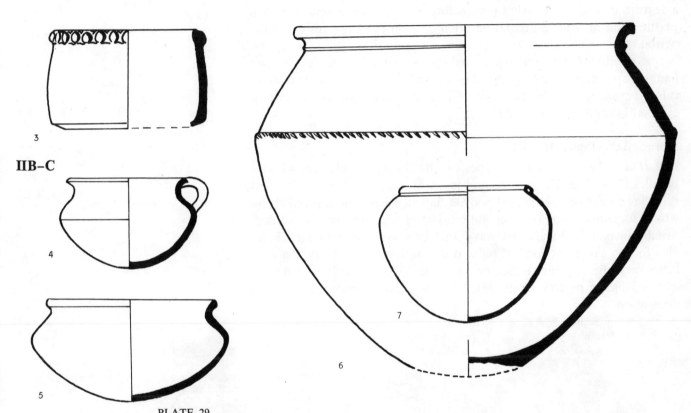

PLATE 29

1.	Krater, pink-buff, red burnished slip	1:5	Megiddo	XIII (T.3118)	Meg. II, pl. 22:6
2.	Krater, pink-buff, red and black decoration, rope decoration	1:5	Megiddo	XIV	Meg. II, pl. 13:11
3.	Krater, buff, red burnished slip	1:5	Megiddo	XIII B	Meg. II, pl. 16:7
4.	Krater, red-buff	1:5	Beth Mirsim G		TBM IA, pl. 5:1
5.	Krater, yellowish, incised decoration	1:5	Hazor	3	H. II, pl. CX:2
6.	Krater, light brown	1:5	Ginossar	Tomb	IDA, no. 847
7.	Krater, pink-buff	1:5	Megiddo	X	Meg. II, pl. 45:24
8.	Krater, yellowish	1:5	Jericho	T.9	AAA XIX, pl. XXXIII:8
9.	Small Krater, cream-buff, irregularly burnished outside	1:5	Megiddo	XI (T.5234)	Meg. II, pl. 34:5
10.	Krater, buff	1 5	Beth Mirsim D		TBM IA, pl. 14:2
11.	Krater, pink-buff	1:5	Megiddo	XI (T.3064)	Meg. II, pl. 38:11

PLATE 30

1.	Cooking-pot, coarse, brown, straw temper, hand made	1:5	Megiddo	XV	Meg. II, pl. 9:19
2.	Cooking-pot, coarse brown, hand made	1 5	Ras el-Ain		QDAP V, p. 123:33
3.	Cooking-pot	1:5	Beth Mirsim D		TBM IA, pl. 13:4
4.	Cooking-pot, brown-grey, numerous red grits	1:5	Megiddo	X (T.3026)	Meg. II, pl. 46:10
5.	Cooking-pot, brown, numerous white grits	1:5	Megiddo	X	Meg. II, pl. 46:4
6.	Cooking-pot, red-brown indented decoration	1:5	Hazor	3	H. II, pl. CX:15
7.	Cooking-pot, brown-grey, numerous grits	1:5	Megiddo	XII (T.3182)	Meg. II, pl. 30:3

Cooking Pots (Plate 30).

MB II A: No. 1 is the commonest form, with straight walls, a row of punctures or holes below the rim, and an applied rope decoration.

No. 2 is a type destined to become very popular in the following periods. The fragment shown here has an inner gutter rim, a feature characteristic of MB II A rims.

MB II B–C: No. 3 is a straight-sided cooking pot. This type is still being produced, but the predominant type is shown in Nos. 4–7. Of these, No. 5, the commonest, is the ancestor of the LB cooking pot. The large specimen shown in No. 6 has a rim which is triangular in section, a feature unusual in cooking pots before LB. It is ornamented with a plastic band of rope, a decoration often seen on the large vessels of the period.

No. 4 resembles the commonest cooking pot (No. 5), but has a loop handle. Specimens with two handles are unknown. Other examples of this type are of smaller size. No. 7 is a very uncommon variant; of especial interest is its folded rim.

Storage Jars (Plates 31—32).

MB II A: Two clear-cut jar types can be distinguished: jars without handles (Nos. 1–3, Photo 102), and jars with handles (No. 4). The first type has a relatively short oval body, a flattened base and a profiled rim which sometimes has an inner gutter. The jars are frequently painted, usually in parallel bands, but wavy lines or even concentric circles are also found. The same kind of painted decoration is also found on contemporary jugs and juglets (see below, Plate 33:14). This type is related to the Khabur pottery (Plate 35), both in general appearance and in decoration.

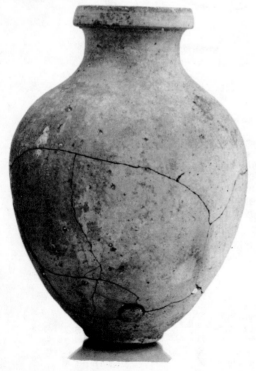

Photo 102. Jar, Ras el-Ain, IDA 36.2078.

Photo 103. Jar, painted, Ajjul, IDA 33.1397.

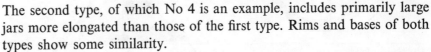

Photo 104. Context to Tomb H, Farah(N), *RB*, 1948, Pl. XXI.

Photo 105. Jar, Megiddo, IDA P.3029.

The second type, of which No 4 is an example, includes primarily large jars more elongated than those of the first type. Rims and bases of both types show some similarity.

MB II B–C: The most characteristic feature of the MB II B–C jar is the ovoid body; the fairly thin walls are of uniform thickness from rim to base. All the jars shown in Plate 32, with the exception of No. 9, belong to this type, in spite of the diversity of features such as the presence and number of handles, their place of attachment, and the form and decoration of the rims.

The two most frequently found variants are jars with two handles attached below the shoulder (No. 6) and handleless jars (No. 1, Photo 105). No. 2 is very similar, but has four handles. No. 7, which could be classified either as a jar or a jug, has a shoulder handle (Photo 104). No. 8 is an uncommon variant of the two-handled jar, with angular handles and a distinctive plain rim.

Two types of jar-rims can be distinguished — plain flaring rims and thickened profiled (stepped) rims.

The decoration is of two kinds: a narrow band on the shoulder consisting of wavy or straight incisions made with a comb, and black or bluish-grey and red alternating wavy and straight lines painted over a white slip covering the shoulder of the vessel (Photo 103). This painted decoration goes back to the preceding period. No. 9 shows a number of features which are related to MB II A, such as the stylized applied rope decoration, the handles attached to this rope, and the flat base (cf. Plate 29:2). The dating of this jar is difficult, because it was found outside of any archaeological context. However, its size and shape, as well as the thickened flat rim, are characteristic of MB II B.

Photo No. 104 shows the assemblage of finds from Tomb H at Tell el-Far'ah (N), which includes two jars like No. 7 on Plate 32, kraters resembling Nos. 6 and 11 on Plate 29, a carinated bowl of the type shown on Plate 27:6, a bowl like Nos. 3 and 7 on Plate 26, three dipper juglets, and three piriform juglets of the type represented on Plate 34, discussed below.

PLATE | 31

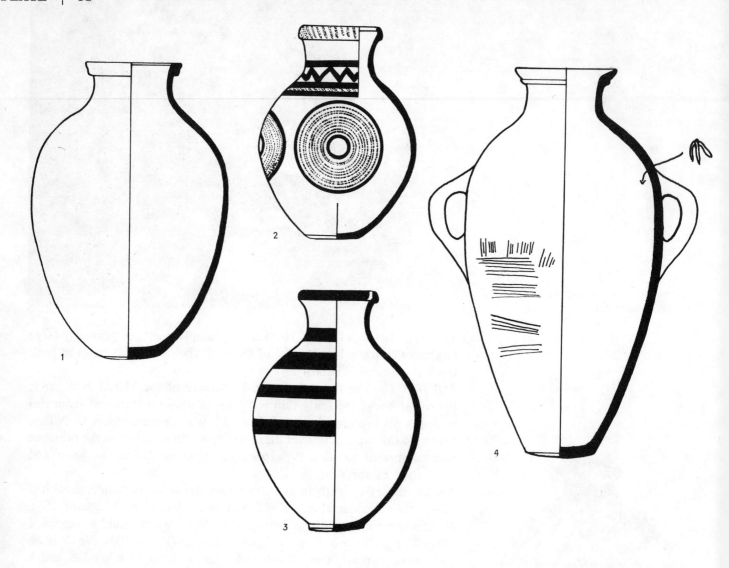

PLATE 31

1. Jar, pink-buff · 1:5   Megiddo   XIV (T.3138)   Meg. II, pl. 12:17
2. Jar, pink-buff, comb-finished, red and
   black decoration · · · · · · · · · · · · · · · · 1:5   Megiddo   XIV   Meg. II, pl. 13:5
3. Jar, pink-buff, burnished, red decoration 1:5   Megiddo   XIV (T.5181)   Meg. II, pl. 12:22
4. Jar, red-buff, comb-finished · · · · · · · · · · 1:5   Megiddo   XIII B   Meg. II, pl. 16:10

PLATE 32

1. Jar, pink-buff · 1:10   Megiddo   XII   Meg. II, pl. 27:8
2. Jar · 1:10   Beth Mirsim   E   TBM IA, pl. 6:1
3. Jar · 1:10   Beth Mirsim   D   TBM IA, pl. 14:10
4. Jar · 1:10   Beth Mirsim   E   TBM IA, pl. 7:10
5. Jar · 1:10   Beth Mirsim   E   TBM IA, pl. 7:3
6. Jar, green-buff, potter's mark on handle 1:10   Megiddo   XII (T.3095)   Meg. II, pl. 27:3
7. Jar, green-buff · · · · · · · · · · · · · · · · · · · 1:10   Megiddo   X (T.3070)   Meg. II, pl. 40:5
8. Jar · 1:10   Far'ah (N.)   5   RB 1951, p. 397, Fig. 2
9. Jar, pink-buff · 1:10   Megiddo   XIII   Meg. II, pl. 21:4

PLATE | 32

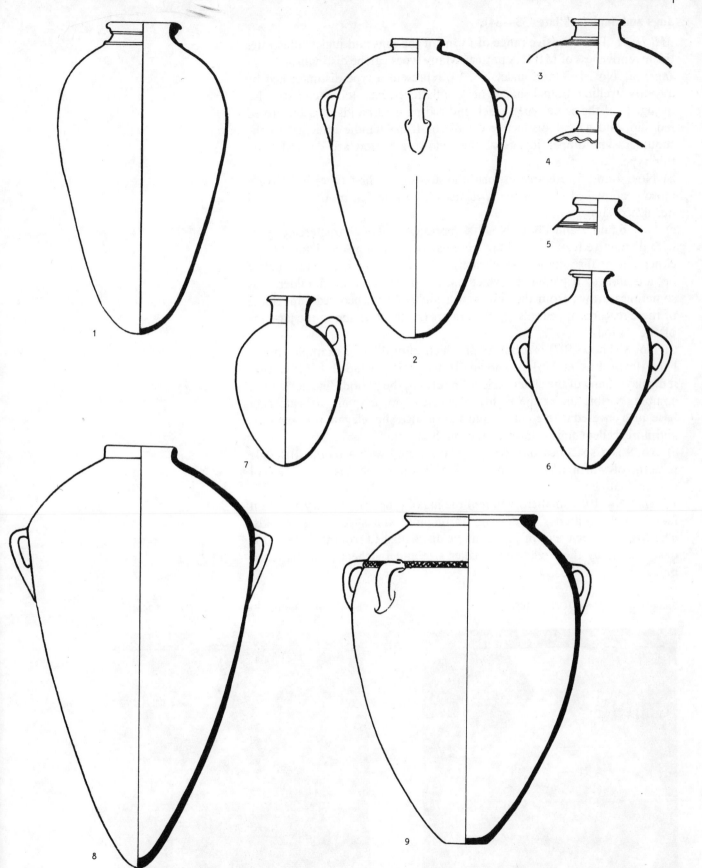

Jugs and Juglets (Plates 33—34).

MB II A: The extensive range of forms of the jugs and juglets illustrates the inventiveness of MB II A potters. Many types can be distinguished:

Jugs: a) Nos. 1–3 (and juglet No. 10) represent a type distinguished by a gently swelling, funnel-shaped neck, a flattened base (characteristic also of juglets of the same type), black and red painted bands or a burnished red slip, and a very distinctive double or triple handle attached to the shoulder. The dipper juglets of the following period are derived from this type.

b) Nos. 4 and 5 resemble in form the jugs of the first type, but have a more pronounced base. Some specimens have a trefoil mouth and a red burnished slip.

c) Nos. 6 and 7 and Photo No. 106 represent a very characteristic type, with distinctive features: a short, globular body with a well-defined base, either flat or disc-shaped, a delicately profiled rim with an inner gutter lip, a double or triple handle which usually perches on the shoulder or is sometimes drawn from the rim, and a highly burnished red slip. Some of these features appear also in the kraters (Plate 29:3) and in the jar-rims of the period.

d) No. 8 (Photo 107) is a bottle, of which only the one example shown here (from Ras el-Ain) is known. It has been included here because it displays many of the characteristic features of the period: fine horizontal combing visible under the highly burnished slip, a small, delicate ring base, also covered with combing and a burnished slip, elegant proportions, and an excellent finish down to the smallest detail.

e) No. 9 is a specimen of the jug-type decorated with a painted triangle pattern, of which further examples are shown in Photos 106, 112–114 and in Plate 35.

Juglets: No. 10, a smaller version of the jug of type a), is a very common form which continues to develop throughout the succeeding periods. The MB II A juglets of this type can be distinguished from their MB II B descendants by their relatively smaller size and by their small flattened base.

Photo 106. Jug, Amr, IDA 59–105.

Photo 107. Bottle, Ras el-Ain, IDA 35.3437.

Photo 108. Juglet, Megiddo, *Meg.* II, Pl. 118, The Oriental Institute, Chicago, No. A23851.

No. 11 is an example of the piriform juglet, which will branch out into many variations and reach the peak of its development in the following period. The MB II A piriform juglet still has an oval body; it has a characteristic ridge below the rim, with the handle springing from it. Inside the rim, a kind of gutter is formed. Both these features disappear in MB II B. Body and rim are thus the main features distinguishing between piriform juglets of MB II A and MB II B. The oval body of the MB II A juglet develops gradually into the pear-shaped body with pronounced shoulder of MB II B (Plate 34:15–16). The rim described above is common in MB II A, while in MB II B an everted, funnel-shaped rim is dominant. We shall return to this distinction in connection with the Tell el-Yahudiyeh juglets (Plate 36). MB II A juglets of the type described above have a red burnished slip and a very small flat base, and frequently a double handle (Photo 108).

Nos. 12 and 13. This cylindrical juglet with a pyxis-like body is common in MB II B and appears already in MB II A. No. 12 is a unique specimen which has peculiar walls.

No. 14 is decorated with concentric circles, a design which we have already encountered on a jar of the same period (Plate 31:2).

No. 15 is piriform, has an ovoid body and all the properties of a jug. The cut-away rim is not native to Palestine but is characteristic of Hittite pottery.

PLATE 33

1.	Jug, buff, red decoration	1:5	Megiddo	XIII B (T.5268)	Meg. II, pl. 16:5
2.	Jug, brown-ocher, red and blue-black decoration	1:5	Megiddo	T.911 D	Meg. T., pl. 31:21
3.	Jug, pink-buff, comb-finished, red and black decoration	1:5	Megiddo	XIV (T.3150)	Meg. II, pl. 11:21
4.	Jug, pink-buff, red vertically burnished slip	1:5	Megiddo	XIV (T.3157)	Meg. II, pl. 11:12
5.	Jug, pink-buff, red burnished slip	1:5	Megiddo	XIV (T.5181)	Meg. II, pl. 11:17
6.	Jug, pink-buff, red vertically burnished slip	1:1	Megiddo	XIV (T.3155)	Meg. II, pl. 10:2
7.	Jug, pink-buff, red burnished slip	1:5	Megiddo	XIV (T.5186)	Meg. II, pl. 10:8
8.	Bottle, red, wheel-combed, red vertically burnished slip	1:6	Ras el-Ain		QDAP V, p. 125:74
9.	Jug, brown-red, white slip, red and black decoration	1:6	Ras el-Ain	T.4	Stra. Comp. Fig. 149:4
10.	Juglet, pink-buff, orange-red vertically burnished slip	1:5	Megiddo	XIV (T.3148)	Meg. II, pl. 12:3
11.	Juglet, pink-buff, red vertically burnished slip	1:5	Megiddo	XV (T.3171)	Meg. II, pl. 7:18
12.	Juglet, brown, red burnished slip	1:5	Ras el-Ain	T.2	QDAP VI, p. 118:87
13.	Juglet, white-yellow, light red vertically burnished slip	1:5	Megiddo	T.911 A	Meg. T., pl. 28:39
14.	Juglet, pink-buff, irregularly burnished, red and black decoration	1:5	Megiddo	XIII	Meg. II, pl. 19:13
15.	Juglet, grey-buff, red vertically burnished slip	1:5	Megiddo	XIII B (T.5114)	Meg. II, pl. 16:2

108

PLATE | **33**

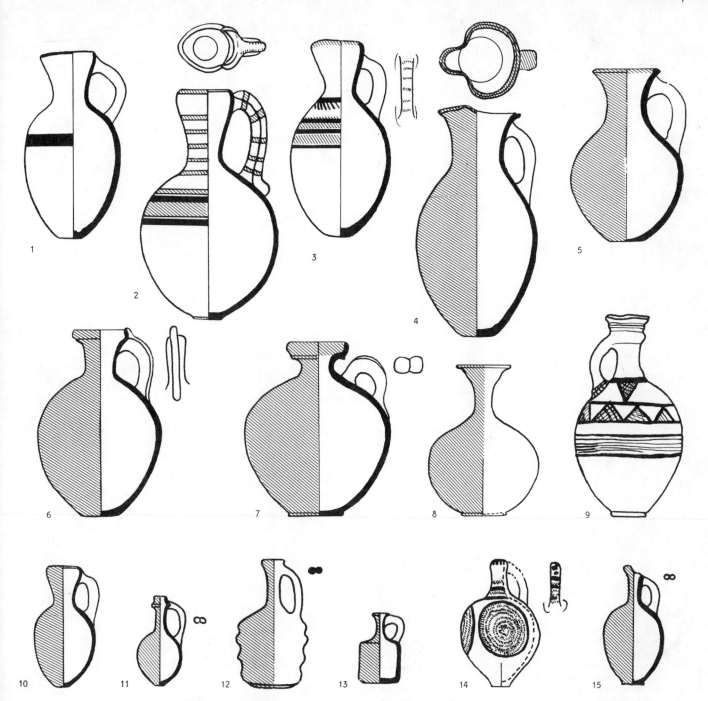

PLATE 34

1.	Jug, orange-buff, vertically burnished	1:5	Megiddo	XI (T.2130)	Meg. II, pl. 34:11
2.	Jug, pink-buff	1:5	Megiddo	XII (T.4099)	Meg. II, pl. 25:3
3.	Jug, buff	1:5	Megiddo	XII (T.3122)	Meg. II, pl. 25:4
4.	Jug, brown, irregularly burnished	1:5	Megiddo	T.24	Meg. T., pl. 23:18
5.	Jug, pink-buff, comb-finished, red burnished slip	1:5	Megiddo	XII (T.5106)	Meg. II, pl. 25:12
6.	Jug, pink-buff	1:5	Megiddo	X	Meg. II, pl. 39:1
7.	Jug, blue-grey, metallic ware, white burnished slip	1:5	Megiddo	XII	Meg. II, pl. 23:2
8.	Jug, buff, vertically burnished	1:5	Megiddo	XI (T.4053)	Meg. II, pl. 31:6
9.	Jug, buff	1:5	Megiddo	X	Meg. II, pl. 41:9
10.	Juglet, buff, orange-red vertically burnished slip	1:5	Megiddo	XII (T.4107)	Meg. II, pl. 26:10
11.	Juglet, pink-buff, orange-red burnished slip	1:5	Megiddo	XII	Meg. II, pl. 24:28
12.	Jug, cream-buff, vertically burnished	1:5	Megiddo	XI (T.5250)	Meg. II, pl. 31:8
13.	Jug, grey, brown horizontally burnished slip	1:5	Lachish	T.173	La. IV, pl. 74:669
14.	Juglet, cream-buff burnished slip, red-brown decoration	1:6	Ajjul	T.1551	AG IV, pl. LIV:60 N 7 and photo PAM 35:4053
15.	Juglet, pink-buff, dark red burnished slip	1:5	Megiddo	XII (T.3122)	Meg. II, pl. 24:10
16.	Juglet, buff, orange vertically burnished slip	1:5	Megiddo	XII (T.5067)	Meg. II, pl. 24:22
17.	Juglet, pink-buff	1:5	Megiddo	XII (T.3095)	Meg. II, pl. 23:14
18.	Juglet, pink-buff, red burnished slip	1:5	Megiddo	XII	Meg. II, pl. 23:18

PLATE | 34

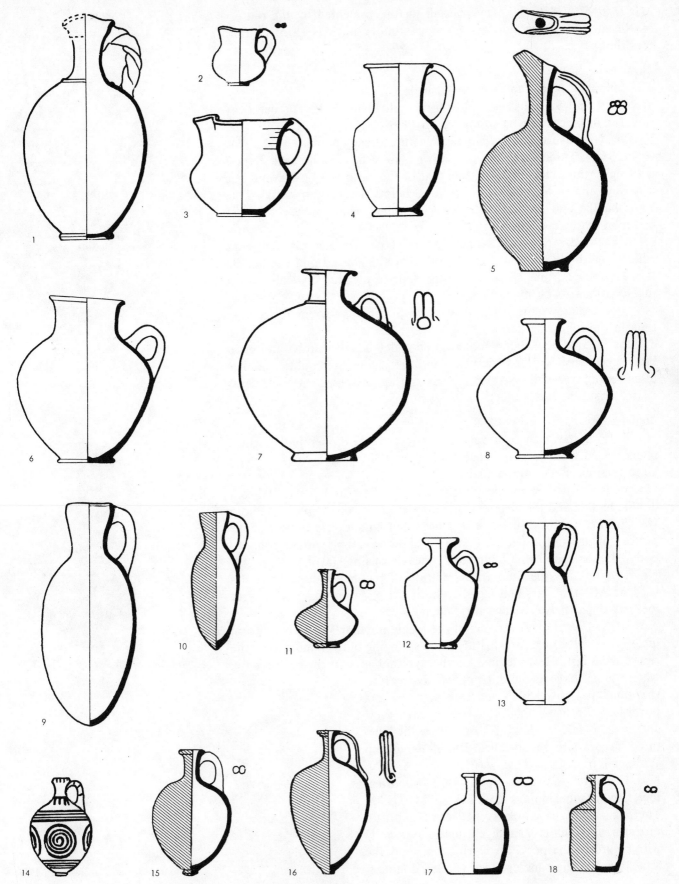

MB II B–C: (Plate 34). The over-all picture presented by the pottery of this period shows a pronounced continuity of MB II A ceramic tradition.

Jugs:

The following types can be distinguished:

a) Nos. 1 and 5 are like MB II A forms (cf. Plate 33:4). The cut-away rim, for instance, can be compared to Plate 33:15.

b) Nos. 6–8 have a shoulder handle, a feature already popular in MB II A (Plate 33:7). Three variations are shown: No. 6 has a wide neck; No. 7 is of light, thin, metallic ware, like that of the carinated bowls, and has a flaring, almost folded-over rim; No. 8 is found very frequently — the triple handle and the slipless surface burnished to an ivory colour are common features of the period.

c) Nos. 2 and 3 represent a new, cup-like type. The neck is almost as wide as the body of the vessel, the rim is trefoil-shaped and the handle is often double. Some specimens of this type of jug are very small. Such jugs continue to be made in LB I.

No. 4 foreshadows the jug-form which will remain current for a long time in the following periods.

d) Nos. 12 and 13. The pronounced shoulder is a feature common to both specimens. No. 12 is derived from the jugs with shoulder handles discussed above, while No. 13, though unusual, displays many elements characteristic of this period.

Juglets:

No. 10 is a specimen of a very common type of dipper juglet which is descended from jugs and juglets of type a) in MB II A. No. 9 is a large version of the same juglets.

No. 11 is unusual in the proportion between base and body. It has a double handle and the characteristic burnished slip of the period. Photo 109 shows a biconical juglet, with a neck and handle very typical of the piriform juglets of this period. Photo 110 shows a variant with bag-shaped body. (It was found in J. Garstang's excavations at Hazor.)

No. 14 continues the decorative tradition of painted concentric circles used on MB II A jars and juglets. Photo 111 shows a juglet with three ibexes painted between concentric circles.

Nos. 15 and 16 are two variants of the highly popular MB II B piriform juglet. A very characteristic feature is the springing of the handle from the rim or from just below the rim. Another typical feature is the button base, which must have evolved from its predecessor, the small flat base. Such juglets usually have a burnished slip in all shades of red, brown, grey, and even black. Juglets of this type with punctured decoration, the so-called Tell el-Yahudiyeh Ware, will be discussed below (Plate 36).

Nos. 17 and 18 are two examples of the cylindrical juglet, whose beginnings go back to MB II A. There is a family resemblance between cylindrical, piriform, and Tell el-Yahudiyeh juglets, especially with regard to the neck, the flaring rim, and the attachment of the handle, which is often double.

112

Photo 111. Juglet, Ginosar, IDA 56–845.

Photo 109. Juglet, Menahat, HU 2204.

Photo 110. Juglet, Hazor, IDA I.5964.

MB II A Pottery and the Khabur Ware (Plate 35).

Plate 35 has been arranged with the intention of illustrating certain features of the MB II A pottery which can be traced back to their origin through Byblos and Qatna to the Khabur region. The ultimate origins of the Khabur Ware are beyond the scope of this work. This chapter follows up a suggestion of Albright's,[2] made many years ago, concerning the affinity between MB II A pottery and the Khabur Ware.

The juxtaposition of MB II A pottery and the Khabur Ware reveals differences as well as similarities in form and decoration: the Khabur Ware (Nos. 1–4) is distinguished by vessels without handles, and the typical MB II A jars (Nos. 11 and 12) are strikingly similar in form to the jars from Chagar Bazar (Nos. 1–3). The characteristic MB II A goblet in Palestine (No. 10, Photo 98), appears to have developed from the Khabur goblet (No. 4), which, in turn, has a long history of its own. However, when we come to compare the decorated Palestinian jugs (Nos. 7–9) with the decorated jars from the Khabur, we find that their shapes are entirely different, and that only the distinctive ornamentation has been adopted by Greater Canaan. As for the decoration itself, two patterns, both characteristic of the Khabur Ware, are found on the examples from Byblos (No. 5), Qatna (No. 6) and Palestine (Nos. 7–9, 11 and 12): simple painted bands around the body of the vessel, or a more complex pattern consisting of bands of painted triangles or rhomboids around the upper part of the vessel (Photos 112–114 and 106).

Photo 112. Jug, Ras el-Ain, IDA 36.2088.

Photo 113. Jug, Ras el-Ain, IDA 36.2081.

Photo 114. Jug, Ras el-Ain, IDA 36.2087.

To what extent this comparative study, which indeed requires much more work, may affect historical and chronological conclusions, remains to be seen. However, in view of Mallowan's statement that at Chagar Bazar no Khabur Ware was found below the stratum attributed to Shamshi-Adad I[3], and in view of the absence of any analogies between MB II B pottery in Palestine and the Khabur Ware and the plentiful analogies in the preceding period, any stylistic connections between

2. W. F. Albright, *TBM*, IA, pp. 67–75.
3. M. E. L. Mallowan, "White painted Subartu Pottery," *Mélanges Syriens offerts à M. Dussaud*, I, Paris, 1939, p. 891, n. 1.

PLATE 35

1.	Jar, red decoration	1:5	Chagar Bazar	I	Iraq IV, Fig. 21:2
2.	Jar, black decoration	1:5	Chagar Bazar	I	Iraq III, Fig. 16:5
3.	Jar	1:5	Chagar Bazar	I	Iraq III, Fig. 16:1
4.	Goblet	1:5	Chagar Bazar	I	Iraq III, Fig. 14:13
5.	Jar	1:10	Byblos, foundation jar		Stra. Comp. Fig. 59:P
6.	Jug, red, black and brown decoration	1:6	Qatna	T.1	Les Ruines, Fig. 49
7.	Jug, red, whitish slip, red and black decoration	1:6	Ras el-Ain	T.4	Stra. Comp., Fig. 149:3
8.	Jug, brown-green, whitish slip, red decoration	1:6	Ras el-Ain	T.2	Stra. Comp., Fig. 148:19
9.	Jug, dark brown, horizontally burnished, black decoration	1:3	Gezer	T.30 III	Gezer I, p. 298:7
10.	Goblet, red, red slip, combed	1:6	Ras el-Ain		QDAP V, p. 125:76
11.	Jar, buff, red decoration	1:5	Megiddo	XIV	Meg. II, pl. 12:21
12.	Jar, pink-buff, burnished, red decoration	1:5	Megiddo	XIV (T.5181)	Meg. II, pl. 12:22

114

PLATE | 35

PLATE 36

1. Bowl, grey-buff, brown-red irregularly bur-
   nished slip, white-filled punctured decoration 1:5   Megiddo   XIV   Meg. II, pl. 14:35
2. Bowl, buff, red burnished slip,
   white-filled punctured decoration   1:5   Megiddo   XV (T.5202)   Meg. II, pl. 9:10
3. Juglet, grey, burnished, white-filled
   punctured and incised decoration   1:5   Afula   IDA, No. 50–804
4. Juglet, grey, burnished, white-filled
   punctured and incised decoration   H.U. No. 1964
5. Juglet, grey, burnished, white-filled
   punctured and incised decoration   1:5   H.U. No. 2203
6. Juglet, burnished between bands of white-
   filled incised and punctured decoration   1:5   Megiddo   XIV (T.5177)   Meg. II, pl. 11:1
7. Juglet, brown, brown vertically burnished slip 1:5 Megiddo   T.911 A 1   Meg. T., pl. 28:40
8. Juglet, charcoal grey, white-filled incised
   and punctured decoration   1:5   Megiddo   T.24   Meg. T., pl. 23:23
9. Juglet, black-grey, white-filled incised
   and punctured decoration   1:5   Megiddo   XII (T.3123)   Meg. II, pl. 24:31
10. Juglet, black-grey traces of burnish white-
    filled incised and punctured decoration   1:5   Megiddo   XI (T.3110)   Meg. II pl. 32:32
11. Juglet, grey-black, burnished, white-filled
    punctured decoration   1:5   Megiddo   XI (T.3085)   Meg. II, pl. 32:31
12. Juglet, pink-buff, dark red burnished slip,
    punctured decoration   1:5   Megiddo   XII (T.3129)   Meg. II, pl. 24:32
13. Juglet, brown, dark brown burnished slip,
    white-filled incised and punctured decoration 1:5 Lachish   T.1552   La. IV, pl. 77:728
14. Juglet, charcoal-grey, white-filled
    punctured decoration   1:5   Megiddo   T.24   Meg. T., pl. 23:30
15. Juglet, dark grey, grey slip, incised and
    punctured decoration   1:5   Lachish   T.157   La. IV, pl. 77:750
16. Juglet, grey, burnished, white-filled incised
    and punctured decoration   1:5   Ginossar   T.3   IDA, No. 56–724
17. Juglet, grey, burnished, punctured decoration 1:5 Gibeon   Tomb   PAM, 45–127
18. Zoomorphic vessel, grey-black white-filled
    incised and punctured decoration   1:5   Megiddo   XII (T.5137)   Meg. II, pl. 247:1
19. Juglet, grey, punctured decoration   1:5   Enkomi   T.11   Astrom, Fig. XXX:21
20. Juglet, grey, punctured decoration   1:5   Enkomi   T.11   Astrom, Fig. XXX:24
21. Juglet, grey, burnished, incised and
    punctured decoration (after a photograph)   Majdalouna   Tomb   BMB IV, Fig. 3:a
22. Juglet, grey, incised and punctured decoration   Sin el-Fill Tomb   Stra. Comp., Fig. 73:2
23. Juglet, grey, incised and punctured decoration   Sin el-Fill Tomb   Stra. Comp., Fig. 73:3
24. Juglet   Byblos   Tomb   Stra. Comp., Fig. 65:E
25. Juglet   Byblos   Tomb   Stra. Comp., Fig. 56:F
26. Juglet   1:5   Ugarit   T. LVII   Stra. Comp., Fig. 48:H
27. Albastron   1:5   Ugarit   T. LVII   Stra. Comp., Fig. 48:G
28. Juglet   1:5   Yahudiyeh   T.37   HIC, pl. VIII:50
29. Juglet   1:4   Yahudiyeh   T.3   HIC, pl. VII:25
30. Juglet   1:6   Yahudiyeh   T.16   HIC, pl. VIII:40
31. Juglet   1:4   Yahudiyeh   HIC, pl. VIIIa:65
32. Juglet   1:4   Yahudiyeh   T.3   HIC, pl. VII:26
33. Juglet   1:5   Kerma   Kerma IV–V, Fig. 264:25

116

PLATE | **36**

Photo 116. Juglet, Afula, IDA 50–801.

Photo 117. Juglet, Afula, IDA 51–728.

Photo 118. Juglet, Afula, IDA 50–803.

MB II A pottery and the Khabur Ware would point to Smith's high chronology[4] rather than to Albright's low chronology.[5] It is difficult to reconcile the low date proposed by Albright for Hammurabi and his contemporary, Shamshi Adad I, with the ceramic evidence from Palestine and the entire region. A date corresponding to the Thirteenth Dynasty, that is, to the first half of the 18th century B.C., when MB II A pottery flourished in Palestine, seems to be in better accord with the archaeological evidence.

Tell el-Yahudiyeh Ware (Plate 36).

The distinctive Tell el-Yahudiyeh Ware is characterized by the punctured design arranged in geometric patterns. Two important points should be noted: first, this type of decoration has been found, up to the present, only on juglets (with the exception of the two small carinated bowls from Megiddo[6] on Plate 36:1, 2, which will be discussed below). Secondly, the Tell el-Yahudiyeh juglets are similar in form to the two main juglet types of the period and their variants, which usually have a burnished slip. Both facts have a bearing on the problem of the geographic and ethnic origin of this ware, named after Tell el-Yahudiyeh in the Nile Delta, where Petrie first uncovered such juglets.[7]

Photo 115. Juglet, Afula, IDA 50–804.

4. Sidney Smith, *AJA* 49 (1945), pp. 1 ff.
5. W. F. Albright, *BASOR* 144 (1956), pp. 26 ff.
6. G. Schumacher, *Tell el-Mutesellim*, I, Leipzig, 1908, figs. 41–42.
7. W. F. Petrie, *Hyksos and Israelite Cities*, London, 1906. The Tell el-Yahudiyeh Ware, the Hyksos, and related problems have been the subject of numerous books and papers, of which we give here only a brief selection: W. F. Albright *TBN*, I–III; ibid., *The Archaeology of Palestine*; E. A. Speiser, "Ethnic Movements in the Near East in the Second Millennium B.C.," *AASOR* XIII (1933), pp. 13 ff.; R. M. Engberg, *The Hyksos Reconsidered*, Chicago, 1935; T. Save-Söderberg, "The Hyksos Rule in Egypt," *JEA* (1951), pp. 37 ff.; A. Alt, "Die Herkunft der Hyksos im neuen Licht," *Kleine Schriften*, III, pp. 72 ff.; Ruth Amiran, "Tell el-Yahudiyeh Ware in Syria," *IEJ* 7 (1957), pp. 93 ff.

Photo 119. Juglet, Ajjul, IDA 32.2088.

Photo 120. Juglet, Gibeon, IDA 45.127.

MB II A and B–C: Two main types of juglet with several variants can be distinguished, as well as some unusual forms:

a) The piriform juglets: The distinctions between earlier and later piriform juglets described above apply also to the Tell el-Yahudiyeh Ware. Oval to start with (Nos. 3–6, Photos 115–118), the juglet becomes gradually more piriform and the shoulder more strongly marked, evolving into the typical MB II B–C juglet (Nos. 6–12, Photo 119), one of whose hallmarks is the pronounced shoulder. At the same time, a number of features, such as the tendency towards squat shapes (Nos. 11 and 12), point to a certain degeneration of the type. The rim is another feature which differentiates between MB II A and B juglets: the earlier forms have a profiled rim appearing in many variations, and especially a ridge below the rim, just like the ordinary juglets; in the later juglets, the predominating rim is everted, usually rounded and thickened, and a handle is attached to the rim or immediately below. The combination of narrow neck, everted rim, and handle attached just below the rim is one of the marked features of MB II B–C pottery.

b) The cylindrical juglet: Such juglets are found already in MB II A (No. 7), but it is difficult to differentiate between such early specimens and similar, though later, juglets like No. 15.

A few unusual forms are shown on Plate 36 in order to illustrate the creative imagination of the craftsmen who produced this ware: No. 17 (Photo 120) has a lower part resembling that of a characteristic MB II B dipper juglet, while the upper part belongs to a piriform juglet and is decorated on the shoulder with lines of punctures. No. 18 is a bird-shaped vessel whose neck, rim, and handle are taken from the common piriform juglet.

Decoration: The clay of the Tell el-Yahudiyeh juglets is usually grey or light brown, with numerous grits. The burnished slip is gray, brownish-black, or yellowish. The decoration consists entirely of punctures made in the clay after slip and burnish had been applied and filled with white chalk, which often is still preserved.

Two main types of punctured decoration can be distinguished: designs delineated by grooves, and areas without delineation filled with straight, diagonal, or zig-zag lines of punctures. In both types horizontal designs are more common, but vertical designs, usually segment-shaped, are also fairly frequent. The predominant motifs are triangles, squares, and rhomboids, and only three instances of concentric circles are known: No. 16, from Ginossar, No. 21, from a tomb at Majdaluna in Lebanon, and a fragment picked up on the surface at Hazor (Photo 121). In all three the concentric circles are contained in a plain horizontal band enclosed by puncture-filled bands.

Photo 121. Juglet fragment, Hazor, IDA 55–104.

Distribution: The thirty-three specimens on Plate 36 show that Tell el-Yahudiyeh Ware has been found on the coast of northern Canaan (Nos. 21–27), in all of southern Canaan (Palestine) Nos. 1–18, in eastern Cyprus (Nos. 19–20, Photo 122), and in Egypt, from the Delta to Nubia (Nos. 28–33, Photo 123). It should be noted that, up to the present, this ware has not been found in inland Syria, i.e. on the upper Orontes and farther east.

Date: As we have seen above, the Tell el-Yahudiyeh Ware first appears in MB II A, and the examples known, though few, are dated with a fair measure of certainty by their context. The cylindrical juglet also makes its appearance already at this early stage. The two small carinated bowls (Nos. 1–2) which, in our opinion, belong to the Tell el-Yahudiyeh Ware, are also dated to MB II A. Interestingly enough, bowls disappear from the repertoire of this ware in MB II B–C. The evidence from Egypt and Phoenicia also points to the first appearance of this ware in the earlier part of the Middle Bronze Age. At Kahun,[8] fragments of Tell el-Yahudiyeh juglets were found together with other Canaanite vessels characteristic of MB II A. At Sin el-Fil,[9] the context in which two juglets (Nos. 22–23) were found, includes vessels which can be dated to MB II A. However, the Tell el-Yahudiyeh Ware reaches the peak of its popularity in MB II B, and is found very frequently on sites of that period. In LB I, the last descendants of this ware still occur.

Origin: The form of the Tell el-Yahudiyeh juglet is firmly rooted in Canaanite ceramic tradition, and can be traced back through earlier periods to such prototypes as, for instance, the juglets from Tomb A at Jericho. The origin of the distinctive punctured decoration, on the other hand, requires further investigation, but there is some evidence that it should be sought somewhere north of Canaan. However, mention should be made of the juglet with white-dotted decoration (Plate 20:20, Photo 73), also from Tomb A at Jericho.

Of particular significance is the potter's kiln excavated at Afula,[10] where both complete vessels and numerous fragments of Tell el-Yahudiyeh Ware were found, including many fragments of unbaked juglets (Photo 124). Thus it appears that this ware was manufactured in Canaan and exported from there to Egypt and Cyprus.

Ethnic Associations: Can any ethnic or historical significance be attached to the fact that the Tell el-Yahudiyeh juglets are characteristic of MB II B, a period when the Hyksos ruled in Canaan and in Egypt, and that they first appear in MB II A, when the Hyksos were already present in Canaan? There is some evidence of a connection, but any identification must remain tentative and should be accepted with caution.

Photo 122. Juglet, Enkomi (Cyprus), Musée du Louvre, No. 18598.

8. C. F. A. Schaeffer, *Stratigraphie comparée et chronologie de l'Asie Occidentale*, Oxford, 1948, fig. 53.
9. Ibid., fig. 73.
10. The excavation at Afula was carried out by Dr. E. Ben-Dor on behalf of the Israel Department of Antiquities.

120

Photo 123. Juglet, Tell el-Yahudiyeh (Egypt), Collections of the PBI, Jerusalem.

Imported Cypriot Wares (Plate 37).

Specimens of Cypriot wares found in Palestine are grouped on Plate 37. The wide range of forms bears witness to the close commercial ties between Cyprus and Canaan in that period, already demonstrated by the presence of Tell el-Yahudiyeh Ware in Cyprus (see above).

Cypriot pottery in this and the following period is characterized by several distinctive features: it is always hand made; jugs as well as bowls are globular; the handles of jugs and juglets are inserted in a special way into the wall of the vessel.

Plate 37 is arranged according to the Cypriot classification of wares:

a) *Red-on-Black Ware:* Nos. 1 and 2. Such vessels are covered with a dark brown or black slip, and are painted with groups of red lines produced with a multiple brush. Bowls as well as jugs of this ware have been excavated in Palestine.

b) *White-Painted Ware:* A wide range of White-Painted Ware characterized by brownish-black painted decoration on a light background has been found in Palestine.

White-Painted VI (No. 3): Only the jug shown here is known up to the present. A distinctive feature of this ware is the lengthwise division of the body by three groups of painted bands meeting at the base, with groups of diagonal bands in between. We shall meet this kind of division again in LB I, in one of the jug types of the Bichrome Ware.

White-Painted V (Nos. 4–8) This is abundantly represented in Palestine in MB II B and continues into LB I. Jugs Nos. 5 and 6, set apart by a frame, are quite different from the other jugs shown on this plate: they have a distinct base, their body is piriform instead of globular, and they appear to be wheel-made. Their whole appearance is that of the piriform juglet, whose birthplace was Canaan. The decoration and the division of the surface are also not of Cypriot character. Their origin appears to be northern Canaan, perhaps Ugarit or its vicinity. In Cyprus, this type of jug has been included in White Painted V Ware for reasons of technical convenience, because of the similarity in the colors of background and decoration.

No. 8 is a type of small teapot frequently found in Palestine, which we shall encounter again in the following period.

White-Painted IV: Cypriot archaeology distinguishes four styles of this ware, but only two have been found outside Cyprus: Nos. 9–11 and Nos. 12 and 13. They feature a decoration covering the entire surface of the vessel and consisting of closely spaced straight lines with vertical or diagonal wavy lines in between. As in the other wares, neck and rim are decorated with horizontal lines. No. 11 is a lentoid flask, which is of special interest as it is the only example of its kind, even in Cyprus itself.

c) *White-Slip I Ware:* This ware makes its appearance already at the end of the Middle Bronze Age, as No. 14 shows, but enjoys the peak of its popularity in the Late Bronze Age. The ware has a thick, grayish-white slip, painted in brown or in two colors — brown and red — in an abundance of designs resembling embroidery patterns.

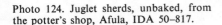

Photo 124. Juglet sherds, unbaked, from the potter's shop, Afula, IDA 50–817.

PLATE 37

1. Bowl, buff, lustrous black slip inside and out,
   red decoration (RoB)   1:5   Megiddo   XI   Meg. II. pl. 38:16
2. Jug, buff, handmade, black burnished slip,
   red decoration (RoB)   1:5   Megiddo   XII (T.5134)   Meg. II, pl. 26:14
3. Jug, pink-buff, handmade, burnished,
   black decoration (WP VI)   1:5   Megiddo   XI (T.5243)   Meg. II, pl. 34:4
4. Bowl (WP V)   1:5   Ajjul   AG III, pl. XXX:19 Q
5. Juglet, green-buff, handmade, black
   decoration (WP V)   1:5   Megiddo   X (T.3046)   Meg. II, pl. 41:30
6. Juglet, green-buff, handmade (?) burnished,
   black decoration (WP V)   1:5   Megiddo   XI (T.5050)   Meg. II, pl. 34:16
7. Jug, buff, handmade, burnished,
   black decoration (WP V)   1:5   Megiddo   XI (T.4109)   Meg. II, pl. 34:13
8. Spouted jug, buff, handmade, black
   decoration (WP V)   1:5   Megiddo   X   Meg. II, pl. 41:32
9. Jug, buff, handmade, burnished, black
   decoration (WP IV)   1:5   Megiddo   XII   Meg. II, pl. 26:16
10. Jug, green-buff, white slip, brown
    decoration (WP IV)   1:5   Beth-shemesh T.3   Beth Semesh, p. 127:649
11. Flask, buff, handmade, burnished,
    brown-red decoration (WP IV)   1:5   Megiddo   X   Meg. II, pl. 46:11
12. Juglet, buff, handmade, burnished,
    black decoration (WP IV)   1:5   Megiddo   XI (T.4109)   Meg. II, pl. 34:9
13. Juglet, cream-buff, handmade, burnished,
    black decoration (WP IV)   1:5   Megiddo   XI   Meg. II, pl. 34:8
14. Bowl, red-buff, handmade, white burnished
    slip, inside and out, red-brown decoration
    (WS I)   1:5   Megiddo   X   Meg. II, pl. 45:21

PLATE | 37

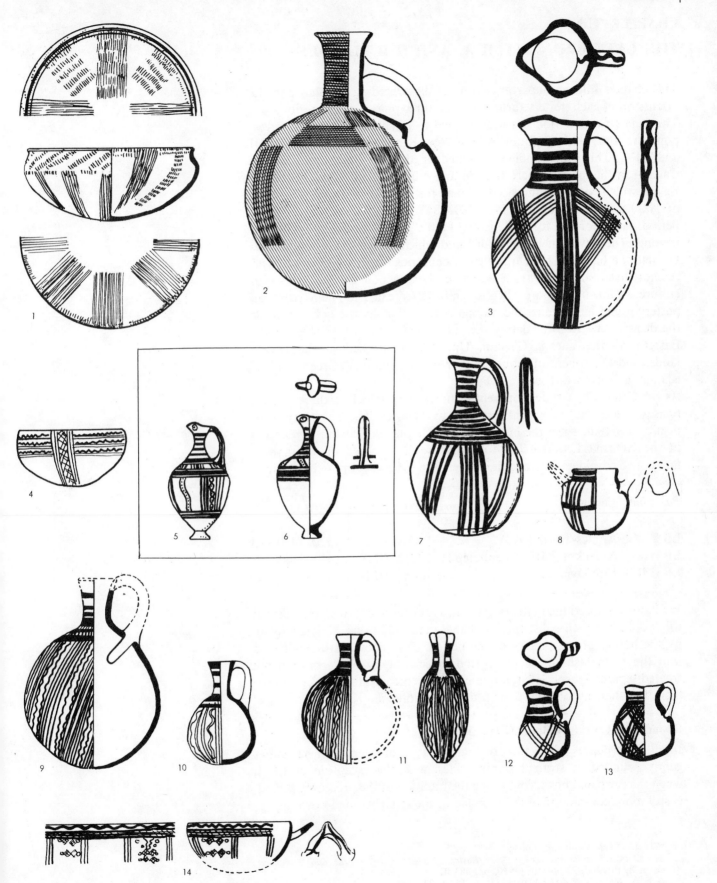

CHAPTER TEN

THE LATE BRONZE I, II A, AND II B PERIODS

This chapter follows the arrangement of the preceding chapter, and the discussion of each pottery form covers all three phases of the period.

The Late Bronze period has been pegged to Egyptian history: it corresponds to the whole duration of the New Kingdom (Dynasties XVIII and XIX). This synchronology is based on the fact that the history of Canaan in this period, more than in any other, is tied to the history of Egypt, which ruled or influenced Canaan for most of this time. The reign of Akhenaton (Amenhotep IV, 1380–1363 B.C.), that is, the Amarna period, is important for the history of the period both in Egypt and beyond. The city Akhenaton built,[1] and which he made his capital, has become the basis for the chronolgy of countries far from Amarna itself. A short-lived site is always a welcome phenomenon for the history of culture, so much the more when it can be dated exactly. The Mycenaean pottery found in the ruins and dumps of that short-lived city has become the decisive criterion for dating the cultures of countries situated in the Eastern Mediterranean: Canaan, Upper Canaan, Cilicia, the Hittite lands, and the sphere of influence in Western Anatolia, Greece and its islands, and even farther westward.

As for Canaan — the development of the pottery falls into three general phases, the second of which is pegged to Amarna. There is every justification for that, since the history of this chapter in Canaan is reflected in the Amarna Letters.[2] The following Table is based on the above-mentioned considerations and the Mycenaean dates as proposed by Wace.[3]

Palestine	Egypt	Mycenae	Dates
LB I	Ahmes-Thothmes IV	Myc. I–II	1570–1410 B.C.
LB II A	Amenhotep III–Amenhotep IV	Myc. III A	1410–1340
LB II B	19th Dynasty	Myc. III B	1340–1200

We have organized the Plates of types in the order maintained throughout this book, but with some special changes and additions, dictated solely by the nature of the pottery of the period. Thus, bowls are subdivided into the main fashions of the period; special styles of decoration are treated separately; special attention is paid to 'biconical vessels', grouping them together, away from their usual definitions, as 'Kraters' or 'Jugs.'

Rounded and Straight Bowls (Plate 38).

In all three phases of LB the predominant type of open bowl has either gently rounded or straight sloping sides, with the exception of LB I, when the carinated bowl, continuing the tradition of the preceding period, is still more common than the rounded or the straight-sided bowl.

---

1. F. Petrie, *Tell el-Amarna*, London, 1891, p. 3.
2. See literature given in *Ancient Near Eastern Texts Relating to the Old Testament*, ed. J. B. Pritchard, Princeton, 1950, pp. 483 ff.
3. A. J. B. Wace, *ABSA*, XLVIII (1953), p. 15, n. 22.

Photo 125. Bowl, Abu Hawam, IDA 34.301.

Photo 126. Bowl, Lachish, IDA 36.1812.

LB I: Nos. 1 and 2 are similar rounded bowls: No. 1 is distinguished by the excellent wheel-finish of the concave omphalos on the inside of the base, which, as we shall see below, is a feature mainly of the white-slipped bowls (Plate 49). Straight bowls: Nos. 3–5. No. 3 is a small, coarsely made bowl, which is very common. The base is string-cut. Nos. 4 and 5 are two specimens from Hazor, illustrating the type of bowl decorated on the inside with red-painted bands (Photos 125 and 126). The concave disc-base appears already in this period. No. 6 reflects a mixture of heterogenous elements and illustrates a whole trend: the forms of bowl and handle are of Cypriot origin and tradition, while the decoration seems of Canaanite or rather northern Canaanite style, including the use of red and black in the patterns, very common in other styles of the period in Canaanite pottery (see below, Plates 48 and 50).

LB II A: From LB II A onwards, the disc-base gradually becomes common alongside the ring-base. Nos. 7 and 8 are two examples of the bowl with painted bands already encountered in the previous period. No. 8, which is decorated with red and black bands, is the commoner of the two, and similar bowls often form the upper part of chalices. No. 9 resembles Nos. 7 and 8, but is plain. Nos. 10 and 11 are in MB tradition, especially the thickened rim, which is folded over on the inside. Nos. 13 and 14 are rounded bowls: No. 13 has an ordinary concave disc-base, while No. 14 has an uncommon flat base. No. 15 is a fragment of a bowl, decorated with red and black triangles. The small bar-handle, which we shall see also in the coming period (No. 25 of the same Plate), seems to point to a fashion of imitating metal objects in clay.

LB II B: Nos. 16–19 are variants of the straight-sided bowl. The concave disc-base predominates, and the flat base of No. 19 is uncommon. No. 20–22 are three rounded bowls with either concave or solid disc-bases. The larger bowl has a rim thickened on the inside. Nos. 23 and 24 are two examples of the deep bowl with a single horizontal handle which shows Cypriot influence in the form of the body, and especially in the type of handle. The decoration on No. 24 is placed, as on No. 6, in the zone of the handle. This zone is divided into panels or metopes by triglyphs, a style popular in this period. On this bowl the metopes are irregular in size, and a large metope encloses a stylized palm-tree exactly opposite the hande (see below, Plate 50). No. 25 is a hemispherical bowl, with a small bar-handle. No. 26 has two such handles attached to one side of the bowl. Their rim is unusual and the disc-base is completely flat. The red-painted decoration inside the bowl consists of three rays radiating from the center, dividing the area inside the bowl into three sections: in one of these a palm-tree is painted, with the roots at the center of the bowl and the crown climbing up the side. The rim is also decorated with a red band. This motif will be discussed in Plate 39, and mainly in Plate 50.

Carinated Bowls (Plate 39).

Late Bronze carinated bowls are a direct development of the Middle Bronze, with a gradual degeneration of the forms towards the end of the period.

125

PLATE 38

1.	Bowl, buff		1:5	Megiddo	IX (T.5040 B)	Meg. II, pl. 53:7
2.	Bowl, pink-buff, pink burnished slip inside and out		1:5	Megiddo	IX	Meg. II, pl. 53:8
3.	Bowl, buff		1:5	Megiddo	IX	Meg. II, pl. 53:5
4.	Bowl, light grey, red decoration		1:5	Hazor	3	H. I, pl. CXXII:2
5.	Bowl, grey-buff, red decoration		1:5	Hazor	3	H. I, pl. CXXII:12
6.	Bowl, light grey, dark brown and red decoration		1:5	Hazor	3	H. I, pl. CXXIV:1
7.	Bowl, buff, traces of burnish inside and out, red decoration		1:5	Megiddo	VIII	Meg. II, pl. 61:18
8.	Bowl, pink-buff, red and black decoration		1:5	Megiddo	VIII	Meg. II, pl. 61:17
9.	Bowl, green-buff		1:5	Megiddo	VIII	Meg. II, pl. 61:12
10.	Bowl, light grey		1:5	Hazor	1 B	H. II, pl. CXXVIII:22
11.	Bowl, grey-brown, red slip		1:5	Hazor	1 B	H. II, pl. CXXVIII:24
12.	Bowl, grey-brown		1:5	Hazor	1 B	H. II, pl. CXXVIII:2
13.	Bowl, green-brown		1:5	Hazor	1 B	H. II, pl. XCCVIII:5
14.	Bowl, pink-buff		1:5	Megiddo	VIII	Meg. II, pl. 61:9
15.	Bowl, pink, buff slip, red and black decoration		1:5	Lachish	Temple III	La. II, pl. XLIII:160
16.	Bowl, grey-buff		1:5	Hazor	1 (pit 9024)	H. I, pl. CXXV:18
17.	Bowl, pinkish		1:5	Hazor	1 (pit 9024)	H. I, pl. XCCV:15
18.	Bowl, pinkish		1:5	Hazor	(pit 9017)	H. I, pl. CV:32
19.	Bowl, grey-buff		1:5	Hazor	(pit 7013)	H. I, pl. CXLIII:4
20.	Bowl, yellowish, red slip		1:5	Hazor	1 (pit 9024)	H. I, pl. CXXV:20
21.	Bowl, grey-buff		1:5	Hazor	(pit 7015)	H. I, pl. CXLIII:17
22.	Bowl, grey-buff		1:5	Hazor	1 (pit 9024)	H. I, pl. CXXV:8
23.	Bowl, grey-buff		1:5	Hazor	1 A	H. I, pl. LXXXVII:7
24.	Bowl, pinkish, red decoration		1:5	Hazor	(pit 9017)	H. I, pl. CVIII:4
25.	Bowl, light yellowish, red decoration		1:5	Hazor	(pit 9017)	H. I, pl. CVI:28
26.	Bowl, buff, red decoration		1:5	Lachish	T. 571	La. IV, pl. 72:630

126

PLATE | 38

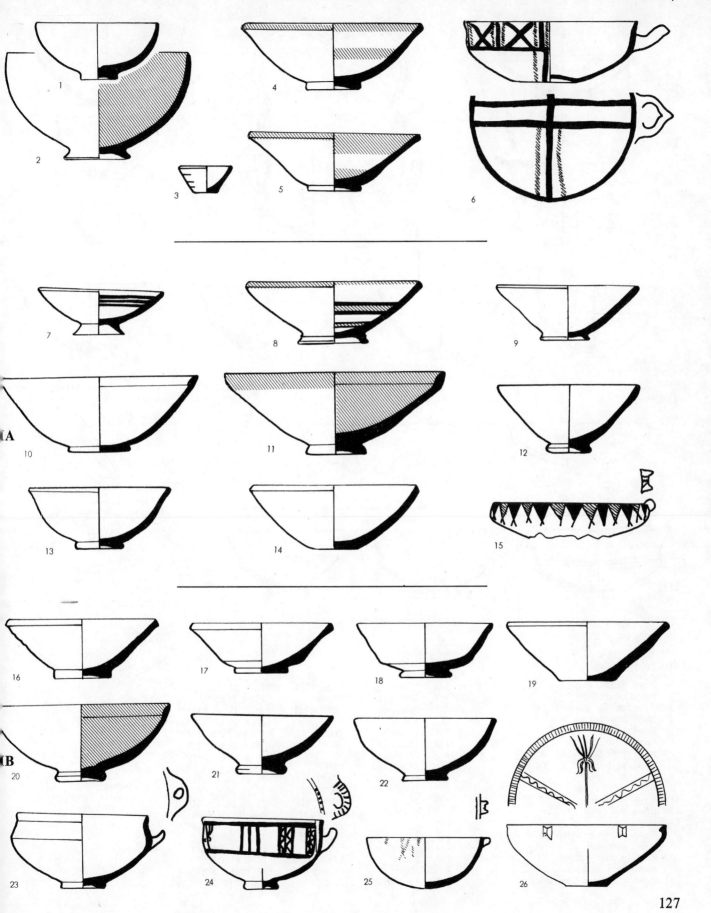

PLATE | **39**

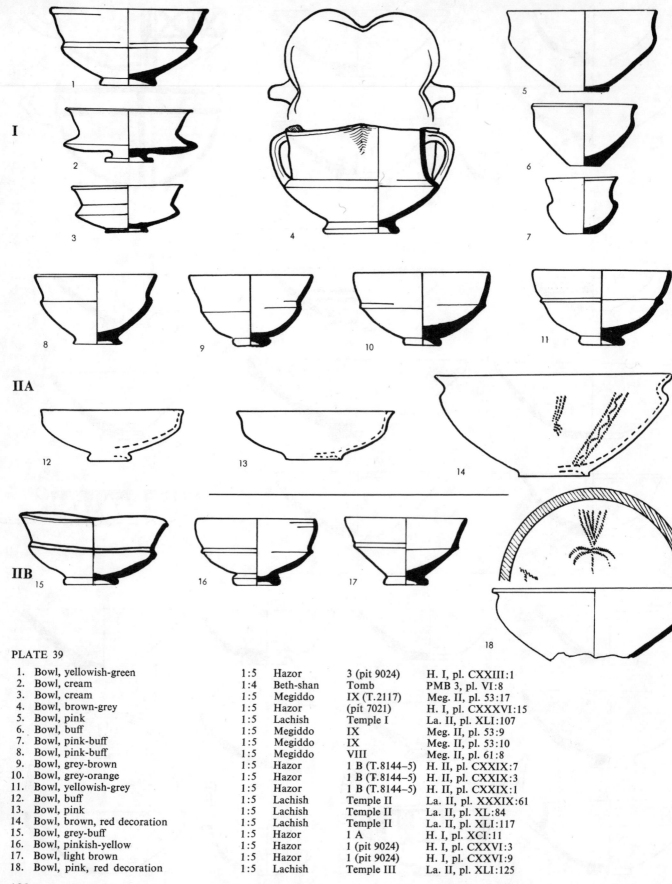

I

IIA

IIB

PLATE 39

1.	Bowl, yellowish-green	1:5	Hazor	3 (pit 9024)	H. I, pl. CXXIII:1
2.	Bowl, cream	1:4	Beth-shan	Tomb	PMB 3, pl. VI:8
3.	Bowl, cream	1:5	Megiddo	IX (T.2117)	Meg. II, pl. 53:17
4.	Bowl, brown-grey	1:5	Hazor	(pit 7021)	H. I, pl. CXXXVI:15
5.	Bowl, pink	1:5	Lachish	Temple I	La. II, pl. XLI:107
6.	Bowl, buff	1:5	Megiddo	IX	Meg. II, pl. 53:9
7.	Bowl, pink-buff	1:5	Megiddo	IX	Meg. II, pl. 53:10
8.	Bowl, pink-buff	1:5	Megiddo	VIII	Meg. II, pl. 61:8
9.	Bowl, grey-brown	1:5	Hazor	1 B (T.8144–5)	H. II, pl. CXXIX:7
10.	Bowl, grey-orange	1:5	Hazor	1 B (T.8144–5)	H. II, pl. CXXIX:3
11.	Bowl, yellowish-grey	1:5	Hazor	1 B (T.8144–5)	H. II, pl. CXXIX:1
12.	Bowl, buff	1:5	Lachish	Temple II	La. II, pl. XXXIX:61
13.	Bowl, pink	1:5	Lachish	Temple II	La. II, pl. XL:84
14.	Bowl, brown, red decoration	1:5	Lachish	Temple II	La. II, pl. XLI:117
15.	Bowl, grey-buff	1:5	Hazor	1 A	H. I, pl. XCI:11
16.	Bowl, pinkish-yellow	1:5	Hazor	1 (pit 9024)	H. I, pl. CXXVI:3
17.	Bowl, light brown	1:5	Hazor	1 (pit 9024)	H. I, pl. CXXVI:9
18.	Bowl, pink, red decoration	1:5	Lachish	Temple III	La. II, pl. XLI:125

Photo 129. Bowl, Lachish, IDA 37.780.

Photo 128. Bowl, Megiddo, IDA I.3465.

Photo 127. Bowl, Megiddo, *Meg*. II, Pl. 134, The Oriental Institute, Chicago, No. A 208/3.

LB I: In shape as well as in the color of the clay and its treatment, the bowls are still much the same as those of the preceding period (Nos. 1–3 and Photo 127). Were it not for their stratigraphic provenience, it would often be difficult to distinguish LB I carinated bowls from their MB II C predecessors. The bases in this period are still mostly ring-bases, but the concave disc-base already makes its appearance. No. 4 is unusual and deserves special mention. We encountered its immediate predecessor in the MB II B–C (Plate 27::12). Interestingly enough, both known occurrences are from Hazor. The LB specimen differs from its forerunner by the addition of two handles placed in the narrow junction of the cusps. Both the MB and the LB specimens are variations of a regular carinated bowl. The Hittite influence can be recognized in both. No. 5 shows a simplified version of the carination, current in all phases of the Late Bronze. Nos. 6 and 7 resemble No. 5 and represent a common form of small heavily built bowl. Such bowls are far removed from the MB II B–C sharply carinated bowls, and have clumsy, flat, often string-cut bases.

LB II A: Three main groups can be distinguished: Nos. 8–11 represent the degeneration of a feature in four different ways: only a slight fold (Nos. 8 and 9) or a bend (No. 10), or something like a ridge (No. 11), are left of the carination. With the exception of No. 8, which has a ring-base, all these degenerated forms have concave disc-bases, more in accord with the general decline of the carination. We have already noted this point in the discussion of the rounded bowls. In Nos. 12 and 13 the carination has survived only in the lower part of the vessel. As far as form is concerned, these bowls continue the tradition of the white-slipped bowls of the Chocolate-on-White Style (see below, Plate 49:1–4). No. 14 is a large bowl, deeply carinated immediately below the everted rim, and having a ring-base. The palm-tree motif painted on the inside is very similar to that inside the rounded bowl shown and discussed in Plate 38:26. This type of bowl continues to be made well into LB II B (No. 18 here) and Iron I (see below, Plate 61:5). This type of Late Bronze bowl has been found up to the present only in excavations in the south of the country. In the Iron I, at least as far as form is concerned, the type also appears to have spread to the north of the country (Plate 60:1–5).

LB II B: The degenerate form noted in LB II A continues to be found, with many variations of the vestigial carination (Nos. 15–17). No. 15 illustrates the general deterioration, in workmanship as well as form. Bowls like No. 14 also occur frequently in LB II B (No. 18). Here the palm-tree serves both as a fill-ornament and as a triglyph. Photos 128 and 129 show degenerate variants of the carinated bowl.

Goblets and Chalices (Plate 40).

For a definition of these forms, see above (p. 95). A glance at Plate 40 shows that in the main the goblets are decorated while the chalices are plain. In both forms it is very difficult to differentiate between the three phases of the Late Bronze. Nos. 1 and 4 are strikingly decorated with horizontal bands from rim to base. No. 2 is a goblet with red and black decoration related to the Bichrome Style (Plate 48). Especially characteristic is the zig-zag band on the upper part of the vessel (cf. Plate 48:7). Nos. 4 and 11 are descendants of the carinated bowl of the MB and LB described above, or should rather be designated as variations on the same

PLATE 40

1. Goblet, pink, red decoration   1:5   Lachish   Temple I   La. II, pl. XLVI:223
2. Goblet, buff, burnished, red and
   black decoration   1:5   Megiddo   IX   Meg. II, pl. 55:13
3. Chalice, pink-buff, burnished below outside   1:5   Megiddo   IX   Meg. II, pl. 54:17
4. Goblet, pink-buff, red decoration   1:5   Megiddo   VIII   Meg. II, pl. 62:8
5. Goblet, brown, burnished, red and white
   decoration   1:5   Lachish   Temple II   La. II, pl. XLVII:230
6. Chalice, grey   1:5   Hazor   1 B (T.8144–5)   H. II, pl. CXXIX:18
7. Chalice, grey-brown, red slip   1:5   Hazor   1 B (T.8144–5)   H. II, pl. CXXIX:17
8. Chalice, brown, red decoration   1:5   Lachish   Temple II   La. II, pl. XLVI:212
9. Goblet, pink-buff   1:5   Lachish   Temple III   La. II, pl. XLVII:236
10. Goblet, pink, red decoration   1:5   Lachish   Temple III   La. II, pl. XLVII:239
11. Goblet, grey, light red burnished slip,
    brown decoration   1:5   Hazor   1 B   H. I, pl. XC:13
12. Chalice, grey, brown-black decoration   1:5   Hazor   1 B   H. II, pl. CXVIII:23
13. Chalice, dark grey, light red burnished slip 1:5   Hazor   1 B   H. I, pl. XC:14
14. Chalice, brown-ocher   1:5   Hazor   1 A   H. II, pl. XCVIII:21
15. Chalice, brown-ocher   1:5   Megiddo   T. 911 A 1   Meg. T., pl. 30:4

130

PLATE | 40

I

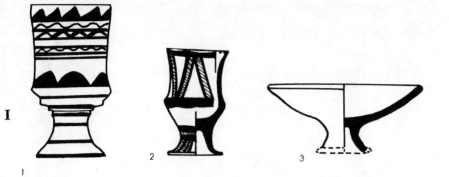

1

2

3

IIA

4

5

6

7

8

IIB

9

10

11

12

13

14

15

PLATE | **41**

I

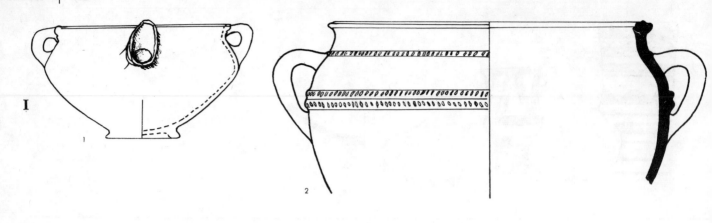

IIA

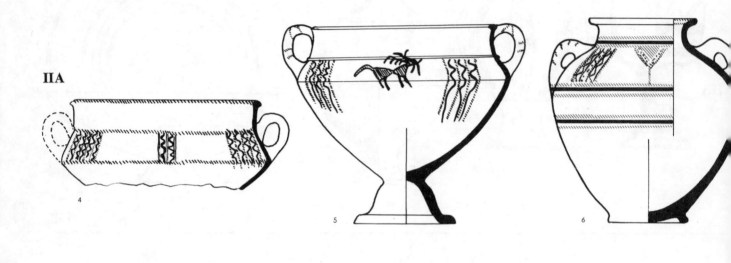

IIB

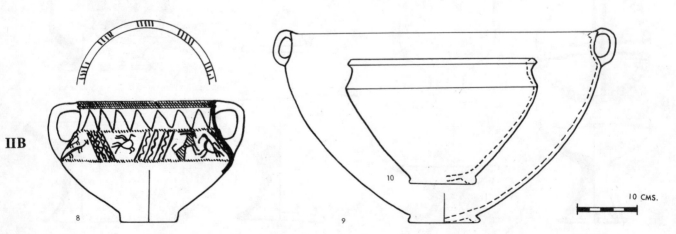

10 CMS.

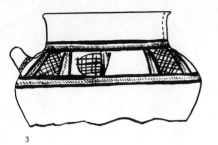

3

PLATE 41

1.	Krater, buff	1:5	Lachish	Temple I	La. II, pl. XLIII:150
2.	Krater, buff	1:5	Megiddo	IX	Meg. II, pl. 52:5
3.	Krater, buff, burnished, black, and red decoration	1:5	Lachish	Temple I	La. II, pl. XLIX:253
4.	Krater, brown, pink slip, black and red decoration	1:5	Lachish	Temple II	La. II, pl. XLVIII:243
5.	Krater, pink, buff slip, black and red decoration	1:5	Lachish	Temple II	La. II, pl. XLVIII:246
6.	Krater, orange-buff, burnished outside, red and black decoration	1:5	Megiddo	VIII (T.3006)	Meg. II, pl. 60:5
7.	Krater, pink, burnished, red decoration	1:5	Lachish	Temple II	La. II, pl. XLVIII:245
8.	Krater, pink, burnished, red decoration	1:5	Lachish	Temple II	La. II, pl. XLVIII:251
9.	Krater, pink	1:5	Lachish	Temple III	La. II, pl. XLIII:162
10.	Krater, pink	1:5	Lachish	Temple III	La. II, pl. XLII:149
11.	Krater, pink-buff, red decoration	1:5	Megiddo	VII B	Meg. II, pl. 66:4

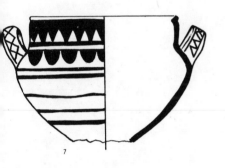

7

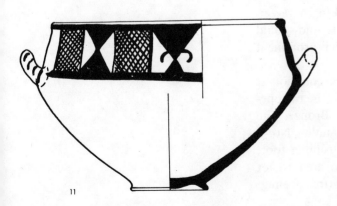

11

133

Photo 130. Chalice, Lachish, *Lachish*, II, Pl. L:267.

subject. Nos. 7, 11, and 13 are typical for their rosy-red slip and the good burnishing. No. 11 has a brown decoration of the metope-style painted on a slip. These three belong to the only group of burnished vessels in the Late Bronze, mainly in LB II A and LB II B. To this group belongs also the jug in Plate 46:17. No. 5 is spherical in shape. The entire body is divided into elongated metopes by triglyphs made up of straight and wavy lines, somewhat reminiscent of a melon. No. 10 consists of two parts, as it were, both ornamented in the metope style. In the lower part the metopes are blank, while in the upper part one of the metopes encloses a running ibex. Photo 130 shows a chalice of a different shape with four handles, decorated with painted metopes. No. 12 shows on the inside the painted cross-pattern known in bowls of the period. No. 15 is characterized by the sharply cut rim (the profile of the rim is triangular in section) which is common at the end of the Late Bronze.

Kraters (Plate 41).

The kraters in all three phases of the Late Bronze can be divided into two main groups: vessels with perpendicular loop-handles, and vessels with horizontal loop-handles. The horizontally placed handles seem to be a feature loaned from the Aegean pottery. In addition to these two groups, the plate includes some vessels which are not strictly speaking kraters, like Nos. 2 and 6.

LB I: Nos. 1 and 2 are more Middle Bronze than Late Bronze in character, both in shape and in decoration. The applied rope decoration on No. 2 is very characteristic for the MB, but is still fairly common on vessels of various shapes in LB I. The profile of No. 1 is still MB in character. No. 3 is related in shape and decoration to the Bichrome Style, and should perhaps be considered as a crude imitation of this style, which is prominent in this very period.

LB II A: There is no doubt that the painted kraters are commonest among the kraters of this period. And, within this group, it is the metope-style which is most in vogue. No. 6 is traditionally Middle Bronze. The handles of No. 4 are placed in the manner of horizontal handles. No. 5 is something like a hybrid krater-chalice. It has a high trumpet foot, but in every other respect it is a krater. The ornamented area is not delimited at the bottom, which lends the whole design a free feeling,

134

leaving the triglyphs and the horned animal as if hanging in the air. No. 6 has affinities in form[4] to the Chocolate-on-White and the Bichrome Wares (Plates 48 and 49). No. 7 is a krater with two horizontal handles, less common than those with a single such handle. It is painted with an uncommon pattern of red triangles and half circles, recalling the decoration of the goblet shown on Plate 40:1. Another point of resemblance is the fact that the pattern covers the whole surface of the vessel — in the case of the krater, even the handles.

LB II B: The forms described above occur in the LB II B almost without distinctive changes. In No. 8 we see two zones of decoration, one on the neck and the other on the shoulder, a division similar in outlook to that on No. 4 of the previous phase. However, in No. 8 both zones are decorated, even lavishly. This trait may perhaps be considered a guide for distinguishing between the phases: that in LB II the decoration becomes too elaborate, a trait typical for a style in decadence. The unusual diagonal triglyphs also point to 'over-doing.' Nos. 9 and 10 are two plain kraters, of which No. 9 deserves comment: its general shape, its rim, and the absence of handles give it the appearance of a cooking-pot. No. 11 seems to be a local shape with a type of handle which is not local in origin. The decoration is again a variation on the palm motif. The ibexes have been dropped, and the palm appears to stand for the complete motif. The style of the palm (two triangles and two curls) is also of decadent character, with imaginative stylization replacing naturalistic representation.

Cooking-Pots (Plate 42).

The ware of the cooking-pots is very distinctive, and even small fragments, without rim or curvature, can be easily identified. The color of the ware, or the fired clay, is brownish-red or near black. Large quantities of relatively large white calcite grits are conspicuous. Very often the pots or their fragments are found blackened by the soot of the cooking-fire, the blackening penetrating through the thickness of the wall. The rim is the best guide for distinguishing between cooking-pots of the various phases of the Late Bronze, since the form of the rounded body does not vary much and is essentially the same as in MB II B–C.

LB I: There are mainly two types of rim in this period, the everted and rounded rim, and the everted triangular rim. The first remains in the tradition of the preceding period, while the second is a new development, which will continue in the coming phases of the Late Bronze. Nos. 7 and 8 illustrate the first type. No. 8 has one handle, also in the tradition of the MB. Nos. 1, 2, and 6 have the second type of rim, which in section looks like a squat triangle. No. 4 is an example of a group of large cooking-pots, which have a flattened base decorated, or rather strengthened, by a coil of clay attached to the base all around and also twice across. The coil is incised all over No. 4a. Nos. 3–5 are variants of a kind of cooking-pot with double rim, known only in LB I, which has neither forerunners in the preceding period nor any descendants in the following. This device may have been intended to receive a lid. No. 3 is the commonest form of this group. It has an inner ledge rim, sometimes pierced by holes.

4. R. Amiran and A. Eitan, *IEJ*, 14 (1964), pp. 221–222.

PLATE 42

1. Cooking-pot, coarse brown, incised
   strokes on base   1:5   Lachish   Temple I   La. II, pl. LV:358
2. Cooking-pot, dark grey   1:5   Beth-shemesh   IV a   AS IV, pl. LV:14
3. Cooking-pot, coarse brown   1:5   Lachish   Temple I   La. II, pl. LV:360
4. Cooking-pot, red-brown, white grits   1:5   Hazor   Temple II   H. III–IV, pl. CCLXV:18
5. Cooking-pot, red-brown, black and
   white grits   1:5   Hazor   Temple II   H. III–IV, pl. CCLXV:21
6. Cooking-pot, coarse brown   1:5   Lachish   Temple I   La. II, pl. LV:353
7. Cooking-pot, coarse brown   1:5   Lachish   Temple I   La. II, pl. LV:359
8. Cooking-pot, red-brown, white grits   1:5   Hazor   Temple II   H. III–IV, pl. CCLXV:1₃
9. Cooking-pot, coarse brown   1:5   Lachish   Temple II   La. II, pl. LVI:370
10. Cooking-pot, pink-buff, numerous grits   1:5   Megiddo   VIII   Meg. II, pl. 61:27
11. Cooking-pot, coarse brown   1:5   Lachish   Temple II   La. II, pl. LVI:369
12. Cooking-pot, pink   1:5   Lachish   Temple II   La. II, pl. LVI:373
13. Cooking-pot   1:5   Beth Mirsim   C   TBM I, pl. 47:11
14. Cooking-pot, grey-brown, white grits   1:5   Hazor   1 (pit 9024)   H. I, pl. CXXVII:7
15. Cooking-pot, brown, burnished on base   1:5   Lachish   T. 532   La. IV, pl. 78:801
16. Cooking-pot, pink   1:5   Lachish   Temple III   La. II, pl. LVI:371
17. Cooking-pot, red-brown, white grits   1:5   (pit 9017)   H. I, pl. CVII:7

136

PLATE | 42

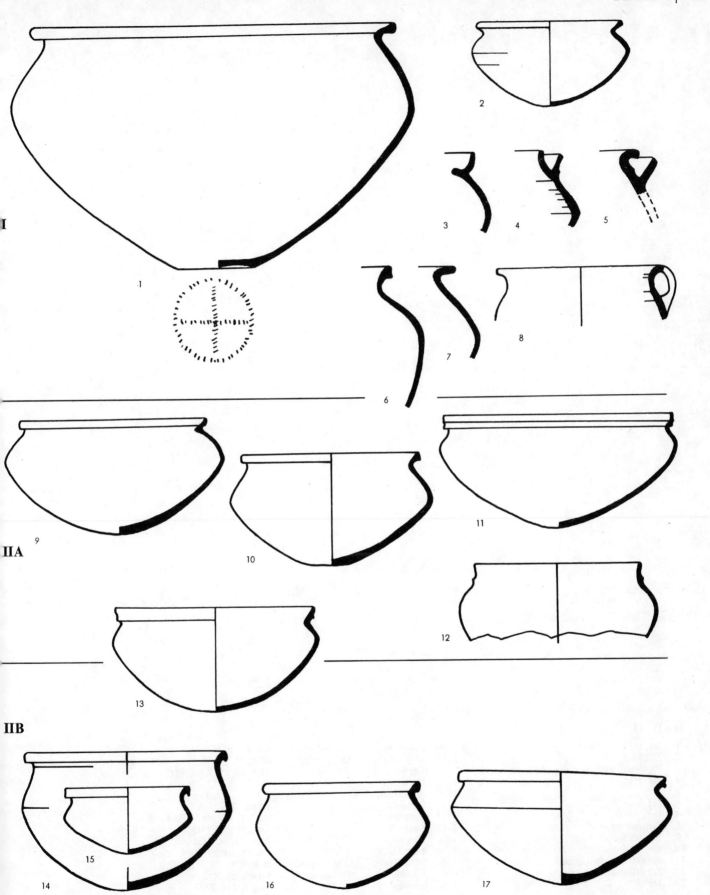

PLATE 43

1.	Jar, pink	1:10	Lachish	T. 1005	La. IV, pl. 87:1015
2.	Jar, buff	1:10	Megiddo	IX (T.3028)	Meg. II, pl. 52:1
3.	Egyptian wall painting, Amenhotep III		Thebes	T. 162	JEA 33, 1947, pl. VIII
4.	Jar, pink	1:10	Lachish	T. 216	La. IV, pl. 87:1018
5.	Jar	1:10	Abu Hawam	V	TAH, p. 13, Fig. 16
6.	Jar	1:10	Athens	Tomb	Grace, Fig. 5:3
7.	Jar	1:12	Amarna		CoA I, LII:XLIII/260
8.	Jar, brown	1:10	Lachish	T. 532	La. IV, pl. 87:1020
9.	Jar, pink-buff	1:10	Megiddo	VII B	Meg. II, pl. 64:1
10.	Jar, buff	1:10	Lachish	T. 501	La. IV, pl. 87:1019
11.	Jar (after a photograph)		Mycenae	Citadel House	ABSA, L, 1955, pl. 20 b
12.	Jar (after a photograph)		Menidi	Tholos tomb	Grace, pl. X:2
13.	Jar	1:10	Thebes	T. 356	Nagel, Fig. 2:33

138

PLATE | 43

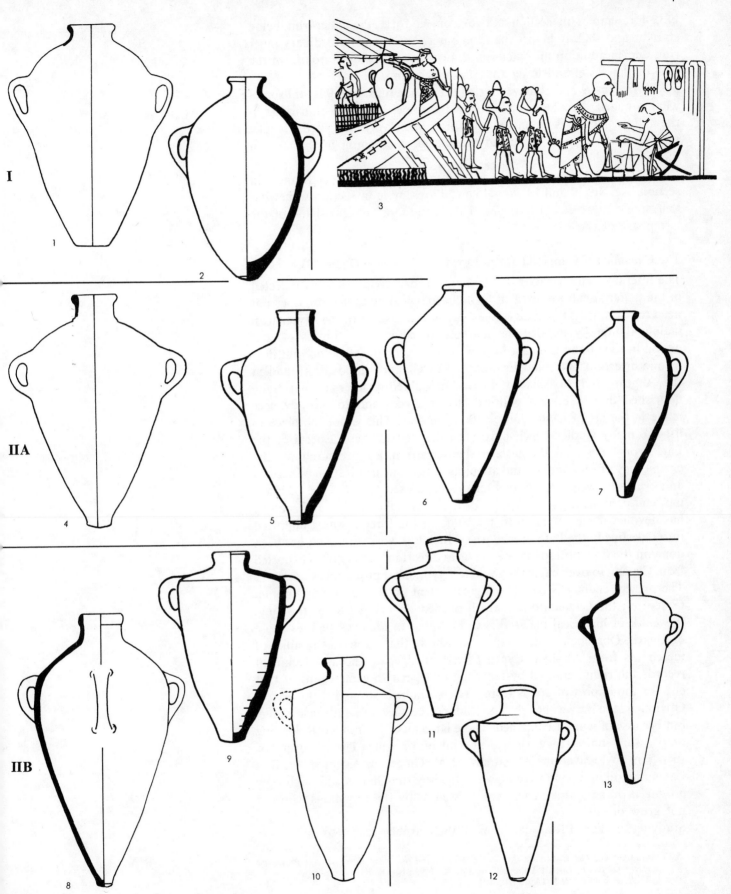

I

1

2

3

IIA

4

5

6

7

IIB

8

9

10

11

12

13

No. 4 resembles in section a two-pronged fork, the inner rim being straight and slightly higher than the outer. No. 5 has an ordinary inner rim, and in addition an outer rim drawn diagonally outwards from the wall of the vessel and lower than the inner rim.

LB II A: Nos. 9 and 10 have everted triangular rims. No. 9 is still somewhat rounded. No. 11 is a variant of the same and has a thin ridge in the middle. No. 12 is an uncommon form, like a very elongated triangle. No. 13 is the type of elongated triangle most common in this and in the coming phase.

LB II B: The rims of Nos. 14 and 16 are still like a squat triangle in section like Nos. 6 and 10. Nos. 15 and 17 resemble in section somewhat longer and more edged triangles. This is the most typical shape of the last phase of the LB.

The Canaanite Commercial Jar in Egypt and Mycenae (Plate 43).

The international character of the Late Bronze civilization, as reflected in the material culture revealed by archaeological investigation, does not need reassessment. Products of the Aegean Islands and of the Mycenaean mainland literally flooded the markets, dwellings, and tombs of that period in Egypt and Canaan. Moreover, commercial traffic does not flow in one direction only, and Egyptian and Canaanite goods are found in the Aegean and Mycenaean areas. Undoubtedly, international trade flourished due to certain political circumstances and to the advances made in the art of navigation on the open seas. This is not the place to list the many studies which have been devoted to these aspects of the Late Bronze Period in the Eastern Mediterranean. Both research into the chronology of each region, and attempts at the synchronization of periods and events between the various regions have used the evidence of international commerce as their point of departure. Palestinian archaeology has devoted much attention to the study of the foreign wares imported into Palestine in the Late Bronze Age. Much less work, however, has been done on the flow of trade in the opposite direction — the goods exported from Canaan to oversea markets and to Egypt, most probably by sea.

The present chapter is based to a great extent on the studies of Virginia Grace[5] on the Canaanite jar, which opened up new vistas of thinking. A wealth of historical material is to be found in archives such as those of Ugarit. One document, for instance, shows that numerous families of merchants from Alashya (Cyprus) lived in Ugarit. Another document records the rights granted by the King of Ugarit to a merchant of that city for the import of goods from Crete without customs fees.[6]

Obviously, the jar was bought and sold, not because of its intrinsic value, but because of what it contained. These large jars were not worth loading onto a ship, unless they were filled with oil or wine. The discovery of such jars in excavations at Athens or at Thebes in Egypt shows that Canaanite oil and wine were highly valued by the Greeks, although they produced oil and wine themselves, as well as by the Egyptians who did not grow olives.

Studying the Late Bronze jar from all these aspects led us to investigate

---

5. Virginia Grace, *The Canaanite Jar in the Aegean and the Near East, Studies Presented To Hetty Goldman*, Locust Valley, 1956, pp. 80–109, pls. IX–XII.
6. Cl. F. A. Schaeffer, *ILN* (April 10, 1954), p. 574.

the form of the jar in relation to its function, an investigation which resulted in the classification of the Late Bronze jars into two main classes (Plates 43 and 44): a) Jars made purposely for trading, called the 'Canaanite jars;' b) jars for everyday household use, designated here as 'decorated jars.' The first class is never decorated (why is commerce of more utilitarian character than household usage?), has thick walls, and a most appropriate shape for transportation. Plate 43 illustrates the development of this commercial jar throughout the period, as well as such jars found outside Canaan.

The two columns on the left side of Plate 43, which show jars from *Palestine*, manifest clearly the trend of development of the jar through the three phases of the Late Bronze: from delicately oval, the body becomes vigorously shouldered; the narrow rounded base turns into a thickened, heavy, button-like base; the placement of the handles rises from the middle of the body to the pronounced shoulder, and the rim becomes plain. There is every reason to think that this trend is dictated by the function of the jar, in accordance with the expanding commerce towards the 14th century B.C.

Egypt: Canaanite exports to Egypt started with the extension of Egyptian rule over Canaan in the time of Thothmes III. In the wake of the heavily laden caravans bringing Canaan's tribute to Pharaoh's court, trade began to develop between the two countries. We have reproduced in Plate 43:3 a tracing of a wall painting from Tomb No. 62 at Thebes,[7] which dates from the reign of Amenhotep III. It illustrates the import of characteristic Canaanite goods into Egypt and affords a glimpse of daily life in Egypt in the golden days of the *pax aegyptiaca*. The drawing shows the ship in which the Canaanite merchants brought their goods to Egypt; it is of Egyptian type, in striking evidence of the prevailing *koiné*, while the merchants are dressed in typical Canaanite attire. They carry Canaanite jars with lids, and one of them carries a vessel we designate today as 'pilgrim flask' (Plate 51 below). On shore, lively trading is going on between the crew and the local inhabitants. In his small shop, an Egyptian wearing the characteristic loincloth is visible. Canaanite jars have been found in considerable numbers in Egyptian tombs; we shall mention here only one example, from the tomb of Queen Meryet-Amun, the wife of Amenhotep II.[8] No. 7 was found near Tell el-Amarna, the city of Akhenaton, and is a fine example of the features described above. No. 13 was found in Tomb No. 356 at Deir el-Medineh (one of the large Theban cemeteries in Upper Egypt), dating from the reign of Ramses II (13th century B.C.). This jar may have been made in Egypt according to Canaanite models. If this proves true (only petrographical analysis can furnish this proof), we may perhaps speculate that this shape of jar proved so suitable for commerce, that it was imitated locally. Photo 131 shows a sealed jar with a hieratic inscription testifying to the measure of oil it contained. On the stopper is a seal impression of Queen Hatshepsut. The jar must have been brought from Canaan.

Photo 131. Canaanite jar, Thebes (Egypt), Metropolitan Museum, N.Y. No. 36.3.83.

---

7. N. de Garis Davies and R. O. Faulkner, "A Syrian Trading Venture to Egypt," *JEA*, 33 (1947), pp. 40–46, pl. VIII.
8. H. E. Winlock, *The Tomb of Queen Meryet-Amun at Thebes*, New York, 1932, p. 31, fig. 17:e.

Mycenaean Greece: Commercial relations between Mycenaean Greece and Canaan began in an early phase of the Mycenaean civilization. The jar shown on Plate 43:6 was found in a tomb on the north slope of the Areopagos in Athens, together with Mycenaean pottery of Myc. III A.[9] The jar itself is clearly a Canaanite jar of LB II A. Many other specimens have been found in various places in Mycenaean Greece, even in Mycenae itself. The two jars shown on Plate 43:11 and 12 are of the 13th century and bear the hallmark of the later phase in the evolution of the Canaanite jar: strongly emphasized, almost horizontal shoulders, handles springing from the shoulder, a thickened strong base, and a thickened simple rim.
Photo 132 shows the reconstruction in the Agora Museum of the above-mentioned chamber-tomb on the Areopagos. The contents of the tomb serve to illustrate the international commerce flourishing in the Eastern Mediterranean in this period.

Photo 132. Reconstructed model of a tomb, Areopagos Athens, Agora Museum.

Decorated Jars (Plate 44).

A designation like 'domestic jar' in contrast to the 'Canaanite-Commercial jar' would perhaps be more appropriate. The two classes differ fundamentally from each other, indicating different functions and different purposes: The Canaanite jar has much thicker walls, a thick, somewhat button-like base, a slanting body, and pronounced shoulders. The decorated or domestic jar has thinner walls, a rounded base, and an ovoid body. Both classes can be traced back to MB II prototypes. We have already encountered decoration on shoulders of jars in MB II, but in the LB this feature is much commoner. Now, the handles are included in the decoration, often bearing simple painted bands crossing each other. The specimens assembled in the Plate demonstrate the similarity of form throughout the three phases of the LB. Nos. 1, 2, and 5 closely approximate MB shapes, especially the protruding loop-handles on the middle of the body. The shortened form of No. 1 and the bichrome decoration of No. 2 assign them, however, to the beginning of LB. Nos. 3 and 4 stand between the two classes just mentioned. In shape they belong to the Canaanite jar, but their decoration places them in the present class. Nos. 6 and 7 are decorated (No. 6 in the metope-style) and

---

9. T. L. Shear, *Hesperia*, IX (1940), pp. 274–291.

both have painted handles. The metope-style is fairly rare on jars. Nos. 8 and 9 are amphoriskoi, characteristic of the end phases of the Late Bronze, and of the first period of the Iron (cf. Plate 83). The decoration of No. 8 is in the metope-style. No. 9 comes from Tomb 571 at Lachish,[10] which is dated by its contents to the end of the LB. A glass-bottle (Photo 261) found in Temple III at Lachish[11] seems to imitate the shape of a pottery amphoriskos. The long slender neck of the glass amphoriskos may have been the result of the technical process used in making glass vessels, that is, the thread-winding process. Interestingly enough, the glass-amphoriskos was in its turn imitated in pottery, including the long slender neck, which is not a form native to the potter's craft.

The Pithos (Plate 45).

The pithos (Photo 133) is a very large container, reaching 1.20 m. or more in height, whose shape clearly indicates that it was used for domestic storage. It probably had its place in one of the rooms of the house or in a corner of the courtyard, and served to store liquids or dry substances. The pithos is characterized by several features, in addition to size: a body gradually tapering to a small flattened base, intended perhaps to be sunk into the floor; a thickened rim, often profiled; two ridges, one at the junction of the body and the shoulder, and the other at the base of the neck, serving perhaps to strengthen these very junctions. The method of making these pithoi, which is still used in village-potteries in Crete,[12] may be designated as a coil-and-wheel method. The ridges, mainly the lower one, are sometimes decorated with incisions to imitate a rope. Other traces of the manufacturing process are visible on the surface of the pithoi from the lower ridge downwards, where the string which the potter used to bind the vessel during drying left its imprint in the wet clay.

It is interesting that such pithoi are known until now almost exclusively from Hazor, where they turn up in quantities in strata of the Late Bronze,[13] but appear already in MB II C.[14] A pithos bearing some resemblance to those from Hazor was found in Stratum VIII–VII at Beth Shan.[15] The vessel thus seems to belong to the northern Canaanite ceramic culture. It is noteworthy that a very similar pithos was found in the excavations of Tell es-Salihiya near Damascus.[16]

Looking ahead, we can trace back to this Late Bronze form the development of the Iron I pithoi, as shown on Plate 77. No 1 on that Plate appears to be a transitional form between the Canaanite and the Israelite pithos of the Iron I period. It shows many features of the Late Bronze type, such as the tapering body, the small base, the wide neck, the lower ridge, as well as the ridge at the base of the neck. At the same time some changes are already evident: the shoulder is concave instead of rounded, and the vessel has two handles, a feature unknown in the Canaanite pithoi.

Photo 133. Pithos, Hazor, *Hazor* II, Pl. CLXXVIII.

10. *Lachish*, IV, pp. 60–61, fig. 6.
11. *Lachish*, II, pl. XXIV:77
12. R. Hampe and A. Winter, *Bei Toepfer und Toepferinaan in Kreta Messenien und Zypern*, Mainz, 1962.
13. *Hazor*, I, p. 131.
14. *Hazor*, II, p. 85.
15. *Beth Shan*, II:II, pl. XLII:9.
16. H. H. von der Osten, *Die Grabung von Tell es-Salihiyah*, Lund, 1956, pl. 35.

PLATE | 44

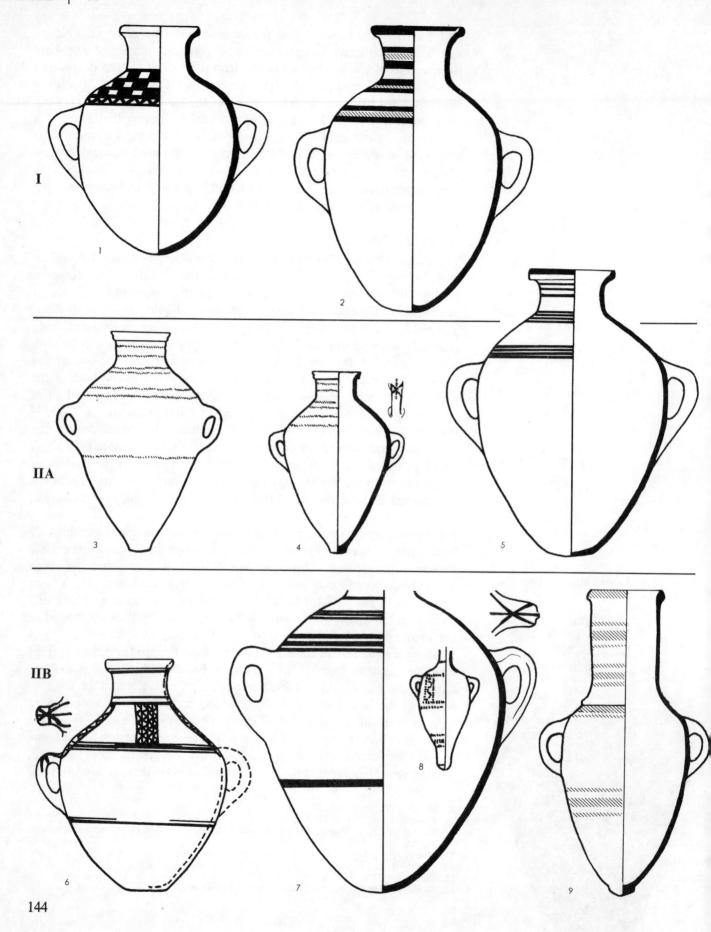

PLATE | 45

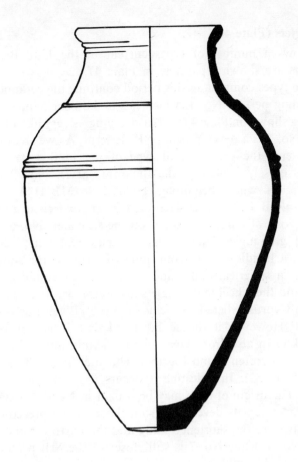

PLATE 44

1.	Jar, brown-ocher, red decoration	1:5	Megiddo	T.1100 C	Meg. T., pl. 48:7
2.	Jar, white-yellow, burnished, brown and light red decoration	1:5	Megiddo	T.1145 B	Meg. T., pl. 51:7
3.	Jar, buff, red and white decoration	1:10	Lachish	Temple II	La. II, pl. LVII:393
4.	Jar, brown, red decoration	1:10	Lachish	T. 216	La. IV, pl. 87:1022
5.	Jar, cream-buff, red decoration	1:15	Megiddo	VIII (T.3005)	Meg. II, pl. 60:2
6.	Jar, grey-buff, light brown decoration	1:5	Hazor	2 (pit 9027)	H. I, pl. CXXXI:4
7.	Jar, brown-pink, dark brown decoration	1 5	Hazor	1 (pit 9024)	H. I, pl. CXXIX:1
8.	Amphoriskos, coarse pink, cream vertically burnished slip, red decoration	1:5	Lachish	T. 4004	La. IV, pl. 85:977
9.	Amphoriskos, brown, horizontally burnished, red decoration	1:5	Lachish	T. 571	La. IV, pl. 85:984

PLATE 45

1.	Pithos, grey	1:10	Hazor	1 B	H. II, pl. CXXIX:2

Jugs and Juglets (Plate 46).

Plate 46 shows a number of types current in the Late Bronze. The biconical jugs are shown separately in Plate 47.

LB I: All the types common in this period continue the ceramic tradition of the preceding period. No. 1, which has a shoulder-handle, resembles closely the jug shown on Plate 43:6; No. 4, a mug, is very like Plate 34:2.3; the form of No. 5 is a development of Plate 34:4. As we shall see below, No. 5 represents the predominant type of jug in this period and in decoration is closely related to the Bichrome Style. Nos. 2 and 3 are cylindrical juglets, whose beginnings go back to MB II A, and whose vogue ends in LB I. No. 3 is decorated in characteristic Late Bronze style, with a zone of painted metopes on the shoulder. No. 6 belongs to a class called 'grey juglets,' and deserves special treatment: it has a long, narrow neck, a handle drawn from under the rim to the shoulder in a perfect curve, a spherical body, and a flattened or rounded base. The clay is grey and the wheel-made juglets are well burnished. This juglet is also found in Cyprus, where it is included in the "Black Lustrous Wheelmade Ware." However, it should be noted that it is not of Cypriot origin; it is known also from Ugarit and Alalakh, and as well as from Egypt, where it is often found together with the 'Syrian flask' in tombs (see below, Plate 52). In Palestine it occurs more frequently than the Syrian flask. The origin of both may be sought in North Canaan. Nos. 7 and 8 are dipper juglets developed from those of the preceding period. Typical of LB I are the shortened body and the narrower and straighter neck, as in No. 8, while No. 7 is still closer to the MB prototype, with its long body and swollen neck.

LB II A: No. 9 is a jug with a shoulder handle, which continues to be popular. Nos. 10–12 are a development of No. 5, and represent the predominant type of jug decorated with zones of painted metopes. In No. 9 the metopes enclose painted elongated triangles. The metopes of No. 11 are left empty. The decoration of No. 12 resembles the Bichrome Style. The form of No. 13 is a development of the 'grey juglet'; the ware of this specimen is pink and it is painted with dark brown decoration. The dipper-juglet is represented by three specimens. No. 14 has a rounded base and is elliptical in shape. This type continues to be popular in LB II B, especially in the south of the country, and later in the Iron period. No. 15 imitates the Cypriot knife-pared juglet (see below, Plate 55:12), which itself is a Cypriot imitation of the Canaanite dipper juglet. This specimen illustrates the general trend of development of the dipper-juglet: the shoulder tends to disappear and the neck becomes shorter and wider. No. 16 combines features of both types shown in Nos. 14 and 15.

LB II B: Jugs with shoulder handles disappear completely in this phase, and the predominant type of jug has a loop-handle springing from the rim to the shoulder. No. 17 belongs to the rosy-red burnished class discussed above in Plate 40.
Nos. 18 and 19 belong to the same type. The coarse, thick base is often string-cut. No. 20 has a debased form of metope decoration: straight and wavy lines fill the decorated zone, and the functions of the triglyph and metope are confused. No. 21 is a development of Nos. 6 and 13,

Photo 134. Mug, Megiddo, IDA I.3348.

Photo 135. Krater, bi-conical, Beth-shan, IDA I.3287.

and belongs to the 'grey juglet' type. Nos. 22 and 23 are dipper juglets. No. 22 is more characteristic of southern Palestine and tends to be cylindrical in form, while No. 23 resembles No. 16 of the preceding phase.

Biconical Jugs and Kraters (Plate 47).

Two distinct groups of biconical vessels have been brought together on Plate 47, although there is some measure of doubt whether they should be associated: a) biconical jugs; b) biconical amphorae-kraters. Three features are common to both groups: the biconical body, the shoulder handle (either one or two), and the metope zone decorating all the vessels.

Biconical jugs: These are very common throughout the Late Bronze Age, but it is difficult to trace back either the form or the ornamentation. The typical form is symmetrical, that is, the upper part of the vessel is about equal in height to the lower part, as in Nos. 6, 7, and 10. The usual rim is everted and triangular.

Side by side with the most typical form appear a number of variants: a) a biconical jug in which the two parts of the vessel are not symmetrical (Nos. 1, 2, Photo 134); b) a vessel on a high, trumpet-like ring base (No. 1); c) a vessel with a basket handle and a trough-like spout with strainer (No. 11).

Biconical amphorae-kraters: This group includes jug-like types such as Nos. 5, 9, 14, and krater-like types, such as Nos. 3, 4, 12, 13 and Photo 135. No. 4 has two tilted horizontal handles, and may show some Mycenaean influence. All the vessels of this group have high, wide necks.

The decoration follows the metope style so popular in the Late Bronze Age, the lower part of the vessel always remaining undecorated. The triglyphs consist of alternating straight and wavy lines, or of criss-cross or checker board patterns. Sometimes the metopes are left blank, but often they enclose stylized trees (Nos. 2, 5, 10), elongated triangles (No. 6), or an inverted lotus blossom (No. 13). No. 7 shows metopes enclosing a motif called a sea anemone in Mycenaean archaeology.[17] Here the flower appears to be suspended from a stalk. For further examples illustrating this group see the photographs accompanying the discussion of Plate 50.

17. A. Furumark, *Mycenaean Pottery*, Stockholm, 1941, Motif 27.

PLATE | 46

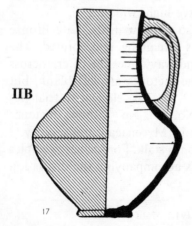

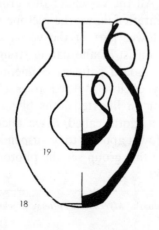

I

IIA

IIB

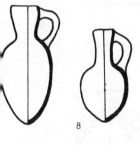

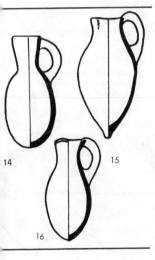

PLATE 46

1.	Jug, pink-buff	1:5	Megiddo	IX (T.3169)	Meg. II, pl. 48:2
2.	Juglet, warm sepia, vertically burnished	1:5	Megiddo	T.1100 B	Meg. T., pl. 47:11
3.	Juglet, buff, traces of burnish, black decoration	1:5	Megiddo	IX (T.3025)	Meg. II, pl. 50:6
4.	Jug, pink-buff	1:5	Megiddo	IX	Meg. II, pl. 50:24
5.	Jug, buff, red and black decoration	1:5	Megiddo	IX (T.3137)	Meg. II, pl. 49:11
6.	Juglet, black-lead, horizontally burnished	1:5	Megiddo	T. 75	Meg. T., pl. 41:24
7.	Juglet, green-buff, burnished	1:5	Megiddo	IX (T.3018 F)	Meg. II, pl. 50:19
8.	Juglet, buff	1:5	Megiddo	VIII (T.2104)	Meg. II, pl. 58:5
9.	Jug, orange-buff, vertically burnished, red decoration	1:5	Megiddo	VIII (T.3014)	Meg. II, pl. 57:2
10.	Jug, grey-brown	1:5	Hazor	I B (T.8144–5)	H. II, pl. CXXXIII:10
11.	Jug, pink-buff, red decoration	1:5	Megiddo	VIII (T.3015)	Meg. II, pl. 57:13
12.	Jug, cream-buff, burnished, red and black decoration	1:5	Megiddo	VIII	Meg. II, pl. 57:21
13.	Jug, pink-buff, brown decoration	1:5	Jerusalem	Tomb	Ey VI, p. 37, Fig. 3:40
14.	Juglet, pink-buff, vertically burnished	1:5	Megiddo	VIII (T.3018 B)	Meg. II, pl. 58:12
15.	Juglet, green-buff	1:5	Megiddo	VIII	Meg. II, pl. 58:10
16.	Juglet, pink-buff	1:5	Megiddo	VIII	Meg. II, pl. 58:6
17.	Jug, pink, light red burnished slip	1:5	Hazor	1 A	H. II, pl. CXXIV:18
18.	Jug, brown ocher	1:5	Megiddo	T. 989 C 1	Meg. T., pl. 19:23
19.	Jug, buff	1:5	Megiddo	VII B	Meg. II, pl. 63:2
20.	Jug, buff, red decoration	1:5	Megiddo	VII A	Meg. II, pl. 67:10
21.	Jug, orange-buff, red decoration	1:5	Megiddo	VII	Meg. II, pl. 71:6
22.	Juglet, brown	1:5	Lachish	Temple III	La. II, pl. LII:317
23.	Juglet, buff	1:5	Megiddo	VII	Meg. II, pl. 71:11

149

PLATE | **47**

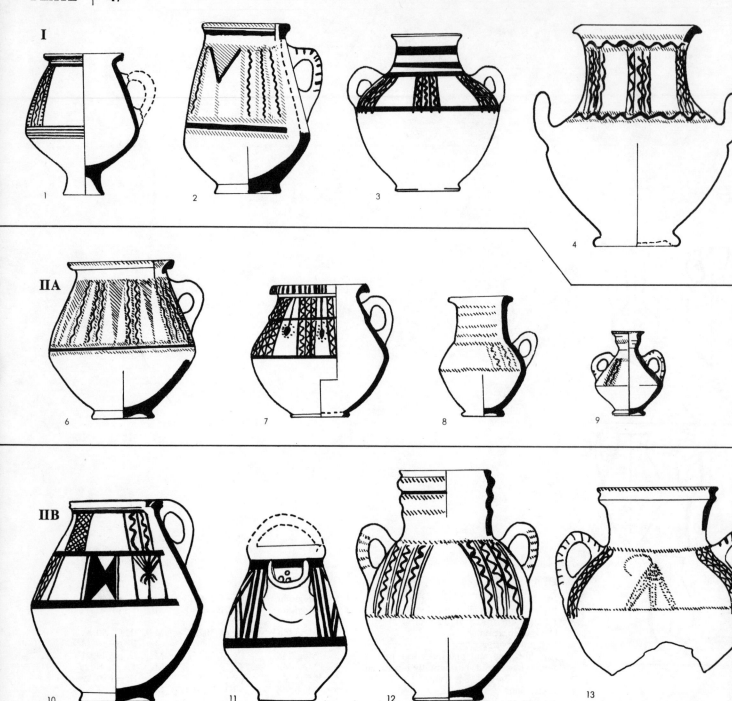

5

14

PLATE 47

1.	Jug, pink, brownish-red decoration	1:5	Far'ah (North)	Tomb	RB, 1951, p. 579, Fig. 9:15
2.	Jug, orange-buff, irregularly burnished, red and black decoration	1:5	Megiddo	IX (T.3018 C)	Meg. II, pl. 49:18
3.	Amphora, light brown, red and black decoration	1:5	Beth-shemesh	II a	AS III, Fig. 2:3
4.	Amphora, pink, red and black decoration	1:5	Lachish	Temple I	La. II, pl. XLIX:259
5.	Amphora, yellow, pink slip, brown decoration	1:5	Far'ah (North)	Tomb	RB, 1951, p. 579, Fig. 9:10
6.	Jug, pink-buff, red and black decoration	1:5	Megiddo	VIII (T.3006)	Meg. II, pl. 58:3
7.	Jug, grey-brown, brown decoration	1:5	Hazor	1 (Tunnels)	H. II, pl. CLII:5
8.	Jug, pink, cream slip, red decoration	1:5	Lachish	T.1003	La. IV, pl. 74:687
9.	Amphora, light brown, red and black decoration	1:5	Jerusalem	Tomb	Ey, VI, p. 37, Fig. 3:38
10.	Jug, pink-buff, red decoration	1:5	Megiddo	VII B	Meg. II, pl. 63:3
11.	Jug, pink-buff, red decoration	1:5	Megiddo	VII B	Meg. II, pl. 63:7
12.	Amphora, pink, red and black decoration	1:5	Lachish	T. 571	La. IV, pl. 85:992
13.	Amphora, pink, red and black decoration	1:5	Lachish	T. 571	La. IV, pl. 85:990
14.	Amphora, black, pink slip	1:5	Lachish	Temple III	La. II, pl. LIV:342

151

Photo 137. Krater, Nagila, IDA 66.921.

Photo 136. Krater, Lachish, IDA 39.814.

Photo 138. Krater, Megiddo, *Meg.* II, Pl. 134:3.

Photo 141. Jug, Megiddo, IDA 34.2173.

The Bichrome Ware (Plate 48).

The Bichrome Ware is one of the few subjects in Palestinian archaeology to which the analytical methods of art history have been applied. Using such methods, Heurtley,[18] in a careful stylistic analysis, reached the conclusion that many of the vessels painted in the Bichrome Style could be ascribed to a craftsman-painter working at Tell el-Ajjul, and called him the Ajjul painter. While it is difficult to accept the premise that one individual potter was responsible for all the vessels found which are painted in this style, it appears likely that they can be ascribed to a school of master potters and painters, working in one of the centers on the coast of Greater Canaan, somewhere between Ugarit in the north and Gaza in the south. The assumption that this school included both potters and painters — although these did not sign their work like their colleagues in classical Greece — is confirmed by the fixed repertoire of the Bichrome Style and by the uniformity of manufacturing technique and of decorative style. Both ware and surface finish are of high quality. The clay is well levigated and has a light color, from sandy yellow to pink. The vessels are wheel-made, and careful attention has been given to details. Usually the vessel was well burnished before the painter took it over and decorated it in his distinctive personal style, or rather, in the style of the school to which he belonged.

A glance at the repertoire of the Bichrome Style shows that most of the forms are peculiar to that style. It follows that we have not only a distinctive decoration and a superior technical execution of ordinary forms,

18. W. A. Heurtley, "A Palestinian Vase-Painter of the Sixteenth Century B.C., *QDAP*, VIII (1938), pp. 21–34, pls. VIII–XIX.

Photo 142. Jug. Ajjul, IDA 35.4036.

Photo 139. Krater, Ajjul, IDA 35.4109.

but a well-defined pottery class with a special range of forms. We shall endeavor to distinguish between the forms common to this and other classes of pottery and the forms peculiar to this class in the following discussion.

Forms common to the Bichrome Style and to other pottery classes: a) Jugs with a shoulder handle (Nos. 1, 3); b) jugs with handle drawn from rim to shoulder (Nos. 2, 4, 5, Photo 141); c) cylindrical juglets (No. 16); d) Vessels with a basket handle and a troughlike spout with strainer (No. 11); e) 'Jars' with two shoulder handles (Photo 139); f) Kraters with two shoulder handles (Nos. 8, 10, 14, Photos 135–137).

Forms peculiar to the Bichrome Style: a) Jugs with high, wide, cylindrical necks. Although these are variants of a jug already well known in MB II B, the form in which they appear here is found only in the Bichrome Style (Nos. 4 and 5, Photo 141); b) Spherical jugs, with a flattened base, a narrow concave neck (No. 7, Photo 144). This is a Cypriot type, in form as well as in decoration. In Cyprus, it is classified as White-Painted V–VI ware; c) Jugs (Nos. 6, 15, Photo 142) with bodies and necks like

Photo 140. Krater, fragement, Ajjul, IDA 35.4114.

No. 7, but with a base and a handle springing from the rim like the ordinary jug-forms — these are a variant of a); d) Bowls, all of which have one horizontal handle. Nos. 12 and 13 have ring bases. The bowl shown in Photo 145 has a rounded base. All three specimens imitate Cypriot bowls either partially or entirely; e) Kraters with a single horizontal handle (No. 9, Photo 138), mentioned above in Plate 41.

Decoration: Heurtley analyzed in detail all the motifs used in the Bichrome Style, and here we shall touch only briefly on some general characteristics: the decoration covers the upper part of the vessel only and emphasizes the shoulder zone. It consists of a frieze-like broad band, bordered below and above by bands composed of red lines between two black ones. The triglyphs which break the frieze into metopes vary in their compositional patterns: straight lines, hatched triangles, 'union jacks', checker-boards, sand-clock, etc. The motifs enclosed within the metopes are ibexes, birds, and fish.

Distribution: This class of painted pottery is found all over Canaan, and especially on the coast, from Alalakh[19] to Gaza. Two sherds of this style have been found at Tarsus.[20] We have already mentioned that vessels painted in the Bichrome Style are common in Cyprus and have been found in Egypt.

Date: Long ago Albright pointed out that the Bichrome Style begins to appear in the MB II C, that is, in Stratum X at Megiddo, but that it flourishes mainly in LB I, that is, Stratum IX at Megiddo. Albright's assumption is confirmed by Locus 3037 at Megiddo which contains, together with typical MB II C material, a krater fragment decorated in distinctive Bichrome Style (Photo 146).[21] Vessels of Bichrome Style still occur in LB II A, for instance, in the lower phase of Stratum V at Tell Abu Hawam (No. 14) and Stratum VIII at Megiddo (Nos. 15 and 16).

The Bichrome Style represents a high point in the Canaanite potters' art. At the same time, another superb decorative style was developed; this is the 'Chocolate-on-White' Ware, discussed below.

Photo 143. Jug, Ajjul, IDA 35.4110.

Photo 145. Bowl, Ajjul, IDA 35.4038.

Photo 146. Krater fragment, Megiddo, The Oriental Institute, Chicago, No. A28437.

---

19. L. Woolley, *Alalakh*, Oxford, 1955, pl. XCIV and passim.
20. Hetty Goldman, *Excavations at Gozlu Kule, Tarsus* II, 1956, p. 200, fig. 315.
21. This fragment has not been published. I am grateful to the Oriental Institute for the permission to publish it and for the photographs.

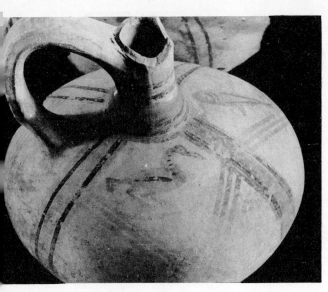

Photo 144. Jug, Archangellos (Cyprus),
A 38.2155.

PLATE | 48

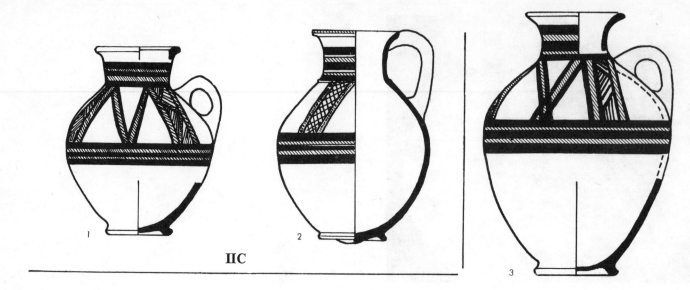

ΙΙC

I

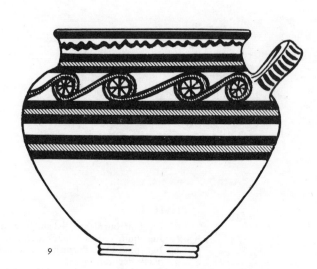

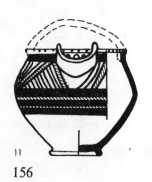

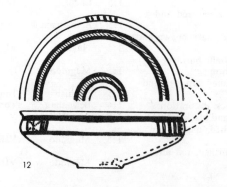

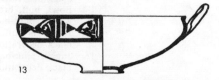

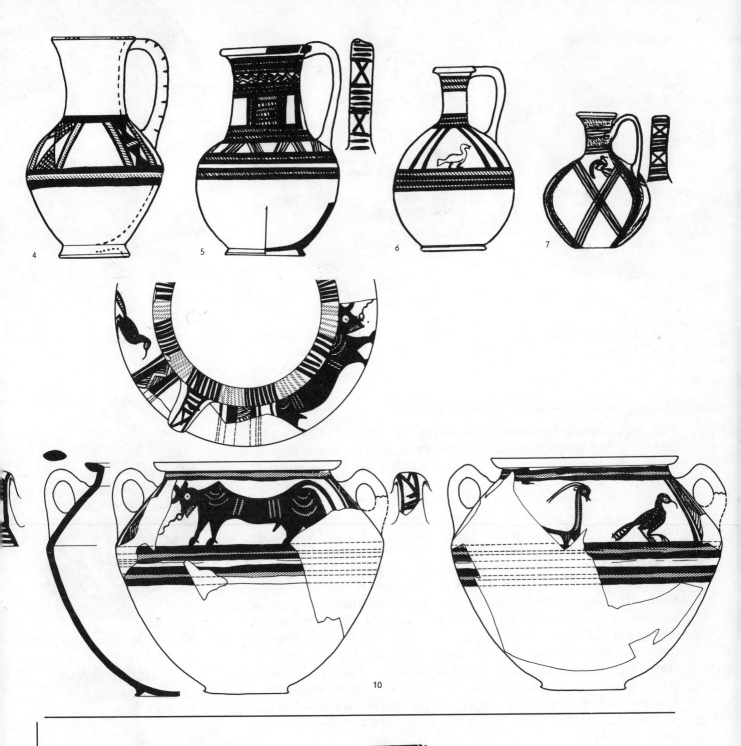

4   5   6   7

10

IIA

14   15   16

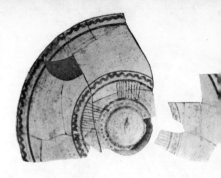

Photo 149. Bowl, *Meg.*, II, Pl. 134:7.

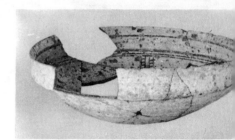

Photo 147. Bowl, Megiddo, *Meg. T.*, Pl. 45:10, The Oriental Institute, Chicago, No. A 16671.

Photo 148. Bowl, *Meg. T.*, Pl. 143:4, The Oriental Institute, Chicago, No. A16679.

150. Bowl, Megiddo, *Meg.* II, Pl. 134:8.

The 'Chocolate-on-White' Ware (Plate 49).

This term, coined by Petrie,[22] has not taken root in archaeological literature, for the simple reason that the ware was never properly studied. When we came to do so, it became clear that Petrie was right in defining it as a separate class. We found that this ware (or family), comprises a surprisingly wide variety of vessels, which have in common a series of stylistic criteria, pertaining to shape, finish, and decoration, but mainly to workmanship. The vessels we suggest belong to this ware are assembled on Plate 49 and in Photos 147–156. Only a close examination of the Krater from Jericho (Photo 151) in the Louvre enabled us to attribute it to this ware, and there may be other cases of this sort.

Form: This ware comprises mostly the same forms which are common in other wares of the period. However, the workmanship in general and mainly the execution of the details is excellent, and leaves no doubt concerning the attribution of specimens to this ware. The wheel-work is evidence of the high technical standard of the potter. The perfectly made details include: the ring-base with an omphalos and a raised ring around it on the inside of bowls (Nos. 1, 2, 4); the rim, very broad and well made, of the large jugs (No. 9 and Photos 153, 155); the harmonious globular forms (No. 8).

Finish: In the case of this ware we make a distinction between finish and decoration because the perfect finish constitutes the main criterion of this ware. In contrast to the inconspicuous finish of the Bichrome Ware, discussed above, the main feature of the 'Chocolate-on-White' Ware is the excellent finish of the surface of every individual vessel. The thick creamy-white slip was applied to the vessel while it was turned on the wheel — the wheel-marks are clearly visible in the burnishing. In every

Photo 152. Jug, Jericho, IDA 32.1821.

22. F. Petrie, *AG*, I, p. 10; *idem*, *AG*, II, pp. 11–12.

Photo 151. Krater, Jericho, *AAA*, XX, Pl. XXXI, Musée du Louvre.

Photo 155. Jug, Zerqa (Jordan), Collections of PBI, Jerusalem.

Photo 156. Jar. Zerqa (Jordan), Collections of PBI, Jerusalem.

Photo 153. Jug, Megiddo, *Meg. T.*, Pl. 144. The Oriental Institute, Chicago, No, A 16554.

Photo 154. Amphoriskos, Farah(N), *RB*, 1951, Pl. XXIV.

case the slip covers the entire surface of the vessel, whether it be a bowl or a closed vessel, or even a jar, as in Photo 156. The burnishing is always executed before the decoration with painting, since only the white areas are shiny, an effect of the burnishing.

Decoration: This is made with thick chocolate-brown or reddish-brown paint usually. A good idea of the color-scheme may be obtained from the color-photo in *Lachish*, II, pl. 162:2. The decoration is also neatly carried out with a sure hand, perhaps even with the aid of instruments. It appears probable that the decoration was partly made on the wheel, hence the exactitude of the horizontal lines. Very characteristic is the accuracy of the design on the rim: the jug in Plate 49:9 and Photo 153 is decorated not only on the rim itself but also on the edge of the rim. The handles are also decorated as in jug No. 9 and the jar in Photo 156.

The patterns are to a great extent geometric. Only two fragments from Megiddo show designs of birds.[23] Straight and wavy lines, triangles, squares, and lozenges are painted in solid color or filled with dots, or sometimes half-circles are also filled with dots. The metopic division of a zone is known also in this style, as e.g. in the biconical amphoriskos No. 10, and on the inside of bowl No. 5.

Distribution: It is of interest to note that this ware has also been found in Transjordan (Photos 155–156).[24]

Date: The contexts in which vessels of this ware were found, and typological analysis, indicate that this decorative style flourished simultaneously with the Bichrome Ware, at the end of MB II C and during LB I. This seems to have been a period of vigorous artistic versatility.

23. *Megiddo*, II pl. 134:21; the second has not been published: Field Reg. No. b 314, in the collections of the Oriental Institute, Chicago.
24. These two vessels have been acquired by Father Mallon in Transjordan.

PLATE | 49

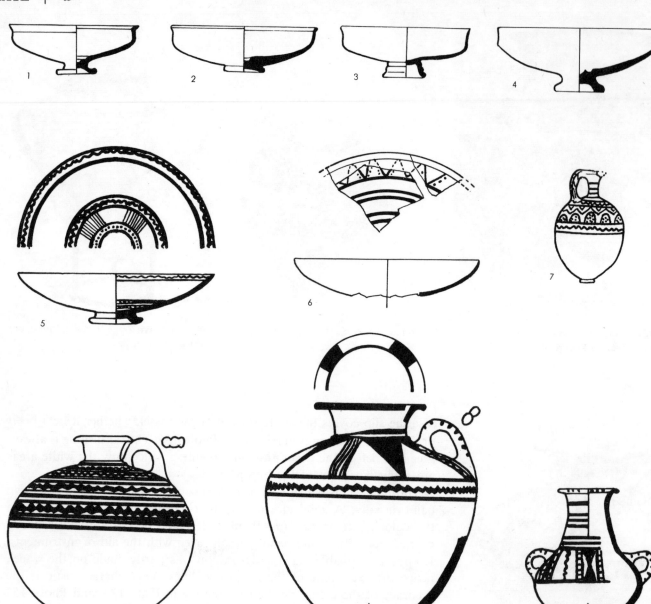

PLATE 49

1. Bowl, dark-grey, white-yellow ring-
   burnished slip   1:5   Megiddo   T. 251   Meg. T., pl. 26:12
2. Bowl, white-yellow, ring-burnished outside   1:5   Megiddo   T. 1100 A   Meg. T., pl. 45:10
3. Bowl, brown-ocher, horizontally
   burnished outside   1:5   Megiddo   T. 251   Meg. T., pl. 26:11
4. Bowl, light buff, cream slip   1:4   Beth-shan   PMB 3, pl. VI:4
5. Bowl, pink-buff, burnished white slip
   inside and out, red decoration   1:5   Megiddo   IX   Meg. II, pl. 54:11
6. Bowl, buff, white burnished slip,
   red decoration   1:6   Ajjul   I–II   AG II, pl. XL:26
7. Juglet, green, white slip, brown decoration   1:6   Jericho   Tomb   Sellin-Watzinger, pl. 22:B.2
8. Jug, brown, white slip, red decoration   1:5   Jericho   T. 9 C   AAA XIX, pl. XXX:11
9. Jug, buff, white-yellow horizontally
   burnished slip, indian red decoration   1:5   Megiddo   T. 1100 A   Meg. T., pl. 46:14
10. Amphora, pink, white, red decoration   1:5   Far'ah (North)   T. 11   RB, 1951, p. 579, Fig. 9:12

Photo 157. Goblet, Lachish, IDA 34.7714.

Photo 158. Goblet, Lachish, IDA 36.1481.

Photo 159. Krater, Beth-shan, IDA I.3862.

◀ Photo 160. Krater, Lachish, IDA 39.797.

The Palm-tree and Ibex Motif (Plate 50).

We have devoted a special plate to this motif because it is the most characteristic decoration of the Late Bronze Period. The antithetic design consists of a tree flanked by two facing ibexes; frequently it appears between the triglyphs of the metope style on a varied range of pottery shapes.

By definition, the nature of the metope style is that of a frieze. This frieze, divided by triglyphs into metopes, is usually placed on the upper part of the vessel, either on the shoulder or in the zone of the handles. It occurs on all kinds of closed vessels, such as jars, jugs, goblets (Photos, 157–158), kraters (Photos, 159–160), bowls with upright walls, and even on local imitations of the Mycenaean amphoriskos (Photo 161). The metope style was so well-rooted in the potter's art of that age that ways were found of applying it even where the form of the vessel was quite unsuited, as for instance on the inside of a bowl (Photo 163, Plate 50:12 — Plate 38:26. cf. also Plate 39:14, 18), or on the hemispherical wall of a pilgrim-flask (Plate 51:7, see also discussion). The division of the inner surface of the bowl into three areas, such as is frequently seen in this period, should be regarded as an application of the metopic division to a hemispherical surface. The triglyphs dividing such surfaces into metopes confirm this interpretation, as they resemble closely the triglyphs used in the usual metopic bands. Generally these consist of alternating straight and wavy lines, but sometimes vertical bands of checkerboard, criss-cross, or other patterns are used.

The commonest motif enclosed in the metopes is the palm-and-ibex; only rarely is a fish or crab represented (Photo 166). Generally the entire decoration is carried out in one color — red. However, sometimes black and red are used to paint both triglyphs and the palm-and-ibex (No. 5).

The vessels on Plate 50 are arranged in chronological order, according to stratigraphic provenience. The development of the style through the three phases of LB has yet to be studied.

LB I: Nos. 3–4. The motif appears already at the beginning of the period, on vessels of the Bichrome Style (see also Plate 48). However, these two specimens are the only ones known which are decorated with the palm-and-ibex, and they are unusual also in other details. Neither the antithetic arrangement nor the birds with heads turned backwards (No. 3) are usual in the Bichrome Style. Both decorative elements appear to be influenced by the palm-and-ibex style best represented in glyptic art (see cylinder seal, Plate 50:2). No. 4 has triglyphs in the Bichrome Style, while the metope is filled with a palm-and-ibex motif.

LB II A: Nos. 5–8. Here we find the full flowering of this motif as used in the metope style. The representation of the animals is either linear (No. 6) or naturalistic (No. 5), while the schematic representation by two triangles (Nos. 7–8) may be a further development. Already in this period, the motif spreads and evolves into a complete picture, such as No. 7, where two animals flank the palm on each side, or Photos 164–165, where whole flocks of animals are shown. To this period or to LB II B belongs the richly decorated biconical jug from Tomb 912 D at Megiddo shown in Photo 166. Ibexes and birds of various kinds are arranged on both sides of the palm tree, while another metope under the handle encloses a solitary crab.

161

LB II B: In this group the motif appears in various forms, some of which are debased, as if the motif had begun to disintegrate. Sometimes there is a multiplicity of animals, such as on krater No. 9, where ibexes and ostriches appear in asymmetrical confusion, or on a krater on Plate 41:8, on which animals and birds, single or in pairs, fill the metopes. A complicated picture is shown on the inside of a chalice from Beth-shemesh (Photo 163): an entire zoo is assembled around a pool indicated by dots. Here the metope style is completely degenerated — the division into three zones remains, but the triglyphs have disappeared and the trees, which originally filled the metopes, serve as triglyphs. The motif also begins to be used in abbreviated form, that is, *Pars pro toto:* either the ibex or a fish (No. 10), or, more frequently, the palm-tree appears alone (Nos. 11 and 12). The abbreviated form of the motif appears in earlier phases, although very rarely (Plates 41:5, 47:5).

The two seal-impressions shown (Nos. 1 and 2) illustrate the wide distribution of the palm-and-ibex motif, encompassing glyptic art, ceramic decoration, and other forms of art. No. 1 is the impression of a cone-shaped seal found at Ta'anach, showing two animals flanking a palm tree. The publication does not state clearly to which stratum this seal belongs. No. 3 is a rolled-out impression of a cylinder seal found in Temple III at Lachish: the two ibexes flanking the tree are represented with their backs to the tree and their heads turned backwards. The seal is carved in Mitannian style. This motif in the art of the Ancient Near East, its origin and symbolic significance as the 'Tree of Life' have been the subject of many studies.

An Iron I jar (No. 10) is included on Plate 50 in order to demonstrate that the abbreviated form of the motif, in which the stylized tree stands for the whole, continues to occur. We shall meet even more stylized forms of this tree in the Iron Period (see Plates 61:4,5; 69:5; 78:4; 79:7; 83:1,7).

Photo 163. Chalice, Beth-shemesh, IDA I.5884.

Photo 164. Jug, Farah(S), IDA I. 7003

Photo 161. Local imitation of Mycenaean piriform jar, Beth-shemesh, IDA I.5884.

Photo 162. Bowl, Gezer, HU 109.

Photo 165. Jug, Farah(S), *BP*, II, Pl. XLIX.

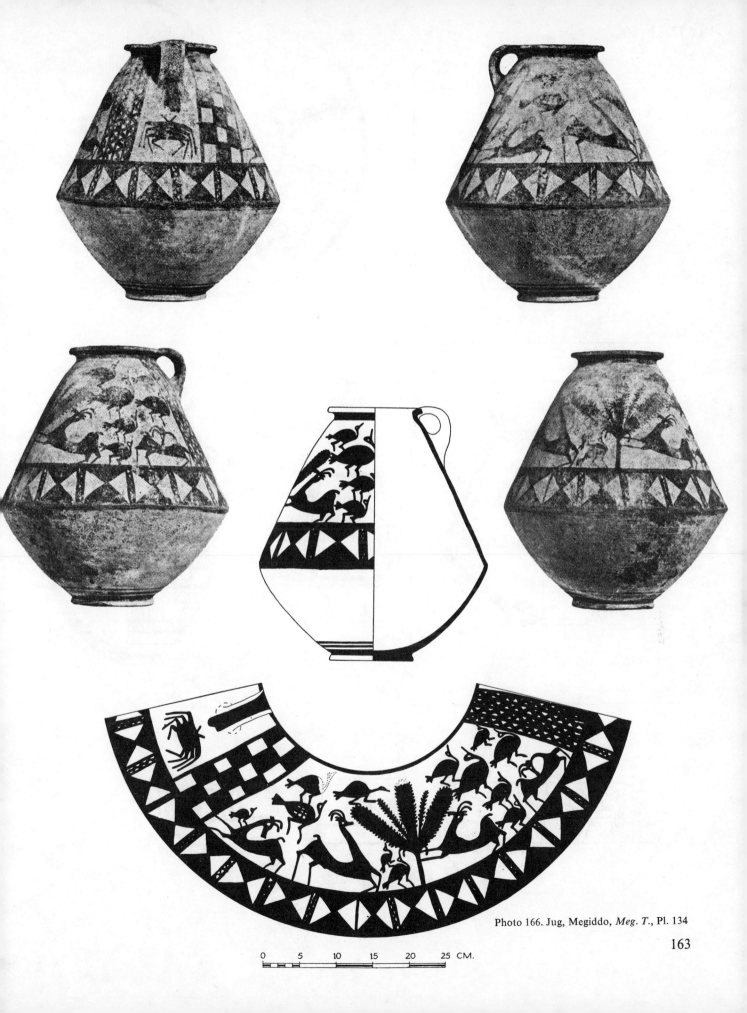

Photo 166. Jug, Megiddo, *Meg. T.*, Pl. 134

0   5   10   15   20   25 CM.

PLATE | 50

1

I

2

3

IIA

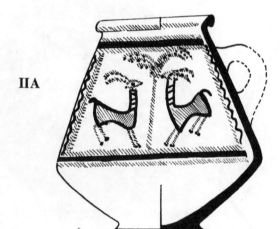

5

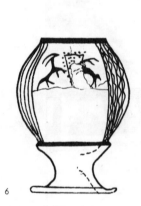

6

7

IIB

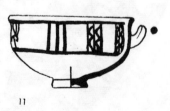

10

11

4

PLATE 50

1.	Impression of a basalt seal	1:1	Ta'annach		Ta'annek, p. 73, Fig. 98
2.	Impression of faience cylinder seal	1:1	Lachish	Temple III	La. II, pl. XXXIII:43
3.	Jug, brown-ocer, red and black decoration	1:5	Megiddo	T. 1100 A	Meg. T., Fig. 111
4.	Jug, pink-buff, red and black decoration	1:5	Megiddo	IX (T.2010)	Meg. II, pl. 56:8
5.	Jug, orange-buff, red and black decoration	1:5	Megiddo	VIII	Meg. II, pl. 58:2
6.	Goblet, pink, vertically burnished, red and black decoration	1:5	Lachish	Temple II	La. II pl. XLVII:229
7.	Jar, pink-buff, burnished, red decoration	1:5	Megiddo	VII B	Meg. II pl. 64:4
8.	Chalice, pink-buff, red decoration	1:5	Megiddo	VII	Meg. II pl. 72:3
9.	Krater, brown, buff slip, red decoration	1:5	Lachish	Temple III	La. II XLVIII:250
10.	Goblet, pink, buff burnished slip, red decoration	1:5	Lachish	Temple III	La. II pl. XLVII:238
11.	Bowl, pinkish, black-brown decoration	1:5	Hazor	pit 9017	H. I pl. CVIII:4
12.	Bowl, buff, red decoration	1:5	Lachish	T. 571	La. IV pl. 72:630
13.	Jar, buff, red decoration	1:5	Megiddo	VI	Meg. II pl. 84:5

8

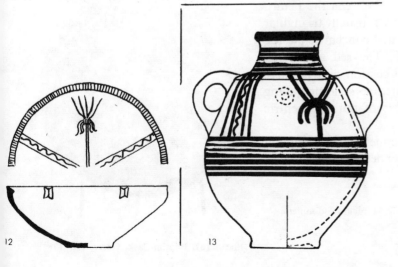

12

13

Pilgrim Flasks (Plate 51).

The pilgrim flask appears to originate in the Late Bronze Period. We do not know for the present whether its birthplace was Canaan or whether its appearance was due to foreign influence, but very soon it became one of the most popular and most characteristic forms in the ceramic repertoire of the Late Bronze Age and the following periods.

The pilgrim flask differs from other pottery vessels not only in its shape but in the technique of manufacture imposed by this shape. The lentoid flask cannot be thrown on the wheel in one operation, and had therefore to be manufactued in several stages: a) two plates were thrown on the wheel and joined together; b) the neck, also wheel-made, was joined to the body; c) the handles were attached.

Before we discuss the pilgrim flask in the various phases of the Late Bronze Age, we should like to mention a number of MB II B flask-like vessels, which may have some significance in relation to the beginnings of the pilgrim flask: a) a flask with one handle, decorated with concentric circles, was found in Tomb 66 in the cemetery of Kafer Garra near Sidon,[25] in a context of MB II B; b) a ring-shaped vessel with the neck and handle of a piriform juglet has been found in various excavations in Palestine and Syria: Tomb LVII at Ugarit, which is dated by the excavator to Bronze Moyen III (part of the group may belong to LB I),[26] mixed tombs at Gezer[27] and Tell Jeriseh; c) a flask-shaped vessel of 'White Painted IV Ware' found at Megiddo, which we include in the plate devoted to Cypriot imports of MB II B (Plate 37:11). As we pointed out, this is the only example of its kind, even in Cyprus itself.

LB I: The earliest pilgrim flask, and the only one belonging to this phase, as far as we know, was found in a tomb on the Mount of Olives in Jerusalem (No. 1). Our flask appears to belong to the second period of interment in this cave. It differs from the later examples especially in the form of its neck, which is wide and slightly swollen, rather like the necks of MB II B–C and LB I dipper juglets. The handles, too, which do not spring from the base of the neck, unlike those of the later pilgrim flasks, are an indication of an earlier date.

LB II A: The pilgrim flask of this phase is characterized especially by the way the handles are attached to the neck and body (Photo 167). This attachment is effected by spreading clay on the neck so as to form petals. In this phase the short neck is planted, as it were, between the petals, and the wide rim, which appears to rest on the handles, is usually triangular in section. Some flasks are decorated with red painted concentric circles, a decoration well suited to their spherical shape. The red and black decoration on No. 7 is more complicated (see discussion above): here the concentric circles have been adapted to the metope style prevailing in the period, and the resulting decoration consists of both concentric circles and metopes.

In this phase they are usually lentoid in section, symmetrical and pointed at the base (Nos. 2, 3). Sometimes the section is rounded (No.4) or asym-

Photo 167. Pilgrim-flask, Gezer, HU 178.

---

25. B. E. Guiges, "Lebea, Kafer Garra, Qraye, Necropoles de la region Sidonnienne," *PMB*, I (1938), pl. IV:e.
26. Cf. F. A. Schaeffer, *Ugaritica*, II (Paris, 1949), pl. XL.
27. *Gezer*, III, pl. LXXXI:20 and pl. CLXI:3.

metrical, with one of the halves deeper than the other (No. 6). At times, the deeper of the two halves has a protuberance at the centre (No. 7).

LB II B: In this phase, the development of the pilgrim flask follows a number of directions. On the one hand, the type prevalent in the preceding phase continues to develop (No. 8). No. 10 still has a short neck, but the method of attaching the handles is already different. No. 9 has a completely different neck — it is high and ridged, with the handles springing from the ridge. Nos. 11–15 (Photo 168) represent the commonest type in this phase, which continues well into Iron I. These flasks are small, and the proportion between body and neck is completely different from that of LB II flasks. Now the neck is about half as high as the body. The outline of the handles resembles that of jugs, while the handles of the earlier flasks were nearer shoulder handles. The handles still spring from the middle of the neck, like those of one specimen of the preceding period. The decoration with concentric circles continues to be popular, but now the circles are broader and more closely spaced. Nos. 9 and 12 have protuberances on both sides. No. 9 is plumper than the flasks we have discussed above.

Photo 168. Pilgrim-flask, Lachish, IDA 36.1809.

Imported Syrian Wares (Plate 52).

The decision to devote a special Plate to the Syrian flask and the grey juglets (see above, Plate 46:6) requires some explanation. First of all, the term 'Syrian' seems to contradict to some extent the opinion we have expressed on a number of occasions concerning the uniform civilization prevailing in the Middle and Late Bronze Ages in Greater Canaan, that is, in the area between Alalakh in the north, the desert to the south, and the desert to the east. However, within this cultural unit there were a great many regional variations, and in Plate 52 we have shown two types of vessel produced in one region within the Canaanite cultural sphere and imported into another region of the same sphere. Further study of the pottery of these periods will certainly reveal additional instances of interregional exports and imports or of mutual stylistic influence between parts of Greater Canaan.

The definition of this flask (and the grey juglet) as 'Syrian' also requires explanation. It is found over a very extensive area, including the Hittite cultural sphere, Cyprus, Canaan, and Egypt. Although occuring in Cyprus in considerable numbers, this flask is plainly a foreign element there. In Egypt, it should undoubtedly be classed as an imported vessel. Relatively few such flasks have been found in Palestine, where the vessel appears to be somewhat alien to the native Canaanite pottery repertoire. Turning now to an examination of the flask, we find that shape, technique of manufacture, and decoration indicate a combination of Canaanite and Hittite features.

Plate 52 shows most of the specimens of the 'Syrian' flask found in Palestine, and especially those from stratified deposits. This flask occurs in LB I (No. 1) and in LB II (Nos. 3–5, Photos 169, 170).

PLATE | 51

I

IIA

IIB

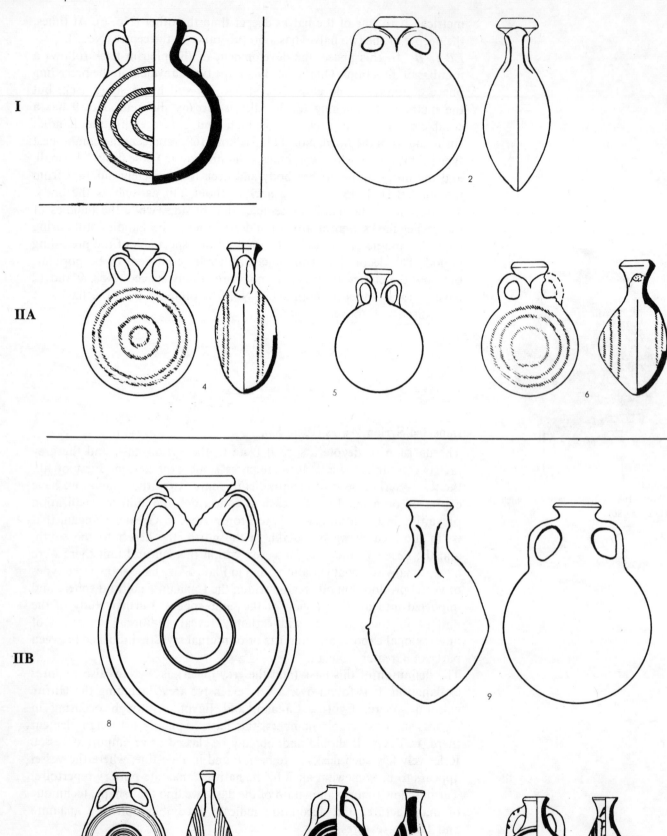

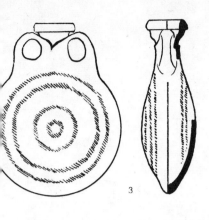

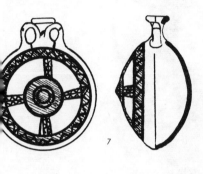

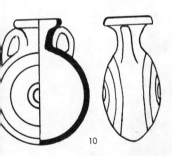

PLATE 51

1.	Flask, light brown decoration	1:3	Jerusalem	Tomb	Olivet, Fig. 55:1
2.	Flask, pink-grey, white slip	1:5	Abu Hawam	V A	TAH, p. 42:255
3.	Flask, reddish, whitish, slip red decoration	1:5	Hazor	1 B (T.8144–5)	H. II, pl. CXXX:12
4.	Flask, black, light grey slip, red decoration	1:5	Hazor	1 B (T.8144–5)	H. II, pl. CXXX:10
5.	Flask (Corrected after the photograph)	1:6	Ajjul	Governer T.	AG III, pl. XI:51
6.	Flask, light grey, red decoration	1:5	Hazor	1 B (T.8144–5)	H. II, pl. CXXX:13
7.	Flask, brown, red and black decoration	1:5	Hazor	1 B (T.8144–5)	H. II, pl. CXXX:14
8.	Flask, pink, red decoration	1:5	Lachish	Temple III	La. II, pl. LIV:349
9.	Flask, pink	1:5	Lachish	Temple III	La. II, LIV:348
10.	Flask, brown, cream slip, dark red decoration	1:5	Lachish	T. 532	La. IV, pl. 84:955
11.	Flask, pink, burnished, red and black decoration	1:5	Lachish	Temple III	La. II, pl. LIV:351
12.	Flask, buff, irregularly burnished, red decoration	1:5	Megiddo	VII B	Meg. II, pl. 67:1
13.	Flask, brown-ocher, red decoration	1:5	Megiddo	T. 877 B	Meg. T., pl. 14:6
14.	Flask, brown-ocher, burnished, red decoration	1:5	Megiddo	T. 912 B	Meg. T., pl. 34:16
15.	Flack, burnt umber, burnished, red decoration	1:5	Megiddo	T. 912 B	Meg. T., pl. 34:13

The 'grey juglet' (Nos. 2 and 8, Photo 171) has already been discussed above (Plate 46:6); here it is shown together with the 'Syrian flask' found in Temple I at Lachish. This juglet can certainly be described as Canaanite, within the mainstream of MB II B tradition. However, it also appears to have been influenced to some extent by the globular shape and the absence of a pronounced base characteristic of contemporary Cypriot jugs and juglets. The 'Syrian' flask and the grey juglet appear very frequently together in their country of origin (as e.g. in Temple I at Lachish, Nos. 1–2) as well as in Cyprus and in Egypt (Nos. 7 and 8,

Photo 171. Juglet, grey, Lachish, IDA 35.3000.

Photo 169. 'Syrian' flask, Jerusalem Tomb, *EI*, VI, Pl. III, IDA 68–81.

Photo 170. 'Syrian' flask, Azor, Collection Dayan.

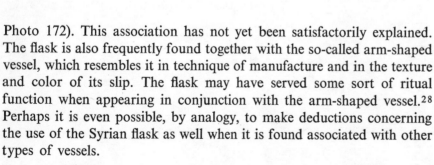

Photo 172). This association has not yet been satisfactorily explained. The flask is also frequently found together with the so-called arm-shaped vessel, which resembles it in technique of manufacture and in the texture and color of its slip. The flask may have served some sort of ritual function when appearing in conjunction with the arm-shaped vessel.[28] Perhaps it is even possible, by analogy, to make deductions concerning the use of the Syrian flask as well when it is found associated with other types of vessels.

Photo 172. 'Syrian' flask, Egypt, Metropolitan Museum No. 30.8.206.

---

28. Ruth Amiran, "The Arm-Shaped Vessel and Its Family," *JNES*, XXI (1962), pp. 161 ff.

PLATE | **52**

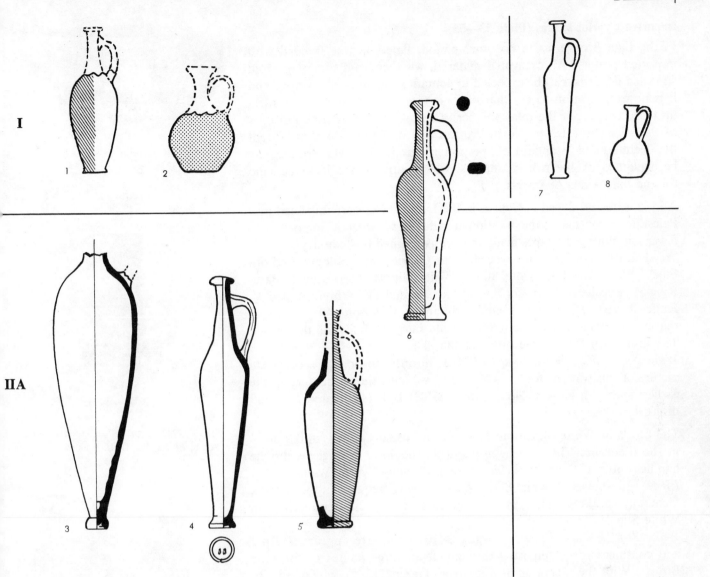

I

IIA

PLATE 52

1.	Jug, pink, red burnished slip	1:5	Lachish	Temple I	La. II, pl. LI:273
2.	Juglet, grey, burnished	1:5	Lachish	Temple I	La. II, pl. LI:276
3.	Jug, grey-brown, grey-brown burnished slip	1:5	Abu Hawam V		TAH, p. 44, Fig. 274
4.	Jug, brown, red burnished slip	1:5	Jerusalem	Tomb	Ey VI, pl 35, Fig. 1:2
5.	Jug, brown, red vertically burnished slip	1:5	Lachish	T. 555	La. IV, pl. 79:815
6.	Jug, brown red burnished slip	1:5	Gezer		Hebrew University, No. 2211
7.	Jug, brown, red burnished slip	1:8	Sediment	T. 256	Sediment, II, pl. LXIII:T. 256
8.	Juglet, grey, burnished	1:8	Sediment	T. 273	Sediment, II, pl. LXIII:T. 273

Imported Cypriot Wares (Plate 53—55).

In the Late Bronze, as in no other period, Palestine was flooded with imported pottery. All excavated material, whether from tombs or from stratified deposits, can be expected to contain some imported wares, and it is no exaggeration to say that in some tomb-groups such wares form up to 50 percent of the total number of vessels.[29] This is true, not only of Palestine, but also of North Canaan and of Egypt. To some extent the decline in the standard of the potter's art in the Late Bronze may be explained by the rise in imports, which satisfied the local demand for the finer kinds of vessels.

All the wares produced in Cyprus in the Late Bronze were imported into Palestine, in contrast to the situation in MB II B–C, when the imports were fewer and not all the types made in Cyprus reached this country.

We shall list here the wares according to Cypriot terminology: Red-on-Black, Black Slip III, White Slip I, White Slip II, Base-Ring I, Base-Ring II, Bucchero, Monochrome, White Painted IV, White Painted V, Knife-Shaved. All these are handmade and have a common feature in the characteristic insertion of the handle into the body of the vessel. The discussion follows the order of the plates.

White Slip I Ware (Plate 53): MB II B: In order to present a complete picture of this ware as found in Palestine, we have shown here again the earliest specimen known (No. 1), from MB II B–C (see Plate 37:14 and discussion there).

The bowls of White Slip I and II Wares are usually called 'milk-bowls' in the literature. They are hemispherical, and have a single wishbone handle (Photo 173), which is characteristic of many Cypriot wares.

LB I: Milk-bowls of White Slip I Ware are very frequent in this period. Generally speaking, this ware is found in Palestine less frequently than White Slip II Ware.

White Slip II Ware (Plate 53): Nos. 3–10: This ware appears in LB I and continues to be imported throughout all three phases of the Late Bronze. With the exception of a jug from Gezer (No. 7), which remains unique in Palestine, all the vessels of this ware are bowls.

White Slip I Ware differs from White Slip II only with respect to details of decoration. Clay and slip remain the same, and the decorative scheme also remains unchanged: the inside of the bowl is always white, while the outside is decorated with a horizontal band around the rim and vertical bands running down towards the centre. However, in White Slip II the pattern has become more rigid and schematic and the ladder-pattern predominates. Other patterns are placed between two lines, such as the row of lozenges in Nos. 3 and 7. Often two horizontal bands run around the rim. The lozenges and the delicate embroidery-like patterns of White Slip I disappear and are often replaced by rows of dots (Nos. 5, 6, 8).

Jug No. 7 has all the characteristic features of the ware — the lower part is decorated like the bowls, while the upper is covered with vertical

---

Photo 173. Cypriot bowl, Ajjul, IDA 35.3935.

Photo 174. Cypriot juglet, Jerusalem Tomb, *EI*, VI, Pl. III, IDA 68.46.

Photo 175. Cypriot juglet, Jerusalem Tomb, *EI*, VI, Pl. III, IDA 68.85.

Photo 176. Cypriot jug, imitating a 'Syrian' flask, Jerusalem Tomb, *EI*, VI, III, IDA 68.39.

---

29. As for instance the group of vessels from the tomb found in Jerusalem, items of which are presented in these plates, published by Ruth Amiran, *EI*, VI (1961), (Hebrew).

bands. The handle terminates in a horned projection, characteristic of many vessels in this period.

On specimens like Nos. 9 and 10, which stand at the end of the series, the ladder-pattern has declined into a group of lines.

Base-Ring I and II Wares (Plate 54): Base-Ring I Ware appears in LB I and II A, while Base-Ring II Ware is current in LB II A and B. Both wares are found in considerable quantities in Palestine. The predominant type is a jug, the so-called 'bilbil.' The main features of these two wares (as well as of the Bucchero and Monochrome Wares) are the hard well-fired metallic clay and the brownish-grey reddish slip resembling copper. The main differences between the two wares are the size and proportions of the vessels and the decoration. While Base-Ring I ornament is chiefly plastic (Photos 174, 175) with very few cases of white painted decoration, Base-Ring II decoration is usually white painted (Photos 176, 177), with a few survivals of the plastic ornament. The jugs of Base-Ring II are more squat, as a comparison of Nos. 15 and 20 of this ware with Nos. 1, 6, and 7 of Base-Ring I Ware will show. Frequently the jugs of Base-Ring II are considerably larger than those of Base-Ring I (Nos. 12 and 18).

Bucchero Ware (Plate 54): No. 17 belongs to LB II A and No. 21 to LB II B. In Cyprus, Bucchero Ware does not appear before LB II.

Monochrome Ware (Plate 55): As far as clay and technique are concerned, this ware forms part of the Base-Ring Ware, but the forms are different (Nos. 3, 4, 10, 11). Like Base-Ring I Ware, Monochrome Ware occurs in LB I and II.

Red-on-Black Ware (Plate 55): This ware is a survival from MB II B and C and is still found in LB I (Nos. 1 and 2). Of special interest is the hemispherical bowl with a round horizontal handle and a trough-shaped spout on the rim opposite the handle.

Black-Slip III Ware (Plate 55): This ware, too, is a carry-over from MB II B and C; only a few specimens have been found in Palestine. No. 5 is a juglet with black slip and incised decoration made before the slip was applied.

White-Painted IV Ware (Plate 55): The ware continues into LB I (No. 6) from MB II B and C; it was discussed and described on p. 125 (Plate 38).

White-Painted V Ware (Plate 55): The ware is not discussed by Sjöqvist[30] or by Astrom,[31] although it is very common. No. 7 is an ordinary juglet; Nos. 8 and 9 are small teapots, and Nos. 13 and 14 resemble small dipper juglets. This ware is closely related to the shaved wares, as the lower part of the vessels shows some signs of knife-paring.

Knife-Shaved Ware (Plate 55): Nos. 12 and 15: This Cypriot juglet is an imitation of the Canaanite dipper juglet. It is hand-made and knife-shaved all over. This ware occurs in LB II A and B.

Photo 177. Cypriot juglet, Jerusalem Tomb, *EI*, VI, Pl. III, IDA. 68.48.

30. E. Sjöqvist, *Problems of the Late Cypriote Bronze Age*, Stockholm, 1940.
31. P. Astrom, *The Middle Cypriote Bronze Age*, Lund, 1957.

PLATE 53

1. Milk bowl, red-buff, handmade, burnished
   white slip, brown decoration (WS I)   1:5   Megiddo   X   Meg. II, pl. 45:21
2. Milk bowl (WS I)   1:6   Ajjul   PB 988   AG, II, pl. XXVIII:19 Q 1
3. Milk bowl, grey, white slip, brown
   decoration (WS II)   1:5   Lachish   Temple I   La. II, pl. XLIII:154
4. Milk bowl, pink, white slip, dark brown
   decoration (WS II)   1:5   Lachish   T. 216   La. IV, pl. 79:831
5. Milk bowl, grey, white slip, brown
   decoration (WS II)   1:5   Lachish   Temple I   La. II, pl. XLIII:157
6. Milk bowl, buff, white irregularly burnished
   slip, brown decoration (WS II)   1:5   Lachish   T. 501   La. IV, pl. 79:833
7. Jug, white slip (WS II)   1:6   Gezer   T. 30   Stra. Comp., Fig. 158:7
8. Milk bowl, red-brown to blue, handmade,
   white slip inside and out, black decoration
   WS II)   1:5   Megiddo   VII B   Meg. II, pl. 65:26
9. Milk bowl, brown, white slip, dark brown
   decoration (WS II)   1:5   Lachish   T. 532   La. IV, pl. 79:835
10. Milk bowl, grey, handmade, cream slip
    inside and out, black decoration (WS II)   1:5   Megiddo   VII B   Meg. II, pl. 65:25

PLATE | 53

IIC

1

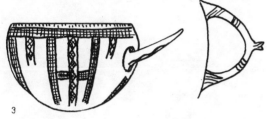

2

I

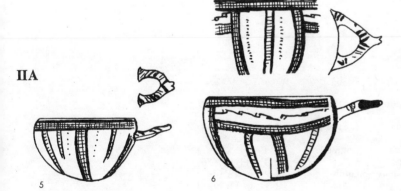

3

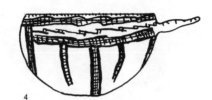

4

IIA

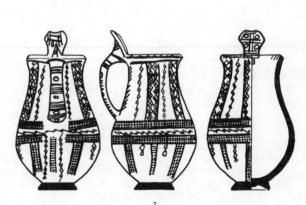

5

6

7

IIB

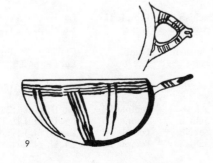

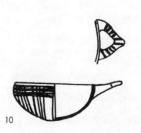

8

9

10

PLATE 54

1.	Bilbil, black-burnt umber slip (BR II)	1:5	Megiddo	T. 855	Meg. T., pl. 43:7
2.	Jug, blue-black, irregularly burnished, raised decoration (BR I)	1:5	Megiddo	T. 1100 C	Meg. T., pl. 47:13
3.	Jug, black-burnt umber burnished slip, raised decoration (BR I)	1:5	Megiddo	T. 1145 B	Meg. T., pl. 50:12
4.	Krater, grey-brown, red and brown slip (BR I)	1:5	Lachish	Temple I	La. IV, pl. XLIV:170
5.	Bilbil, brown, brown-grey slip (BR I)	1:5	Lachish	T. 216	La. IV, pl. 80:856
6.	Bilbil, brown, brown-grey slip (BR I)	1:5	Jerusalem	Tomb	EI VI, p. 35, Fig. 1:5
7.	Bilbil, brown-pink, brown-grey slip (BR I)	1:5	Jerusalem	Tomb	EI VI, p. 35, Fig. 1:8
8.	Jug, yellowish-brown, brown-grey slip (BR I)	1:5	Jerusalem	Tomb	EI VI, p. 35, Fig. 1:4
9.	Twin bilbils, brown, brown-grey slip (BR I)	1:5	Jerusalem	Tomb	EI VI, p. 35, Fig. 1:13
10.	Bowl, grey, brown-grey slip (BR II)	1:5	Lachish	Temple II	La. II, pl. XLIV:174
11.	Bilbil (after a photograph) (BR II)	1:5	Jerusalem	Tomb	EI VI, p. 35, Fig. 1:18
12.	Bilbil, brown, brown slip, white decoration (BR II)	1:5	Lachish	Temple II	La. II, pl. LI:279
13.	Flask, brown, black slip, white decoration (BR II)	1:5	Lachish	Temple II	La. II, pl. LIV:339
14.	Jug, brown-yellow, brown-grey slip (BR II)	1:5	Jerusalem	Tomb	EI VI, p. 35, Fig. 1:14
15.	Bilbil, brown-pink, brown-grey slip, white decoration	1:5	Jerusalem	Tomb	EI VI, p. 35, Fig. 1:10
16.	Jug, brown, brown-grey slip (BR II)	1:5	Lachish	T. 216	La. IV, pl. 80:836
17.	Jug, yellowish-brown, brown-grey slip, ridged (Bucchero)	1:5	Jerusalem	Tomb	EI VI, p. 35, Fig. 1:19
18.	Bilbil, brown, black slip, white decoration (BR II)	1:5	Lachish	Temple III	La. II, pl. LI:283
19.	Bilbil, brown-black, black slip (BR II)	1:5	Lachish	Temple III	La. II, pl. LII:312
20.	Bilbil, pink (BR II)	1:5	Lachish	Temple III	La. II, pl. LII:313
21.	Jug, brown, black slip (Bucchero)	1:5	Lachish	Temple III	La. II, pl. LI:285

176

PLATE | 54

I

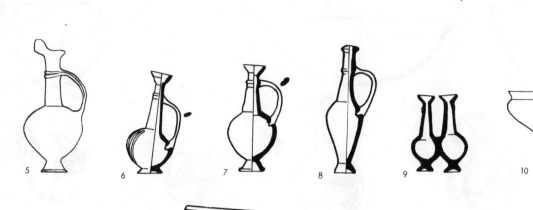

1   2   3   4

5   6   7   8   9   10

IIA

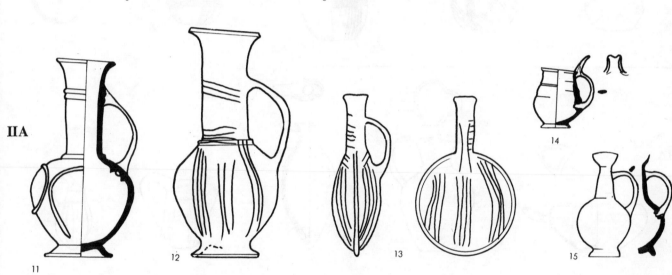

11   12   13   14   15

IIB

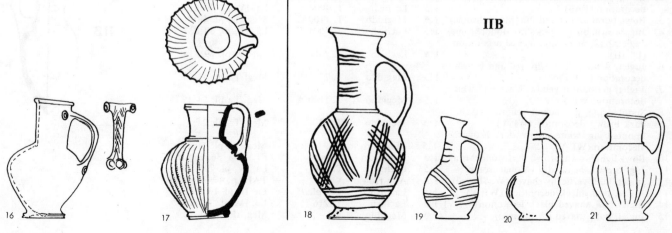

16   17   18   19   20   21

PLATE | 55

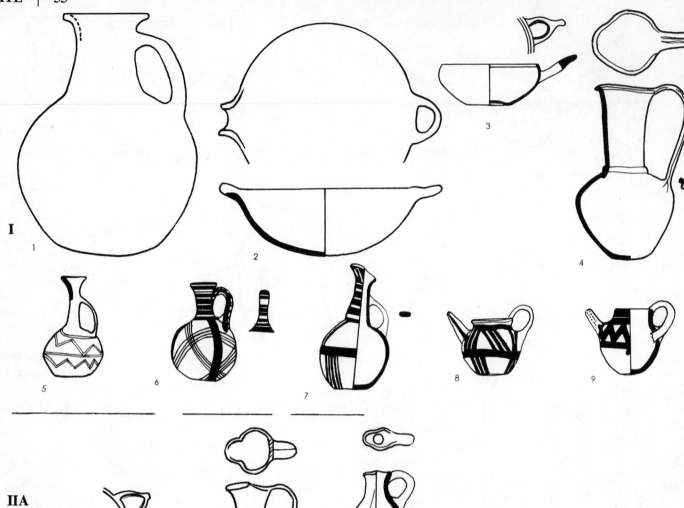

I

1

2

3

4

5

6

7

8

9

IIA

10

11

12

13

14

IIB

15

PLATE 55

1. Jug, buff, traces of black slip and red
   decoration (RoB) ... 1:5 Lachish Temple I La. II, pl. LI:274
2. Bowl, buff, traces of black slip and red
   decoration (RoB) ... 1:5 Lachish T. 4004 La. IV, pl. 79:816
3. Bowl, burnt umber, red slip (Monochrome) 1:5 Megiddo T. 1100 C Meg. T., pl. 48:8
4. Jug, brown, brown-grey slip (Monochrome) 1:5 Lachish T. 4004 La. IV, pl. 80:837
5. Juglet, buff, black slip, incised decoration
   (BS III) ... 1:5 Lachish T. 7011 La. IV, pl. 79:814
6. Juglet, white-yellow slip, red and brown
   decoration (WP IV) ... 1:5 Megiddo T. 77 Meg. T., pl. 41:27
7. Juglet, permanent yellow, black and white
   decoration (WP V) ... 1:5 Megiddo T. 1100 A Meg. T., pl. 54:19
8. Spouted jug, permanent yellow, shaved,
   dark brown decoration (WP V) ... 1:5 Megiddo T. 42 Meg. T., pl. 24:3
9. Spouted jug, white-yellow, dark brown
   decoration (WP V) ... 1:5 Megiddo T. 77 Meg. T., pl. 41:28
10. Bowl, light brown, brown slip (Monochrome) 1:5 Jerusalem Tomb EI VI, p. 36, Fig. 2:25
11. Jug, brown, black slip (Monochrome) 1:5 Lachish T. 216 La. IV, pl. 79:829
12. Juglet, buff, vertically shaved (W. Shaved) 1:4 Abu Hawam V TAH, p. 47, Fig. 288
13. Juglet, buff, black decoration (WP V) 1:5 Lachish Temple II La. II, pl. LI:282
14. Juglet, buff, shaved, black decoration (WP V) 1:5 Lachish T. 216 La. IV, pl. 79:824
15. Juglet, buff, shaved (W. Shaved) 1:5 Megiddo VII Meg. II, pl. 71:12

Photo 178. Kylix, Lachish,
IDA 36.2248.

Imported Mycenaean Wares (Photos 178—194).

The Mycenaean imported vessels are shown here in photographs only, as this pottery loses much of its striking appearance and character in profile drawings.

The origin of this pottery, designated as Mycenaean, is a problem which has given rise to an extensive literature. Were these vessels, commonly found in excavations in all the civilized centres of that period, made only in mainland Mycenae, and exported from there? Or did they also reach the markets from Mycenaean settlements and colonies in the Aegean Islands, such as Crete, Rhodes, Cos, and Cyprus? The discussion pertains mainly to material of Mycenaean III B, a period when many Mycenaean settlements flourished in these islands.[32]

Mycenaean vessels are of excellent workmanship. The clay is very fine, and well-fired. The wheel-made vessels are expertly executed. The decoration, also carried out mostly on the wheel, consists of simple line-drawing (the concentric circles were made with an instrument). The texture of the liquid paint contained some glossy element which lends the vessel a lustrous look after firing. All these details bear witness to the high technical standard of the Mycenaean potter's art.

The group of 15 photos and line-drawings assembled here represent the types of Mycenaean pottery which were imported into Canaan during all phases of the LB.

LB I (*No.* 1 *Photo* 178): In this period Mycenaean imports into Palestine are sparse. The few specimens known belong to Mycenaen II, such as the kylix, with one high loop handle, excavated in Temple I at Lachish. In addition, a few fragments of Mycenaean II are known, such as a sherd from Tell el-Ajjul.[33]

LB II A (Nos. 2–9 — Photos 179–186): Mycenaean imports rise sharply and spread over Canaan and Egypt. The Mycenaean III vessels and sherds found at Tell el-Amarna are among the main pegs to which Mycenaean as well as Palestinean chronology are anchored. The following is a list of the types of Mycenaean pottery found in Palestine in this period, all of the Mycenaean III A classes:

---

32. F. H. Stubbings, *Mycenaean Pottery from the Levant*, Cambridge, 1931.
33. *AG*, III pl. XLII:42.

Photo 179. Kylix, Jerusalem Tomb,
EI, VI, Pl. III, IDA 68.36.

Photo 180. Piriform jar,
Gezer, HU 149.

Photo 181. Pyxis,
Beth-shemesh, IDA I.43.

Photo 182. Globular pilgrim-flask,
Beth-shemesh, IDA I.42.

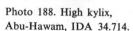

Photo 187. Kylix, Lachish,
La. II, Pl. XLIV.

Photo 188. High kylix,
Abu-Hawam, IDA 34.714.

Photo 189. Pyxis,
Abu-Hawam, IDA 34.718.

Photo 190. Globular pilgrim-flask,
Megiddo, IDA I.2891.

No. 2 Photo 179: two-handled kylix found in a tomb in Jerusalem,
resembling most kylixes with spiral decoration from
Rhodes.
No. 3 Photo 180: piriform small amphora with three handles.
No. 4 Photo 181: pyxis.
No. 5 Photo 182: globular pilgrim flask with ring-base.
No. 6 Photo 183: stirrup jar.
No. 7 Photo 184: juglet with piriform body and cutaway neck.
No. 8 Photo 185: alabastron.
No. 9 Photo 186: mug.

180

Photo 183. Stirrup-jar, Beth-shemesh, IDA I.41.

Photo 184. Juglet, Beth-shemesh, IDA I.44.

Photo 185. Alabastron, Gezer, IDA V.513.

Photo 186. Mug, Beth-shemesh, IDA 33.1853.

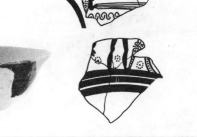

Photo 191. Stirrup-jar, Gezer, HU 2210.

Photo 192. Jug, Abu-Hawam, IDA 34.312.

Photo 193. Cup, Abu-Hawam, IDA 34.710.

Photo 194. Krater sherds, Charioteer scenes, Beth-shemesh, *Stubbings*, p. 65, Fig. 21.

LB II B: The majority of the Mycenaean wares imported into Canaan are of the Mycenaean III B wares, excavated in LB II B strata, or in tomb deposits. The following is a selection of the types of this period excavated in Palestine:

No. 10 Photo 187: kylix with one handle. The vessel is given in line-drawing because it is very fragmentary.

No. 11 Photo 188: kylix of unusual shape and size.

No. 12 Photo 189: pyxis.

No. 13 Photo 190: globular pilgrim flask with ring-base.

No. 14 Photo 191: stirrup jar.

No. 15 Photo 192: jug with globular body.

No. 16 Photo 193: shallow cup.

No. 17 Photo 194: fragment of a krater with charioteer[34] drawing.

---

34. On the charioteer style, cf. Sjöqvist, *Problems of the Late Cypriote Bronze Age;* Levanto-Helladic Pictorial Style.

Imported Cypriot Vessels and their Local Imitations (Plate 56).

Plate 56 shows several examples of local imitations of vessels imported from Cyprus. The imitations differ from their prototypes mainly in that they are wheel-made, following native Canaanite custom, instead of hand-made, like all Cypriot vessels. This is the main reason for the different shape of the local imitations, since a vessel thrown on the wheel is bound to be much more symmetrical than a handmade vessel. The imitation products differ also in the quality of the clay and the firing.

The plate is arranged in pairs, with the imported prototype appearing on the left, with the exception of Nos. 7–9, where two local imitations are shown. The most popular subject for imitation by local potters was the 'bilbil' jug, (Base-Ring II Ware), such as Nos. 8 and 9, which imitate No. 7 (Photos 195 and 196). Photos 197 and 198 show a White Slip milk-bowl and a local imitation.

Photo 195. Cypriot 'Bilbil', Beth-shemesh, IDA I.1.

Photo 197. Cypriot 'Milk-bowl', Beth-shan, IDA 32.80.

Photo 198. Local imitation of Cypriot 'Milk-bowl', Beth-shemesh, IDA I.58.

Photo 196. Local imitation of Cypriot 'bilbil', Beth-shemesh, IDA I.64.

PLATE 56

1. Cypriot bowl, handmade (WP IV)	1:5	Cyprus	Lapitos	Astrom, Fig. XII:2
2. Local bowl, pink-buff, burnished outside, red-brown decoration	1:5	Megiddo	X (T.3070)	Meg. II, pl. 45:20
3. Cypriot milk bowl, brown, white slip, dark brown decoration handmade (WS II)	1:5	Lachish	T. 532	La. IV, pl. 79:835
4. Local milk bowl, light brown, red decoration, wheel-made	1:5	Beth-shemesh	T. 11	Beth Shemesh, p. 191:481
5. Cypriot spouted jug, white-yellow, sepia decoration, handmade (WP V)	1:5	Megiddo	T. 77	Meg. T., pl. 41:28
6. Local spouted jug, brown-ocher	1:5	Megiddo	T. 38	Meg. T., pl. 41:16
7. Cypriot bilbil, pink, grey slip, white decoration, handmade (BR II)	1:5	Lachish	T. 4019	La. IV, pl. 81:878
8. Local bilbil, brown, cream horizontally burnished slip, red decoration, wheel-made	1:5	Lachish	T. 532	La. IV, pl. 81:893
9. Local bilbil, brown, cream burnished slip, red decoration, wheel-made	1:5	Lachish	T. 532	La. IV, pl. 82:905
10. Cypriot bowl, brown-pink, brown slip, handmade (BR II)	1:5	Lachish	T. 216	La. IV, pl. 81:868
11. Local bowl, pink, brown slip, red decoration, wheel-made	1:5	Lachish	T. 559	La. IV, pl. 82:907
12. Cypriot flask, brown-pink, brown-grey slip, handmade (BR II)	1:5	Lachish	T. 501	La. IV, pl. 81:873
13. Local flask, brown	1:5	Lachish	T. 556	La. IV, pl. 82:908
14. Cypriot jug, brown, brown-grey slip (BR I)	1:5	Lachish	T. 216	La. IV, pl. 80:850
15. Local jug, brown, red slip	1:5	Lachish	T. 216	La. IV, pl. 84:964

PLATE | 56

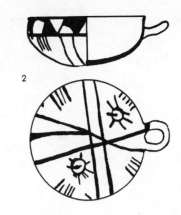

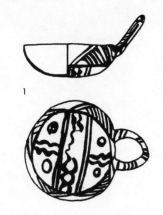

1

2

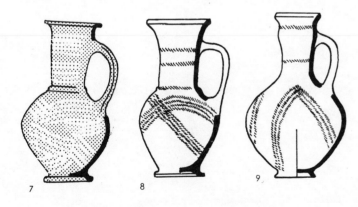

3

4

5

6

7

8

9

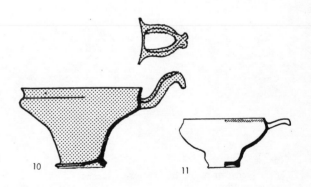

10

11

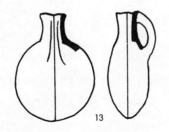

12

13

14

15

PLATE 57

1.	Mycenaean pyxis, buff, brown lustrous decoration	1:5	Beth-shemesh	T. 11	Beth-shemesh, p. 189:508
2.	Local pyxis, brown, buff horizontally burnished slip, red decoration	1:5	Lachish	T. 508	La. IV, pl. 82:923
3.	Local pyxis, buff, red decoration	1:5	Lachish	T. 4011	La. IV, pl. 82:924
4.	Local pyxis, red, red decoration	1:5	Lachish	T. 4013	La. IV, pl. 82:920
5.	Local pyxis, brown, horizontally burnished, black and red decoration	1:5	Lachish	T. 524	La. IV, pl. 82:914
6.	Local pyxis, red, purple decoration	1:3	Beth-shemesh	E. Grotto	PMB 3, pl. VII:6
7.	Local pyxis, brown-ocher, horizontally burnished, red decoration	1:5	Megiddo	T. 989 C	Meg. T., pl. 20:5
8.	Mycenaean piriform jar, buff, brown-red decoration	1:5	Lachish	T. 216	La. IV, pl. 83:945
9.	Local piriform jar, buff, red and black decoration	1:5	Lachish	T. 1006	La. IV, pl. 82:942
10.	Mycenaean stirrup jar	1:6	Ajjul	Governer T.	AG III, pl. XI:42
11.	Local stirrup jar	1:6	Ajjul	Governer T.	AG III, pl. XI:44
12.	Mycenaean (?) bowl, brown-ocher, brown decoration	1:5	Megiddo	T. 912 B	Meg. T., pl. 34:9
13.	Local bowl, burnt umber, red decoration	1:5	Megiddo	T. 912 D	Meg. T., pl. 35:30

184

PLATE | 57

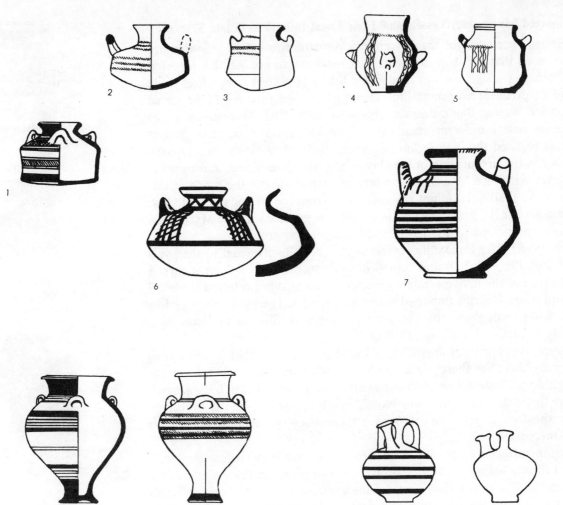

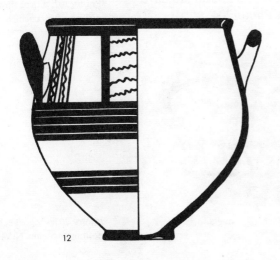

Imported Mycenaean Vessels and Their Local Imitations (Plate 57).

Selected specimens of the Mycenaean repertoire found in Palestine are shown on Plate 57, together with their local imitations. All the imported Mycenaean vessels used as models for the local potters were wheel-made and of excellent workmanship. Therefore, unlike the case of imported Cypriot wares, the differences between local and Mycenaean wares mainly reflect different standards of workmanship. Canaanite potters never reached the high technical level of their Mycenaean counterparts, either in the preparation of the clay or in making, finishing, and painting the vessels. Since Mycenaean pottery as such is outside the scope of this book, we shall not attempt any evaluation from the artistic point of view. Plate 57, like the preceding one, is arranged in groups, with the Mycenaean prototype placed to the left at the head of each group.

The Pyxis: The Canaanite potters were especially attracted to the pyxis (Photos 199 and 200) and copied it so frequently that it almost turned into part of the native ceramic repertoire, just as they preferred the bilbil to all other Cypriot imported wares as a model. The pyxis continued to be made throughout the Late Bronze Age and most of the Iron Age, until it finally disappeared in Iron II C.

Several types of local imitations of the imported pyxis (No. 1) are shown in Nos. 2–7, but there are a number of other variants, which have not been drawn here. Of special interest are Nos. 4 and 5, which have a waist, and the large pyxis shown in No. 7, which appears to be the prototype for the Iron I type. Nos. 4–6 have taken over the metopic decoration of the period.

Piriform Amphoriskos: No. 8 and Photo 201 are imported, while No. 9 and Photo 202 are local imitations, of which there are several additional variants. Photo 161 shows one of these variants, already fairly different in shape from the prototype and decorated with metopes in the fashion of the period.

Stirrup Jar: No. 10 is the prototype and No. 11 the imitation. This oddly shaped vessel whose name has now been read in Linear B inscriptions, was copied only infrequently (cf. also Plate 88 and discussion of Philistine pottery).

Krater: Nos. 12 and 13. The Mycenaean provenience of No. 12 is doubtful.

Mug: The Mycenaean cup (Photo 186 — Photo 203) also appears to have served as a model for local imitations, such as in Photo 204.

Photo 199. Mycenaean pyxis, Beth-shemesh, I.43.

Photo 200. Local imitation of Mycenaean pyxis, Lachish, IDA 37.819.

Photo 201. Mycenaean piriform jar, Ajjul, IDA 33.1463.

Photo 202. Local imitation of Mycenaean piriform jar, Lachish, IDA 35.2983.

Photo 203. Mycenaean mug, Beth-shemesh, IDA 33. 1853.

Photo 204. Mug, Megiddo, *Meg. T.,* Pl. 139.

Photo 207. Jug, Thebes (Egypt), Metro-politan Museum N.Y. No. 35.3.98.

Photo 205. Jar, Thebes (Egypt), Metropolitan Museum N.Y. No. 36.3.161.

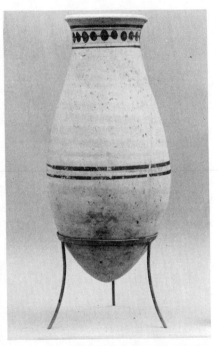

Photo 206. Jar, Thebes (Egypt), Metropolitan Museum N.Y. No. 36.3.164.

Imported Egyptian Wares (Plate 58).

We have grouped in this plate a number of examples of Egyptian vessels imported into Palestine in the Late Bronze Age. Together with Plate 43, this plate illustrates the flow of trade between Canaan and Egypt.

The vessels have not been arranged according to the three phases of the Late Bronze Age, because some (Nos. 2, 3 and 8) are of uncertain stratigraphic provenience, while those which come from tomb-groups (Nos. 4, 5 and 7) cannot be precisely dated. Five of the eight vessels shown (Nos. 1–4 and 7) are definitely Egyptian types, thoroughly at home in the native Egyptian ceramic tradition. Both are handleless and have an elongated rounded base; two are drop-shaped (Nos. 1 and 7), and one (No. 4) date-shaped. The vessels from Thebes in Egypt (Photos 205 and 206) are shown here for purposes of comparison.

Nos. 5 and 6 are pyxides whose shape appears to be influenced by Aegean types, while their decoration approaches the Canaanite style. No. 8 and Photo 207 are particularly interesting: they represent a vessel imported into Palestine from Egypt, which in its turn, goes back to a Canaanite prototype of a much earlier age (Plates 47:8 and 48:3). The development of the amphoriskos (Plate 83) follows similar lines.

We have not illustrated here the profusely decorated and colourful Egyptian pottery of the Amarna period, of which a few fragments have been found in Palestine — for instance, in a pit at Tell el-Ajjul.[35] The decoration consists of leaf patterns, mainly lotus leaves, painted in bright colours, among which blue predominates, followed by red, white, black and even yellow. Guy[36] may have been right in attributing the rarity of this Egyptian pottery in Palestine to the inferior quality of the paints used, which deteriorated under local climatic conditions, and was therefore not in great demand locally. A similar view has been taken by Nagel.[37]

Egyptian imported pottery is found in Palestine in quantities which, although much smaller than those of Aegean or Cypriot origin, are more considerable than is usually thought. However, due to the nature of Egyptian pottery (see below), imports from Egypt do not stand out from Palestinian pottery as a whole. Plate 58 presents a picture of ceramic relations which lends itself to several interpretations. However, any attempt to draw conclusions concerning political and cultural relations between Palestine and Egypt in the Late Bronze Age from the quantity of Egyptian pottery of that period found in Palestine would be misleading. The presence of considerable quantities of pottery imported from a certain country is not necessarily a measure of the political relations with that country. Inversely, political relations, such as the fact that Canaan formed part of the Egyptian Empire, need not be reflected in the ceramic material. In other words, we should not expect to find a strong flow of pottery imports from the ruling country to that of the ruled. We have stressed pottery imports, because trade in pottery is dependent not only on the thriving pottery production of the exporting country, but to a great extent (see above, Plate 43) on other goods

---

35. *AG*, III, pl. LIV:77.
36. *Megiddo Tombs*, p. 155.
37. O. Nagel, *La ceramique du Nouvel Empire à Deir el-Medineh*, Le Caire, 1938, p. ix.

PLATE | 58

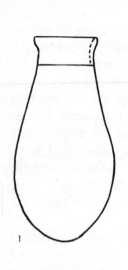

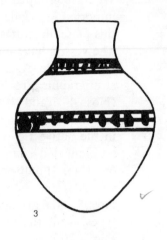
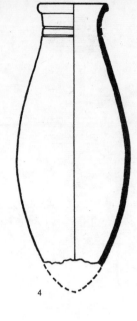

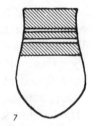

PLATE 58

1.	Drop-shaped vessel, coarse buff	1:5	Lachish	Temple I	La. II, pl. LIV:335
2.	Jar-bottle	1:6	Ajjul	TCP 870	AG IV, pl. LII:41 E 5
3.	Jar	1:6	Ajjul	Pl. 960	AG II, pl. XXXI:41 E 3
4.	Date-shaped vessel, brown	1:5	Megiddo	T. 26	Meg. T., pl. 57:9
5.	Pyxis-shaped vessel, burnt umber, white-yellow horizontally burnished slip, sepia decoration	1:5	Megiddo	T. 38 B	Meg. T., pl. 41:17
6.	Pyxis-shaped vessel	1:6	Ajjul	Palace IV	AG II, pl. XXX:32 A 9
7.	Drop-shaped vessel	1:6	Ajjul	T. 1166	AG II, pl. XXXV:75 N 6
8.	Jug	1:6	Ajjul		AG I, pl. XLIV:34 E 2

PLATE 59

1.	Lamp, buff, traces of burning	1:5	Megiddo	XIV	Meg. II, pl. 15:22
2.	Lamp, buff, traces of burning	1:5	Megiddo	XIV	Meg. II, pl. 15:21
3.	Lamp, buff, traces of burning	1:5	Megiddo	XIII B	Meg. II, pl. 16:20
4.	Lamp, buff, string-cut base	1:5	Megiddo	XIII A	Meg. II, pl. 19:18
5.	Lamp, buff, pink-red slip inside, traces of burning	1:5	Megiddo	X	Meg. II, pl. 47:4
6.	Lamp, pink-buff, traces of burning	1:5	Megiddo	XI (T.3085)	Meg. II, pl. 38:22
7.	Lamp, buff, traces of burning	1:5	Megiddo	X (T.3070)	Meg. II, pl. 47:1
8.	Lamp	1:5	Beth Mirsim	D	TBM IA, pl. 15:18
9.	Lamp	1:5	Beth Mirsim	D	TBM IA, pl. 15:20
10.	Lamp, pink	1:5	Lachish	Temple I	La. pl. XLV:188
11.	Lamp, pink-buff	1:5	Megiddo	IX (T.3018 C)	Meg. II, pl. 55:1
12.	Lamp, orange-buff, traces of burning	1:5	Megiddo	VIII (T.3014)	Meg. II, pl. 62:52
13.	Lamp, brown	1:5	Lachish	Temple II	La. II, pl. XLV:1 094
14.	Lamp, buff, traces of burning	1:5	Megiddo	VIII	Meg. II, pl. 62:4
15.	Lamp, buff, traces of burning	1:5	Megiddo	VIII	Meg. II, pl. 62:4
16.	Lamp, pink-buff, traces of burning	1:5	Megiddo	VIII (T.3015)	Meg. II, pl. 62:3
17.	Lamp, pink	1:5	Lachish	Temple III	La. II, pl. XLV:204
18.	Lamp, pink	1:5	Lachish	Temple III	La. II, pl. XLV:203
19.	Lamp, buff, traces of burning	1:5	Megiddo	VII B	Meg. II, pl. 66:10
20.	Lamp, brown, string-cut base	1:5	Abu Hawam	V A	TAH, p. 45:279

PLATE | 59

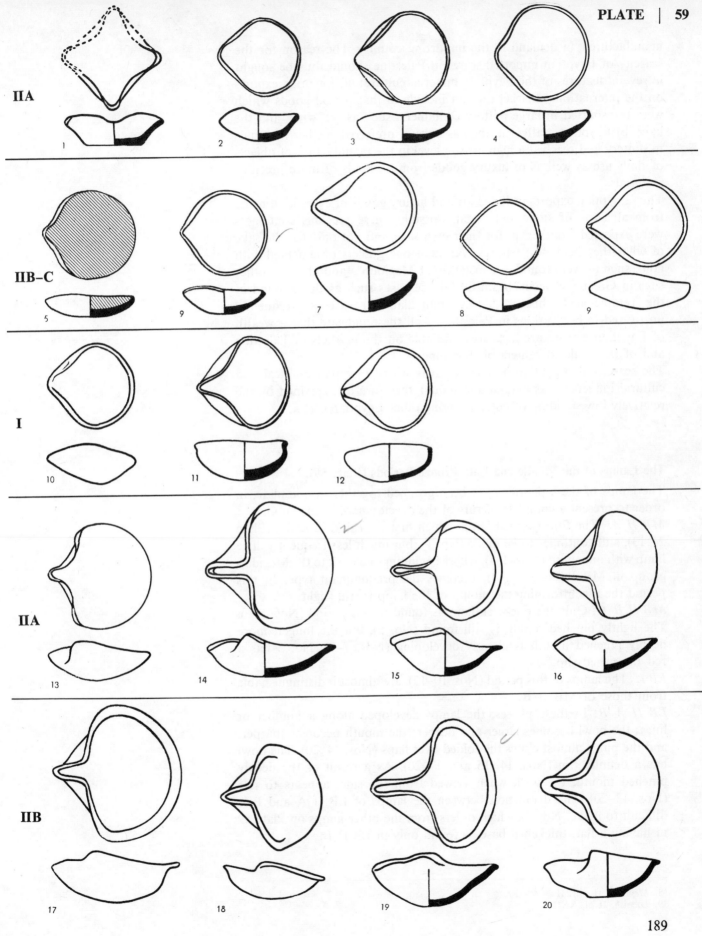

manufactured, in demand in the importing country. The reason for the scarcity of Egyptian imported wares in Palestine should thus be sought in several features of the Egyptian material culture: a) Egyptian exports on the international market did not include in that period goods which were transported in large pottery containers, such as oil, wine, and the like; b) Egyptian craftsmen, then as always, preferred costlier materials to pottery and reached a high artistic level in the manufacture of objects of daily use as well as of luxury goods from all kinds of more precious materials.

Thus Egyptian exports included art and luxury goods of every kind made from all sorts of stone and metal. Possibly, these precious containers were exported from Egypt for their own sake and not only for the sake of what they held: toilet boxes, various stone goblets ornamented with gold, such as were found, for instance, at Megiddo[38] and at many other sites in Greater Canaan, beautiful faience vases such as those found in the Temple at Lachish,[39] the Egyptian alabaster vases so frequently uncovered in excavations in Palestine — all these indicate that a wealth of Egyptian artistic products was available on the markets of Palestine and of the civilized centers of that time.

The scarcity of Egyptian pottery in areas where Egyptian political and cultural influence was paramount should therefore be explained by the relatively low standing of pottery among other Egyptian crafts.

The Lamps of the Middle and Late Bronze Periods (Plate 59).

The lamps of these periods have been grouped together in one plate, in order to present a complete picture of the development of the lamp.

MB II A: The four-spouted lamp, which first appeared in MB I (Plate 24:13), still continues to be made (No. 1), but much less frequently. The lamp with one spout (Nos. 2–4), whose beginnings go back to the Megiddo group in MB I (Plate 24:14), becomes the predominant type. In this period the pinch forming the mouth of the lamp is still slight.

MB II B–C: Only the one-wick lamp is found in this period (Nos. 5–9). The lightly pinched mouth is still found (No. 5), but the longer, more deeply pinched mouth is already developing (Nos. 7–9). No. 5 has a red burnished slip.

LB I: The lamps of this period (Nos. 10–12), are almost indistinguishable from those of MB II B.

LB II A–B: In these phases, the lamps developed along a number of lines: the bowl becomes larger and deeper; the mouth becomes sharper, and the pinch almost closes the folded-over flaps (Nos. 14–20). The bowl has a definite rim (Nos. 14, 15 and 17–20). As a result of the deeply pinched mouth, the wall, when viewed from the side, appears to rise (Nos. 13–20). The distinction between the lamps of LB II A and B is difficult to make. No. 20, which differs from the other lamps on Plate 59 in having a flat, thickened base, is found only in LB II B.

---

38. *Megiddo*, II pl. 231.
39. *Lachish*, II pl. XXII.

CHAPTER ELEVEN

THE IRON I, IRON II A–B, AND IRON II C PERIODS

We follow here the chronological system according to which the development of the Iron Age culture is subdivided into three main periods.[1] This system is based on the conception that there are two main 'shifts' from phase to phase in the cultural history of the country during this long period: the first around 1000 B.C., with the consolidation of the Kingdom, and the second around 800 B.C., with the dwindling of Phoenician influence and the strengthening of Assyrian influence and intervention. The following comparative Chronological Table. showing various systems, is self-explanatory:

Dates	Aharoni-Amiran	Albright-Wright	Encyclopedia of Excavations
1200–1150	I A	I	I A
1150–1000	I B		I B
1000–918/900	I C	II	II A
900–800	II A		II B
800–587	II B	III	II C

To gather material for the plates of this, as of the other chapters of this book, we have worked through all the published excavation reports. We found an almost insurmountable difficulty in finding stratigraphically reliable material typical for the South in Iron II A–B (10th–9th centuries). Assuming that this is not an inherent difficulty, we may take it as a directive for planning future excavations and investigations.

In the arrangement of the material of these periods, we were also guided by the assumption that differences exist between the pottery cultures of the North and the South, that is, of Israel and Judah. Albright,[2] Wampler,[3] and others have already pointed out some distinguishing features of the pottery of the two kindgoms. The relatively recently excavated material from Hazor[4] indeed provides evidence for this regional difference, within the broader cultural-political unity. Thus the following Type-Plates are arranged both according to the 'tripartite' division of the long Israelite period, and according to the regional division into Israel and Judah.

In the discussion pertaining to the transition from the Early Bronze period to the Middle Bronze, we have emphasized the sharp cultural break between these two worlds. From the MB I onwards, the development of the material culture (to judge by its reflection in the pottery) is continuous, gradual, and evolutionary to the end of the Iron Age, or even later. This continuity does not, however, stand in any conflict with the distinctive changes taking place from period to period, and characterizing

---

1. This system has recently been worked out by the editorial committee of the *Encyclopaedia of Excavations* (Jerusalem, Israel), to be published shortly. A similar system has been suggested by Y. Aharoni and Ruth Amiran, *IEJ*, 8 (1958).
2. *TBM*, I, pp. 82–3.
3. *TN*, II, p. 21.
4. All three authors of this book have participated in the excavations of Hazor.

every new trend and new influence, brought about either by ethnic influx, by political changes, or by commercial intercourse. The continuity between the Canaanite pottery culture of the Late Bronze and the Iron Age pottery culture, including both Israelite and other pottery, is clearly apparent in each of the Plates from Nos. 60 to 101. Almost every pottery type can be traced back to its origins in the Bronze Age. On the other hand, the profound changes brought about in Canaan by the settlement of the Israelite tribes are easily discernible in various material phenomena, first and foremost in the pottery. There is no doubt that the pottery of the 12th–11th centuries (Iron I), although the Canaanite legacy is well in evidence, is already a different entity, which will develop gradually into a new set of ceramic ideas in the following phase.

Both technically and aesthetically, the pottery of the Iron Age is of manifold interest. Technically, great progress in wheel-work and in firing must have taken place. The abundance of types and of variants within each type is perhaps the most conspicuous feature of the period. Aesthetically, such highlights of form, manufacture, finish, and decoration as the Samaria bowl or the water-decanter should be considered as evidence of the high standard of the potter's art. The Israelite period shows a predilection for angular pottery shapes instead of the rounded outlines favoured in the Canaanite period. In the finish and decoration of the exterior, there is a new approach: little use is made of painted decoration, and only some faint echoes remain of the painting styles of the Late Bronze. Instead, the entire surface of the vessel or a good part of it is covered with slip, mainly red, but also yellow, black, or brown, which is expertly burnished to a high lustre.

Many of these developments are due to contacts with neighboring cultures, which served as catalysts fertilizing the local culture. Relations with Phoenicia (apparently of more than mere commercial nature); with Cyprus (probably of commercial character); with the Aramean Kingdoms and with Assyria to the north, and with Egypt to the south — all these are reflected in the pottery collected in the Plates. Egypt is an exception, since the material interrelations with that country are reflected in materials other than pottery.

Bowls: Iron I — North and South (Plates 60—61).

North (Plate 60): Generally speaking, the bowls on Plate 60 are of coarse workmanship, with thick walls and little ornamentation. Three main types can be dinstinguished: 1) large, carinated bowls (Nos. 1–5); 2) small, slightly carinated bowls (Nos. 6 and 7); 3) rounded bowls, which are often decorated (Nos. 8–15).

1) A characteristic feature of the carination is the 'canal' formed just below the rim; this canal can be either deep or shallow. The base is generally a shallow or even flattened ring-base. These bowls are usually plain. We have encountered this type of bowl in LB II B (Plate 39:18) and even in LB II A (Plate 39:14).

2) A similar, though slighter, carination characterizes the small bowls.

3) The rounded bowls have rounded or flattened bases, and sometimes even shallow ring-bases. They have been grouped together here because of their decoration, which consists of painted bands or groups of bands, generally of one color. Of particular interest is No. 15, whose ornamenta-

192

PLATE | 60

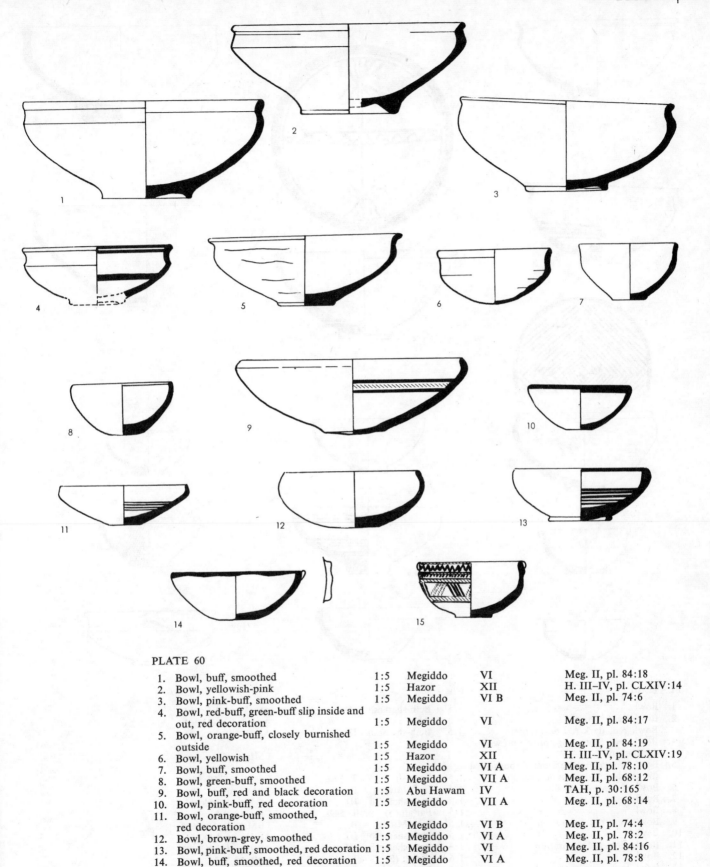

PLATE 60

1.	Bowl, buff, smoothed	1:5	Megiddo	VI	Meg. II, pl. 84:18
2.	Bowl, yellowish-pink	1:5	Hazor	XII	H. III–IV, pl. CLXIV:14
3.	Bowl, pink-buff, smoothed	1:5	Megiddo	VI B	Meg. II, pl. 74:6
4.	Bowl, red-buff, green-buff slip inside and out, red decoration	1:5	Megiddo	VI	Meg. II, pl. 84:17
5.	Bowl, orange-buff, closely burnished outside	1:5	Megiddo	VI	Meg. II, pl. 84:19
6.	Bowl, yellowish	1:5	Hazor	XII	H. III–IV, pl. CLXIV:19
7.	Bowl, buff, smoothed	1:5	Megiddo	VI A	Meg. II, pl. 78:10
8.	Bowl, green-buff, smoothed	1:5	Megiddo	VII A	Meg. II, pl. 68:12
9.	Bowl, buff, red and black decoration	1:5	Abu Hawam	IV	TAH, p. 30:165
10.	Bowl, pink-buff, red decoration	1:5	Megiddo	VII A	Meg. II, pl. 68:14
11.	Bowl, orange-buff, smoothed, red decoration	1:5	Megiddo	VI B	Meg. II, pl. 74:4
12.	Bowl, brown-grey, smoothed	1:5	Megiddo	VI A	Meg. II, pl. 78:2
13.	Bowl, pink-buff, smoothed, red decoration	1:5	Megiddo	VI	Meg. II, pl. 84:16
14.	Bowl, buff, smoothed, red decoration	1:5	Megiddo	VI A	Meg. II, pl. 78:8
15.	Bowl, pink-buff, smoothed, red and black decoration	1:5	Megiddo	VI	Meg. II, pl. 85:2

PLATE | 61

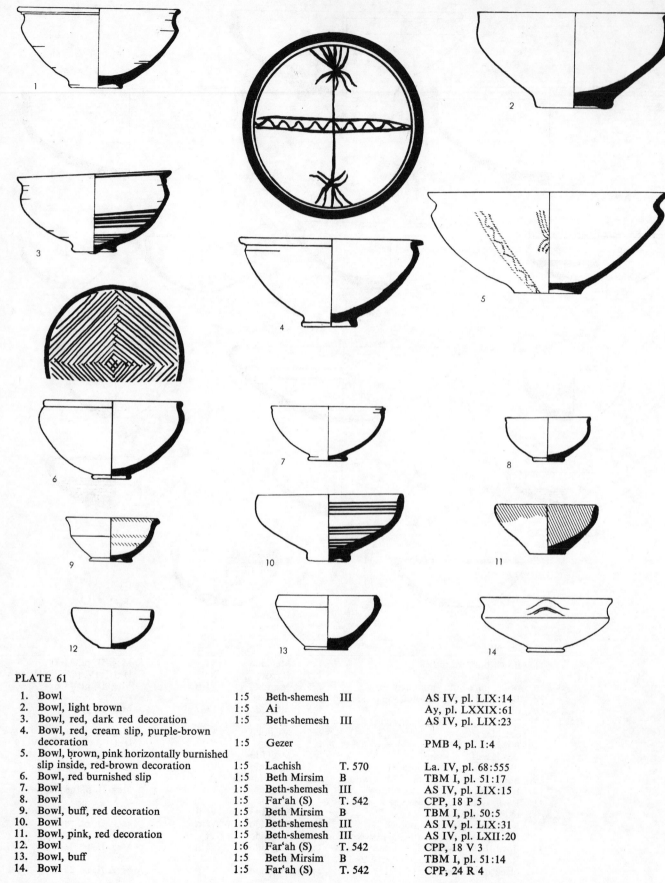

PLATE 61

1.	Bowl	1:5	Beth-shemesh III	AS IV, pl. LIX:14
2.	Bowl, light brown	1:5	Ai	Ay, pl. LXXIX:61
3.	Bowl, red, dark red decoration	1:5	Beth-shemesh III	AS IV, pl. LIX:23
4.	Bowl, red, cream slip, purple-brown decoration	1:5	Gezer	PMB 4, pl. I:4
5.	Bowl, brown, pink horizontally burnished slip inside, red-brown decoration	1:5	Lachish T. 570	La. IV, pl. 68:555
6.	Bowl, red burnished slip	1:5	Beth Mirsim B	TBM I, pl. 51:17
7.	Bowl	1:5	Beth-shemesh III	AS IV, pl. LIX:15
8.	Bowl	1:5	Far'ah (S) T. 542	CPP, 18 P 5
9.	Bowl, buff, red decoration	1:5	Beth-shemesh III	TBM I, pl. 50:5
10.	Bowl	1:5	Beth-shemesh III	AS IV, pl. LIX:31
11.	Bowl, pink, red decoration	1:5	Beth-shemesh III	AS IV, pl. LXII:20
12.	Bowl	1:6	Far'ah (S) T. 542	CPP, 18 V 3
13.	Bowl, buff	1:5	Beth Mirsim B	TBM I, pl. 51:14
14.	Bowl	1:5	Far'ah (S) T. 542	CPP, 24 R 4

tion is more complex. It echoes the LB tradition of the metope style. Nos. 14 and 15 have one small bar-handle on the rim, also a trait encountered in the LB.

Bowls decorated in the Bichrome Style with alternating black and red bands (No. 9) are also found and continue down into Iron II.

In conclusion, several features of these bowls can be described as a legacy of the Late Bronze Age: the carination, the decoration, especially the band filled with triangles, and the small bar-handle.

South (Plate 61): In this period, there is a close similarity between northern and southern types. We find on Plate 61 the carinated bowls (Nos. 1–5), as well as the rounded bowls (Nos. 6–8, 10–12). In addition to the painted bands (No. 10), found also in the North, a complex pattern appears on bowls from the South, which divides the inside of the bowls by radial bands into sectors containing representations of trees (Nos. 4 and 5). Such a metopic division of the inside of the bowl has been discussed above (cf. Plates 38, 39, and 50), and is obviously a survival of a Canaanite element.

The degenerated horizontal handle on Bowl No. 14, found more frequently in the south than in the north, appears to be a survival of the influence of the Philistine krater (see below, Plate 90).

Nos. 9 and 13 are examples of bowls derivated from the Canaanite carinated bowl. No. 6 is irregularly hand-burnished, a decorative style which has its beginnings in this period.

The bowls bearing Philistine designs have been grouped separately (Plate 90).

Bowls: Iron II A—B — North and South (Plate 62—63).

North (Plate 62): In Iron II A–B workmanship improves: the clay is well levigated and fired and the vessels are well finished. The red burnished slip predominates. Especially common is the irregular hand-burnish, but wheel-burnishing is found on bowls and jugs. A number of definite types can be distinguished among the many bowl forms of the period:

1) Carinated bowls: In this period the wall of the bowls is carinated fairly high up, so that the part above the carination is relatively short. The carination is either slight, almost approaching a rounded outline (Nos. 1–5), or sharper (Nos. 6 and 7). The sharply carinated bowls usually have a rim no thicker than the wall, and low ring- or disc-bases.

2) Straight-sided bowls: Four variants of this not very common bowl have been shown (Nos. 8–11), from Megiddo, Samaria, and Hazor. The two bowls from Samaria have a high ring-base, which recalls the 'Samaria ware.' No. 8 is a forerunner of the straight-sided bowl which will predominate, with slight variations, in the following period. No. 11 combines features of the straight-sided and the carinated types.

3) Rounded bowls: This is one of the commonest forms, which can be subdivided into three main types: a) shallow bowls with a low ring-base (Nos. 12, 13, and 16, Photo 208); b) round-bottomed-bowls (Nos. 14 and 15); c) small, deep bowls with a small flat base (Nos. 17 and 18). In this period, the slip is usually applied to the entire vessel, but a painted band on the rim is also found.

Photo 208. Bowl, Hazor, *Hazor*, II, Pl. CLIII.

195

PLATE 62

1.	Bowl, pink	1:5	Hazor	VIII	H. II, pl. LIII:14
2.	Bowl, pink, yellow burnished slip inside and out	1:5	Hazor	VIII	H. II, pl. LV:38
3.	Bowl, grey-buff, red slip	1:5	Hazor	X	H. II, pl. LI:1
4.	Bowl, pink	1:5	Hazor	VIII	H. II, pl. LIII:17
5.	Bowl, brown-red	1:5	Abu Hawam	III	TAH, p. 21:75
6.	Bowl, pink, burnished	1:5	Hazor	VIII	H. II, pl. LIII:8
7.	Bowl, brown	1:5	Hazor	IX	H. II, pl. LII:1
8.	Bowl, pink, brown decoration	1:5	Hazor	VIII	H. II, pl. LIII:32
9.	Bowl, pink	1:5	Samaria	III	SS III, Fig. 4:14
10.	Bowl, red	1:5	Samaria	III	SS III, Fig. 4:15
11.	Bowl, brown, brown horizontally burnished slip	1:5	Hazor	VIII	H. II, pl. LIII:30
12.	Bowl, pink, yellowish slip	1:5	Hazor	IX	H. III–IV, pl. CCVIII:18
13.	Bowl, light brown	1:5	Hazor	IX	H. III–IV, pl. CCVIII:22
14.	Bowl, pink	1:5	Hazor	IX	H. III1IV, pl. CCVIII:11
15.	Bowl, brown, greyish slip	1:5	Hazor	IX	H. III–IV, pl. CCVIII:5
16.	Bowl, brown, red hand-burnished slip	1:5	Hazor	VIII ?	H. II, pl. XCIII:15
17.	Bowl, pink, red slip	1:5	Hazor	VIII	H. II, pl. LIII:22
18.	Bowl, pink, red burnished slip	1:5	Hazor	X	H. II, pl. LI:3
19.	Bowl, yellow, red and black decoration	1:5	Hazor	IX	H. III–IV, pl. CCVIII:29
20.	Bowl, brown, red and black decoration	1 5	Hazor	IX–X	H. III–IV, pl. CLXXVII:11
21.	Bowl, red-buff, red and black decoration	1:5	Abu Hawam	IV	TAH, p. 29:153
22.	Bowl, pink, brown burnished slip	1:5	Hazor	VIII	H. II, pl. LIV:9
23.	Bowl, grey-buff	1:5	Hazor	VIII	H. II, pl. LIII:24
24.	Bowl, pink	1:5	Hazor	VIII	H. II, pl. LIII:12
25.	Bowl, pink, red slip	1:5	Hazor	VIII	H. II, pl. LIV:25
26.	Bowl, pink, brown slip	1:5	Hazor	VIII	H. II, pl. LIV:24
27.	Bowl, brown	1:5	Hazor	VIII	H. II, pl. LIV:22
28.	Bowl, burnt umber	1:5	Megiddo	V	Meg. I, pl. 31:146

PLATE | 62

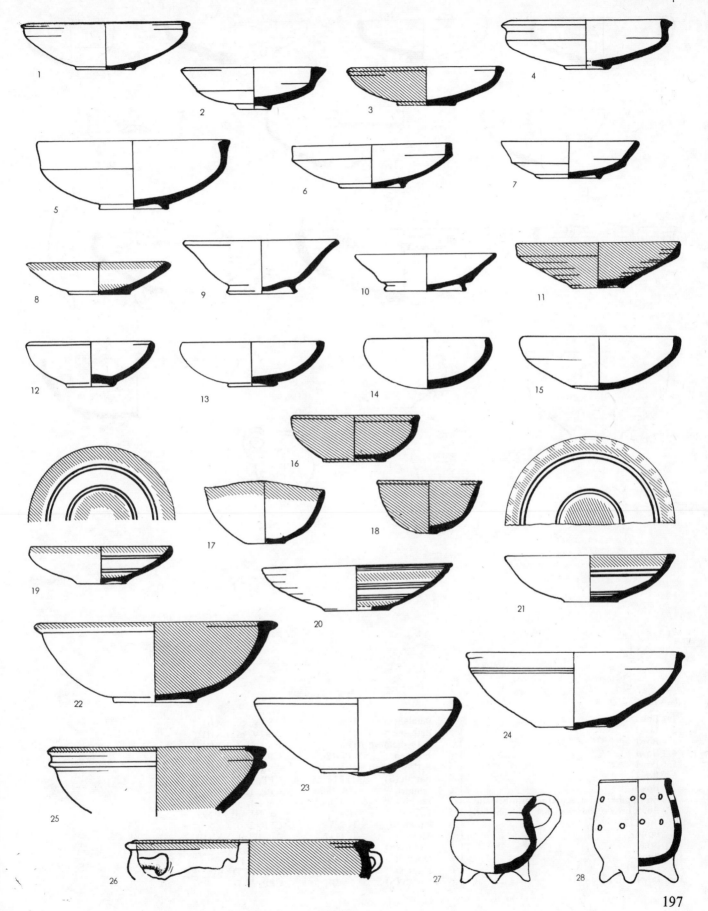

PLATE | 63

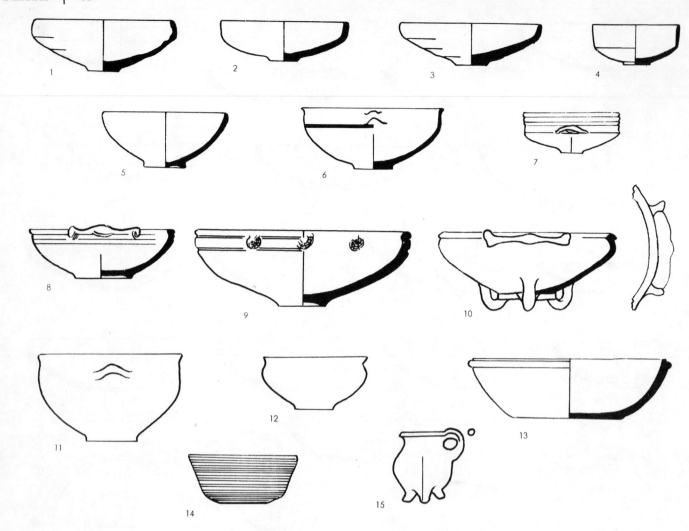

Photo 209. Bowl, Megiddo, IDA 36.1953.

Some of the rounded bowls are decorated with alternating black and red painted concentric rings applied without slip and filling the entire inner surface of the bowl (Nos. 19–21). This bichrome style appeared in the preceding period on bowls (Plate 60:9) as well as on globular jugs.

4) Deep bowls: The three deep bowls shown (Nos. 22–24) demonstrate that the main difference between types is found in the rim. The first bowl has a projecting ledge-rim, the second a sharp, slightly inverted rim, and the third a slightly thickened rim. These large bowls resemble in outline the small rounded bowls. In Iron II, these deep bowls are not common, while in Iron II C they are one of the commonest bowl-forms.

5) Bowls with bar-handles or a ridge below the rim: Nos. 25 and 26, Photo 209. The bar-handle appears in this period in the form later found in Iron II C.

6) Bowls on three stump legs: The bowl or one-handled cup, usually with three stump legs, begins to appear in this period both in the North and in the South (Nos. 27 and 28, Plate 63:15), and is mainly popular in Iron II C. Sometimes the body of the vessel is perforated like a sieve.

South (Plate 63): Three main groups can be distinguished on this plate, as well as a number of forms which are difficult to classify: a) rounded-carinated bowls; b) bowls with degenerated horizontal handles; c) bowls with bar-handles. Albright, in his analysis of the excavations of Tell Beth Mirsim, defined a very important feature of Iron II pottery, especially of southern wares: the hand-burnished, often also termed "irregularly burnished' slip. Usually this is applied only on the inside, but sometimes also on the upper part of the outside of the bowls, as well as on kraters and storage jars. Photo 210 shows the inside of a bowl, with the irregular burnishing lines clearly visible. Photo 211 shows a bowl burnished partly by hand, partly on the wheel.

1) Nos. 1–5 are bowls which are difficult to classify as either carinated or rounded. The angle in those specimens which do have a carination is always obtuse. These generally have a small ring-base.

2) The bowl with two small horizontal degenerated handles is one of the commonest types (Nos. 6, 7 and 11), and is probably a debased derivation from the Philistine two-handled krater (Plate 90:1–4). The upper part of these bowls is often grooved. No. 12 is similar in form, but has no handles.

Photo 210. Bowl, Safi, Dayan Collection.

Photo 211. Bowl, Ruqeish, IDA 40.515.

3) The bowls with bar-handles form a distinct group (Nos. 8–10). Here, too, the upper part is often grooved. Of special interest is No. 10, which stands on three loop-handles. This feature, which is found as far back as the Middle Bronze Age, recurs in the Iron Age. Bowl No. 9, from Lachish, has three knobs, which appear to be the last vestiges of a bar-handle (cf. also Photo 212). However, since the material from levels V–VI at Lachish is scanty, and not enough is known about it, the attribution of this bowl to Iron II is not certain.

No. 13 has a marked ridge immediately below the rim. It bears a family resemblance to the bowls with bar-handles. No. 14 is grooved all over, including the base (Photo 213). Only a few such bowls have been found (one at Tell en-Nasbeh[5] and another at Samaria[6]). The same grooving technique occurs also on pilgrim-flasks of a certain type (Plates 94:8; 95:16). A bottle from Tell en-Nasbeh, whose lower part is grooved in a similar fashion, and which is dated to Iron II C,[7] should also be mentioned. This technique begins in Iron II A.

No. 15 is a cup from Tell el-Far'ah (S). Although the publication does not give the number of the tomb in which it was found, it appears to belong to Iron II A. The cup has three stump feet, a feature we have already noted in the northern wares.

Photo 212. Bowl, Far'ah(S), IDA I.7005.

Photo 213. Bowl, Jemmeh, IDA B.710.

Bowls: Iron II C — North and South (Plates 64—65).

North (Plate 64): The bowls of Iron II C are a direct continuation of Iron II A–B forms, and the same types can be distinguished. The carinated bowl becomes one of the commonest vessels of the period, while the straight-sided bowl and the shallow bowl (platter), of which the first specimens appeared in Iron II A–B, are also frequently found. The rounded bowl, which was so common in Iron II A–B, appears in new variants, but its popularity is on the wane, and its place seems to be taken by the large, deep bowls.

Generally speaking, the Iron II C bowls — large or small — are decorated in one of three ways: a) overall red burnished slip inside and outside; b) red burnished slip only on the inside; c) painted red band on the rim.

1) Carinated bowls: In Iron II C, the carination occurs lower down on the wall of the bowl than in the preceding period, and the vessel is rather more flared above the carination (Nos. 1–5). No. 5 has a profiled rim and a shallow disc-base, sometimes more like a ring-base.

2) Straight-sided bowls: The five specimens shown here (Nos. 6–11) differ from each other mainly in the rims, which are often more everted than the bowl-walls. The bases are flat or sometimes concave and are often string-cut (Photo 214).

3) Rounded bowls: We have already mentioned the decrease of the rounded bowls of the preceding period. Two forms of the rounded bowl are shown on Plate 64:12, a shallow bowl with rounded walls, which continues the tradition of the Iron II A–B rounded bowls; and No. 13,

Photo 214. Bowl, Hazor, *Hazor*, I, Pl. CXLVII.

5. *TN*, II, pl. 54:1204.
6. *SS*, III, fig. 26:8.
7. *TN*, II pl. 27:440.

a thin-walled hemispherical bowl. Some variants of the bowl have a small flat base, others are thin-walled without either slip or burnish, or are painted on the rim only. This type of bowl resembles a certain kind of thin Samarian bowl, as far as its fine ware and form are concerned, but there are differences in the finish, and it is difficult to determine whether it really belongs in the Samarian bowl class.

The medium-sized bowls in Nos. 14–18 are difficult to classify. In size, they are close to the large, deep bowls, while in form they stand between the carinated and rounded bowls on the one hand and the deep bowls on the other. However, the moulding of the rim assigns this type to the deep bowls.

4) Deep Bowls: The large, deep bowls (Nos. 19–25) are common in Iron II C. Their walls are generally rounded, and sometimes a very slight carination is noticeable. The most characteristic feature is the rim, which is thickened in a number of ways: a) a flat rim thickening outwards (Nos. 14, 18 and 21); b) a rim sloping inwards and thickened on the outside (No. 20); c) a rim sloping outwards and thickened on the outside, which is often grooved (Nos. 22–24); d) a turned-over rim (Nos. 15, 17 and 19). This turned-over rim is highly characteristic of bowls and kraters of various sizes made in southern Palestine in Iron II C (see below, Plate 65). The fact that bowls with such rims found in the North are often wheel-burnished in a fashion common in the South, may perhaps indicate that these bowls were imported from the South.

5) Bar-handled and ridged-rim bowls: (Nos. 25–28, Photos 215–217). The bar-handle of Iron II C, unlike that of the Late Bronze Age, has become a merely ornamental feature. Usually two such handles are found which almost encircle the bowl. Sometimes these handles resemble an uninterrupted ridge below the rim. Further study of imitations in pottery of metal vessels is required to answer the question whether the Iron Age bar-handle is a development of the small bar-handle of the Late Bronze Age.

6) Bowls on three stump legs: This form (No. 29) is found also in Iron II C, in the North as well as in the South (cf. Plate 65:21). The vessel is often perforated to serve as a sieve. However, it is less common in Palestine than in Transjordan in the same period (see below, Plate 101 and discussion).

Photo 215. Bowl, Hazor, *Hazor*, II, Pl. CLV.

Photo 216. Bowl, Megiddo, IDA 36.968.

Photo 217. Bowl, Hazor, *Hazor*, III-IV, Pl. CCCXLIX.

PLATE 64

1.	Bowl, grey	1:5	Hazor	V A	H. II, pl. LXXX:23
2.	Bowl, light brown, red slip	1:5	Hazor	IV	H. II, pl. XCVIII:5
3.	Bowl, brown, red decoration	1:5	Hazor	V A	H. II, pl. LXXX:4
4.	Bowl, light brown, red slip	1:5	Hazor	IV	H. II, pl. XCVIII:4
5.	Bowl, light brown, red decoration	1:5	Hazor	V B	H. II, pl. LXXIX:3
6.	Bowl, grey-buff	1:5	Hazor	V B	H. II, pl. LXXIX:12
7.	Bowl, pink, red decoration	1:5	Hazor	V A	H. II, pl. CVII:1
8.	Bowl, light brown	1:5	Hazor	V A	H. II, pl. LXXXI:11
9.	Bowl, light brown, red decoration	1:5	Hazor	V A	H. II, pl. LXXXI:1
10.	Bowl, grey, red decoration	1:5	Hazor	V A	H. II, pl. LXXXI:9
11.	Bowl, grey-buff, red decoration	1:5	Hazor	VII	H. II, pl. LXIII:11
12.	Bowl, yellowish, red burnished slip	1:5	Hazor	VI	H. III–IV, pl. CCXIX:3
13.	Bowl, pink, brown burnished slip	1:5	Hazor	VI	H. II, pl. LXVII:3
14.	Bowl, grey-buff, red decoration	1:5	Hazor	IV	H. II, pl. XCVIII:24
15.	Bowl, brown, red slip	1:5	Hazor	V B	H. II, pl. LXXIX:6
16.	Bowl, brown-buff, red decoration	1:5	Hazor	V A	H. II, pl. LXXXI:25
17.	Bowl, light brown, red decoration	1:5	Hazor	V	H. II, pl. LXXXI:19
18.	Bowl, grey-buff, brown slip	1:5	Hazor	VI	H. II, pl. LXVI:8
19.	Bowl, grey, red decoration	1:5	Hazor	V	H. I, pl. LIV:1
20.	Bowl, brown, red decoration	1:5	Hazor	V B	H. II, pl. LXXIX:7
21.	Bowl, pink	1:5	Hazor	VI	H. II, pl. LXVI:20
22.	Bowl, pink, brown slip	1:5	Hazor	VI	H. II, pl. LXVI:26
23.	Bowl, grey-buff, red decoration	1:5	Hazor	V A	H. II, pl. XCIII:5
24.	Bowl, grey-brown, red decoration	1:5	Hazor	V	H. I, pl. LXXI:13
25.	Bowl, grey-buff, red burnished slip	1:5	Hazor	V A	H. II, pl. LXXXII:2
26.	Bowl, light brown, red slip	1:5	Hazor	IV	H. II, pl. XCVIII:27
27.	Bowl, grey-buff, burnished inside and out	1:5	Hazor	V A	H. IIIIV, pl. CCXXX:2
28.	Bowl, pink, red slip	1:5	Hazor	VI	H. I, pl. LI:21
29.	Bowl, green-brown	1:5	Megiddo	IV–II	Meg. I, pl. 23:22

PLATE | 64

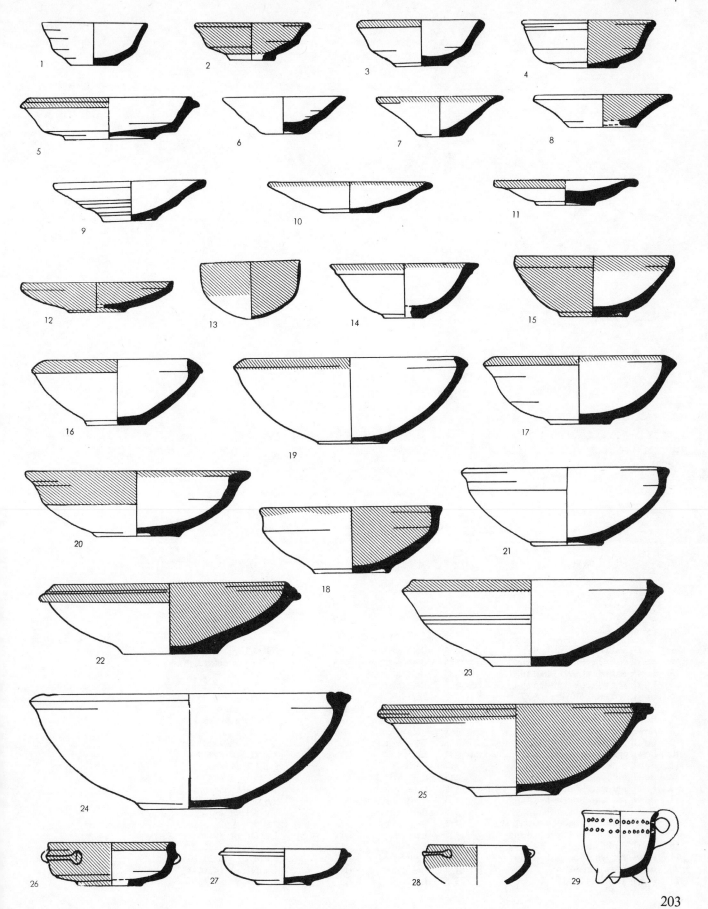

PLATE 65

1.	Bowl, red wheel-burnished slip	1:5	Beth Mirsim	A	TBM I, pl. 51:1
2.	Bowl, red wheel-burnished slip	1:5	Beth Mirsim	A	TBM I, pl. 62:5
3.	Bowl, red wheel-burnished slip	1:5	Beth Mirsim	A	TBM I, pl. 61:2
4.	Bowl, red wheel-burnished slip	1:5	Beth Mirsim	A	TBM I, pl. 64:1
5.	Bowl, brown, buff slip	1:5	Lachish	III	La. III, pl. 80:28
6.	Bowl, dark grey, wheel-burnished	1:5	Beth Mirsim	A	TBM I, pl. 63:2
7.	Bowl, red decoration	1:5	Beth Mirsim	A	TBM III, pl. 26:7
8.	Bowl, dark brown, red slip	1:5	Beth-shemesh	II b	AS IV, pl. LXIII:25
9.	Bowl, red wheel-burnished slip	1:5	Beth Mirsim	A	TBM I, pl. 64:18
10.	Bowl, pink, pink irregularly burnished slip	1:5	Lachish	III	La. III, pl. 81:100
11.	Bowl, pink, red slip	1:5	Lachish	III	La. III, pl. 80:63
12.	Bowl, buff	1:5	Beth Mirsim	A	TBM I, pl. 65:29
13.	Bowl, red wheel-burnished slip	1:5	Beth Mirsim	A	TBM III, pl. 21:5
14.	Bowl, red wheel-burnished slip	1:5	Beth Mirsim	A	TBM III, pl. 21:15
15.	Bowl, red wheel-burnished slip	1:5	Beth Mirsim	A	TBM I, pl. 64:5
16.	Bowl, red-buff wheel-burnished slip	1:5	Beth Mirsim	A	TBM III, pl. 15:13
17.	Bowl, brown, red burnished slip	1:5	Lachish	III	La. III, pl. 80:86
18.	Bowl, pink, smoothed	1:5	Lachish	III	La. III, pl. 81:120
19.	Bowl, red wheel-burnished slip	1:5	Beth Mirsim	A	TBM III, pl. 20:16
20.	Bowl, brown, red slip	1:5	Lachish	III	La. III, pl. 102:651
21.	Bowl, grey, buff slip	1:5	Lachish	III	La. III, pl. 90:380

PLATE | **65**

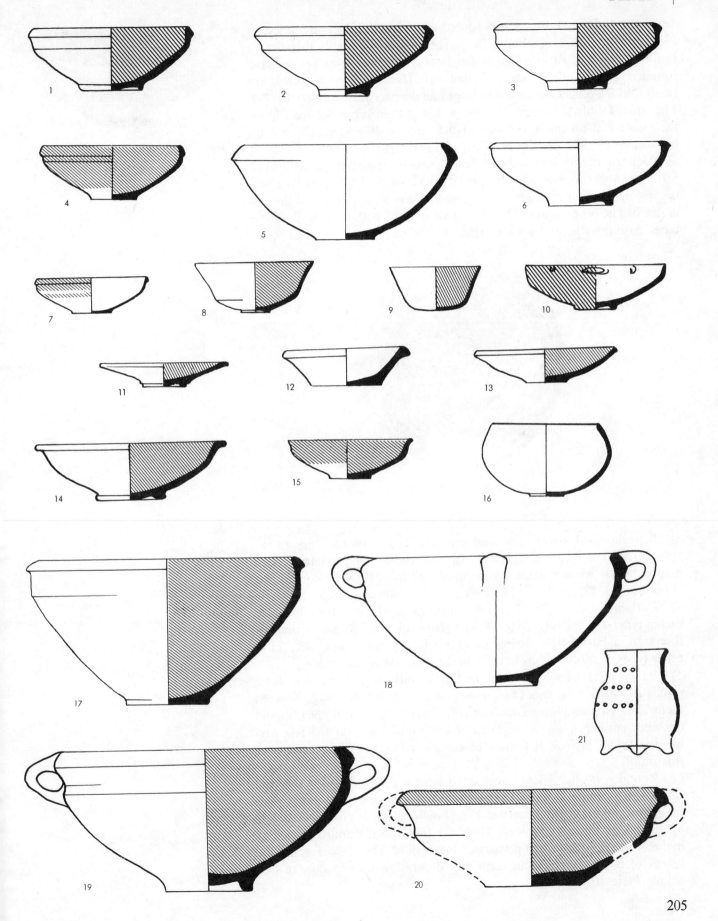

South (Plate 65): 1) Bowls with turned-over rims are the commonest in the South in Iron II C (Photo 218). The predominance of this rim in southern bowls of various shapes and sizes is striking: some vessels have rounded (No. 4), others have carinated walls (Nos. 1–3); some bowls are small (No. 7), others are almost as large and deep as kraters (Nos. 17–20). The entire family is further characterized by a light brownish-red slip on the inside and on the upper part of the outer wall, and regular wheel-burnishing all over the slip on the inside and the rim.

Photo 218. Bowl, Beth Mirsim, IDA I.8956.

2) Delicate flaring bowls: These bowls, which are somewhat conical in form, are also common. One of the variants (No. 8), has a ring base and is carinated not far above the base. The upper part is flaring and the rim is sharp. The other variant (No. 9) is a small bowl with a broad flattened base, flaring walls, and a sharp rim.

Photo 219. Bowl, Lachish, IDA 38.728.

3) Straight-sided bowls: The southern type, which corresponds to the straight-sided bowl common in the North, is shallower, and is characterized mainly by the wheel-burnish on the inside (Photo 219). The commonest variant is No. 12, but bowls like Nos. 11 and 13 are also found.

4) Carinated bowls: Two kinds of carinated bowls have been included under types (1) and (2). A third type (Nos. 14 and 15) has a ring- or disc-base, a fairly slight carination and a flaring rim. These, like most other types of southern bowls, are wheel-burnished on the inside.

5) Bar-handles now appear in the South only in a degenerate form (No. 10), which consists of two knobs with a small isolated ridge between them. The rich and varied material of Stratum A at Tell Beth Mirsim does not contain a single specimen of bar-handle, so that the few bar-handles found in Iron II C may be considered as the last offshoots of this motif.

6) Rounded bowls: These bowls often have walls so rounded that the rim has a holemouth appearance (No. 16). To some extent, that is, as far as size and finish are concerned, these bowls belong to group No. 2.

7) Bowls on three stump legs: These are found in the South as well as in the North, and are often perforated like a sieve. The vessel reaches the height of its development in form and decoration in Transjordan (see below, Plate 101:11).

The Samaria Bowls (Plates 66—77).

The term 'Samaria Bowls' is generally used in archaeological literature, though it still lacks exact definition. Interestingly enough, the publication of the excavations at Samaria itself does not use this term. Here we have included under this heading various types of bowls, which have in common the high level of workmanship, and especially the beautiful slip and burnish.

The bowls can be divided into two groups: thin-walled bowls (Plate 66 and thick bowls (Plate 67). Both groups occur in Iron II A–B and II C.

Plate 66, where the thin bowls are attributed, according to stratigraphical provenience, to Iron II A–B and II C, shows clearly that our present knowledge is insufficient to distinguish any particular features characteristic for each period. Such a differentiation can, however, be made in the thick bowls.

Thin bowls (Plate 66): This group includes several types of rounded and of carinated bowls. The rounded vessels often have a completely rounded bottom (Nos. 4, 6 and 15) or a wide flattened base (No. 14). Various angles are found among the carinations of the bowls: some are softly carinated (Nos. 1, 2, 3 and 5) and others are sharply carinated (Nos. 9, 11, 12, 16 and 17). Sometimes the wall above the carination break is inverted (No. 19).

Photo 220. Bowl, Hazor, *Hazor*, I, Pl. CXLVII.

Photo 221. Bowl, Hazor, *Hazor*, III-IV, Pl. CCCLV.

The bases of the carinated bowls are either rounded (Nos. 16 and 19, Photo 220), flattened (No. 7), or small ring-bases (Nos. 1, 3, 8 and 17, Photo 221).

The workmanship of all the thin bowls is excellent: eggshell-thin, fine, throughly baked ware; thick slip, continuously burnished on the wheel, or, rarely, by hand. The color or color of the slip are very striking: red slip inside and outside, or red and yellow slip alternating in bands, or sometimes, red inside and yellow outside, or vice versa. The red and yellow alternating bands, the commonest, are emphasized by groups of grooves in the red slip, through which shows the native yellow of the clay. Nos. 17 and 18 (Photo 221) are unusual in that they have thin black lines between the red and yellow bands.

207

PLATE 66

1. Bowl, yellowish, red slip, wheel-burnished
   outside and irregularly burnished inside 1:5   Hazor   IX   H. III–IV, pl. CCVIII:26
2. Bowl, yellowish, red slip, wheel-burnished
   outside and irregularly burnished inside 1:5   Hazor   IX   H. III–IV, pl. CCVIII:24
3. Bowl, red, dark brownish-red slip, wheel-
   burnished outside and hand burnished
   inside   1:5   Samaria   III   SS. III, Fig. 4:10
4. Bowl, yellowish, red burnished slip   1:5   Hazor   IX   H. III–IV, pl. CCVIII:25
5. Bowl   1:5   Abu Hawam   III   TAH, Fig. 9
6. Bowl, buff, red burnished slip   1:5   Samaria   III   SS III, Fig. 4:8
7. Bowl, buff, red slip, concentric incised
   circles on the base   1:5   Samaria   SS III, Fig. 19:1
8. Bowl, buff, red burnished slip   1:5   Samaria   SS III, Fig. 19:3
9. Bowl, red, whitish-grey burnished slip   1:5   Hazor   IX   H. III–IV, pl. CCVIII:30
10. Bowl, yellowish-pink, red burnished slip   1:5   Hazor   VII   H. III–IV, pl. CCXIV:16
11. Bowl, pink, brown burnished slip   1:5   Hazor   V   H. I, pl. LIV:7
12. Bowl, reddish-brown   1:5   Samaria   E. 207   SS III, Fig. 18:7
13. Bowl, pink, red burnished slip   1:5   Hazor   VII   H. III–IV, pl. CCXIV:19
14. Bowl, pinkish-brown, red burnished slip   1:5   Hazor   V   H. I, pl. LXVII:24
15. Bowl, red   1:5   Samaria   E. 207   SS III, Fig. 18:5
16. Bowl, pink, red burnished slip   1:5   Hazor   V A   H. III–IV, pl. CCXXX:12
17. Bowl, pink, red burnished slip, red and
    black decoration   1:5   Hazor   VII   H. III–IV, pl. CCXIV:24
18. Bowl, light brown, burnished, red and
    black decoration   1:5   Hazor   V B   H. III–IV, pl. CCXXIII:19
19. Bowl, pink, red burnished slip   1:5   Hazor   V   H. I, pl. LIV:6

PLATE | 66

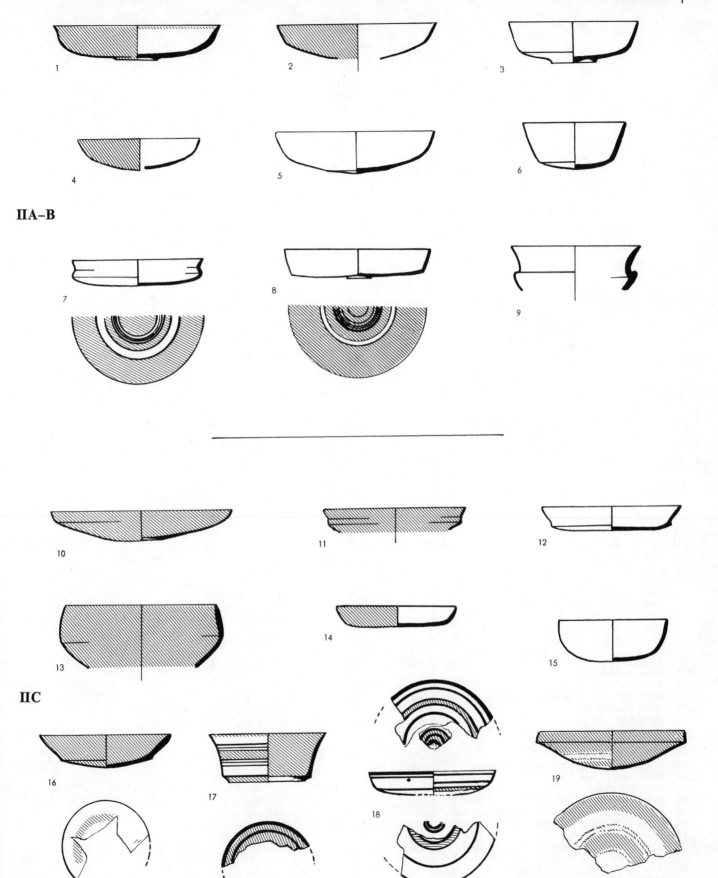

IIA–B

IIC

PLATE 67

1.	Bowl, brown, red wheel-burnished slip	1:5	Hazor	IX–X	H. I, pl. XLV:15
2.	Bowl, brown, red burnished slip	1:5	Hazor	VIII	H. II, pl. LV:22
3.	Bowl, pink, burnished	1:5	Hazor	VIII	H. II, pl. LIII:33
4.	Bowl, pink, red burnished slip, incised decoration	1:5	Hazor	VIII	H. II, pl. LV:21
5.	Bowl, light brown, red wheel-burnished slip	1:5	Hazor	VIII	H. III–IV, pl. CCXIII:25
6.	Bowl, reddish-buff	1:5	Samaria	III	SS III, Fig. 4:8
7.	Bowl, buff, red slip	1:5	Samaria	III	SS III, Fig. 4:13
8.	Bowl, light brown, red burnished slip	1:5	Samaria	III	SS III, Fig. 4:17
9.	Bowl, red, red slip	1:5	Samaria	III	SS III, Fig. 4:16
10.	Bowl, buff, red slip	1:5	Samaria	V–VI	SS III, Fig. 13:12
11.	Bowl, yellow, brown burnished slip	1:5	Hazor	V	H. I, pl. LIV:10
12.	Bowl, pink-brown, red wheel-burnished slip	1:5	Hazor	V A	H. II, pl. LXXXII:6
13.	Bowl, grey-buff, dark brown burnished slip	1:5	Hazor	VII	H. I, pl. XLIX:25
14.	Bowl, light brown, brown-red burnished slip	1:5	Samaria		HU, No. 5348
15.	Bowl, pink, red burnished slip	1:5	Samaria		HU, No. 608
16.	Bowl, light brown, red burnished slip	1:5	Samaria		HU, No. 3522
17.	Bowl, grey, black burnished slip	1:5	Samaria	E. 207	SS III, Fig. 14:13
18.	Bowl, grey, black burnished slip	1:5	Samaria		HU, No. 3274
19.	Bowl, brown-buff, yellowish burnished slip	1:5	Hazor	V A	H. III–IV, pl. CCXXVI:10
20.	Bowl, brown, red slip	1:5	Hazor	V A	H. III–IV, pl. CCXXVI:11
21.	Bowl, pink, buff burnished slip inside and out	1:5	Hazor	VI	H. II, pl. LXVII:8

210

PLATE | 67

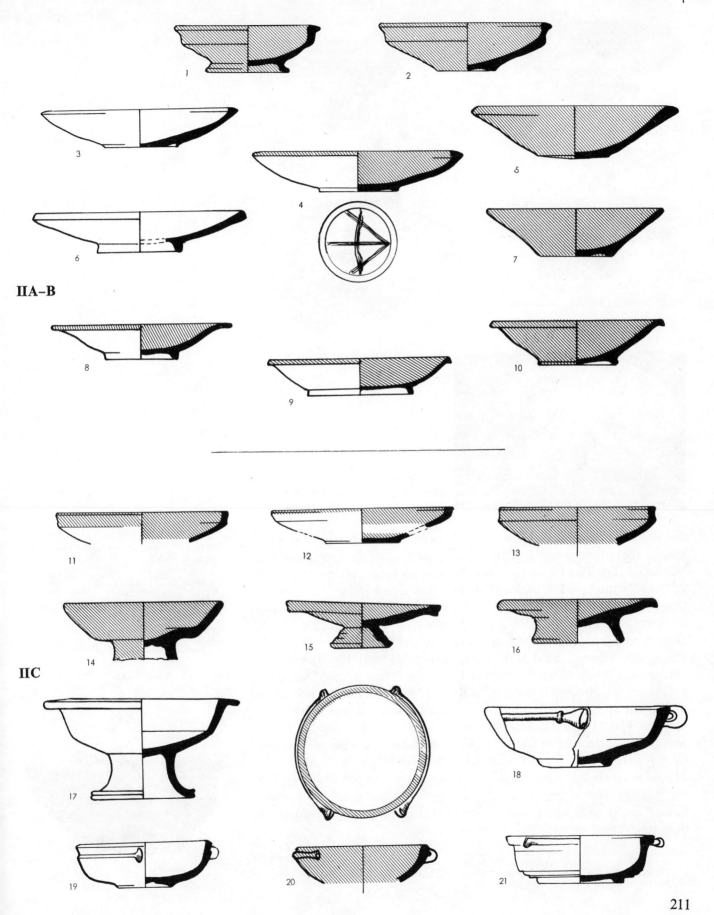

IIA–B

IIC

Photo 222. Bowl, Hazor, *Hazor*, III-IV,
Pl. CCCXLVIII.

Photo 223. Bowl, high-footed,
Samaria, IDA 32.2446.

Photo 224. Bowl, high-footed, Samaria,
HU 608.

Photo 225. Bowl, stepped, Hazor,
Hazor, II, Pl. CLVI.

Photo 226. Bowl, stepped, Jemmeh
Institute of Archaeology, London.

Thick bowls (Plate 67): Here we find forms similar to those current among the ordinary wares of the period, the main difference being the burnished slip. This group also includes various types: carinated (Photo 222) and straight-sided (Photo 224) bowls. Very characteristic are the trumpet bases (Photos 223 and 224) occurring in both carinated and straight-sided vessels, and the stepped bases (No. 21, Photo 225), which are not found among the ordinary wares of the period.

Photo 226 shows a bowl with a stepped profile near the base which belongs to a group of bowls found at Tell Jemmeh and termed 'Assyrian' by Petrie. An interesting parallel to these bowls is found in the palace of Kapara at Tell Halaf,[8] which may possibly de dated to the Assyrian period.[9] Photos 227–228 represent two variants of the rounded bowl. Such bowls, especially in Iron II C, are often decorated with bar-handles or with a ridge under the rim, as in the plain bowls (Plate 64:25–28).

The thick bowls also have the superb Samaria slip, the colours being red and yellow, used either separately or together. Black slip also occurs, though rarely (No. 18). It should be noted that the grooved decoration does not appear on the thick Samaria bowls.

Photo 227. Bowl, Samaria, IDA 33.2170.

Photo 228. Bowl, Samaria, HU 3545.

8. M. von Oppenheim, *Der Tell Halaf*, Leipzig, 1931, pl. 55.
9. W. F. Albright, Anat. St., VI (1956), 75 ff.

Chalices and Goblets — North and South (Plate 68).

Iron I – North: The chalice is a very characteristic Iron I form. Two main types can bs distinguished: a) an open, rather shallow bowl on a high foot; 2) a deep bowl on a low foot, here termed 'goblet.' There are, of course, borderline cases which are difficult to classify.

1) Nos. 1–3 represent variants of rim and foot profiles. The step in the lower part of the foot is a characteristic feature. Generally, the chalices are plain, without decoration, slip, or burnish.

2) The goblet (Nos. 4–6) is contemporary with the chalice. It has a spherical body, a relatively narrow neck and a low trumpet foot, and is usually decorated.

Though already known in preceding periods, the chalice reaches the height of its popularity in Iron I. The goblet, on the other hand, attains its greatest development in the Late Bronze Age, and the isolated specimens found in Iron I should be considered as the last descendants of that form.

Iron I — South (Nos. 7–10): The chalice was just as popular in the South as in the North. We shall attempt to outline here a few points of difference between southern and northern specimens: the southern chalice has a carinated rim, rather more flaring than that of the North, and always a stepped foot. Another difference is that decorated chalices are found only in the South (Photo 229). The goblet does not seem to occur in the South in this period.

Iron II A–B — North and South: The fashion for decorated chalices grows in this period; we find in the South chalices whose entire surface is decorated with a delicate pattern, rather like embroidery (Nos. 14 and 15). In form, there is hardly any difference between North and South (Nos. 14–16). Perhaps a slight difference in the depth of the bowl can be perceived.

Iron II C — North and South: The popularity of the chalice wanes in this period. At the same time, there is a decline in size and form, and the chalice turns into a kind of small goblet on a high stand. No. 22, from Tell Qasile, recalls Nos. 4 and 5, of Iron I.

Photo 229. Chalice, Far'ah(S), IDA V.1944.

213

PLATE | 68

I

IIA–B

IIC

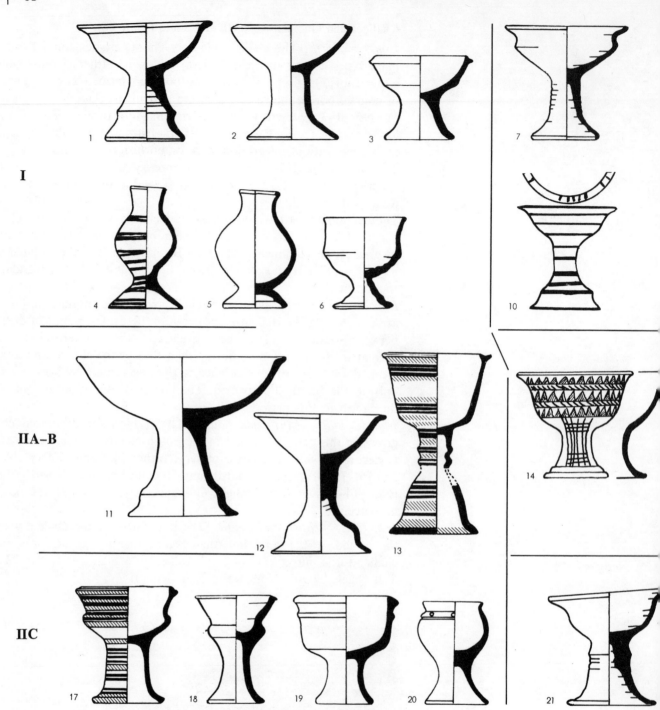

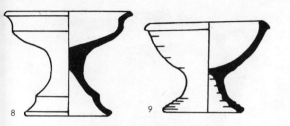

PLATE 68

1.	Chalice, burnt umber	1:5	Megiddo	T. 76 A	Meg. T., pl. 74:25
2.	Chalice, white-yellow	1:5	Megiddo	T. 39	Meg. T., pl. 68:19
3.	Chalice, pink-buff, smoothed	1:5	Megiddo	VII A	Meg. II, pl. 70:11
4.	Goblet, orange-buff, smoothed	1:5	Megiddo	VI	Meg. II, pl. 87:3
5.	Goblet, pink-buff, smoothed	1:5	Megiddo	VI	Meg. II, pl. 87:2
6.	Goblet, red-buff	1:5	Abu Hawam	IV	TAH, p. 30:170
7.	Chalice	1:5	Beth-shemesh	III	AS IV, pl. LIX:26
8.	Chalice	1:5	Qasile	X	Qasile, Fig. 6:2
9.	Chalice	1:5	Beth-shemesh	III	AS IV, pl. LIX:22
10.	Chalice	1:6	Far'ah (S)	T. 542	CPP, 17 E 4
11.	Chalice, red-buff	1:5	Abu Hawam	III	TAH, p. 23:88
12.	Chalice, burnt umber	1:5	Megiddo	T. 39	Meg. T., pl. 68:20
13.	Chalice, buff, red and black decoration	1:5	Megiddo	VI	Meg. II, pl. 91:12
14.	Chalice	1:6	Far'ah (S)	T. 201	CPP, 17 L 5
15.	Chalice	1:6	Far'ah (S)	T. 213	CPP, 17 K 6
16.	Chalice	1:5	Qasile	IX	Qasile, Fig. 12:c
17.	Chalice, yellow, light red and black decoration	1:5	Megiddo	III	Meg. I, pl. 33:12
18.	Chalice, light brown	1:5	Hazor	V A	H. II, pl. XCIII:21
19.	Chalice, yellow, brown-ocher slip outside	1:5	Megiddo	III	Meg. I, pl. 33:10
20.	Chalice, brown-ocher	1:5	Megiddo	III	Meg. I, pl. 33:13
21.	Chalice, light brown, buff slip	1:5	Beth-shemesh	II c	AS IV, pl. LXVII:3
22.	Chalice	1:5	Qasile	VII	Qasile, Fig. 10:a

Kraters: Iron I — North and South (Plates 69—70).

North (Plate 69): Here, as in many other forms, the Canaanite tradition is marked: a) the form of the body, the base, and sometimes even of the rim, recall Canaanite prototypes; b) the painted decoration is entirely Canaanite in character — a frieze in the zone of the handles, often made up of a fairly debased form of metope (Nos. 5, 7, and 9); c) the krater with two or four horizontal handles is a development of the krater of the Late Bronze Age; d) the krater standing on three loop-handles (No. 9) is also well known in LB.

However, in addition to the above-mentioned features taken over from Canaanite tradition, there are a number of genuinely Iron I elements:

a) Multiple handles: many kraters have four, eight, or more handles (No. 1, Photo 230); b) rope decoration in the handle-zone: this kind of decoration is commoner on kraters found in the North than on those found in the South; c) a rim thickened inwards and outwards, forming a sort of ledge: this rim develops further and becomes one of the characteristic features of Israelite pottery.

The incised decoration on the broad sloping rim of No. 6 is, for the present, unknown from other examples.

Photo 230. Krater, Megiddo, IDA I.3790.

Photo 231. Krater, very large, Safi, Dayan Collection.

South (Plate 70): This plate demonstrates the scarcity of kraters in Iron I southern pottery. Since the same scarcity also prevails in the following periods, the conclusion is unavoidable that kraters are almost entirely absent from the range of southern pottery types. Kraters and jugs with Philistine decoration are represented on Plate 90 (below).

Nos. 1–3 are standard kraters. No. 4 is a very large vessel (scale 1:10) and could just as well be classified as a pithos.

Photo 231 shows a large krater from Tell es-Safi with multiple handles and rope decoration, resembling No. 1 on this Plate.

216

Photo 232. Krater, Ruqeish, IDA 40.478.

Photo 233. Krater, Ruqeish, IDA 40.505.

Photo 234. Krater, Ruqeish, IDA 40.474.

Photo 235. Krater, Ruqeish, IDA 40.512.

Kraters: Iron II A—B — North and South (Plates 71—72).

North (Plate 71): Six types can be distinguished among the kraters assembled on this Plate:
1) Kraters with pronounced carination (Nos. 1 and 2).
2) Kraters with a ridge in the zone of the handles (Nos. 3 and 4).
3) Kraters with necks (No. 6).
4) Kraters resembling group 1 in form, but with a 'forked' rim, that is, a moulded rim something like a fork in profile (No. 5); No. 4 also has a 'forked' rim.
5) Kraters with horizontal handles (No. 8).
6) Kraters without handles (Nos. 9–11), often standing on three loop-handles.

The thickening of the rims, which we have already noted in Iron I, is also evident in most of the Iron II kraters, for instance, in groups 1, 2, and 3. On the other hand, the popularity of the multiple handles is now on the decline, although many kraters are still equipped with four or eight handles. In the eight-handled kraters, the handles are drawn from the middle of the neck, that is, from the ridge, towards the carination.

Krater No. 2 has, in addition to a rope pattern forming the ridge, also a row of reed impressions immediately below the rim. Both these elements, as well as the multiple handles, still belong to the ceramic fashion of Iron I (see above, Plate 69). Rope decoration and reed impressions are also found on other vessels of Iron I, such as incense stands. Iron I pithoi (Plate 77) are also frequently decorated with reed impressions.

Kraters with 'forked' rims (group 4) are characteristic of Stratum VIII in Hazor, though many have only two handles. Of special interest is No. 4, a small krater from Samaria, Stratum III.

Kraters with horizontal handles (group 5) are uncommon, and should be considered as the last offshoots of Late Bronze Age traditions.

The kraters without handles of group 6, and especially No. 10, recall to some extent cooking-pot forms.

South (Plate 72): We have already emphasized the scarcity of kraters in the Iron I southern repertoire of forms. The same scarcity prevails in the South of Iron II, as shown by the few examples we have been able collect on Plate 72.

The krater from Tell Beth Mirsim (No. 1) resembles, on the one hand, an Iron I specimen from the same site, and, on the other, Iron II C kraters. This type differs from contemporary bowls only in having two handles. Most of the elements characteristic of northern kraters are absent in the south.

Nos. 3–6 are small vessels with an opening narrower than that of the northern kraters. They have a pronounced neck, sometimes ridged in the middle (No. 4), a piriform body, and a relatively small base. With the exception of the handles, which are drawn from the rim to the shoulder in characteristic krater fashion, these vessels resemble jars, and especially Plate 80:6.

No. 6 (Photo 232) is a peculiar vessel. Nos. 3–6 should, in fact, be considered as belonging to the Phoenician-Israelite pottery (Plate 92) and its satellites, like the Punic pottery. Photos 232–235 come from the Abu Ruqeish cemetery.

PLATE | 69

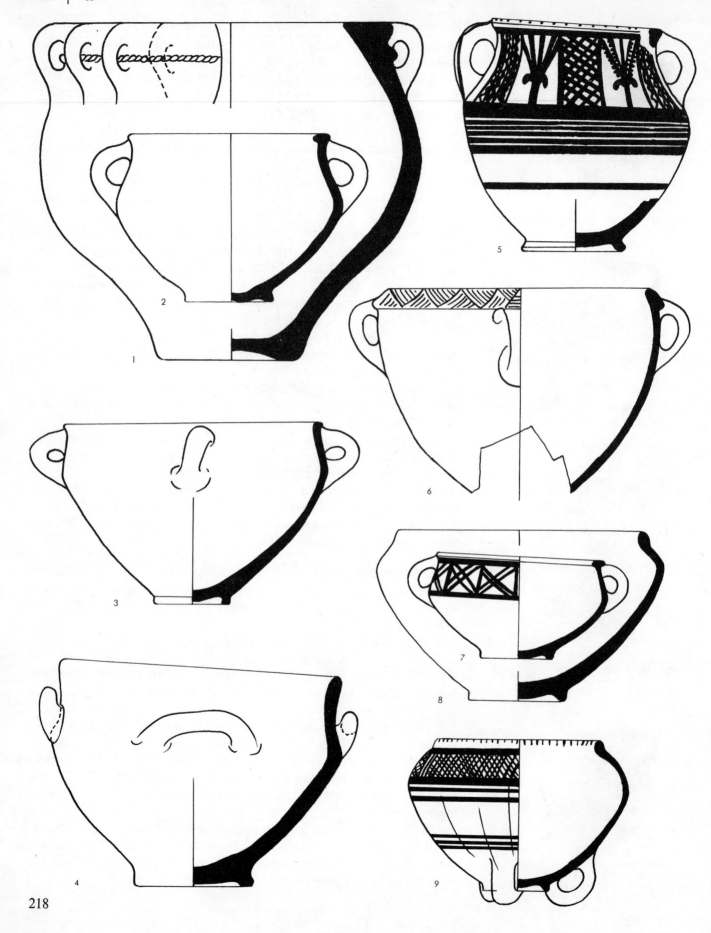

PLATE | 70

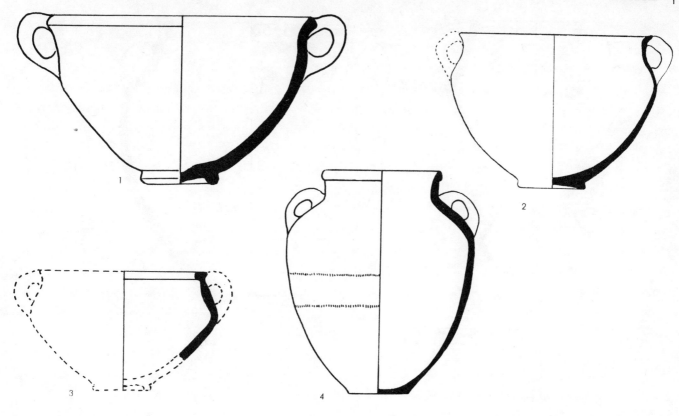

PLATE | 71

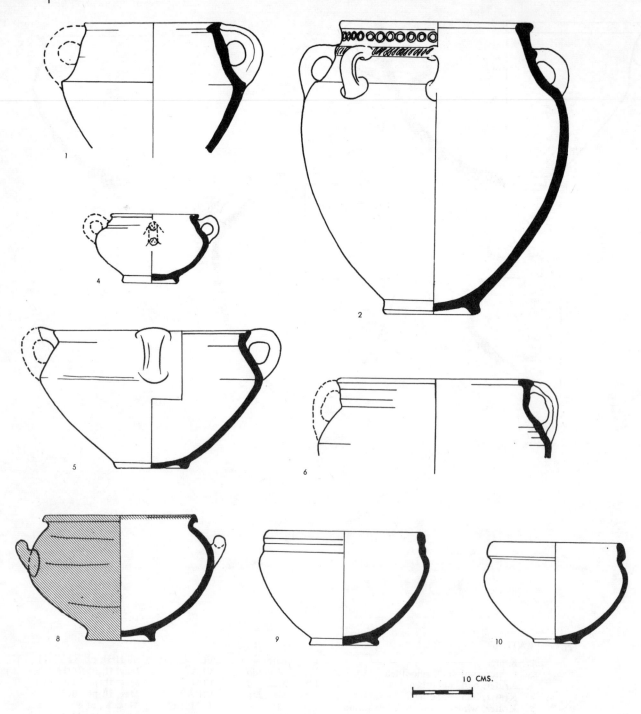

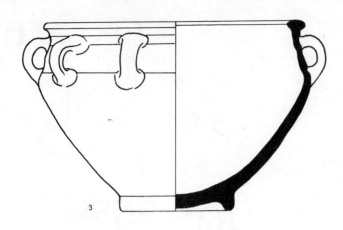

3

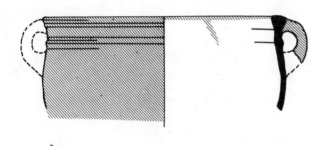

7

11

PLATE 71

1.	Krater, pink	1:5	Hazor	X	H. III–IV, pl. CCVII:6
2.	Krater, brown-ocher, incised decoration	1:5	Megiddo	V	Meg. I, pl. 21:125
3.	Krater, yellow	1:5	Megiddo	V	Meg. I, pl. 32:167
4.	Krater, grey, whitish slip	1:5	Samaria		SS III, Fig. 20:2
5.	Krater, pink	1:5	Hazor	VIII	H. II, pl. LVI:14
6.	Krater, pink	1:5	Hazor	VIII	H. II, pl. LVI:3
7.	Krater, pink, brown slip	1:5	Hazor	VIII	H. II, pl. LVI:6
8.	Krater, pink-buff, burnished red slip	1:5	Megiddo	V A	Meg. II, pl. 89:15
9.	Krater, brown-ocher	1:5	Megiddo	V	Meg. I, pl. 29:111
10.	Krater, burnt umber	1:5	Megiddo	V	Meg. I, pl. 31:154
11.	Krater, red-brown, red decoration, four grooves under the rim (after a photograph)	1:5	Abu Hawam	III	TAH, pl. XIII:81

PLATE | 72

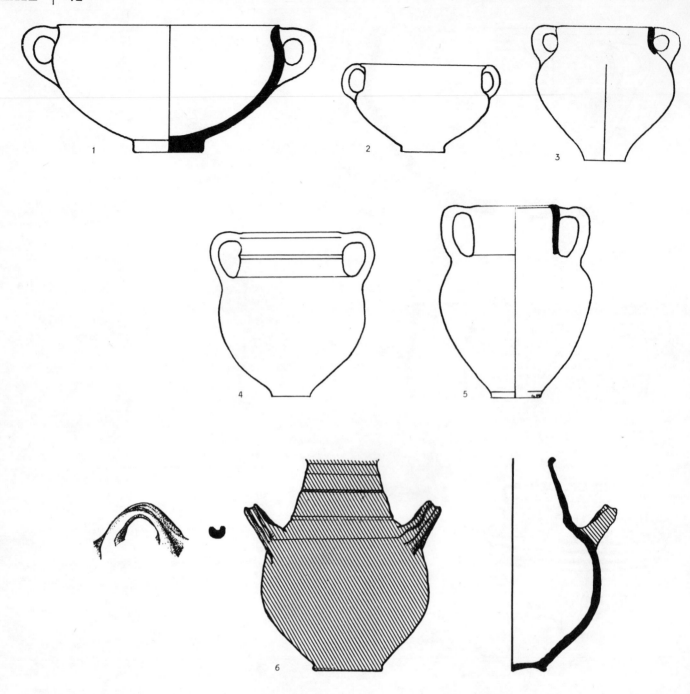

Plate 72

1. Krater, buff   1:5   Beth Mirsim   B   TBM I, pl. 50:7
2. Krater   1:6   Jemmeh   GQ 185   CPP, 28 H
3. Krater   1:6   Far'ah (S)   T. 263   CPP, 33 C
4. Krater   1:6   Ajjul   T. 1024   AG II, pl. XXIX:31 L 3
5. Krater   1:6   Far'ah (S)   T. 251   CPP, 33 U
6. Krater, red, red burnished slip   1:5   er-Ruqeish   IDA 40.478

Photo 236. Krater, Hazor, *Hazor*, II, Pl. CLVI.

Kraters: Iron II C — North and South (Plates 73—74).

The same groups which we distinguished among the Iron II A–B kraters continue to develop in Iron II C. Like the contemporary bowls, some Iron II C kraters have a slip on the outside which is often burnished. Sometimes there is only a red band on the rim.

1) Kraters with pronounced carination and a thickened everted rim which is sometimes levelled off at the top: the base, which is usually high and flat, differs from that of earlier specimens, and the vessels have generally two handles (Nos. 1 and 2).

2) In this group, the upper part of the vessel, to which the handles are attached, is separated from the rest of the body by a ridge and forms a neck, which is often inclined inwards (Nos. 3–5, Photo 237).

3) This fairly widespread group is characterized by fine plastic decoration evolved from the bar-handle (Nos. 6–8, Photo 236): the usual loop-handles are combined in various ingenious ways with this plastic decoration. The decoration on No. 10, which has wing-like projections on both sides of the handle, forms part of the same play of ideas, perhaps in imitation of metal prototypes.

4) Hole–mouth krater–bowls without handles (No. 9): in addition to the plain specimen shown in Plate 73, such kraters are sometimes decorated with painted bands on the upper part, or with a slip, plain or burnished.

South (Plate 74): In Iron II C, as in the preceding Iron Age phases, kraters are rare in the South. Only five specimens (Plate 74) from southern sites could be collated from stratigraphic deposits. They are not related to each other, either in form or in evolution, and thus bear out our judgment concerning the scarcity of kraters in the South.

No. 1: continues the tradition of the Iron II amphora-like form.

No. 2: of the five specimens on this plate, we believe this to be the most characteristic southern Iron II C form. The rim resembles the standard Iron Age turned-over rim.

No. 3: is a krater which resembles contemporary deep bowls (Plate 65), but is deeper and has four handles (Photo 238).

No. 4: which comes from Tell Qasile, is carinated, and thus resembles group 1 of the northern kraters.

No. 5: is a very large vessel with many handles, which goes back to an Iron I form (Plate 69:1).

Photo 237. Krater, Megiddo, IDA 36.1951.

Photo 238. Two kraters, Beth Mirsim, IDA I.8957 and I.9037.

223

PLATE | 73

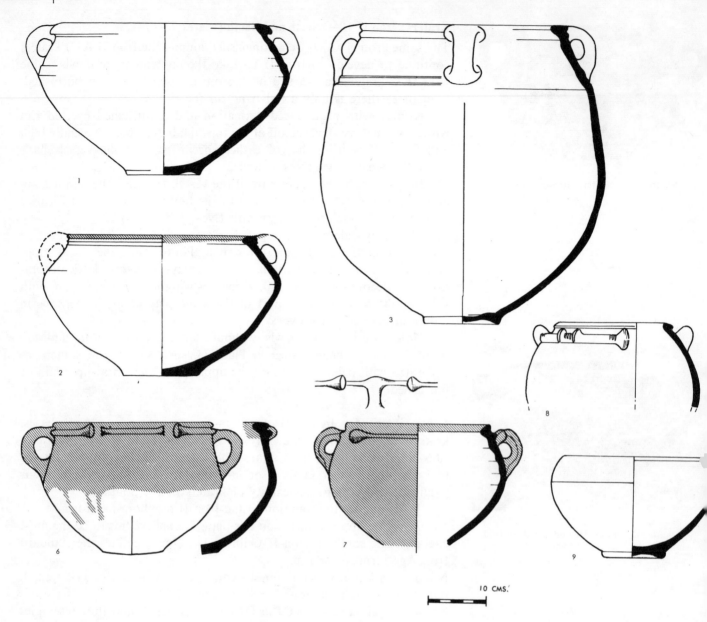

10 CMS.

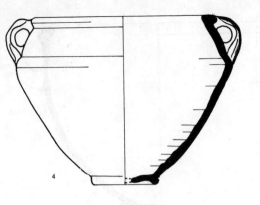

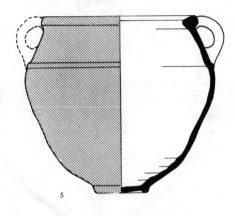

PLATE 73

1.	Krater, grey-buff, wheel-burnished inside, seal impressions	1:5	Hazor	VI	H. II, pl. LXVII:13
2.	Krater, pink, burnished, red decoration	1:5	Hazor	VI	H. II, pl. LXVII:12
3.	Krater, pink-buff	1:5	Hazor	VI	H. II, pl. LXVIII:5
4.	Krater, grey-buff	1:5	Hazor	IV	H. II, pl. CVII:19
5.	Krater, light brown, red slip	1:5	Hazor	V A	H. II, pl. LXXXIII:10
6.	Krater, light brown, red slip	1:5	Hazor	V A	H. II, pl. LXXXIV:2
7.	Krater, grey, red slip	1:5	Hazor	V A	H. II, pl. CCXXVII:4
8.	Krater, yellow, red irregularly burnished slip	1:5	Megiddo	IV–III	Meg. I, pl. 26:73
9.	Krater, grey	1:5	Far'ah (N)	II	RB, 1952, p. 568, Fig. 8:18
10.	Krater, green-brown, red wheel-burnished slip	1:5	Megiddo	IV–III	Meg. I, pl. 26:70

PLATE | 74

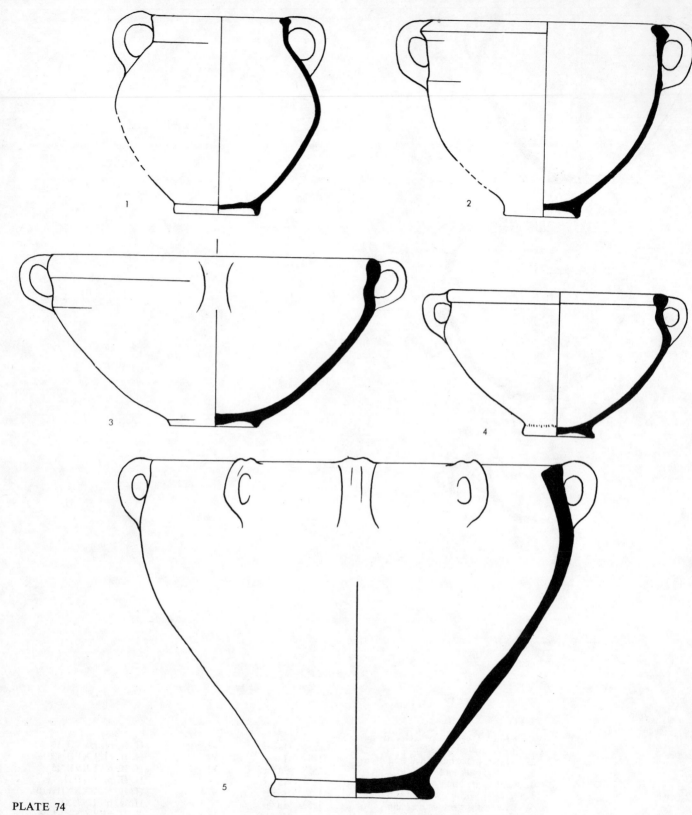

PLATE 74

1. Krater, pink	1 5	Lachish	III	La. III, pl. 91:403
2. Krater, pink, pink slip inside	1:5	Lachish	T. 120	La. III, pl. 82:128
3. Krater, pink, buff burnished slip inside	1:5	Lachish	III	La. III, pl. 82:122
4. Krater, red wheel-burnished slip	1:5	Qasile	VII	Qasile, Fig. 12:d
5. Krater, pink, buff	1:5	Lachish	II–III	La. III, pl. 82:124

Cooking-Pots: Iron I, II A—B, II C — North and South (Plates 75—76).

The Iron Age cooking-pot is directly descended from its Canaanite prototype, and develops in the North and in the South along distinctive lines. We have arranged the cooking-pots of all three phases of the Iron Age in two plates so as to emphasize this development: Plate 75 for the northern, and Plate 76 for the southern material. The clay of the cooking-pot in these periods is also easily distinguishable: it is full of white calcite grits, which seem mostly to be smaller than those in the Late Bronze.

Iron I: The type which prevails in the North as well as in the South is a broad, relatively shallow vessel with a carinated body and a rounded base, and is usually without handles. The rim is elongated and triangular in section. In all periods, the rim is the best criterion for dating cooking-pots. The elongated rim with triangular section first appears in Iron I, and is found in numerous variants. Perhaps the carination and its emplacement on the wall of the vessel can also serve as a criterion for distinguishing between Iron I and Iron II A–B cooking-pots. In Iron II A–B, the placement of the carination appears to be lower, and the upper part of the vessel, above the carination, appears longer in many vessels.

Iron II A–B: Few changes can be discerned in the cooking-pots of this period, with the exception of the lower carination mentioned above. In this period, cooking-pots with handles appear to be more numerous than in Iron I (Plates 75:11–12; 76:7). The rounded shape of the pot in Plate 76:7 is unusual, and we have shown it here because of the scarcity of material from the South. Nos. 8–10 on Plate 76, which come from the South, show that the walls are still carinated.

The northern material (Plate 75) indicates clearly that the rims are still triangular in section but are generally shorter than in Iron I (Plate 75:11–15).

Iron II C: Definite changes in the rim as well as in the general shape of the vessel can be observed in Iron II C cooking-pots, both in the South and in the North.

Iron II C, North: Excavations at Hazor and Samaria show that the transition between cooking-pots of Iron II A–B and Iron II C is fairly abrupt. In Samaria, the late type described below does not appear before Stratum IV and is characteristic of that and later strata. At Hazor, this type predominates from Stratum VII onwards and is not found earlier. This late type has a slightly squat body, the carination has almost disappeared, and the pots always have two handles. The rim has become stepped or ridged and appears in many variants, of which a few are shown on Plate 75.

Iron II C, South: The cooking-pot and its variants follow the same lines of development as in the North. However, the stratigraphical transition is difficult to trace in the excavations carried out in the South up to the present.

Another type has until now been found exclusively in the South; the evidence indicates that its development is not earlier than the 8th century. This is a deep cooking-pot (Plate 76:15–17), almost as wide as it is high,

PLATE | 75

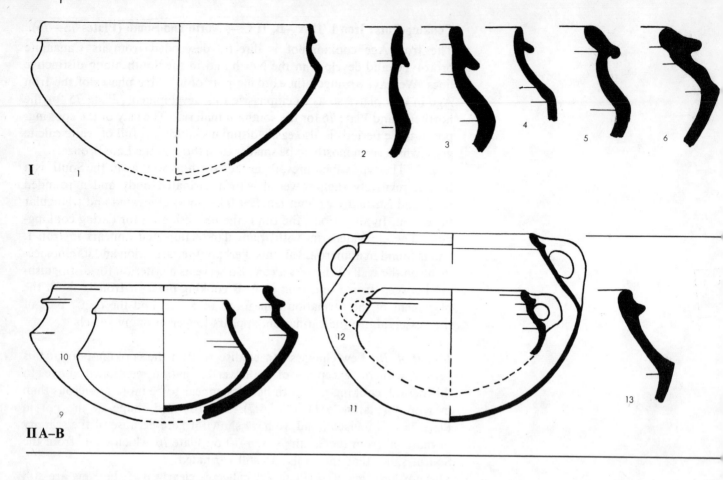

I

II A–B

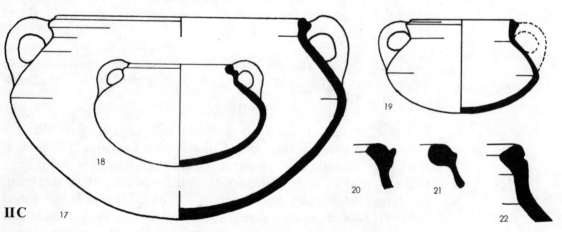

II C

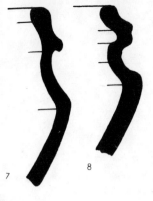

PLATE 75

1.	Cooking-pot, red-buff, crystalline grits	1:5	Megiddo	VI	Meg. II, pl. 85:16
2.	Cooking-pot, red-brown, white grits	1:5	Hazor	XII	H. III–IV, pl. CLXV:17
3.	Cooking-pot, red-brown, white grits	1:5	Hazor	XI	H. III–IV, pl. CCIII:7
4.	Cooking-pot, dark brown, white grits	1:5	Hazor	XII	H. III–IV, pl. CLXVI:7
5.	Cooking-pot, brown, white grits	1:5	Hazor	XII	H. III–IV, pl. CCI:14
6.	Cooking-pot, brown, white grits	1:5	Hazor	XII	H. III–IV, pl. CCI:11
7.	Cooking-pot, black-brown, white grits	1:5	Hazor	XII	H. III–IV, pl. CCI:15
8.	Cooking-pot, black-brown, white grits	1:5	Hazor	XII	H. III–IV, pl. CCI:13
9.	Cooking-pot, red-brown, white grits	1:5	Hazor	IX	H. III–IV, pl. CCIX:1
10.	Cooking-pot	1:5	Abu Hawam	III	TAH, p. 23:90
11.	Cooking-pot	1:5	Far'ah (N)	III	RB 1955, p. 579, Fig. 17:7
12.	Cooking-pot, brown, white grits	1:5	Hazor	VIII	H. II, pl. LVII:15
13.	Cooking-pot, brown, white grits	1:5	Hazor	X	H. II, pl. LI:11
14.	Cooking-pot, brown, white grits	1:5	Hazor	X	H. II, pl. LI:12
15.	Cooking-pot, brown, white grits	1:5	Hazor	VIII	H. II, pl. LVII:4
16.	Cooking-pot, brown, white grits	1:5	Hazor	VIII	H. II, pl. LVII:13
17.	Cooking-pot, brown, white grits	1:5	Hazor	VI	H. II, pl. LXIX:11
18.	Cooking-pot	1:5	Megiddo	IV–I	Meg. I, pl. 39:7
20.	Cooking-pot, fragment	2:5	Samaria	E. 207	SS III, Fig. 30:5
21.	Cooking-pot, fragment	2:5	Samaria	E. 207	SS III, Fig. 30:21
22.	Cooking-pot, fragment	2:5	Samaria	E. 207	SS III, Fig. 30:22
23.	Cooking-pot, red-brown, white grits	1:5	Hazor	V A	H. II, pl. LXXXV:7
24.	Cooking-pot, brown, white grits	1:5	Hazor	V A	H. II, pl. LXXXV:10

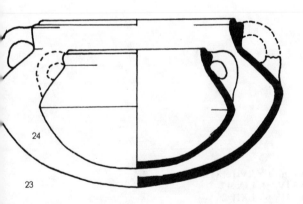

PLATE 76

1.	Cooking-pot	1:5	Ai		Ay, pl. LXXVII:1843
2.	Cooking-pot	1:5	Beth-shemesh	III	AS IV, pl. LIX:17
3.	Cooking-pot, fragment	1:2	Beth-shemesh	III	AS IV, pl. LXII:26
4.	Cooking-pot, fragment	1:2	Beth-shemesh	III	AS IV, pl. LXII:27
5.	Cooking-pot, fragment	1:2	Beth-shemesh	III	AS IV, pl. LXII:28
6.	Cooking-pot, fragment	1:2	Beth-shemesh	III	AS IV, pl. LXII:35
7.	Cooking-pot	1:5	Beth-shemesh	II a	AS IV, pl. LXIII:37
8.	Cooking-pot, fragment	1:5	Beth-shemesh	II a	AS IV, pl. LXIII:31
9.	Cooking-pot, fragment	1:5	Beth-shemesh	II a	AS IV, pl. LXIII:32
10.	Cooking-pot, fragment	1:5	Beth-shemesh	II a	AS IV, pl. LXII:45
11.	Cooking-pot, pink	1:5	Lachish	III	La. III, pl. 93:441
12.	Cooking-pot	1:5	Beth Mirsim	A	TBM III, pl. 19:1
13.	Cooking-pot	1:5	Nasbeh		TN II, pl. 48:1012
14.	Cooking-pot	1:5	Beth-shemesh	II	AS IV, pl. LXIII:36
15.	Cooking-pot	1:5	Beth Mirsim	A	TBM I, pl. 55:3
16.	Cooking-pot	1:5	Beth-shemesh	II b–c	AS IV, pl. LXIV:31
17.	Cooking-pot	1:5	Beth-shemesh	II	Beth Shemesh, p. 205:132
18.	Cooking-pot, red-brown	1:5	Ein Gedi	V	BIES, 27, Fig. 18:4
19.	Cooking-pot, red-brown	1:5	Ein Gedi	V	BIES, 27, Fig. 17:4

PLATE | 76

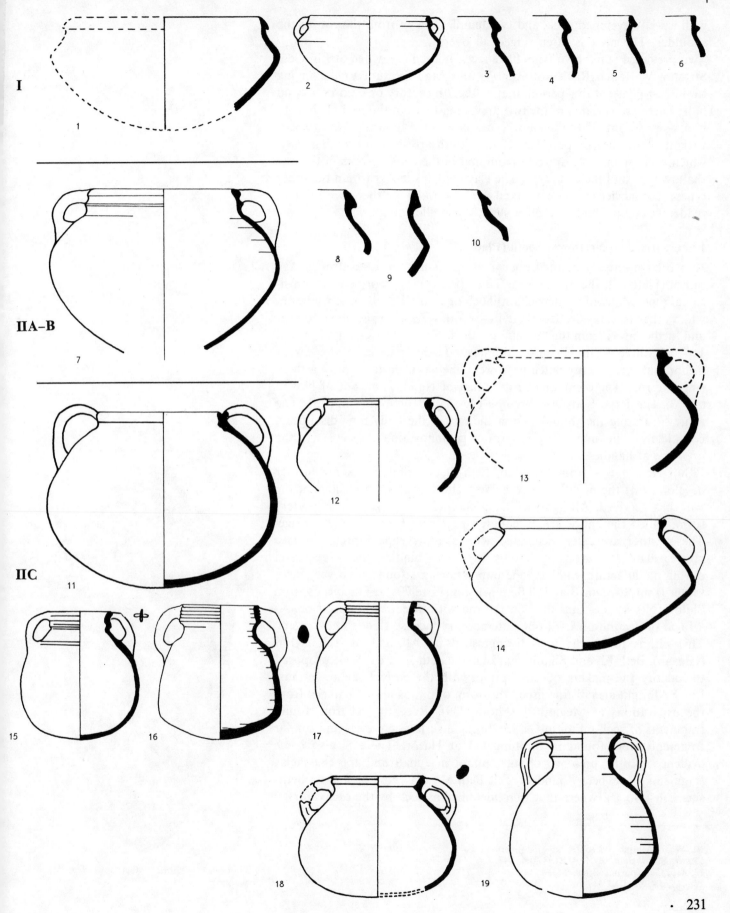

I

1   2   3   4   5   6

IIA–B   7   8   9   10

IIC   11   12   13   14

15   16   17   18   19

with a well-developed neck, and two handles drawn from the rim to the shoulder. The neck is often ridged all over.

Two previously unknown types have recently been excavated at Ein Gedi Stratum V, Ramat Rachel Stratum V, and Arad Stratum VI, belonging to the last phase of this period, that is, the 7th century or even its second half. These are variants of the two prevailing types of the period: No. 18 is a new variant of the shallow type (Nos. 11–14), while No. 19 is a variant of the deep type (Nos. 15–17). Both are made of similar clay, which is conspicuously different from that of the cooking-pots of the late shallow type and the deep type. The clay contains less grit than the other types; it is harder and better baked, and the walls are therefore thinner, redder in colour, and give off a slightly metallic sound.

Pithoi: Iron I — North and South (Plate 77).

As we have already pointed out when discussing the Late Bronze Age pithoi (Plate 45), the pithos from Tuleil (Plate 77:1) represents a transitional type. Many of its elements still belong to the Late Bronze tradition, while other features are Iron Age innovations. Later types move further and further away from the Canaanite pithos. Nos. 2, 3 (neck missing), and 11 — all three from Hazor — still have the high neck of the earlier pithoi, but it is already much narrower. The vessels usually have a thick ring-like rim. The commonest rim is that of No. 11, and not of Nos. 2 and 3. The large body has become egg-shaped or even elliptical. The ridge separating the shoulder from the rest of the body now disappears completely. The most striking Iron Age innovation, however, is the presence of handles.

Pithoi Nos. 4–6 — from Megiddo, Beth-El, and Shiloh — show further development: the neck has become very short and only the ridge at the base has survived. Albright, who was the first to recognize this pottery form, called the entire group 'collared rim' jars, because of this ridge. These pithoi are often decorated with shallow rope-impressions (see above, Plate 45), probably left by the ropes binding the large vessel during manufacture. Similar rope impressions are found on a very large krater from Stratum B at Tell Beth Mirsim (Plate 70:4). The pithos from Shiloh (No. 4) is ornamented on the rim with three reed impressions — a form of decoration used on contemporary incense stands and kraters. This pithos form was first distinguished by Albright at Tell el-Ful (Gibeah), Beth-El, and Shiloh, that is, in the Beth-El area.[10] He proposed to identify the makers of these pithoi with the early Israelite settlers. Later Albright also distinguished this form of pithos in the material from the excavations at Megiddo[11] (Photo 239). Recently, Aharoni found fragments of such pithoi in Galilee during a surface survey,[12] and similar fragments were found in Stratum XII at Hazor. There is also some evidence for the presence of such pithoi in Judah and the Shephela: fragments have been found at Tell Beth Mirsim (No. 9) and at Beth-shemesh (No. 7), where they were identified as such by the excavators.[13]

Photo 239. Pithos, Megiddo, *Meg.* II, Pl. 83:1.

---

10. W. F. Albright, *BASOR*, 56 (1934), pp. 11 ff.
11. W. F. Albright, *AJA*, 41 (1937), p. 147.
12. Up. Gal., pl. 4:1–2; pl. 5:3–4.
13. *AS*, IV, pl. LXI:1.

Similar fragments were also found at Afula (No. 8), Ai (No. 10), and Tell en-Nasbeh (No. 12).

The ethnic identification of the makers of these vessels, as proposed by Albright and confirmed by Aharoni's survey, seems to be in accordance with other evidence in this period. There remain, of course, some problems to be investigated, as for example the absence of a Canaanite prototype in the South as well as in the North.

Storage Jars: Iron I — North and South (Plate 78).

North: Four main groups of storage jars can be distinguished:

1) Ovoid body and ridged neck (Nos. 1 and 2).
2) Ovoid body and straight neck (Nos. 3 and 4).
3) Jars (No. 11) which have a spout and are sometimes decorated with painted bands or metopes: this type seems to be a development of the biconical jars and jugs popular in the Late Bronze Age.
4) Multi-handled jars (Nos. 5–6).

South: Material from stratified deposits in the South is so scarce that it is difficult to determine if the same classification can be followed.

Photo 240. Jar.
Beth-shemesh, IDA I.8679.

Ovoid jars are common in the South, and follow Late Bronze Age tradition both in general outline and in the form of the base. No. 7, a many-handled jar, can be compared to the jars in northern group (4). Photo 240 shows a jar with characteristic Iron I burnishing.

Further excavations may well furnish material to round out this admittedly incomplete picture of Iron I storage jars. A recent dig at Tell Isdar in the Negev [14] produced much complementary material.

---

14. Excavated by M. Kokhavi.

PLATE 77

1. Pithos   1:10 Tuleil   Up. Gal., p. 22, Fig. 4:4
2. Pithos, yellowish-pink, rope impression   1:10 Hazor   XII   H. III–IV, pl. CLXVII:8
3. Pithos, yellowish-pink, rope impression   1:10 Hazor   XII   H. III–IV, pl. CLXVII:10
4. Pithos (after a photograph)   Shiloh   JPOS X
5. Pithos (after a photograph)   Beth-El   BASOR 137, Fig. 2
6. Pithos (after a photograph)   Megiddo   Meg. Mut., I, pl. XLVI:d
7. Pithos, light brown   1:5   Beth-shemesh   III   AS IV, pl. LXI:1
8. Pithos   1:10 Afula   III B   Atiqot I, Fig. 16:4
9. Pithos (after a photograph)   Beth Mirsim   TBM I, pl. 26:18
10. Pithos   1:10 Ai   Ay, pl. LXIX:167 a
11. Pithos, brown   1:10 Hazor   XII   H. II–IV, pl. CLXVII:5
12. Pithos, brown   1:10 Nasbeh   TN II, pl. 2:28

234

PLATE | 77

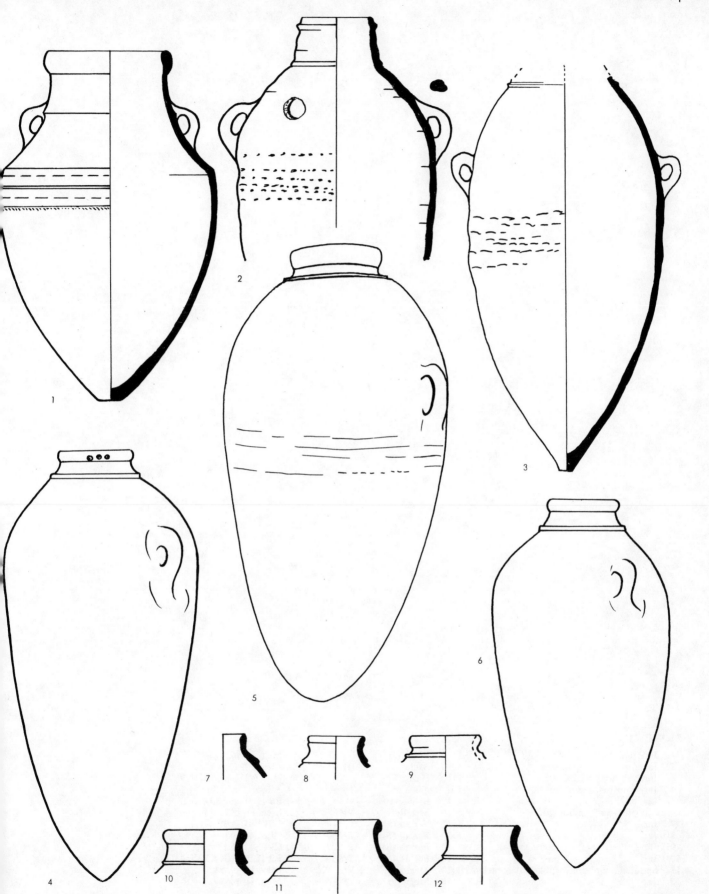

235

236

PLATE | 78

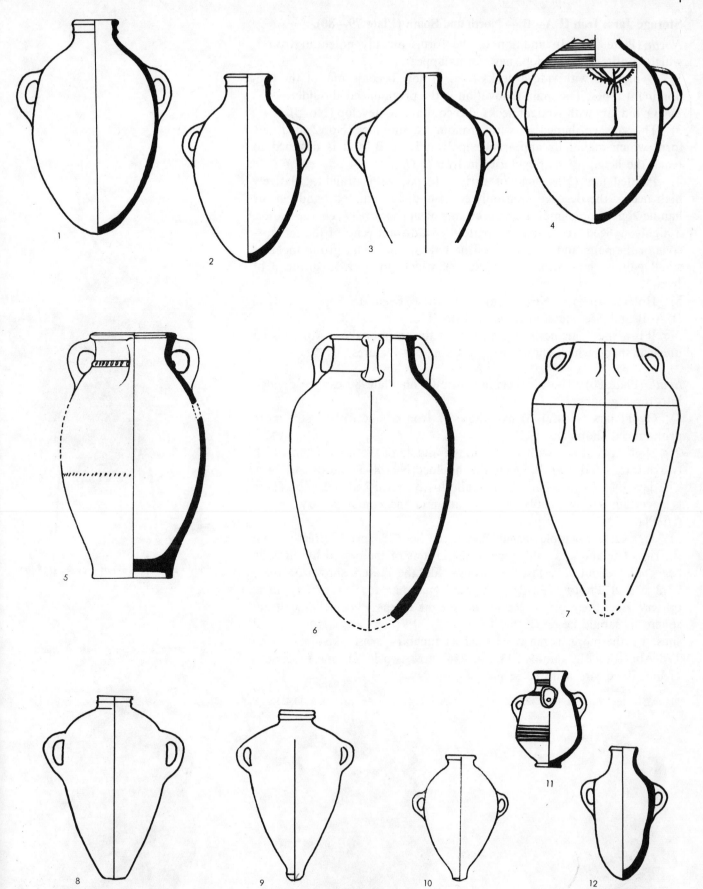

Storage Jars: Iron II A—B — North and South (Plate 79—80).

North (Plate 79): In addition to the forms already noted in Iron I, which continue to develop, new forms appear.

1) Ovoid jars with ridged necks (No. 1) now become one of the predominant types. The main innovation is the pronounced shoulder.

2) Ovoid jars with straight necks also continue to develop (No. 5).

3) The sausage-shaped jar with pronounced shoulder, No. 2, is a new form which makes its appearance in Iron II A–B, and is destined to reach the height of its popularity in Iron II C.

4) Painted jars (Nos. 6–8) of various forms, with straight, relatively high necks: the decoration usually consists of red painted bands in the handle-zone. Sometimes a single ornament appears between the bands, a highly stylized tree or zig-zag pattern — a distant echo of the metope-style or the palm-and-ibex motif of the Late Bronze. This group includes small painted jars with spouts (No. 8), which go back to group 3 of Iron I.

5) Holemouth jars, Nos. 11 and 12: these begin to appear in Iron II A–B and become commoner in Iron II C.

No. 9 is a small jar, perhaps a variant of the amphoriskos. No. 10 is an unusual shape which shows many cooking-pot features.

South (Plate 80): The six specimens shown on Plate 80 can be divided into three groups:

1) Ovoid jars (Nos. 1–3) like those of Iron I, but with a still more pronounced shoulder.

2) High-necked jars with a ridge in the middle of the neck, from which two or three handles are drawn to the shoulder (Nos. 4–5, Photos 241–242). The jars of this type have an overall closely burnished red slip. There is a certain kinship between these jars and the contemporary kraters (cf. Plate 72).

3) Jar No. 6 resembles group 2, but the handles spring directly from the rim. The affinity of this type to the kraters of the period has already been pointed out. The last two groups, like the kraters shown on Plate 72:3–6 and Photos 232–235, appear somewhat foreign among local pottery, and their origin should be sought in the Phoenician cultural sphere. It should be noted that these jars and kraters come from coastal sites. Furthermore, some were used as funerary urns, like those from Tell Abu-Ruqeish. Photos 243 and 244 show two handsome specimens of burnished jars, with some painting on 244.

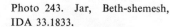

Photo 244. Jar, Unknown prov., HU· 4009.

Photo 243. Jar, Beth-shemesh, IDA 33.1833.

Photo 241. Jar, Ruqeish, IDA 40.476.   Photo 242. Jar, Ruqeish, IDA 40.455.

PLATE | 79

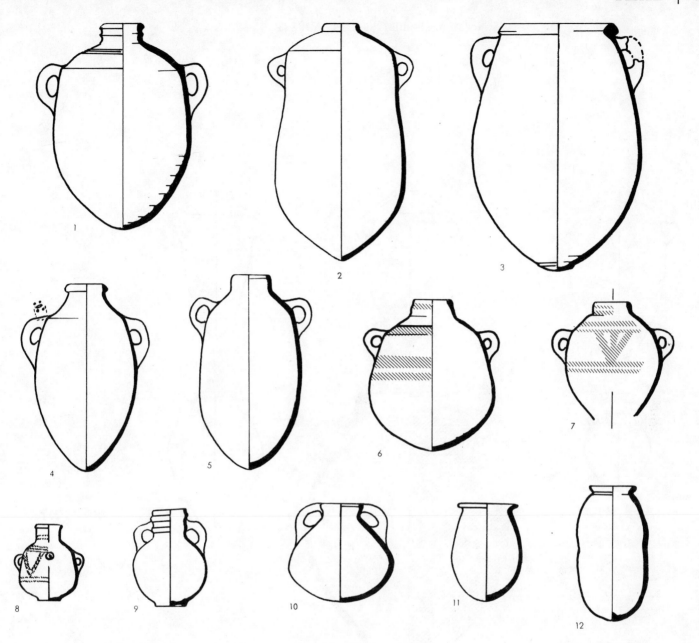

PLATE 79

1.	Jar, grey	1:10	Hazor	VIII	H. II, pl. LX:6
2.	Jar, burnt umber	1:10	Megiddo	V	Meg. I, pl. 20:119
3.	Jar, grey-buff	1:10	Hazor	VIII	H. II, pl. LIX:1
4.	Jar, brown-ocher	1:10	Megiddo	V	Meg. I, pl. 21:123
5.	Jar, brown-ocher	1:10	Megiddo	V	Meg. I, pl. 21:122
6.	Jar, pink, red and black decoration	1:10	Hazor	VIII	H. II, pl. LIX:4
7.	Jar, grey-buff, red decoration	1:10	Hazor	VIII	H. II, pl. LIX:7
8.	Jar, grey, reddish-brown slip, red and black decoration	1:10	Samaria	II–I	SS III, Fig. 2:1
9.	Jar, buff, smoothed	1:10	Megiddo	V A	Meg. II, pl. 89:1
10.	Jar (?), dark burnt umber	1:10	Megiddo	V	Meg. I, pl. 20:115
11.	Jar, brown-ocher	1:10	Megiddo	V	Meg. I, pl. 20:117
12.	Jar, brown	1:10	Hazor	VIII	H. II, pl. LXI:1

PLATE | 80

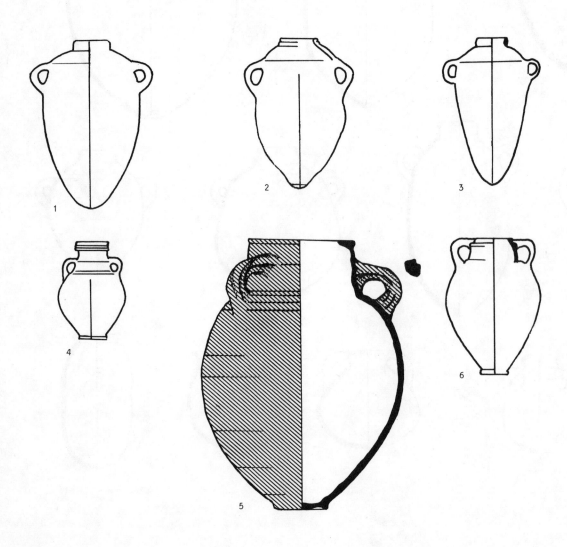

PLATE 80

1.	Jar		1:12	Far'ah (S)	T. 201	CPP, 43 K 4
2.	Jar		1:12	Far'ah (S)	T. 221	BP I, pl. XLI
3.	Jar		1:12	Far'ah (S)	T. 200	CPP, 43 J 10
4.	Jar		1:12	Far'ah (S)	T. 270	CPP, 44 L 4
5.	Jar, reddish-brown, red vertically burnished slip		1:5	er-Ruqeish	Tomb	IDA 40.501
6.	Jar		1:12	Far'ah (S)	T. 255	CPP, 33 T

Storage Jars: Iron II C — North and South (Plate 81—82).

North (Plate 81): Five main groups can be discerned:

1) Ovoid jars with a ridged neck (Nos. 1–3, Photo 245). The ridge is always present, although its placement may change. This group has a widespread distribution and appears in many variants.

2) Sausage-shaped jars with a pronounced shoulder (Nos. 4–8, Photo 246). The neck is so short that it is often only a rim. The rims are various: straight, concave or lightly ridged. The main difference between these two groups, both of which are very common, lies in the quality of the clay. Jars of group 1 are made of characteristic brown-grey, gritty, medium-baked clay resembling that of other contemporary pottery vessels. The clay of the jars of group 2, on the other hand, is well levigated and well-baked to give off a metallic sound, and is yellowish-pink in colour. No. 8 is a variant of this group with a tapering body. Shoulder, rim, and handles follow closely the group-type.

3) The jars are similar in form to those of group 1, but they have straight necks and rail-like rims (Nos. 9–10). Such jars are often painted with red bands on the neck, shoulder, and body.

4) Holemouth jars are infrequently found in the North (Nos. 11 and 12). The entire range of holemouth rim variations (grooved, inverted, etc.), which is plentifully represented in the South, is absent from the northern material.

5) Jars with three handles and spout (Nos. 13, 14). The mouth of the spout served as a seat for a dipper-juglet, in order to catch and return to the vessel any liquid dripping from the juglet after use. (In the literature this is sometimes designated as pillar-handle). These jars come in two types of clay and decoration: vessels of metallic ware, decorated with grooves on the shoulder, and vessels of "fatty" ware with red slip or red painted bands.

No. 15 is an unusual jar, included in Plate 81 because of some characteristic Iron Age features which are common to several types of jugs, such as decanters, and to the three-handled and spouted jars described above: ridged neck and handles drawn from the ridge to the shoulder. This jar resembles the jars from Gibeon on whose handles Hebrew inscriptions, including the name 'Gibeon,' were incised (Plate 82:14).

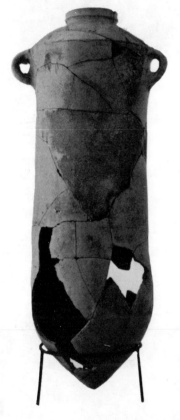

Photo 246. Jar, Hazor, *Hazor*, II, Pl. XCI.

Photo 245. Jar, Hazor, *Hazor*, I, Pl. CLIII.

241

South (Plate 82): The following groups can be distinguished on this plate:

1) Ovoid jars with a wide, rounded shoulder, generally four handles, a relatively high, tapering neck, and a thickened rim (Nos. 1 and 3): this is one of the two predominant Iron II C jar-types in the South. The jar-handles with *la-melekh* seal-impressions, found on all Judaean sites, belong to such jars (Photos 247–248).

2) Ovoid jars with ridged necks (No. 2) are uncommon in the South, in contrast to their prevalence in the North.

3) Holemouth jars: rarely found in the North, they constitute the second widely distributed group in the South, and appear in very numerous variations, especially of the rims. Six specimens are shown (Nos. 4, 5 and 8–11). Of these, Nos. 4 and 8 have a barrel-shaped body, Nos. 9–11 (Photo 249) a cylindrical body. No. 5 is a very large vessel, also with a cylindrical body, but with shoulder and base completely different from Nos. 9–11.

4) Sausage-shaped jars (Nos. 6 and 7): this type is less common than in the North, where it is one of the most frequently found forms. No. 7 is a late development of the type — the carinated shoulder, the characteristic handles, the short rim, and the pointed base are all present, but the body has changed and has become shorter.

5) Jars with three handles and spout (No. 12): we have noted two variants of this jar in the North. The southern jars differ from the northern vessels in the form of the neck and of the rim (Photo 250).

6) Jars with narrow, ridged necks and two handles drawn from the ridge to the shoulder (cf. Plate 81:15, where we already noted their resemblance to the ridged-neck jugs): this type is infrequently found in the South, and the only examples we have been able to trace in the literature are No. 13, from Beth-shemesh, and No. 14, which is one of a group of such jars recently discovered at Gibeon.

Photo 247. Jar, LMLK, Lachish, *Lachish*, III, Pl. 78: Type 484.

Photo 248. Jar-handle, with LMLK HBRN stamp-impression, Lachish, IDA 33.2105.

Photo 249. Jar, Beth-shemesh, IDA 33.1831.

Photo 250. Jar, Beth Mirsim, IDA I 4962.
Juglet has been placed in the cup of the spout.

244

PLATE | 81

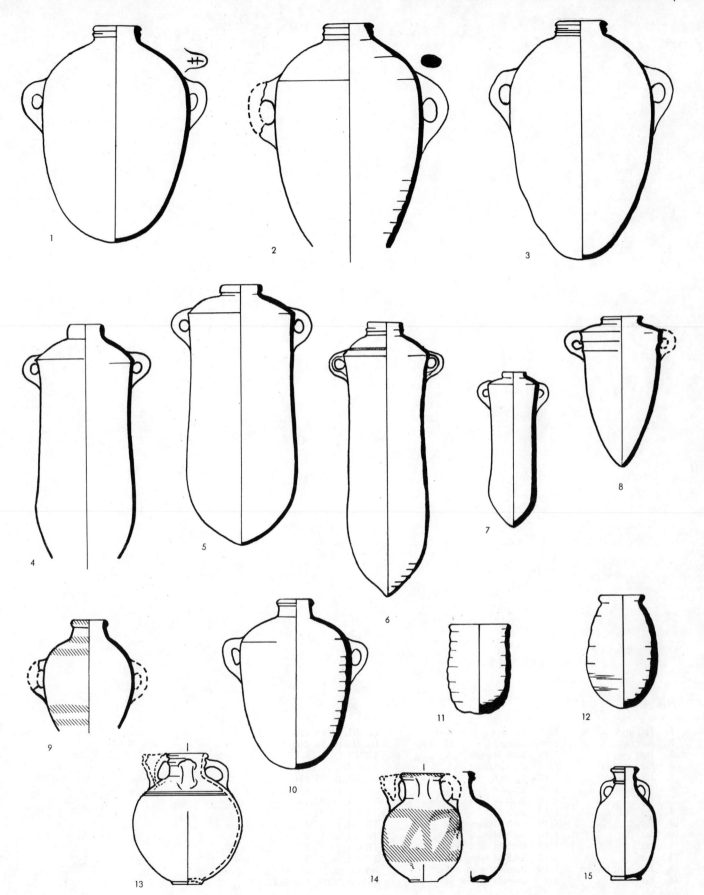

PLATE 82

1.	Jar, grey	1:10	Lachish	II–III	La. III, pl. 95:484
2.	Jar, red	1:10	Lachish	II	La. III, pl. 94–480
3.	Jar	1:10	Beth Mirsim	A	TBM III, pl. 13:3
4.	Jar, red-buff	1:10	Beth Mirsim	A	TBM III, pl. 13:1
5.	Jar, red-buff	1:10	Lachish		La. III, pl. 95:491
6.	Jar, pink	1:10	Lachish	III	La. III, pl. 95:489
7.	Jar	1:10	Beth Mirsim	A	TBM I, pl. 52:14
8.	Jar	1:10	Beth Mirsim	A	TBM I, pl. 52:12
9.	Jar	1:10	Beth Mirsim	A	TBM I, pl. 52:1
10.	Jar	1:10	Beth Mirsim	A	TBM I, pl. 52:2
11.	Jar	1:10	Beth Mirsim	A	TBM I, pl. 52:5
12.	Jar	1:10	Beth Mirsim	A	TBM I, pl. 53:3
13.	Jar, light brown	1:10	Beth-shemesh	II c	AS IV, pl. LXVII:5
14.	Jar	1:8	Gibeon		Gibeon, 1959, Fig. 6:2

PLATE | 82

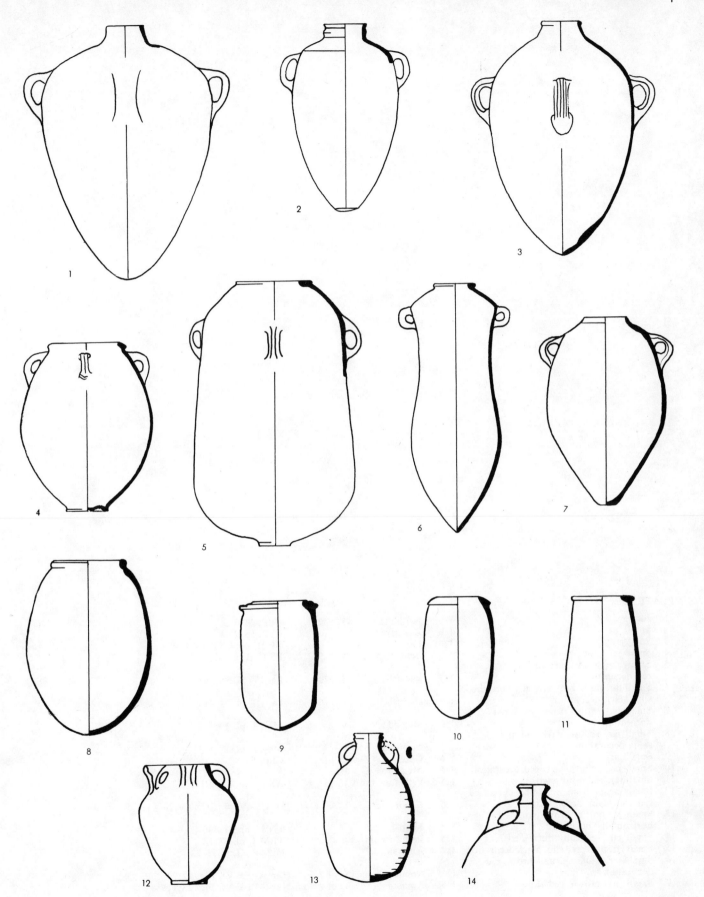

PLATE 83

1.	Jar	1:6	Far'ah (S)	T. 552	CPP, 44 R 2
2.	Small jar	1:6	Zakariya		CPP, 55 W 7
3.	Smal jar	1:6	Far'ah (S)		BP II, pl. LXXXVII:W 6
4.	Small jar, grey	1:6	Beth-shan	VI	BS II:II, pl. XLV:3
5.	Small jar, brown, cream slip red decoration	1:5	Lachish	T. 570	La. IV, pl. 85:985
6.	Small jar, pink, red vertically burnished slip, black decoration	1:5	Lachish	T. 116	La. III, pl. 91:419
7.	Small jar, brown-ocher, dark red decoration	1:5	Megiddo	V	Meg. I, pl. 19:114
8.	Small jar, yellow, dark red and sepia decoration	1:5	Megiddo	V	Meg. I, pl. 19:113
9.	Small jar	1:6	Gezer	T. 142	CPP, 55 X
10.	Small jar, yellow, light red decoration	1:5	Megiddo	III	Meg. I, pl. 9:24
11.	Small jar, reddish-brown	1:5	Beth-shemesh	II	AS IV, pl. LXVII:1
12.	Small jar, pink-brown, wheel-burnished, red and black decoration	1:5	Hazor	V A	H. III–IV, pl. CCXXVIII: 13
13.	Small jar-bottle, brown-red, horizontally burnished	1:5	Nasbeh		TN II, pl. 27:446
14.	Small jar, vertically burnished	1:5	Beth Mirsim	A	TBM I, pl. 53:12
15.	Small jar, pink, red slip, black decoration	1:5	Amman		QDAP XI, p. 71:23
16.	Small jar, buff, red and brown-red decoration	1:5	Amman	T. of Adoni-Nur	APEF VI, Fig. 22:90
17.	Small jar, brown, red slip	1:5	Amman	T. of Adoni-Nur	APEF VI, Fig. 23:119

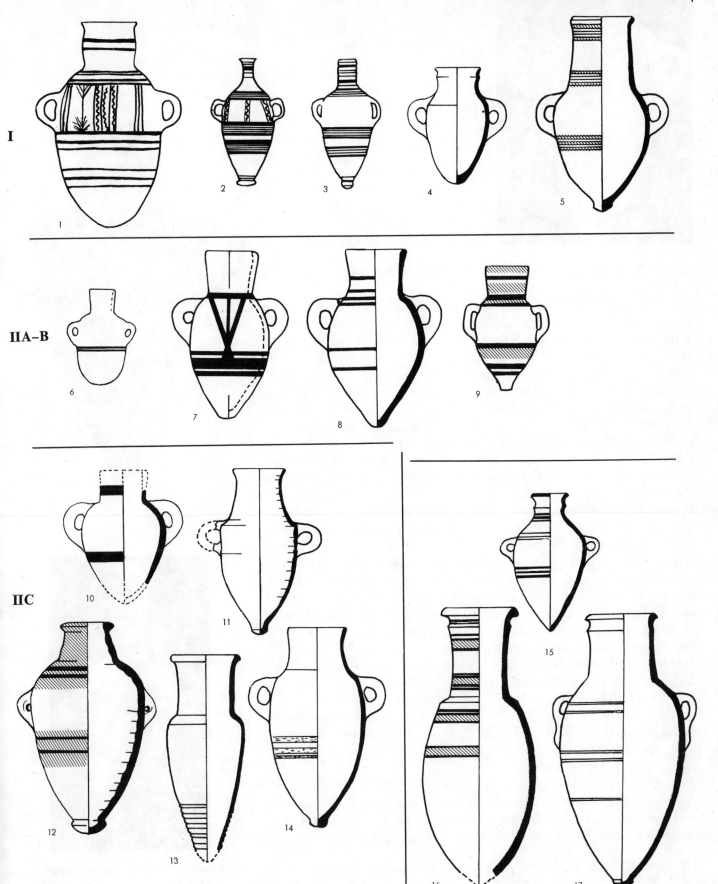

PLATE | 83

I

IIA–B

IIC

Photo 251. Jar, Far'ah(S), IDA I.6981.

Amphoriskoi: Iron I, II A—B, II C — North and South and Transjordan (Plate 83).

A certain type of small jar, the so-called amphoriskos, which is found in all three phases of the Iron Age, derives from the Canaanite jars and amphoriskoi of the Bronze Age. On Plate 83 we have assembled the main types: Nos. 1–5 belong to Iron I, but all five are still typically Canaanite in form and decoration. No. 5, from Tomb 570 in Lachish, closely resembles a vessel found in Tomb 571 at the same site (cf. Plate 44:9); the entire contents of Tomb 571 clearly belong to the Late Bronze Age. No. 1 is a Canaanite jar in every feature except the swollen neck — and this last element was adopted by Canaanite potters under Egyptian influence. Nos. 2 and 3 and Photos 251–254 illustrate an interesting phenomenon; vessels such as that in Photo No. 254 appear to imitate the glass amphoriskos in Photo 253. The narrow, straight, relatively long neck is unsuited to pottery shapes, while it is entirely appropriate to a glass vessel made by the thread-winding process. Some confirmation for this supposition can be found in the fact that the pottery form is very short-lived and appears to have been only a passing fashion. However, it is also obvious that the glass vessel itself is an imitation of a pottery jar or amphoriskos like those in Photos 251, 252. In the Amarna period and in the XIXth Dynasty, glass manufacture in Egypt had already developed sufficiently to produce fairly numerous vessels. Most of these were made in imitation of pottery forms.

Iron II A–B: The amphoriskos appears to have lost some of its popularity, and the range of types becomes more limited (Nos. 6–9). No. 6 can be compared to No. 1 of Iron I. No. 7 is decorated with a stylized tree.

Iron II C: Larger variants of the amphoriskos appear (Nos. 12–14), and also in Transjordan (Nos. 15 and 17). Interestingly enough, the button base, which echoes the thickened base of the Canaanite jar, survives throughout the entire Iron Age.

Nos. 15 and 17, which belong to the Ammonite pottery (cf. Plate 101), deserve special mention. The painted bands, the form of the vessels, and especially the lug-handles shaped like ducks' heads, suggest that these are influenced by Assyrian pottery, such as that found at Nimrud.[15]

Photo 252. Amphoriskos, Beth-shemesh, IDA I.81.

Photo 253. Glass amphoriskos, Lachish, IDA 34.7706.

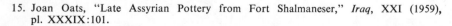

15. Joan Oats, "Late Assyrian Pottery from Fort Shalmaneser," *Iraq*, XXI (1959), pl. XXXIX:101.

Jugs and Juglets: Iron I — North and South (Plates 84—85).

North (Plate 84) — *Jugs:* The six main northern types of jugs in Iron I are shown on Plate 84:

1) Large jugs with short, wide neck, trefoil mouth, and handle drawn from rim to shoulder, often with red slip (Nos. 1 and 2).

2) Large jugs with high, cylindrical neck, and handle drawn from rim to shoulder (Nos. 3 and 4).

3) Jugs with biconical body, rim diameter equal to base diameter, without neck, and handle drawn from rim to shoulder (No. 5); this type goes back to the biconical jugs of the Late Bronze Age.

4) A type whose main features are a long neck and a handle from the centre of the neck to the shoulder; the body is generally piriform, and most of the specimens are decorated or have a slip (Nos. 6–8); the types appear in many variants and derive from a certain type of 'grey juglet' of the Late Bronze Age (cf. Plates 46 and 52).

5) This type is mainly characterized by metope decoration, entirely in Late Bronze Age tradition (No. 9).

6) Jugs with trough-like strainer-spouts (Nos. 10 and 11). The two specimens shown here have only the spout in common and differ in all other respects. No. 10, which has a basket handle, goes back a long way, to the Middle Bronze Age. The handle of jugs like No. 11 is always at right angles to the spout. The upper part of the body, that is, the zone of the handles and the spout, is painted with black and red metopes. This jug is of particular interest because of its kinship to the pilgrim flasks, and to jugs with similar bichrome decoration and handle descending from the middle of the neck to the shoulder (Plate 91).

Juglets: No. 12 is a juglet as far as its shape is concerned, but its size is that of a jug. Most of the juglets have a trefoil mouth, an ovoid body, and a slightly pointed base (Nos. 13–15). However, the juglet with cylindrical body and wide base ending in a blunt point already makes its appearance (No. 15).

South (Plate 85): The pottery vessels assembled on this plate come mainly from tombs excavated at Tell el-Far'ah and Gezer. The ceramic material from Stratum B at Tell Beth Mirsim does not contain any jugs or juglets and thus could not furnish any specimens. Jugs decorated in Philistine style have been relegated to Plate 90.

Jugs: Five main groups can be distinguished:

1) Piriform body, straight or slightly concave neck, often a trefoil mouth, ring-base, and handle drawn from rim to shoulder (Nos. 1–3).

2) No. 4 is similar to the above, but has a thickened button-shaped base characteristic mainly of contemporary storage-jars (cf. Plate 78:8–10).

3) Squat jugs with globular body, ring-base, wide neck, and handle drawn from rim to shoulder (Nos. 5, 6); this type will become popular in the later phases of the Iron Age, especially in the South.

4) The two painted jugs (Nos. 7–9) go back to two different types: No. 7 belongs to a type which is well represented in the North (Plate 84:6–7), while No. 8 evolved from local imitations of the Cypriot bilbil.

5) Jugs with trough-like strainer-spouts, resembling such jugs found in the North (Nos. 10 and 11). No. 11 has a basket handle, and is painted on the body and on the handle. In the publication, this jug is classified as Philistine.

Photo 254. Pottery amphoriskos imitating glass one, Zakariya, IDA V.255.

PLATE 84

1.	Jug, reddish	1:5	Hazor	XII	H. III–IV, pl. CLXVI:12
2.	Jug, pink, red slip	1:5	Hazor	XI	H. III–IV, pl. CCIII:18
3.	Jug, buff, smoothed	1:5	Megiddo	VI	Meg. II, pl. 75:5
4.	Jug, pink-buff, smoothed	1:5	Megiddo	VI	Meg. II, pl. 81:1
5.	Jug, buff, traces of burnish	1:5	Megiddo	VI	Meg. II, pl. 81:2
6.	Jug, orange-buff, irregularly burnished, red decoration	1:5	Megiddo	VI	Meg. II, pl. 81:20
7.	Jug, orange-buff, vertically burnished, red decoration	1:5	Megiddo	VI A	Meg. II, pl. 75:7
8.	Jug, buff, irregularly burnished, red slip	1:5	Megiddo	VI A	Meg. II, pl. 75:6
9.	Jug, pink-buff, vertically burnished, red decoration	1:5	Megiddo	VI	Meg. II, pl. 81:21
10.	Spouted jug, orange-buff, smoothed, red decoration	1:5	Megiddo	VI	Meg. II, pl. 82:2
11.	Spouted jug, buff, burnished, red and black decoration	1:5	Megiddo	VI A	Meg. II, pl. 75:22
12.	Jug, pink-buff, smoothed	1:5	Megiddo	VI	Meg. II, pl. 81:13
13.	Juglet, brownish-pink	1:5	Hazor	XII	H. III–IV, pl. CCI:25
14.	Juglet, buff, smoothed	1:5	Megiddo	VI	Meg. II, pl. 81:10
15.	Juglet, pink-buff, smoothed	1:5	Megiddo	VI	Meg. II, pl. 81:10

PLATE | 84

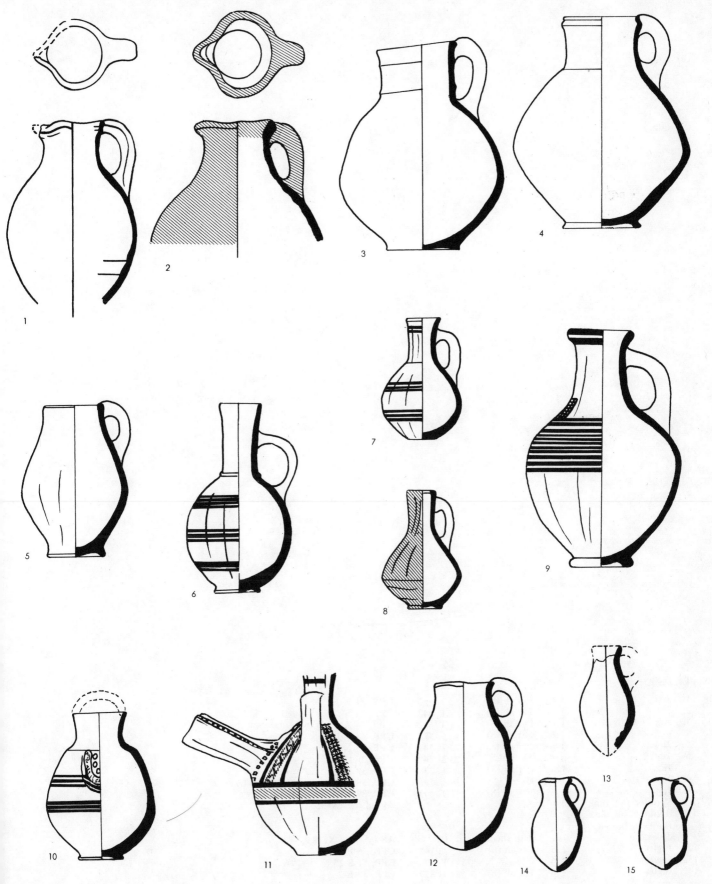

PLATE 85

1.	Jug	1:6	Far'ah (S)	T. 552	CPP, 34 B 3
2.	Jug	1:6	Far'ah (S)	T. 542	CPP, 34, F 2
3.	Jug	1:6	Far'ah (S)	T. 532	CPP, 34 A
4.	Jug	1:6	Far'ah (S)	T. 532	CPP, 38 F 1
5.	Jug	1:6	Far'ah (S)	T. 542	CPP, 36 N 8
6.	Jug	1:6	Far'ah (S)	T. 542	CPP, 36 P
7.	Jug	1:6	Far'ah (S)	T. 236	CPP, 39 H 1
8.	Jug	1:6	Gezer	T. 59	CPP, 59 W
9.	Jug	1:6	Far'ah (S)	T. 543	CPP, 39 N
10.	Spouted jug, pink	1:6	Ai		Ay, pl. LXIX:385
11.	Spouted jug, pink, red slip, brown decoration	1:5	Beth-shemesh	III	AS IV, pl. LX:18
12.	Juglet	1:6	Far'ah (S)	T. 562	CPP, 35 P 1
13.	Juglet	1:6	Gezer	T. 59	CPP, 51 S 2
14.	Juglet	1:6	Far'ah (S)	T. 839	CPP, 37 E 2

254

PLATE | 85

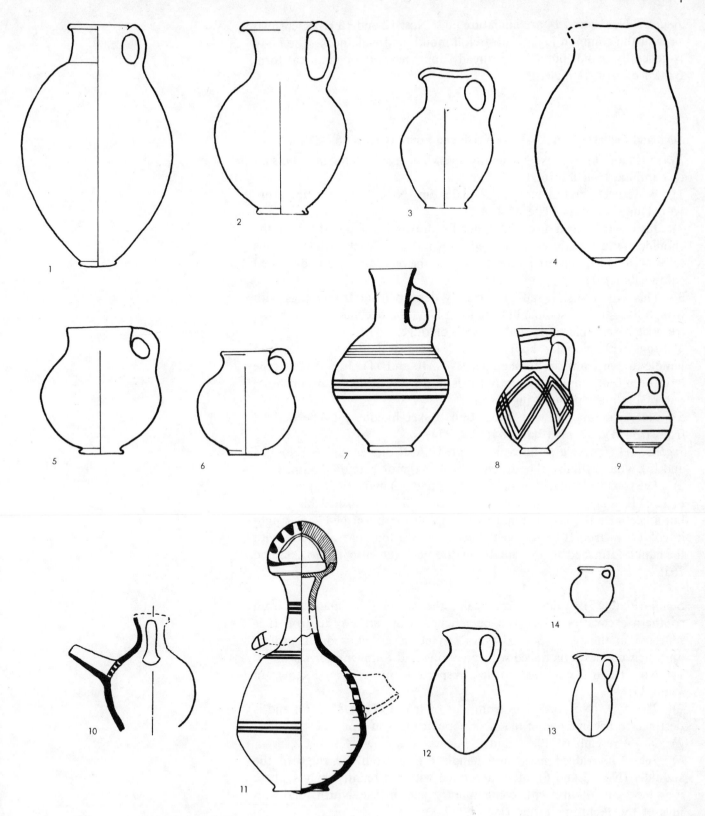

Juglets: Nos. 9 and 14 are miniature jugs. Nos. 12 and 13 represent two sizes of the common juglet with trefoil mouth and wide neck. The body is generally ovoid, but No. 13 already approaches the cylindrical form typical of Iron II juglets.

Jugs and Juglets: Iron A—B — North and South (Plates 86—87).

North (Plate 86) — *Jugs:* Generally speaking, Iron II jugs may be said to continue Iron I forms.

1) Wide neck, trefoil mouth, or plain rim (Nos. 1–3), deriving from Iron I jugs, such as Plate 84:1–4.

2) Jugs with ridged neck, and handle drawn from the ridge to the shoulder, either plain or decorated with red and black painted bands (Nos. 4–6); such jugs are a development of the bichrome group discussed below (Plate 91).

3) This type (Nos. 7 and 8) is clearly derived from Iron I jugs with trough-like strainer-spouts, but the form is on the decline — small body, trumpet base, wide neck, and absence of ridge.

4) Jugs with globular body, rounded base, straight wide neck, and handle drawn from rim to shoulder (Nos. 10 and 11). Jugs of this type have been found in the North, but it is in the South that they constitute one of the most popular jug forms.

5) No. 9, a tiny jug with spout and basket handle, may be derived from Iron Age forms (Plates 84:10, 85:11).

Juglets: 1) These are the typical Iron II A–B dipper juglets (Nos. 14 and 15), whith cylindrical body, either a plain rim or a trefoil mouth.

2) The so-called "black" juglets (Nos. 12 and 13) make their appearance in Iron II. They are usually of grey ware, with a burnished black slip, but sometimes the clay is pinkish-brown and the burnished slip is light in colour. In Iron II these juglets have usually a long narrow neck, with the handle attached to the middle of the neck (cf. also Photo 262 and 263).

South (Plate 87) — *Jugs*: Here again, the scarcity of material from southern excavation which can be assigned with certainty to Iron II is reflected in the plate. Several types can be nevertheless distinguished, and their connections traced with preceding and following forms.

1) Nos. 1 and 2 continue in most respects forms of Iron I shown in Plate 85:1–3.

2) This type (No. 3) derives from jugs of Iron I (Plate 85:5–6), and is destined to become one of the most popular types in Iron II C.

3) No. 4 resembles Nos. 1 and 2, but has a narrow neck.

4) Jugs with ridged neck, and handle drawn from the ridge to the shoulder (Nos. 5 and 6), often decorated with red painted bands; these jugs have an affinity with contemporary jugs in the North, and with jugs of the Bichrome group (Plate 91:7–8).

5) No. 7 has a trough-like strainer spout; such jugs have already been discussed (p. 251 above).

6) No. 8 is a tiny jug with a handle drawn from the middle of the neck to the shoulder.

PLATE | 86

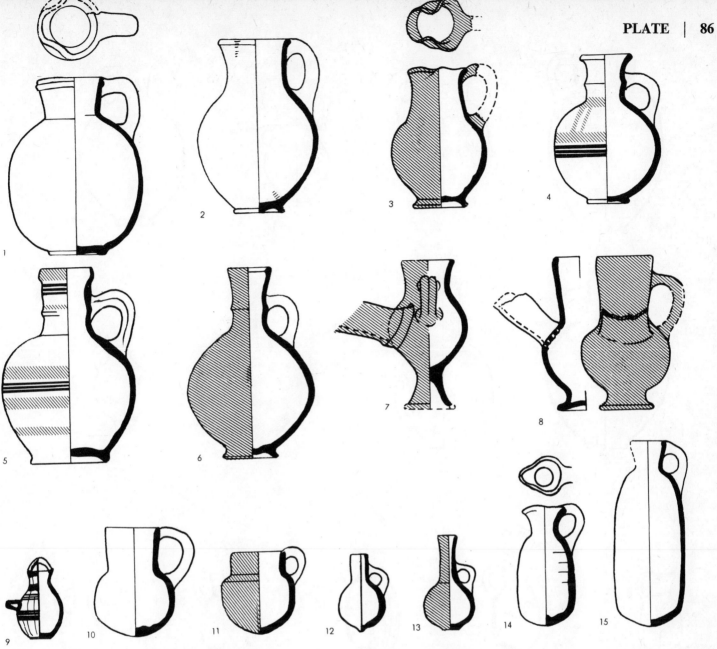

PLATE 86

1.	Jug, pink	1:5	Hazor	VIII	J. II, pl. LVIII:14
2.	Jug, brown-ocher	1:5	Megiddo	V	Meg. I, pl. 6:159
3.	Jug, buff, red burnished slip	1:5	Samaria	III	SS III, Fig. 5:5
4.	Jug, brown-ocher, dark red and black decoration	1:5	Megiddo	V	Meg. I, pl. 8:177
5.	Jug, buff, buff slip, red and black decoration	1:5	Samaria	III	SS III, Fig. 5:1
6.	Jug, brown-ocher, red irregularly hand-burnished slip	1:5	Megiddo	V	Meg. I, pl. 7:171
7.	Spouted jug, brown-ocher, red irregularly hand-burnished slip	1:5	Megiddo	V	Meg. I, pl. 8:175
8.	Spouted jug, buff, red vertically burnished slip	1:5	Samaria	III	SS III, Fig. 5:2
9.	Spouted juglet, pink-buff, burnished, black decoration	1:5	Megiddo	V A	Meg. II, pl. 88:19
10.	Jug, purple	1:5	Samaria	III	SS III, Fig. 5:3
11.	Jug, dark brown ocher, red hand-burnished slip	1:5	Megiddo	V	Meg. I, pl. 8:179
12.	Black juglet, blue-black, hand burnished	1:5	Megiddo	V	Meg. I, pl. 5:124
13.	Juglet, red	1:5	Far'ah (N)	III	RB 1952, p. 563, Fig. 6:4
14.	Juglet, reddish-buff	1:5	Abu Hawam	III	TAH, p. 20:57
15.	Juglet, pink-buff, smoothed	1:5	Megiddo	V A	Meg. pl. 88:13

PLATE | 87

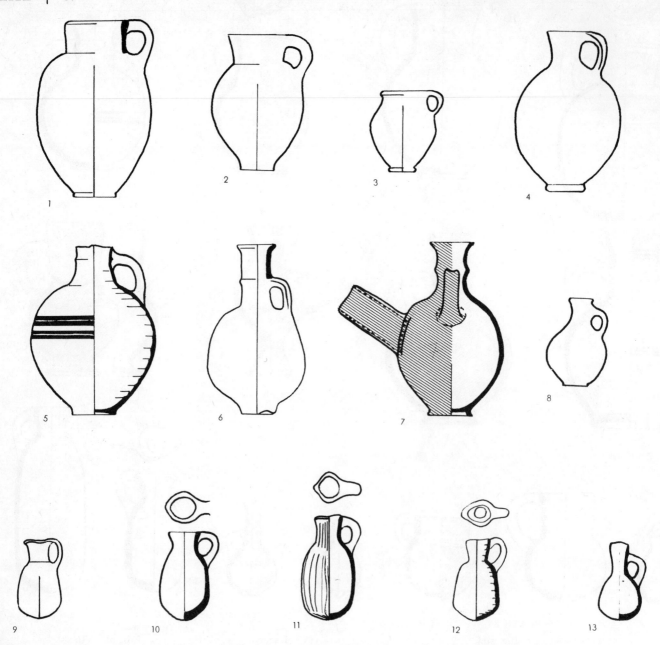

PLATE 87

1. Jug	1:6	Far'ah (S)	T. 215	CPP, 34 U 2
2. Jug	1:6	Far'ah (S)	T. 240	CPP, 34 X 4
3. Jug	1:6	Far'ah (S)	T. 218	CPP, 37 N 8
4. Jug	1:6	Far'ah (S)	T. 213	CPP, 39 E
5. Jug, dark red decoration	1:5	Beth-shemesh	II a	AS IV, pl. LXV:39
6. Jug	1;6	Far'ah (S)	T. 223	CPP, 83 N 2
7. Spouted jug, brown, dark red vertically burnished slip	1:5	Lachish	T. 521	La. III, pl. 89:364
8. Jug	1:6	Far'ah (S)	T. 225	CPP, 34 T 8
9. Juglet	1:6	Far'ah (S)	T. 225	CPP, 54 J 2
10. Juglet	1:5	Beth Mirsim	B 3	TBM I, pl. 51:12
11. Juglet, red vertically burnished slip	1:5	Beth Mirsim	A 1	TBM III, pl. 18:20
12. Juglet, light brown	1:5	Beth-shemesh	II a	AS IV, pl. LXIV:42
13. Juglet, brown-red, vertically burnished	1:5	Beth Mirsim	B	TBM I, pl. 51:2

Photo 255. Jug, 'decanter', Hazor, *Hazor*, I, Pl. CLIII.

Photo 256. Jug, 'decanter', Hazor, *Hazor*, III-IV, Pl. CCCLII.

Photo 257. Jug, Beth-shemesh, IDA I.10515.

Juglets: 1) Nos. 9–12 are four examples of the common dipper juglet of the period.

2) No. 13 belongs to the "black" juglet type, although it is of brownish ware and is very like its northern counterpart; the handle is attached to the middle of the long neck.

Jugs and Juglets: Iron II C — North and South (Plates 88—89).

North (Plate 88) — *Jugs:* The examples assembled on Plate 88 can be classified as follows:

1) The decanter is one of the most characteristic Iron II C forms in the North as well as in the South (Nos. 1–4). The shape of the body and the generally ridged neck, with the handle drawn from the ridge, are common to all the members of this group, but there are significant differences between northern and southern examples.

The four examples in the plate (Nos. 1–4) and Photos 255–256 illustrate the chief variants of the type and underline at the same time the essential homogeneity of the form. The main features of the northern decanter are the 'double,' deeply grooved rim, splayed like a funnel, the metallic well-baked ware, and the frequently found group of grooves on the shoulder. There are also some decanters of 'fatty' ware, which is not well-baked, with a red slip.

2) Two examples (Nos. 5 and 6) are shown here which are derived from the Bichrome group discussed below (Plate 91:7, 8); the neck is ridged.

3) Jugs with a straight, plain neck, trefoil mouth, and painted red or black bands on the body (Nos. 7 and 8).

4) Jugs with a short trough-like strainer-spout (No. 11; Photo 257), whose forerunners we have already encountered in Iron I and II A–B.

5) Two jugs which have a trefoil neck in common (Nos. 9 and 10); both have a red slip; No. 10 bears a relationship to the Phoenician-Israelite pottery described below (Plate 92).

6) No. 13 is a jug with narrow neck and plain thickened rim.

7) These jugs belong to a fairly common type, with globular body, rounded base, a short neck, and a slightly inverted rim (Nos. 14 and 15); the globular base is reminiscent of cooking-pots; slightly divergent variants are common in the South (Plate 89:14–16).

8) No. 12 is a tiny jug with spout, which derives to some extent from spouted jugs of Iron II A–B, but which has a handle drawn from rim to shoulder instead of a basket handle.

Juglets: 1) Dipper juglets (Nos. 16–18) appear in a variety of ovoid and cylindrical forms.

2) The black juglet (No. 19) has declined into a very small vessel with a shorter neck and a handle drawn from the rim; generally, this kind of juglet has a burnished black slip, but in Iron II C the light-colored specimens continue to be made.

PLATE 88

1.	Decanter, red smoothed	1:5	Megiddo	IV	Meg. II, pl. 91:1
2.	Decanter, yellowish-orange, red slip, smoothed	1:5	Hazor	VI	H. III–IV, pl. CCXIX:20
3.	Decanter, grey	1:5	Far'ah (N)	II	RB 1951, p. 415, Fig. 11:23
4.	Decanter, light brown	1:5	Hazor	V A	H. II, pl. LXXXVII:4
5.	Jug, pink, burnished, brown decoration	1:5	Hazor	VI	H. II, pl. LXX:16
6.	Jug, light brown	1:5	Hazor	V	H. I, pl. LVI:18
7.	Jug, pink, red decoration	1:5	Hazor	VI	H. II, pl. LXX:15
8.	Jug, grey, red and black decoration	1:5	Hazor	V A	H. III–IV, pl. CCXXVII:3
9.	Jug, pink, brown slip	1:5	Hazor	V	H. I, pl. LVI:7
10.	Jug, pink, brown slip	1:5	Hazor	VII	H. II, pl. LXIV:19
11.	Spouted jug, grey, red slip	1:5	Hazor	V A	H. III–IV, pl. CCXXVIII:1
12.	Spouted juglet, dark brown ocher, sepia and dark red decoration	1:5	Megiddo	III	Meg. I, pl. 1:34
13.	Jug, green-brown, light red slip	1:5	Megiddo	IV	Meg. I, pl. 3:92
14.	Jug, burnt umber	1:5	Megiddo	III–II	Meg. I, pl. 5:118
15.	Jug, burnt umber	1:5	Megiddo	III	Meg. I, pl. 5:112
16.	Juglet, pink	1:5	Hazor	VI	H. II, pl. LXX:4
17.	Juglet, yellow	1:5	Hazor	VI	H. II, pl. LXX:2
18.	Juglet, brown	1:5	Hazor	V A	H. II, pl. LXXXVI:8
19.	Black juglet, blue-black, vertically burnished	1:5	Megiddo	IV–I	Meg. I, pl. 2:50
20.	Amphoriskos, yellow, light red decoration	1:5	Megiddo	II	Meg. I, pl. 9:3
21.	Bottle, brown ocher, wheel-burnished, sepia decoration	1:5	Megiddo	II	Meg. I, pl. 9:7

PLATE | 88

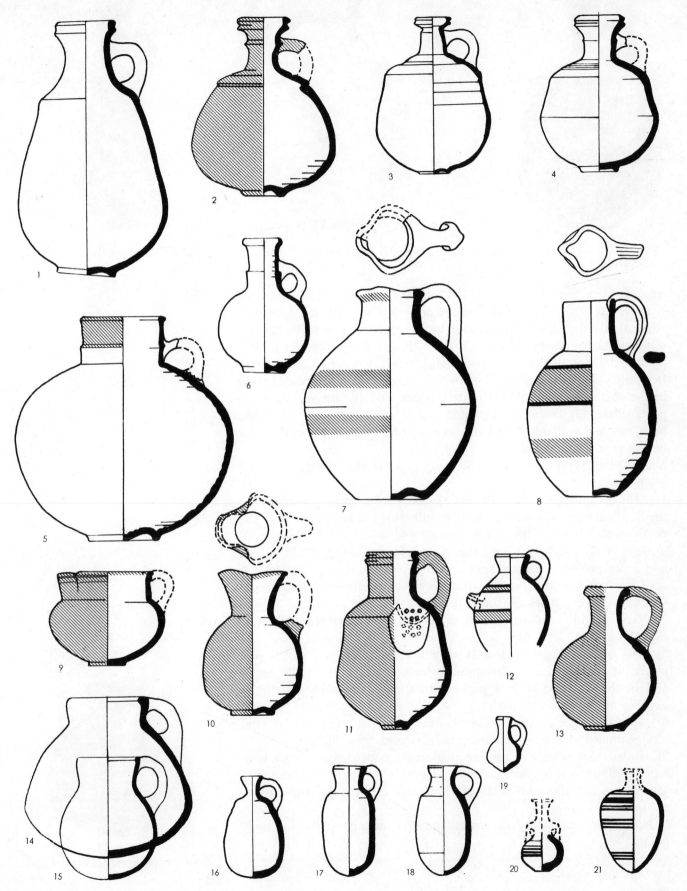

Photo 258. Jug, 'decanter', Unknown prov., HU 619.

Photo 259. Jug, 'decanter', Lachish, IDA 33.1920.

Photo 260. Jug, 'decanter', Ain Tuba, HU 2216.

The tiny amphoriskos (No. 20) is found also in the southern assemblage (Plate 89:23) and in Ammonite pottery (Plate 101:25). Albright's suggestion[16] that this amphoriskos is first made in the tenth century requires further study. The bottle (No. 21) has been included in this plate as well as in the next plate (Plate 89:24) in order to demonstrate that this vessel is found in all parts of the country. It will be discussed in the chapters on Ammonite pottery (Plate 101) and on Assyrian imports (Plate 99). We have included these two vessels with the juglets both here and in Plates 89 and 101, in order to emphasize the parallelism between the three related areas.

South (Plate 89) — *Jugs:* The following types can be distinguished on Plate 89:

1) The decanter (Nos. 1–3, Photos 258–261) has a wide distribution in the South as well as in the North; the southern decanter differs from the northern mainly in the form of its splayed and cut-off rim, and is usually made of "fatty" ware, with a red slip. No. 1 is the prototype, while Nos. 2 and 3 are probably slightly later variants. Nos. 4 and 5 do not form a separate type but are distant variations on the decanter theme. No. 4 (cf.Photo 260) is remarkable for its slender shape.

2) Nos. 6 and 7 are parallel to group 2 of the northern Iron II C assemblage.

3) No. 8 derives from the Iron II jug with trough-like spout and handle placed at right angles to the spout, which occurs both in the South and in the North; No. 9, a juglet with spout and basket handle, is likewise not an innovation.

4) Jugs with a wide neck, a handle drawn from rim to shoulder, and a ridge immediately below the often trefoil mouth (Nos. 10–13).

5) Broad jugs with a squat, often globular body, usually a rounded base, a relatively short neck, a handle drawn from rim to shoulder, and generally a red slip; this is a very common southern jug-form (Nos. 14–16).

6) No. 17 is a small jug which corresponds to contemporary jugs in most points.

Photo 265. Black pyxis, Unknown prov., HU.

16. *TBM*, I, pp. 84–85.

262

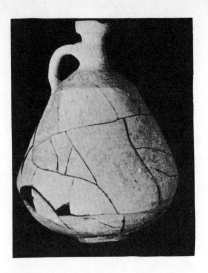

Photo 261. Jug, 'decanter', Beth-shemesh, IDA I.5899.

Photo 262. Black juglet, Unknown prov., HU 3282.

Photo 263. Black juglet, Unknown prov., HU 2512.

Photo 264. Black juglet, Beth-shemesh, HU 346.

Juglets: 1) Broad, piriform body, narrow neck, and wide grooved rim (No. 18); the rim recalls the grooved rims of deep cooking-pots and bowls. 2) Dipper juglets; two examples, both very common, are shown (Nos. 19 and 20; Photo 267).

3) Black juglets (Photo 264), evolved from the black juglets of the preceding period (Photos 262–263); in the South as well as in the North, such juglets have a short neck, a handle drawn from the rim to the shoulder, and a tiny body (No. 22), but the type is more common in the South than in the North; No. 21 combines features of the dipper juglets and of the black juglets.

Amphoriskos: For the amphoriskos (No. 23), see above, Plate 88:20, and Photo 268.

Bottle: For the bottle (No. 24), see above, Plate 88:21, and especially below, Plate 101:25.

Photos 262–268 show three juglets, two pyxides, and an amphoriskos of the grey-black Iron Age II A–B and II C ware, discussed above.

Photo 266. Black elongated pyxis, Artas, HU 2234.

Photo 267. Juglet, Unknown prov., IDA 49–1293.

Photo 268. Amphoriskos, Beth Mirsim, IDA I.4992.

PLATE 89

1.	Decanter, pink, pink wheel-burnished slip	1:5	Lachish	II	La. III, pl. 87:274
2.	Decanter, red-buff, wheel-burnished	1:5	Beth Mirsim	A	TBM I, pl. 59:2
3.	Decanter, wheel-burnished	1:5	Beth Mirsim	A	TBM III, pl. 16:8
4.	Decanter, pink, red burnished slip	1:5	Lachish	II	La. III, pl. 87:277
5.	Jug, red brown	1:5	Beth Mirsim	A	TBM I, pl. 58:2
6.	Jug, brownish-red	1:5	Beth-shemesh	II b ?	AS IV, pl. LXV:42
7.	Jug, pink, red burnished slip	1:5	Lachish	III	La. III, pl. 87:270
8.	Spouted jug, pink, pink slip	1:5	Lachish	III	La. III, pl. 89:361
9.	Spouted juglet with basket handle, grey, brown slip	1:5	Lachish	III	La. III, pl. 89:358
10.	Jug, brown	1:5	Beth Mirsim	A	TBM I, pl. 58:8
11.	Jug, red-buff	1:5	Beth Mirsim	A	TBM I, pl. 58:6
12.	Jug, grey	1:5	Beth Mirsim	A	TBM I, pl. 58:5
13.	Jug, red-buff	1:5	Beth Mirsim	A	TBM I, pl. 58:3
14.	Jug, buff	1:5	Beth Mirsim	A	TBM I, pl. 57:14
15.	Jug, pink	1:5	Lachish	III	La. III, pl. 84:177
16.	Jug, red-buff	1:5	Beth Mirsim	A	TBM I, pl. 57:13
17.	Juglet, buff	1:5	Beth Mirsim	A	TBM III, pl. 16:3
18.	Juglet, pink-buff, vertically burnished	1:5	Beth Mirsim	A	TBM I, pl. 57:15
19.	Juglet, brown, red irregularly burnished slip	1:5	Lachish	T. 191	La. III, pl. 88:296
20.	Juglet, brown-red	1:5	Beth Mirsim	A	TBM III, pl. 17:1
21.	Juglet, red vertically slip	1:5	Beth Mirsim	A	TBM III, pl. 18:14
22.	Juglet, grey	1:5	Beth Mirsim	A	TBM I, pl. 68:31
23.	Amphoriskos, buff, burnished, red decoration	1:5	Beth Mirsim	A	TBM I, pl. 66:17
24.	Bottle, pink, brown decoration	1:5	Lachish	T. 106	La. III, pl. 90:384

264

PLATE | 89

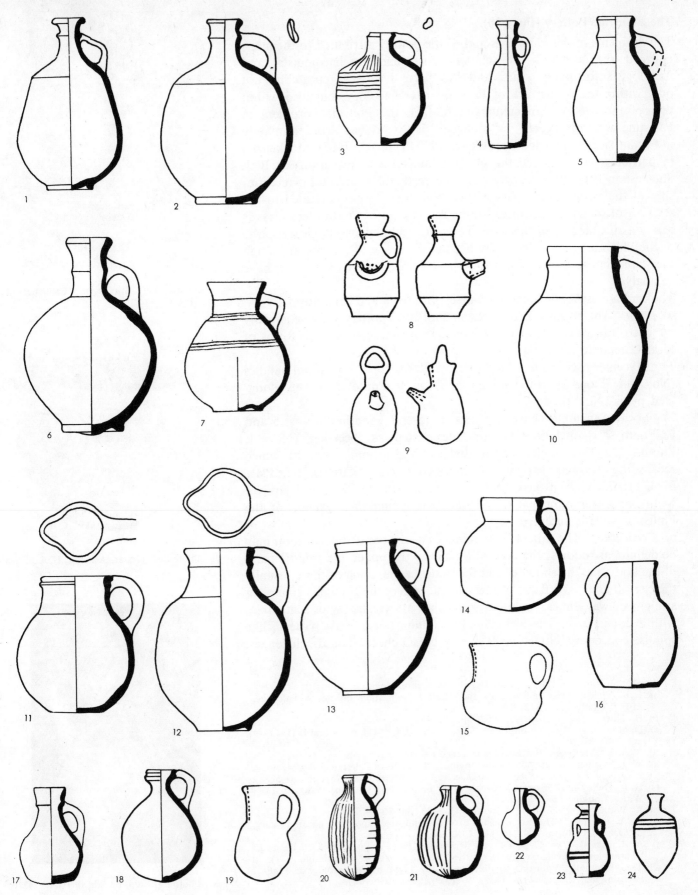

The Philistine Pottery (Plate 90).

The problems of the Philistines and of the pottery attributed to them has engaged the attention of scholars, historians, archaeologists, and philologists for many years, and has been discussed repeatedly, not only within the framework of Palestinian archaeology, but also within that of the the Aegean cultures.[17] In fact, the Philistine problem in Palestine was 'discovered' by archaeologists who had worked mainly in Cretan-Aegean archaeology (Welch, 1900; Thiersch, 1908). Mackenzie, in particular, investigated the problem during his excavations at Beth Shemesh in 1911–1912, he determined correctly the stratigraphic relationship of the pottery and defined it as "Philistine," and as related to the cultures of the Aegean world. Ethnic association of any pottery class is rarely as justified as in this case. The historical and philological aspects of the Philistine phenomenon are beyond the scope of this book, though they are almost inseparable from the ceramic aspect, which we have to analyse.

The ceramic aspect includes, of course, both form and decoration.

a) *Form:* The repertoire of types in Philistine pottery falls generically into two categories: 1) forms of Mycenaean character, and 2) forms of local Canaanite character.

1) Mycenaean character: the krater with two tilted horizontal handles (Nos. 1–4, Photo 269); the stirrup-jar (No. 10, Photo 270); the elongated pyxis (Nos. 6 and 7).

2) Local Canaanite character: jugs in several variations (Nos. 5 and 9, Photo 271), including the one designated as 'beer-jug' (No. 11, Photos 272–274); juglets, even the 'waisted' example (No. 8), which recalls the 'waisted' variants of the local pyxis imitations, (cf. Plate 57:4, 5); the pilgrim flask (Nos. 12 and 13, Photo 275); and jar No. 14, if our assumption that its decoration is a simplified version of the Philistine style is accepted.

b) *Decoration:* The salient characteristics of the painted decoration may be defined as follows: the decoration covers the upper and middle parts of the body, i.e. the shoulder and the central zone. Each of these, usually the central zone, is a frieze of the metopic order: the triglyphs consist of straight or wavy lines, enclosing sometimes a vertical row of semicircles with a dot in each. The metopes may contain a geometric pattern, like spirals, concentric circles enclosing a cross, checkerboards, lozenges,

Photo 270. Stirrup-jar, Beth-shemesh, IDA I.10510.

Photo 269. Krater, Askelon, IDA B. 645.

Photo 271. Jug, Far'ah(S), IDA I. 4276.

---

17. A selection from the wide literature is given here, chronologically arranged:
   a) F. B. Welch, "The Influence of the Aegean Civilization on South Palestine," *PEFQST* (1900), pp. 342–350.
   b) H. Thiersch, *JDAI Anzeiger*, 1908, pp. 378–384.
   c) D. Mackenzie, "Excavations at Ain Shems," *PEFA*, I (1911), p. 84, and II (1912–13), pp. 9–10, 33–36.
   d) R. A. S. Macalister, *The Philistines*, London, 1911.
   e) W. J. Phythian-Adams, "Philistine Origins in the Light of Palestinian Archaeology," *Bulletin of the British School of Archaeology, Jerusalem*, III (1923), pp. 20–27.
   f) H. R. Hall, *The Civilization of Greece in the Bronze Age*, London, 1928, pp. 239 ff.
   g) W. F. Albright, *TBM*, I (1932), pp. 53–56.
   h) K. Watzinger, *Denkmaeler Palaestinas*, I, 1933, pp. 80–84.
   i) W. A. Heurtley, "The Relationship between 'Philistine' and Mycenaean Pottery," *QDAP*, V (1936), pp. 90–110, pls. LIX–LX.
   j) A. Furumark, *The Chronology of Mycenaean Pottery*, pp. 116–122: Appendix: "Chronological Evidence from Derivative Mycenaean Wares" (Stockholm, 1941).
   k) Trude Dothan, "Philistine Civilization in the Light of Archaeological Finds in Palestine and Egypt," *Eretz Israel*, V (1959), 55–66 (Hebrew).

266

Photo 273. Jug, Lyre-playing man and animal-procession, Megiddo, *Meg.* II, Pl. 76. IDA 36. 1921.

Photo 274. Jug, 'Beer-jug', Ashdod, IDA68–321.

Photo 272. Jug, 'Beer-jug', Beth-shemesh, IDA V.504.

or, most characteristically, a bird-motif. The bird is shown in two postures — generally the head is turned backwards, with the beak thrust under the wing-feathers, but sometimes the bird looks straight ahead. Generally this decoration is black and red on a white slip, but it occurs also in one color, with or without the slip.

This style of decoration occurs on all the types enumerated above in the two groups of forms. A very interesting point should now be emphasized: representatives of the types in group 1 were imported into Canaan as early as in the Late Bronze (cf. for krater — Plate 57:12; for stirrup-jar — Photo 191 and Plate 57:10; for pyxis — Photos 181, 199, and Plate 57:1). Even more important is the fact that these very types, among others, were not only imitated by local potters (Plate 57), but were absorbed into the local culture, and continued to develop together with the other more native elements making up the pottery repertoire. They became part of the local culture to such an extent that it could reasonably be suggested that the three types enumerated in group 1 came down to Iron I as direct descendants of the Late Bronze repertoire, in itself a complex amalgamation. In other words, the stirrup-jar was already a native though a 'naturalized' one, when the decorated stirrup-jar started to be made by the newcomers — the Philistines, who decorated it in the style customary in their Aegean homeland.

This suggestion has been brought forward merely to illustrate the complexity of the problems involved, although the ethnic connotation of this pottery seems to be satisfactorily settled.

267

Photo 275. Pilgrim-flask with cup, Megiddo, IDA 36.1999.

PLATE | **90**

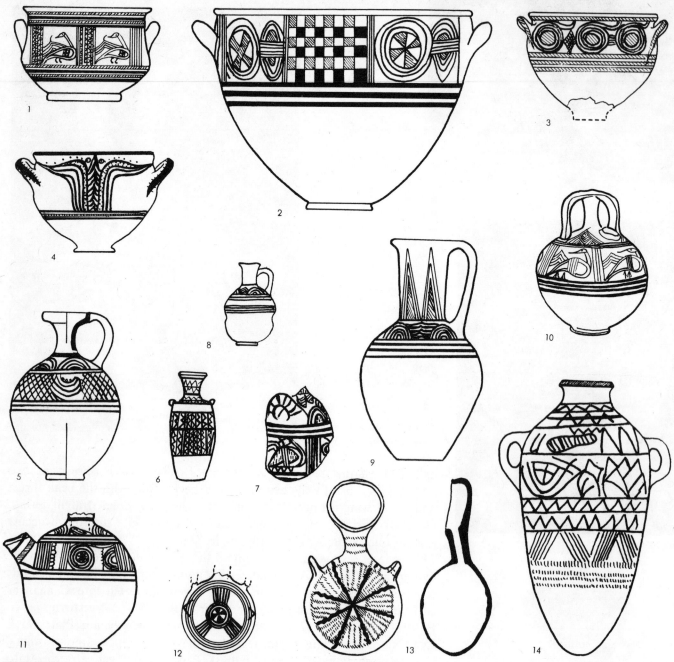

PLATE 90

1.	Bowl	1:4	Gezer	Gezer III, pl. CLXIII:1
2.	Krater	1:6	Gezer	CPP, 27 D 8
3.	Bowl	1:5	Beth-shemesh	AS III, Fig. 2:20
4.	Bowl, red, white slip, red and black decoration	1:4	Askelon	PMB 4, pl. 1:3
5.	Jug	1:6	Far'ah (S) T. 601	CPP, 67 D 2
6.	Pyxis	1:6	Gezer	CPP, 66 X 5
7.	Pyxis-bottle, fragment, pink-grey, red and black decoration	1:4	es-Safi	PMB 4, pl. II:4– EP, pl. 42:163
8.	Juglet	1:6	Far'ah (S) T. 607	CPP, 59 J 1
9.	Jug	1:6	Far'ah (S) T. 552	CPP, 34 Y 4
10.	Stirrup-jar	1:6	Gezer	CPP, 64 R 2
11.	Spouted jug, red and black decoration	1:6	es-Safi	CPP, 67 S 2
12.	Pilgrim flask	1:6	Gezer	CPP, 85 H 16
13.	Pilgrim flask, buff, red and black decoration	1:5	Megiddo VI B	Meg. II, pl. 74:16
14.	Jar	1:6	Far'ah (S) T. 834	CPP, 43 L 2

PLATE | 91

PLATE 91

1. Jug, brown-buff, red and black decoration 1:5   Abu Hawam   IV   TAH, p. 23:152
2. Jug, buff, burnished, red and
   black decoration   1:5   Megiddo   VI A   Meg. II, pl. 75:22
3. Bowl, brown, red and black decoration 1:5   Hazor   IX–X   H. III–IV, pl. CLXXVII:11
4. Bowl, reddish-buff, red and
   black decoration   1:5   Abu Hawam   IV   TAH, p. 29:153
5. Jug-flask, buff, burnished orange-buff
   slip, red and black decoration   1:5   Megiddo   VI   Meg. II, pl. 86:1
6. Jug, pink, red and black decoration   1:5   Hazor   IX B   H. III IV, pl. CLXXVI:6
7. Jug, red, vertically burnished, red and
   black decoration   1:5   Hazor   X B   H. III–IV, pl. CCCLV:13
8. Jug, buff, buff slip, red and
   black decoration   1:6   Carmel   Tomb 7   BBSAJ 5, pl. III:27

Photo 276. Jug. Gharbi, Dayan Collection.

Photo 277. Jug, Abu-Hawam, IDA 34.520.

The Bichrome Style (Plate 91).

A few words of explanation are necessary to introduce the three groups, which are here presented separately: a) The Bichrome Style; b) The Phoenician Pottery; c) The imported Cypriot and Cypro-Phoenician Pottery. These three groups are related to each other by their common connection with the Phoenician problem. Our purpose in selecting the material and arranging it in three groups was to assist in defining the problem, inasmuch as the definition of a pottery group is an indispensable basis for the understanding of its problems, origins, and connections. These plates were arranged before the publication of Joan Du Plat Taylor's work on the pottery from Al-Mina near Alalakh,[18] and it was a particular pleasure to note that her classification corresponds to that proposed here.

The Bichrome Style (Bichrome II in Cyprus) includes the following types:

1) Jugs decorated with concentric circles on opposite sides of the body (No. 1, Photos 276 and 277).

2) Similar jugs, but without a base. These forms stand midway between jugs and pilgrim-flasks (Nos. 5 and probably 6, whose base is broken; Photos 278 and 279).

3) Jug with long, trough-like strainer spout, decorated in the usual way (No. 2).

4) Bowls decorated inside with red and black bands (Nos. 3 and 4, Photo 280).

Photo 280. Bowl, Hazor, *Hazor*, III-IV, Pl. CCCLV.

---

18. Joan du Plat Taylor, "The Cypriote and Syrian Pottery from Al Mina," *Iraq*, XXI (1959), pp. 62–92.

Photo 278. Pilgrim-flask, Farah(N),
RB, 1952, Pl. XVIII.

Photo 279. Pilgrim-flask, Megiddo,
IDA 49–1385.

5) Jugs with a different conception of the decoration: only the neck is decorated (Nos. 7 and 8), This type has been included here with some hesitation.

Types 1 and 2 have a distinctive bichrome pattern: opposite the handle there is always a fill-motif, usually a stylized plant, placed between the two bulging hemispheres painted with concentric circles. Sometimes such a fill-motif is also used below the handle, for instance on a spherical jug from Tell Abu Hawam, Stratum IV.[19]

Origin and date: Vessels of this style are found mainly in the north of the country, in Iron I strata, as for instance No. 2, which comes from Stratum VI at Megiddo. A pilgrim-flask with a similar decoration appears in Megiddo as early as in Stratum VII A.[20] This style continues to be used, and even flourishes in the Iron II A as well, and to a lesser degree in Iron II B, side by side with the other pottery-class to be discussed in the next chapter. The examination of the material from Dikaios' excavations at Enkomi[21] seems to lead to the conclusion that the origin of this style should be sought in the area of Phoenicia and Northern Israel rather than in Cyprus, since no examples of this style have been found in the Late Cypriot III Stratum at Enkomi (which is dated to the 12th–11th centuries, corresponding to the Palestinian Iron I). The development of the Bichrome Style should be considered as one of the first manifestations of the civilization rising in the Phoenician-Israelite area after the collapse of the Canaanite world.

---

19. *TAH*, p. 9, fig. 14.
20. *Megiddo*, II pl. 86:5.
21. The first author is most grateful to Dr. Dikaios for his generosity in explaining to her the material from Enkomi.

The Phoenician Pottery (Plate 92).

At a certain moment of the work on this chapter the term 'Phoenician Pottery' seemed both pretentious and misleading, since most of the type-specimens selected for this Plate, are from excavations within the borders of the Northern Kingdom of Israel, with the exception of one site. The one exception is Akhziv, where two cemeteries were excavated in 1941.[22] We have thought of using for this plate a narrower designation than 'Phoenician,' as e.g. 'The Akhziv Group.' However, since the term 'Phoenician' still has a very general connotation, it seems appropriate enough to use it for this plate. The fact that much of this pottery comes from sites in Northern Israel raises a very important problem pertaining to the history and culture of both Phoenicia and Israel. Is this element foreign within the repertoire of the Northern Israelite pottery, or should it be considered as an organic part of Northern Israelite pottery culture? The answer to this problem requires much more evidence, which must be furnished both by additional excavations in Phoenicia and Northern Israel, and by additional typological studies. Petrographical analysis should also prove a helpful, if not a decisive, instrument in these investigations.

Iron II A–B (Nos. 1–3, Photo 281): Two main features characterize the Iron II A–B group: the strong, clear lines of every part of the vessel (for instance, the base of Nos. 1 and 2) and the highly burnished, thick dark-red slip. The walls are always thick and heavy. Bowl No. 2 and Jug No. 1 resemble each other in all details of manufacture, and it may well be that both are the product of one pottery at Hazor.

We have included here jug No. 3, although at Megiddo it is attributed to Stratum IV (general), because it comes from Room 2096 adjoining the Gate of Stratum IV B.[23] This jug too, though more delicate in form and workmanship than No. 1, resembles it in many details and in the red burnished slip.

Iron II C (Nos. 4–16, Photos 282–287): Jugs as well as bowls of the Iron II C group are characterized by the sharp, clean-cut form of every part of the vessel and by their elegance. Two streams of tradition meet in this group: a) jug No. 4, a very common type in Iron II C, is clearly a natural development of jug No. 3. Furthermore, we believe that No. 3 is the prototype from which are derived jugs such as Nos. 5, 7, 8, and 9 (Photos 284–285), which are distinguished by a conical neck. The link between this prototype (No. 3) and the derivatives appear to be bronze jugs, like the one reproduced in Photo 283. A conical neck was probably easier to produce in metalwork than a narrow neck such as that of jug No. 3. The group of vessels Nos. 5 and 7–9 would then be imitations in pottery of this metal vessel, which served as a connecting link.[24] b) The second tradition, very much in evidence in the Akhziv cemeteries and apparently in the second half of the Iron II C generally, is represented by jugs Nos. 10–12 (Photo 286). The characteristic elements are the small handle

Photo 281. Jug, Safi, IMA 68.32.22.

Photo 283. Bronze jug, Cyprus, Metropolitan Museum N.Y. No. 55.121.1.

---

22. By Dr. I. Ben-Dor. We are grateful to him for drawings 15 and 16 on this plate.
23. *Megiddo*, II, fig. 389.
24. A jug made of glass of this very type is in the collections of the Madrid Museum; cf. A. von Solderen, *Journal of Glass Studies*, I (1959), fig. 14.

spanning the angle between neck and shoulder, the swollen neck, and the broad, splaying, mushroom-like rim. We should like to suggest that this tradition is in fact the tradition of the decanter, one of the most popular shapes of the period, whose characteristic features appear also in various other Iron II forms. As we have seen above, one of these features was the handle drawn from the ridge on the neck to the shoulder, and the other was the grooved rim. Jugs Nos. 10–13 display all the features of the northern version of the decanter, but in a more refined ceramic approach — instead of being ridged, the neck is swollen; the grooved rim has evolved into a mushroom shape, perhaps under the influence of metalwork. The body of No. 10 is still the typical decanter body, and even the group of shallow fine grooves often seen on the shoulder of Northern decanters is still present. No. 13 is a variant. No. 14 (Photo 287) is a decanter in every way, except for the wider neck, and the fact that it is not ridged but slightly swollen. It bears the clear imprint of the Akhziv (Phoenician) ceramic ideas.

Photo 282. Jug, Unknown prov., HU 248.

Photo 284. Jug, Achziv, Nahariya Museum.

Photo 285. Jug, Achziv, HU.

Photo 286. Jug, Achziv, Nahariya Museum.

Photo 287. Jug 'decanter', Achziv, Nahariya Museum.

273

274

PLATE | 92

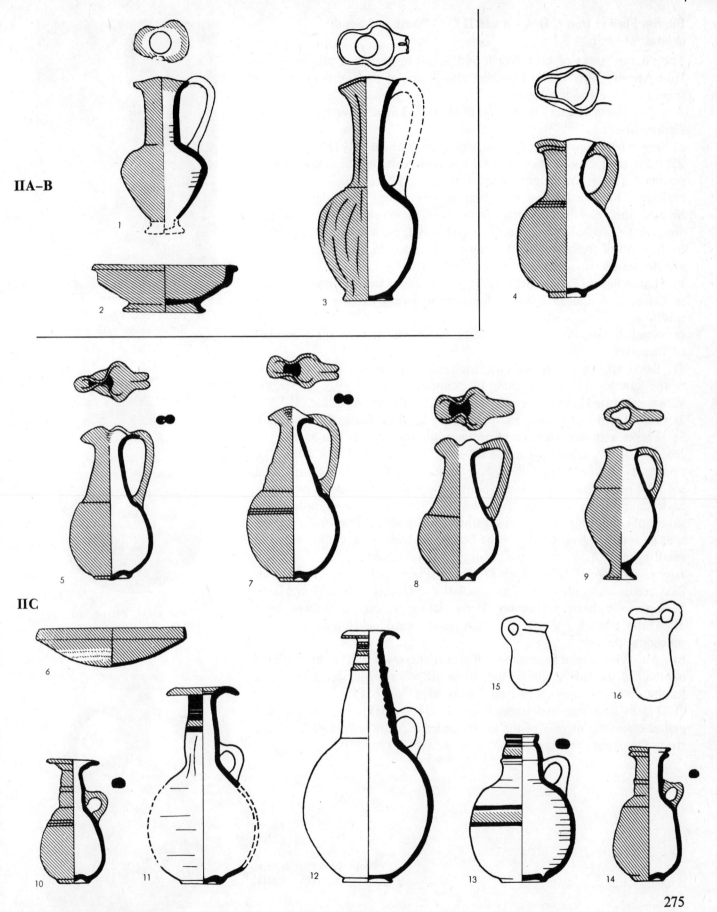

IIA–B

IIC

Pilgrim Flasks: Iron I, II A—B and II C — North and South (Plates 93—95).

The pilgrim flasks of both North and South in the three phases of the Iron Age are here treated together. This is one of the forms taken over from the Late Bronze Age.

Iron I — North (Plate 93); *South* (Plate 95): Three main types can be distinguished:

a) Vessels with spherical body, and usually one handle only (Plate 93:1–4; 95:1–2): their classification as flasks is debatable, as they have a pronounced base — an element quite foreign to pilgrim flasks. We have preferred, however, to include these vessels among the pilgrim flasks because the resemblances, mainly the way in which the decoration is adapted to two halves of a lentil-shaped vessel, outweigh the differences in the form of the base. The Bichrome Style in which these pilgrim flasks are decorated was discussed above (Plate 90).

b) Large flasks (Plates 93:6; 95:7; Photo 288): the specimens shown in Plates 93:6 and 95:7 bear a metopic ornament in Late Bronze Age tradition.

c) Small flasks (Plates 93:7–11; 95:3–6), of which there are a number of variants:

1) flasks still following the Late Bronze Age tradition, with the loops of the handles shaped something like slanting eyes (93:7–9, 11; 95:3, 4); 93:8 is decorated in the Cypriot style of the Late Bronze Age.

2) Flasks with cup-mouth and pierced lug-handles (Plates 93:10; 95:6).

3) Flasks with cup-mouth and ordinary loop-handles (Plate 95:5).

Iron II A–B — North (Plate 94:1–4); *South* (Plate 95:8–10): The popularity of the pilgrim flask now appears to decline in comparison with the preceding period. In the North, the flasks decorated in Bichrome Style continue to be made (Plate 94:1–2; here, too, for completeness' sake, spherical jugs are shown together with spherical pilgrim flasks), as well as small pilgrim flasks. In the South, we were able to find only the small type of flask; there too, a decline is noticeable.

Iron II C — North (Plate 94:5–8); *South* (Plate 95:11–16): The pilgrim flask seems to regain some of its popularity in Iron II C, though the large flask prevails almost exclusively. Three main types can be distinguished:

a) Plates 94:5–6 and 95:11–12: straightforward developments of the preceding periods.

b) An asymmetrical flask ribbed all over (Plates 94:8; 95:16; Photo 289): one half of the flask is almost flat, while the other is bulging. The ribbed technique is also applied to Iron Age bowls (Photo 213).

c) Flasks imitating metal vessels (Plates 94:7; 95:13, 14): this is suggested especially in view of the knobs under the handles, which echo the rivets attaching the handles of a metal vessel (Photo 290).

Photo 288. Pilgrim-flask, Beth-shemesh, IDA I.47.

Photo 289. Pilgrim-flask, Megiddo, IDA I. 3553.

Photo 290. Pilgrim-flask, Lachish, IDA 36.2244. ▶

The Pyxis: Iron I, II A—B, II C — North and South (Plate 96).

Although certainly of Mycenaean origin, the pyxis, after being imitated locally like so many other imported vessels, was adopted, first by Canaanite and later by Israelite pottery to a much greater extent than other forms.

Iron I — North (Nos. 1–7): The Iron I pyxis is already fairly remote both from the Mycenaean prototype and from the contemporary local imitations. The new pyxis, whether made by the Israelite newcomers or by Canaanites, has a tall, generally piriform body with two carinations: a gentle angle setting off the shoulder, and a sharper carination near the base (Photo 291–292). It has two handles, either raised lug handles or small horizontal loop-handles, rising from the shoulder. Side by side with this type, debased variants appear already in Iron I, with a spherical or slightly squat body, like No. 7. In accordance with the taste of the period, pyxides are often decorated with painted bands or with metopes in the zone of the handles (No. 1).

No. 8 is a tall bottle which resembles a pyxis in many details. For this reason it has been included in Plate 96, although the question of its relationship to the pyxis has not been studied.

Iron I — South (Nos. 9–14): A comparison of the pyxides from excavations in the south of the country with those from the North shows that in the South the potters followed more conservatively the prototype and the local imitations. The tall pyxis-bottle is found in the South as well (No. 15).

Iron II A–B — North (Nos. 16–21): Generally, Iron II pyxides resemble those of Iron I, but are squatter and less frequently found.

Iron II A–B — South (Nos. 22–24): The few examples we have been able to collect reflect the scarcity of the stratigraphic material available and may well present a distorted picture. However, it is interesting that the three vessels shown here, from three different excavations, all belong to a greatly degenerated type, which bears little resemblance to the prototype.

Iron II C — North and South (Nos. 25–27): The pyxis gradually disappears from the pottery repertoire, and its last, rare, representatives are small and degenerated.

Photo 291. Pyxis, Afula, IDA 50.822.

Photo 292. Pyxis, Beth-shemesh, IDA I.107.

277

PLATE 93

1.	Jug, brown-buff, red and black decoration	1:5	Abu Hawam	IV	TAH, p. 29:152
2.	Jug-flask, pink-buff, smoothed, brown and red decoration	1:5	Megiddo	VI	Meg. II, pl. 86:2
3.	Jug-flask, orange-buff, traces of burnish, red and black decoration	1:5	Megiddo	VI A	Meg. II, pl. 80:3
4.	Jug-flask, pink-buff, smoothed, red decoration	1:5	Megiddo	VI	Meg. II, pl. 86:3
5.	Flask, orange-buff, smoothed, red and black decoration	1:5	Megiddo	VI	
6.	Flask, buff, smoothed, red decoration	1:5	Megiddo	VII A	Meg. II, pl. 70:9
7.	Flask, buff, red decoration	1:5	Abu Hawam	IV	TAH, p. 30:166
8.	Flask, cream, smoothed, red and black decoration	1:5	Megiddo	VII A	Meg. II, pl. 70:8
9.	Flask, orange-buff, irregularly burnished, red decoration	1:5	Megiddo	VI	Meg. II, pl. 86:6
10.	Flask, burnt umber, red decoration	1:5	Megiddo	T. 39	Meg. T., pl. 68:10
11.	Flask, buff, traces of irregular burnish	1:5	Megiddo	VI B	Meg. II, pl. 74:14

278

PLATE | 93

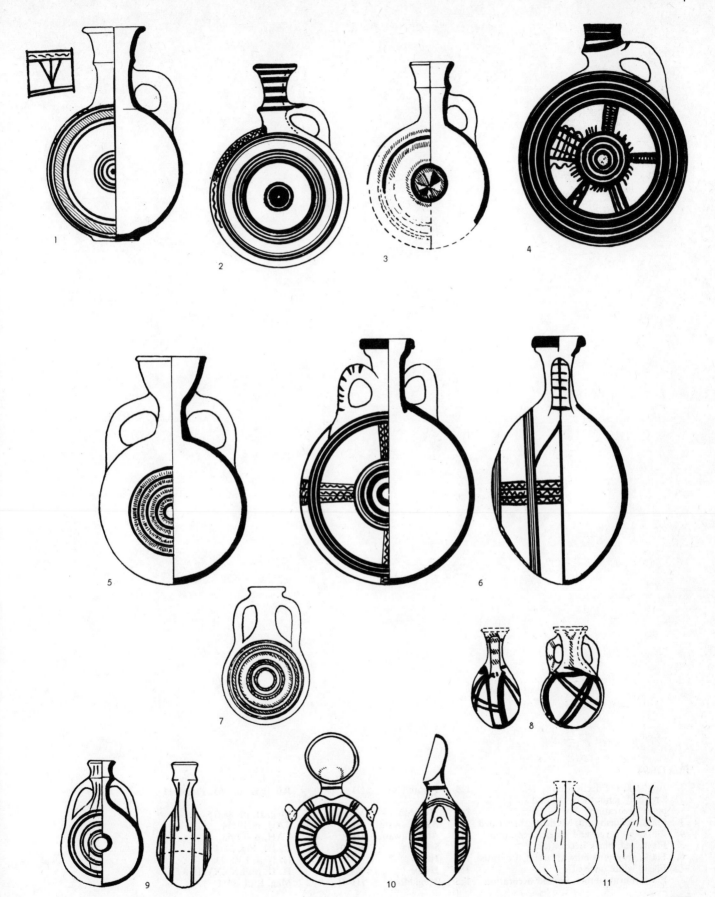

PLATE | 94

IIA–B

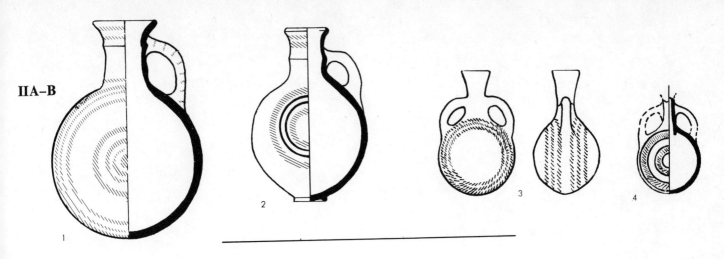

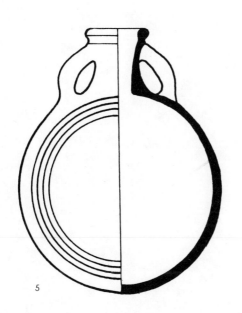

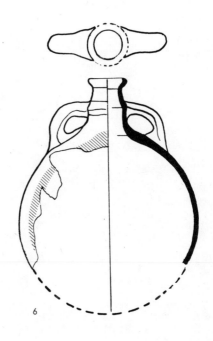

IIC

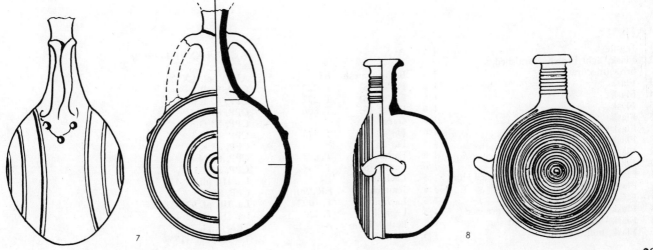

282

PLATE | 95

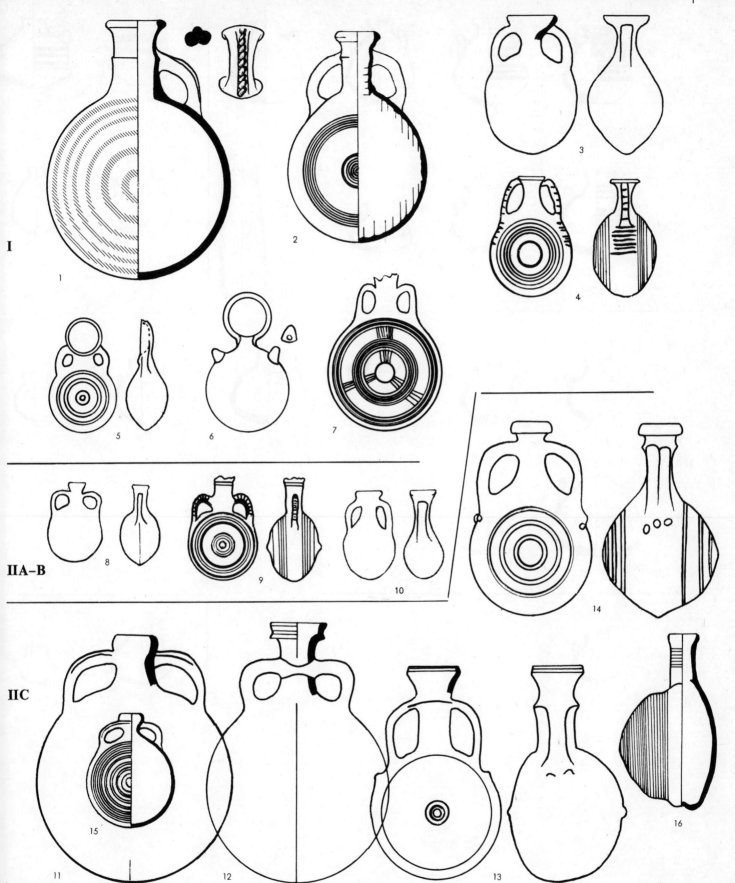

I

1

2

3

4

5

6

7

IIA–B

8

9

10

14

IIC

15

11

12

13

16

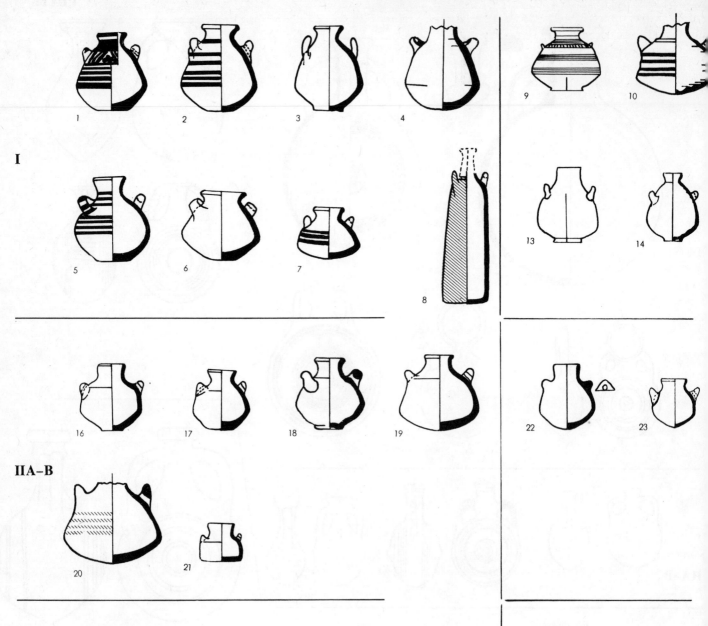

I

IIA–B

IIC

PLATE | 96

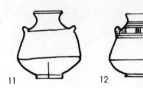

PLATE 96

1.	Pyxis, brown-grey, smoothed, black decoration	1:5	Megiddo	VI A	Meg. II, pl. 77:10
2.	Pyxis, brown-grey, smoothed, red decoration	1:5	Megiddo	VII A	Meg. II, pl. 68:9
3.	Pyxis, buff, smoothed	1:5	Megiddo	VI	Meg. II, pl. 84:11
4.	Pyxis, yellowish-grey	1:5	Hazor	XII	H. III–IV, pl. CCI:26
5.	Pyxis pink-buff, smoothed red decoration	1:5	Megiddo	VI	Meg. II, pl. 84:10
6.	Pyxis, orange-buff, smoothed	1:5	Megiddo	VI	Meg. II, pl. 84:9
7.	Pyxis, buff, smoothed, red decoration	1:5	Megiddo	VI A	Meg. II, pl. 77:7
8.	Pyxis-bottle, buff, vertically burnished dark red slip	1:5	Megiddo	VI B	Meg. II, pl. 73:9
9.	Pyxis	1:6	Far'ah (S)	T. 642	CPP, 55 S 3
10.	Pyxis, reddish-brown, red decoration	1:5	Beth-shemesh	III	AS IV, pl. LIX:21
11.	Pyxis	1:6	Far'ah (S)	T. 642	CPP, 55 S 3
12.	Pyxis	1:6	Far'ah (S)	T. 222	CPP, 55 S 4
13.	Pyxis	1:6	Gezer		CPP, 55 N 6
14.	Pyxis	1:6	Beth-shemesh		AS III, Fig. 6:3.76
15.	Pyxis-bottle	1:6	Far'ah (S)	T. 609	CPP, 66 Y
16.	Pyxis, brown-ocher, dark red wheel-burnished slip	1:5	Megiddo	V	Meg. I, pl. 19:96
17.	Pyxis, brown-ocher, traces of burnish	1:5	Megiddo	V	Meg. I, pl. 19:95
18.	Pyxis, buff	1:5	Abu Hawam	III	TAH, p. 20:60
19.	Pyxis, yellow	1:5	Megiddo	V	Meg. I, pl. 19:98
20.	Pyxis, buff, red decoration	1:5	Abu Hawam	III	TAH, p. 20:61
21.	Pyxis, grey-black, burnished	1:5	Megiddo	V	Meg. I, pl. 19:99
22.	Pyxis, grey, black slip	1:5	Beth Mirsim	B	TBM I, pl. 51:5
23.	Pyxis, grey, black burnished slip	1:5	Beth-shemesh	III	AS IV, pl. LX:17
24.	Pyxis	1:6	Far'ah (S)	T. 231	CPP, 55 Q 2
25.	Pyxis, blue-black, wheel-burnished	1:5	Megiddo	III	Meg. I, pl. 9:35
26.	Pyxis, pink, buff irregularly burnished slip	1:5	Lachish	T. 110	La. III, pl. 91:416
27.	Pyxis	1:5	Beth Mirsim	A	TBM I, pl. 53:11

285

Imported Cypriot and Cypro-Phoenician Wares: Iron I, II A—B, and II C (Plates 97 and 98).

The term 'Cypro-Phoenician' pottery was coined in Palestinian archaeology, and is not used in Cyprus. This term refers in fact to one ware only, the 'black-on-red.' but for convenience we have applied it here to all Cypriot and Cypro-Phoenician wares of the Iron Age found in Palestine. The implications of this term are negative rather than positive. The truth is that our knowledge is insufficient to assign to each of the wares described here a place of origin in the lands along the coasts of Cilicia, Phoenicia, Israel, and Cyprus, where highly developed cultures flourished in the Iron Age. There is some evidence that this kind of pottery was foreign to the Judaean and Israelite ceramic repertoire and that it was imported from abroad.

The arrangement of the plates is based on the stratigraphic provenience of the material from Palestine, as well as on the classification in use in Cypriot archaeology. Thus, Plate 97 contains pottery from strata dated to Iron I and II A–B and Plate 98 includes the pottery from strata of Iron II C. Within each group, the arrangement follows Cypriot ceramic classification, which is based on the colour of the decoration.

We have followed Gjerstad in our analysis of the material, and especially in the classification of the wares, most of which are described in his book.[25] This does not imply that we accept all of Gjerstad's conclusions.

No attempt has been made to collect here all the Cypriot and Cypro-Phoenician material available from excavations in Israel; only representative examples of each period and each type have been given. The description of the types has been omitted, since it is available in Gjerstad and in other works on Cypriot archaeology. The tables attached to Plates 97 and 98 list the types.

The early presence of these imported wares in Stratum VI A at Megiddo (Plate 97:1) indicates, on the one hand, the cultural interchange at the end of Iron I between Palestine and Cyprus, and, on the other, helps Cypriot archaeology in establishing absolute dates. To judge by the amount of such imported pottery found in Palestinian excavations, imports from Cyprus increased considerably in Iron II A–B. Especially numerous are vessels of 'Black-on-Red' I and II (cf. Plate 97). In Iron II C, imports of such pottery are on the decline, as is evident from Plate 98.

The four vessels from Hazor in Plate 98:9–12 are included here, although the question remains open as to whether they are really imported wares or local imitations. Size, as well as shape and workmanship, set them apart from the rest of the pottery shown in Plates 97 and 98.

Photos 293–297 show two bowls and three types of juglet of the 'Black-on-Red' ware.

Photo 293. Bowl, Megiddo, IDA 36.1946

---

25. E. Gjerstad, *The Swedish Cyprus Expedition*, IV:2, Stockholm, 1948.

Photo 296. Juglet, Lachish,
IDA 34.2926.

Photo 295. Juglet-amphoriskos,
Ajjul, IDA 32.1925.

Photo 294. Bowl, Megiddo, *Meg.*, II,
Pl. 147:6.

Photo 297. Juglet, Megiddo,
IDA 36.1940.

I

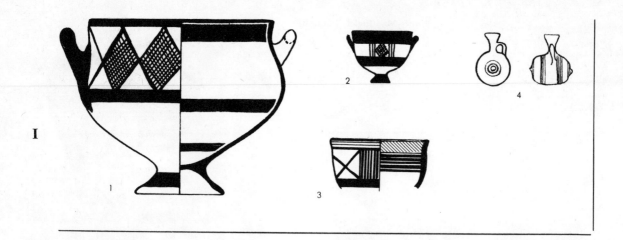

IIA–B

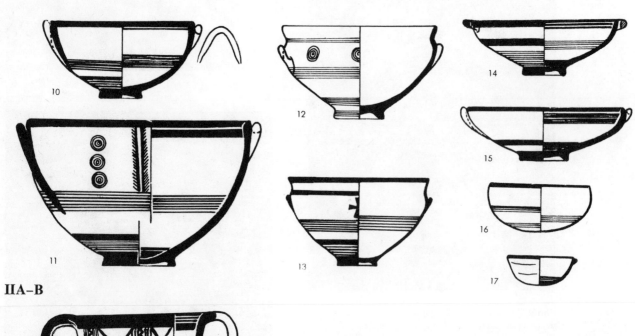

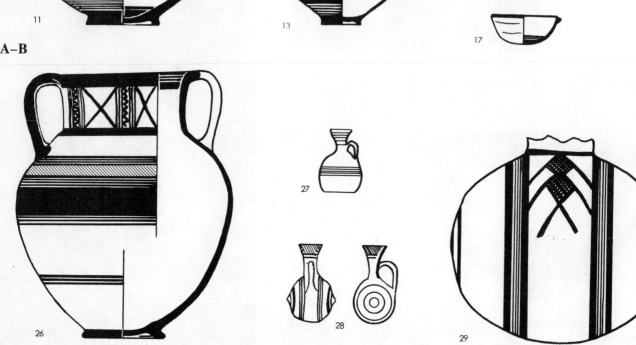

288

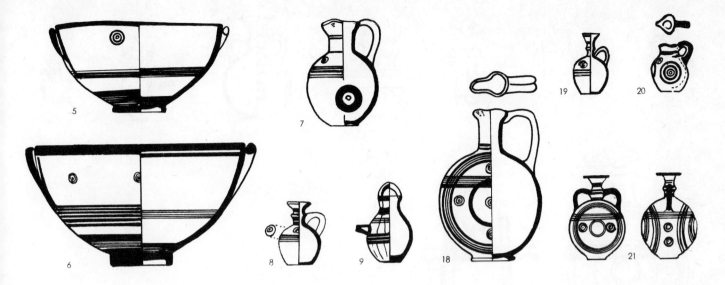

PLATE | **97**

PLATE 97

1.	Bowl, green-buff, black decoration (WP I)	1:5	Megiddo	VI A	Meg. II, pl. 78:20
2.	Bowl (WP I)	1:6	Far'ah (S)		BP I, pl. XXXI:325
3.	Bowl, brown-ocher, cream slip, red and	1:5	Megiddo	V	Meg. I, pl. 30:141
4.	Juglet-flask (WP II)	1:6	Far'ah (S)		BP I, pl. XXXIX:86 D
5.	Bowl, brown-ocher, red burnished slip, black decoration (BoR I)	1:5	Megiddo	V–III	Meg. I, pl. 29:107
6.	Bowl (BoR I)	1:5	Abu Hawam	III	TAH, p. 6, Fig. 8
7.	Jug, brown-grey, close burnished red slip, black decoration (BoR I)	1:5	Megiddo	V A	Meg. II, pl. 88:9
8.	Juglet (BoR I)	1:5	Beth Mirsim	B	TBM I, pl. 51:9
9.	Spouted juglet, pink-buff, close burnished red slip, black decoration (BoR I)	1:5	Megiddo	V A	Meg. II, pl. 88:19
10.	Bowl, pink-buff, burnished red slip, black decoration (BoR II)	1:5	Megiddo	V A	Meg. II, pl. 90:2
11.	Bowl, pink-buff, close burnished red slip, black decoration (BoR II)	1:5	Megiddo	V A	Meg. II, pl. 90:3
12.	Bowl, yellow, light red burnished slip, black decoration (BoR II)	1:5	Megiddo	V	Meg. I, pl. 32:169
13.	Bowl (BoR II)	1:5	Carmel	T. 7	BBSAJ 5, pl. III:33
14.	Bowl, brown ocher, black decoration (BoR II)	1:5	Megiddo	V	Meg. I, pl. 30:140
15.	Bowl, pink-buff, close burnished red slip, black decoration (BoR II)	1:5	Megiddo	V A	Meg. II, pl. 90:1
16.	Bowl, brown-ocher, wheel-burnished, black decoration (BoR II)	1:5	Megiddo	IV	Meg. I, pl. 28:95
17.	Miniature bowl, pink-buff, burnished red slip, black decoration (BoR II)	1:5	Megiddo	V A	Meg. II, pl. 90:4
18.	Jug, grey, black burnished slip, yellow decoration (BoR II)	1:5	Megiddo	V	Meg. I, pl. 8:176
19.	Juglet (BoR II)	1:5	Carmel	T. 1	BBSAJ, 5, pl. II:8
20.	Juglet, pink-buff, close burnished red slip, black decoration (BoR II)	1:5	Megiddo	V A	Meg. II, pl. 88:8
21.	Juglet-flask (BoR II)	1:6	Ajjul	T. 1704	AG II, pl. XXXV:69 P 2
22.	Juglet (BoR II)	1:5	Carmel	T. 7	BBSAJ 5, pl. III:32
23.	Juglet (BoR II)	1:6	Ajjul	T. 1011	AG II, pl. XXXV:82 E
24.	Juglet, pink-buff, close burnished red slip, black decoration (BoR II)	1:5	Megiddo	V A	Meg. II, pl. 88:18
25.	Juglet (after a photograph) (BoR II)	1:4	Lachish		La. III, pl. 36:62
26.	Jar, pink-buff, white slip, mauve and black decoration (Bichrome II)	1:5	Megiddo	V A	Meg. II, pl. 89:7
27.	Juglet (WP II)	1:6	Far'ah (S)	T. 227	CPP, 82 L 1
28.	Juglet-flask, buff, buff slip, red and black decoration (Bichrome III)	1:5	Lachish	T. 110	La. III, pl. 88:329
29.	Jug-flask (WP I)	1:6	Jemmeh	EM 185	CPP, 86 A

PLATE | **98**

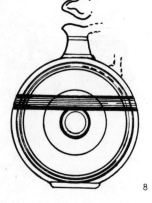

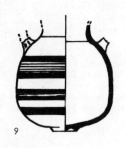
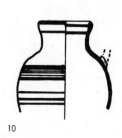
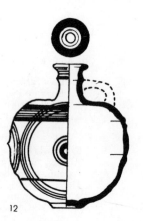

PLATE 98

1.	Juglet (BoR I)	1:5	Lachish	T. 147	La. III, pl. 88:337
2.	Juglet (BoR I)	1:5	Lachish	T. 1002	La. III, pl. 88:336
3.	Juglet (BoR I)	1:5	Lachish	T. 146	La. III, pl. 88:338
4.	Juglet-flask (BoR II)	1:5	Lachish	T. 1002	La. III, pl. 88:339
5.	Juglet-flask, light red, close burnished, black decoration (BoR II)	1:5	Megiddo	V–III	Meg. I, pl. 17:87
6.	Juglet-flask, brown-ocher, brown irregularly burnished slip, black decoration (BoR II)	1:5	Megiddo	V–III	Meg. I, pl. 5:123
7.	Juglet (BoR II)	1:5	Lachish	T. 120	La. III, pl. 88:330
8.	Jug (WP V)	1:5	Lachish	II	La. III, pl. 89:350
9.	Jug, grey-buff, whitish burnished slip, black decoration	1:5	Hazor	V A	H. II, pl. LXXXVIII:3
10.	Jug, pink-brown, white slip (?), burnished, brown decoration	1:5	Hazor	IV	H. II, pl. C:22
11.	Jug, light brown, white slip (?), burnished, black decoration	1:5	Hazor	V A	H. II, pl. LXXXVIII:2
12.	Jug, grey, brown decoration	1:5	Hazor	V A	H. II, pl. LXXXVIII:1

Photo 299. Assyrian bottle, Gibeon, IDA 45.136.

Photo 298. Assyrian bowl, Farah(N), *RB*, 1951, Pl. XV.

Imported Assyrian Ware (Plate 99).

The group of vessels shown on this plate differs strikingly from local wares and is foreign both in shape and in ceramic technique. Petrie was the first to recognize bowls such as Nos. 1–5 as Assyrian, during his his excavations at Tell Jemmeh (Gerar).[26] Since then, such pottery has been found at Samaria, Tell el-Far'ah (N) (Photo 298), and Hazor. In all excavations it appears in strata of the period following the Assyrian conquest of Samaria, that is, after 721 B.C. Commercial relations between Israel–Judah and Assyria are one of the consequences of Assyrian rule over the Northern Kingdom. However, commercial relations are never one-sided, and it is thus not surprising to find Palestinian pottery at Nimrud (Kalhu) in the 7th century. In recent years, the ceramic inter-relations between Assyria and Israel-Judah have been the subject of several studies.[27]

Bottle No. 6 (Photo 299) also belongs to this group. It appeared earlier in Plates 88 and 89, and will be discussed in detail in Plate 101. Its origin should be sought in Assyria rather than in Ammon. Bottle No. 7 (Photo 300) is duplicated in Assyrian pottery found in Assyria proper, and its discovery in Stratum V at Hazor is evidence that commercial relations between Northern Israel and Assyria began before the conquest of Israel by the Assyrians.

Lamps: Iron I, II A—B and II C — North and South (Plate 100).

The Iron I lamp is a direct continuation of the Canaanite lamp. In the North, there are two main Iron I types:

1) a relatively small lamp with flat base, and (2) a larger lamp with rounded base. As far as we know, only type 2 is found in the South.

In Iron II A–B, the lamp with rounded base is the prevalent type in the North as well as in the South; often such lamps have a wider and more pronounced lip than in the preceding period.

In Iron II C, northern lamps are usually smaller, the rounded bases have become wide and flat, and the rim is emphasized. In the South, side by side with the northern type of lamps, a completely new type evolved. It has a relatively small, shallow bowl placed on a thick, high disc base.

Photo 300. Assyrian bottle, Hazor, *Hazor*, II, Pl. CLIX.

---

26. *Gerar*, pp. 7 and 23, pls. XLVIII and LXV.
27. M. E. L. Mallowan, "The Excavations at Nimrud (Kalhu)," *Iraq*, XII (1950), pl. XXXII:1; Ruth Amiran, "A Late Assyrian Stone Bowl from Tell el-Qitaf in the Beth Shan Valley," *Atiqot* II, 1959, pp. 129–132; Joan Oats, "Late Assyrian Pottery from Fort Shalmaneser," *Iraq*, XXI (1959), pl. XXXIX:101.

PLATE | **99**

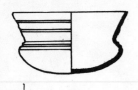

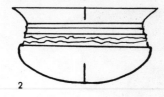

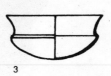

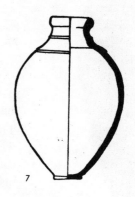

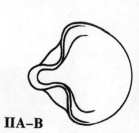

I

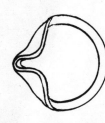

IIA–B

IIC

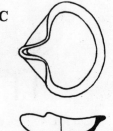

PLATE 99

1.	Bowl, black, hard and thin	1:5	Samaria	VII	SS III, Fig. 11:22
2.	Bowl	1:6	Jemmeh		Gerar, pl. LXV:1
3.	Bowl, pink, hard and thin, traces of burnish	1:5	Far'ah (N)	I	RB 1951, p. 419, Fig. 12:3
4.	Bowl, light brown, closely burnished inside and out	1:5	Hazor	IV	H. II, pl. XCVIII:44
5.	Goblet	1:6	Jemmeh		Gerar, pl. LXV:4
6.	Bottle	1:4	Samaria		Samaria I, p. 288, Fig. 163
7.	Bottle, light brown	1:5	Hazor	V A	H. II, pl. XCVII:11

PLATE 100

1.	Lamp, pink	1:5	Hazor	XII	H. III–IV, pl. CLXIX:10
2.	Lamp, brown-ocher	1:5	Megiddo	V	Meg. I, pl. 38:18
3.	Lamp, buff	1:5	Megiddo	VI A	Meg. II, pl. 79:9
4.	Lamp, pink-buff	1:5	Megiddo	VI B	Meg. II, pl. 74:13
5.	Lamp	1:5	Ai		Ay, pl. LXXI:746
6.	Lamp	1:5	Beth Mirsim	B	TBM I, pl. 51:1
7.	Lamp	1:5	Beth-shemesh	III	AS IV, pl. LIX:19
8.	Lamp	1:5	Hazor	IX B	H. III–IV, pl. CLXXVI:15
9.	Lamp	1:5	Hazor	X A	H. III–IC, pl. CLXXIV:18
10.	Lamp	1:5	Hazor	IX	H. III–IV, pl. CCVIII:47
11.	Lamp	1:6	Far'ah (S)	T. 229	CPP, 91 K 3ii
12.	Lamp	1:6	Far'ah (S)	T. 234	CPP, 91 J 4v
13.	Lamp	1:6	Far'ah (S)	T. 220	CPP, 91 J 3i
14.	Lamp, yellow	1:5	Megiddo	IV–III	Meg. I, pl. 37:13
15.	Lamp, pink	1:5	Hazor	V A	H. II, pl. LXXXVIII:13
16.	Lamp, burnt umber	1:5	Megiddo	IV–III	Meg. I, pl. 37:11
17.	Lamp, green-brown, red decoration	1:5	Megiddo	IV–III	Meg. I, pl. 37:15
18.	Lamp	1:5	Beth Mirsim	A	TBM III, pl. 15:9
19.	Lamp	1:5	Beth Mirsim	A	TBM I, pl. 70:8
20.	Lamp	1:5	Beth Mirsim	A	TBM III, pl. 15:1

PLATE | 100

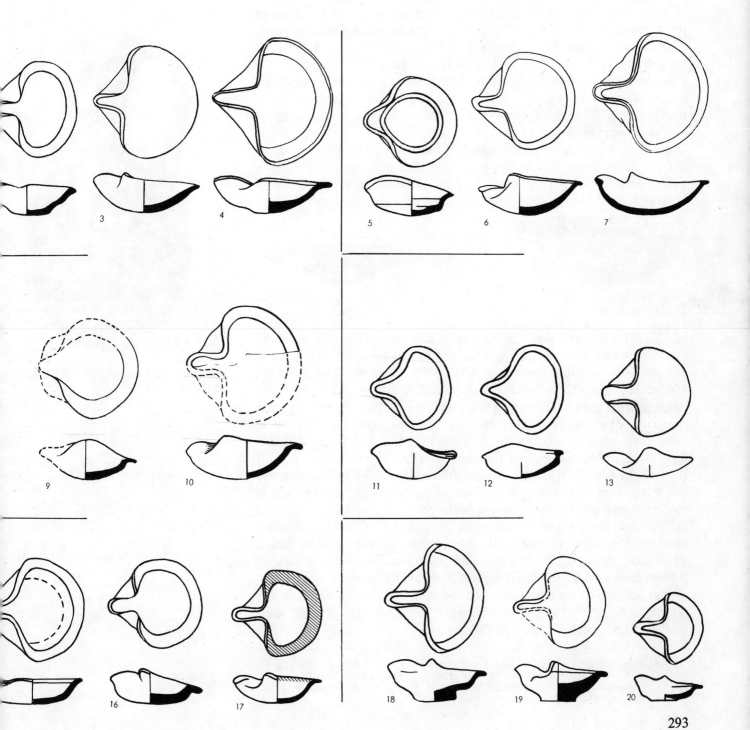

CHAPTER TWELVE

SELECTED TYPES OF AMMONITE POTTERY

Plate 101 represents a distinctive chapter in the history of Ammonite pottery, as revealed in a series of seven tombs excavated in Amman and its vicinity.[1] This chapter is included here in order to give the reader some idea of the ceramic culture of a neighbouring area, which is related to the pottery of Israel and Judah with respect to origins and style.

Although there is a great deal of resemblance between the vessels of the seven tomb-groups, certain differences permit us to spread the dates of these groups over a period of a hundred or a hundred and fifty years. Their attribution to the seventh century is based on the one hand on a comparison with Iron II C pottery in Israel and in Judah, and on the other hand on the seal of Adoni-nur, the servant of Aminadab, uncovered in one of the Amman tombs. Aminadab is known from Assyrian records to be a king of Ammon, who paid tribute to Assyria in the reign of A shurbanipal (668–625 B.C.E.).

The history of Ammon took a somewhat different course from that of her neighbors Israel and Judah, in spite of their geographical proximity and in spite of their being affected by the same world events. Ammon experienced a period of prosperity after the Assyrian conquest of Samaria

Photo 305. Jug, Sahab, *QDAP*, XIII, Pl. XXXV:48.

Photo 301. Bowl, Sahab, *QDAP*, XIII, Pl. XXXV:1.

Pho to 302. Bowl, Sahab *QDAP*, XIII, p. 98:18

in 733–721 B.C.E. and seems to have continued to prosper also after the the Babylonian conquest had put an end to the kingdom of Judah in 587 B.C. On this point, the author differs with Albright,[2] who dates the Muqabelein tomb to the sixth and early fifth centuries. A careful comparison of the material from that tomb with that of the other tombs, and especially of the tomb of Adoni-nur, appears to show that the Maqabelein tomb cannot be much later than the tomb of Adoni-nur, the most likely date being within the span of time encompassed by the second half of the seventh and the first half of the sixth centuries. We believe that for the seven Ammonite tombs a date within the limits of 731–550 B.C. is in closer agreement with historical evidence.

Within the general picture presented by Ammonite pottery, we can distinguish elements attributable to four ceramic horizons: Judah, Israel, Phoenicia, and Assyria. However, the identification and isolation of these elements, which link the pottery of Ammon to that of her neighbours, should not lead to the conclusion that the Ammonite ceramic culture was eclectic in nature and lacking in originality. Below we shall describe some of the characteristic features of this pottery:

---

1. All seven tombs have been excavated and published by G. Lankester Harding, in: *QDAP*, XI (1945); XIII (1948); XIV (1950); *ADAJ*, I (1951); *PEFA*, VI (1953).
2. W. F. Albright, "Notes on Ammonite History," in *Miscellanea Biblica*, ed. B. Ubach (Montserrat, 1954), p. 131, n. 22.

Photo 303. Tripod cup, Amman, *QDAP*, XI, Pl. XVIII:53.

Photo 304. Cup, Sahab, *QDAP*, XIII, Pl. XXXV:66.

Photo 306. Jug, Sahab, *QDAP*, XIII, Pl. XXXV:61.

Photo 307. Jug, Sahab, *QDAP*, XIII, Pl. XXXV:55.

Photo 308. Jug 'decanter', Sahab, *QDAP*, XIII, Pl. XXXV:57.

Bowls: Nos. 1–4 resemble Judaean types. No. 5 appears to be an Assyrian bowl (Photo 301). No. 7 is a bowl of Samaria Ware (Photo 302). No. 9 is decorated with what seems to be a characteristically Ammonite pattern — a band made up of stepped red painted triangles. No. 10 is of a very unusual shape and is perhaps influenced by Assyrian forms. No. 11 (Photo 303) is a vessel which can be defined either as a cup or as a bowl: this is one of the most characteristic forms in all seven Ammonite tomb-groups. No. 12 (Photo 304) is something between a mug and a cup, and belongs to a definitely Judaean type.

Chalices: No. 13 is an unknown form; No. 14, however, is a chalice known in northern Israelite pottery.

Jugs: No. 15 (Photo 305) is a Phoenician type, found mainly in Israel but, as we have seen above, also present in Judah. Nos. 18 and 19 are jug forms known in Israel as well as Judah, including the black decoration on a burnished red background (Photos 306, 307). Nos. 16 and 17 (Photo 308) are examples of decanter types current in Ammonite pottery:

No. 16 approximates the Judaean type in every respect, most noticeably in the form of the rim. No. 17 appears to be a local development, with odd angularities. Here too, the rim is that of a Judaean decanter. Of interest is the fact that a fragment of such a decanter was found in Hazor, Stratum IV.[3]

Photo 309. Amphoriskos, Sahab, *QDAP*, XIII, Pl. XXXV:69.

Photo 310. Bottle, Amman, *QDAP*, XI Pl. XVIII:56.

Photo 313. Lamp, Sahab, *QDAP*, XIII, p. 102:80.

Juglets: The juglets are generally of a common type, the only special feature being their length, recalling the Phoenician juglets.

Lamps: The typical Judaean lamp with a thickened base (No. 22) appears here together with the rounded type (Photo 313).

Jars and Amphoriskoi: Jar No. 24 is a Phoenician type. The amphoriskos No. 25 (Photo 309) is known from excavations in the South (e.g. Tell Beth Mirsim) and in the North (e.g. Megiddo).

Cooking Pots: These vessels belong to the type dominant in Israel and in Judah.

Bottles: The bottle, as exemplified by No. 27 (Photo 310) has been the subject of a study by Henschel-Simon.[4] We have already encountered this form on Plates 88 and 89, and on Plate 99, where it was placed among Assyrian imports, although with some reservations. The form of the vessel, and especially the absence of handles, stamp it, in our opinion, as an Assyrian product. The vessel fits well in the general assemblage of Assyrian ceramics, while among Israelite, or even Ammonite pottery, it appears foreign and unconnected with ceramic tradition, either of the past or of its own time.

---

3. *Hazor*, II, pl. C, no. 32.
4. E. Henschel-Simon, "Note on the Pottery of the Amman Tombs," *QDAP*, XI (1945), pp. 75–80.

Photo 311. Bottle-jar, Muqabelein, *QDAP*, XIV.

Photo 312. Zoomorphic vessel, Amman, *QDAP*, XI, Pl. XVIII.

Bottle-Amphoriskos: The large vessel shown in Plate 101:28 (Photo 311), was discussed in the chapter on the amphoriskos (cf. Plate 83:15,17). We should like to repeat that this form also appears to belong to Assyrian ceramics. Photo 312 shows a zoomorphic vessel with a trough-like spout, resembling the jug spouts.

PLATE 101

1. Bowl, buff, red ring-burnished slip   1:5   Amman   Adoni-nur Tomb   APEF, VI, Fig. 21:63
2. Bowl, grey, red decoration   1:5   Amman   Adoni-nur Tomb   APEF, VI, Fig. 21:66
3. Bowl, red ring-burnished slip   1:5   Amman   Adoni-nur Tomb   APEF, VI, Fig. 21:68
4. Bowl, buff, red ring-burnished slip   1:6   Sahab   Tomb   QDAP, XIII, p. 97, Fig. 3:11
5. Bowl, pink, red ring-burnished slip   1:5   Amman   Tomb   QDAP, XI, p. 69:3
6. Bowl, buff, red ring-burnished slip   1:6   Sahab   Tomb   QDAP, XIII, p. 97, Fig. 3:1
7. Bowl, red ring-burnished slip   1:5   Amman   Adoni-nur Tomb   APEF, VI, Fig. 21:53
8. Bowl, pink, red burnished slip   1:5   Amman   Tomb   QDAP, XI, p. 74:47
9. Bowl, buff, brown ring-burnished slip,
    red decoration   1:5   Amman   Adoni-nur Tomb   APEF, VI, Fig. 21:72
10. Pot, cream slip   1:5   Amman   Tomb   QDAP, XI, p. 70:18
11. Bowl with handle and three legs, pink,
     red burnished slip, black decoration   1:5   Amman   Tomb   QDAP, XI, p. 70:11
12. Mug, buff, pink slip   1:6   Sahab   Tomb   QDAP, XIII, p. 101, Fig. 7:66
13. Goblet, buff   1:5   Amman   Tomb C   ADAJ, I, p. 39, Fig. 1:48
14. Chalice, pink, red burnished slip,
     black and white decoration   1:5   Amman   Tomb   QDAP, XI, p. 70:9
15. Jug, buff, reddish-brown burnished slip   1:5   Amman   Tomb   QDAP, XI, p. 72:36
16. Decanter, red, pink burnished slip   1:5   Amman   Tomb   QDAP, XI, p. 71:29
17. Decanter, pink-buff   1:5   Amman   Adoni-nur Tomb   APEF, VI, Fig. 22:103
18. Spouted jug, brownish, brown slip,
     black and white decoration   1:5   Amman   Tomb   QDAP, XI, p. 71:25
19. Jug, red burnished slip   1:6   Sahab   Tomb   QDAP, XIII, p. 100, Fig. 6:55
20. Juglet, pink, cream slip   1:5   Amman   Tomb   QDAP, XI, p. 71:24
21. Juglet, black, black burnished slip   1:5   Amman   Tomb   QDAP, XI, p. 74:66
22. Lamp   1:6   Sahab   Tomb   QDAP, XIII, p. 101, Fig. 7:72
23. Lamp   1:6   Sahab   Tomb   QDAP, XIII, p. 101, Fig. 7:75
24. Jar, buff, buff slip, red decoration   1:5   Amman   Adoni-nur Tomb   APEF, VI, Fig. 23:117
25. Amphoriskos, pink, red burnished slip,
     black decoration   1:6   Sahab   Tomb   QDAP, XIII, p. 101, Fig. 7:64
26. Cooking-pot, brown   1:6   Sahab   Tomb   QDAP, XIII, p. 101, Fig. 7:67
27. Bottle, pink, pink slip, brown decoration   1:5   Amman   Adoni-nur Tomb   APEF, VI, Fig. 22:97
28. Bottle, buff, buff slip, brownish-yellow
     and red decoration   1:5   Amman   Adoni-nur Tomb   APEF, VI, Fig. 22:90

PLATE | 101

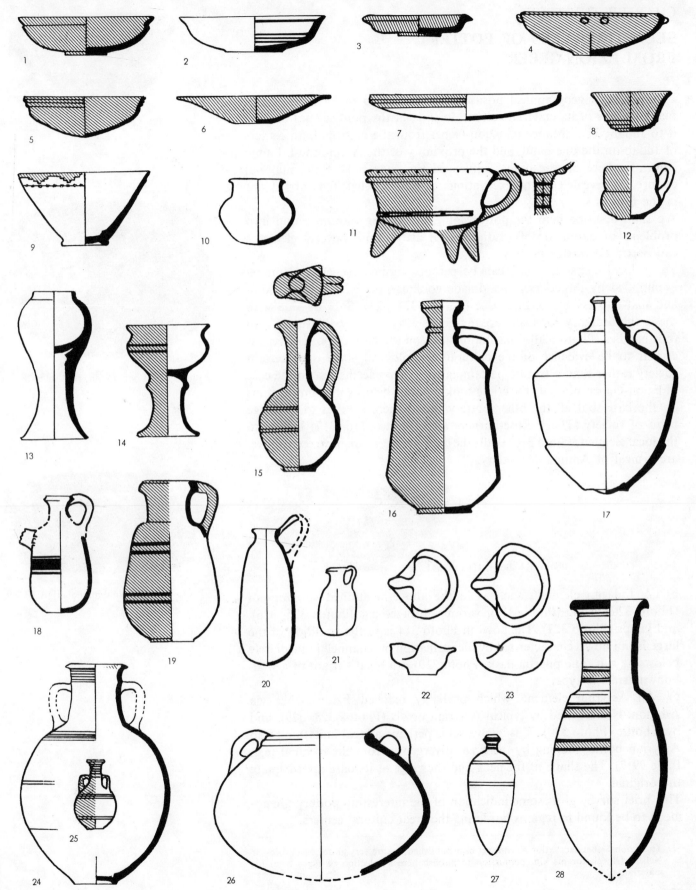

CHAPTER THIRTEEN

SELECTED TYPES OF POTTERY FROM EZION-GEBER

Ezion-Geber's geographical position was bound to make itself felt in many aspects of its material culture, in spite of the political ties binding it to Judah. The distance of Ezion-Geber from the metropolitan centers of Judah on the one hand, and the proximity of the Ammonite-Edomite cultural sphere on the other, influenced the character of the material culture, as revealed in the excavations of Tell el-Kheleifeh carried out in the thirties.[1]

We shall describe here the pottery of Ezion-Geber without going into problems of dating or of stratigraphical attribution. Several elements can be traced in this pottery:

a) A local element, which can be perhaps termed Negebite-Edomite, exemplified by the coarsely handmade cooking-pots with vertical sides, and mat-impressions on the base (Photos 321–323). Side by side with these, the ordinary Judaean cooking-pot is also found, but usually with four handles (Photo 320). Mat-impressions on the base of pottery vessels appear to be evidence of the cultural-technological stage of a certain society rather than a feature pertaining to style or aesthetics. In the case of Ezion-Geber, not only the crude cooking-pots, bearing mat-impressions on the base, but all the other pottery found there testifies to a village form of society. The incense-burners also (Photos 316, 317) belong to the local element. Photo 316 recalls the cups which, as we have seen above, are typical of Ammonite pottery.

Photo 320. Cooking-pot, IDA 40.657.

Photo 314. Bowl, IDA 40.644.

Photo 324. Low cooking-pot, IDA 40.649.

b) A Judaean element, such as in the above-mentioned cooking-pot (Photo 320), a jug (Photo 318), various storage-jars (Photos 325, 326), and lamps (Photo 327). The bowl in Photo 314 is in the tradition of the large Iron I bowls characterized by the carination or 'channel' immediately below the rim. The pilgrim flask (Photo 319) is a local variant of a well-known Israelite type.

c) An Assyrian element, which probably reached Ezion-Geber via Ammon, is illustrated by typical Assyrian bowls (Photos 328, 329), and by a bottle (Photo 330). This last vessel is perhaps a local imitation of an Assyrian bottle, judging by the great divergence from the original (e.g. Plate 99:7). The shape of the neck and the ridge at its base approximate the original.

This brief survey gives some indication of the interesting pottery phenomena to be found in regions bordering the great cultural centers.

---

1. The Ezion-Geber excavation has not yet been published; we are very grateful to Professor Nelson Glueck for his kind permission to publish here a selection of types from his material.

Photo 316. Incense-cup, IDA 40.674.

Photo 317. Chalice, IDA 40.557.

Photo 318. Jug, IDA 40.575.

Photo 319. Pilgrim-flask, IDA 40.599.

Photo 321. Cooking-pot, IDA 40.629.

Photo 322. Cooking-pot, IDA 40.602.

Photo 323. Fragment of a base of cooking-pot, IDA 40.656.

Photo 325. Jar, IDA 40.714.

Photo 326 Jar, IDA 40.715.

Photo 327. Lamp, IDA 40.551.

Photo 328. Assyrian bowl, IDA 40.577.

Photo 329. Fragment of an Assyrian bowl, IDA 40.616. ▶

Photo 330. Local imitation of Assyrian bottle, IDA 40.585. ▶

CHAPTER FOURTEEN

CULT VESSELS

The thirteen foregoing chapters have dealt solely with 'pots and pans,' a limitation imperative to a book of this sort, and, as a result, many subjects have had to be excluded. We should like to end the book, however, with one of the most intriguing of the many subjects omitted — cult vessels made of clay.

'Cult vessels' is a term which includes many categories both from sanctuaries and from tombs which we do not pretend to systematize here, either according to the type of the cult, or according to the type of vessel involved. A purely typological list of categories includes figurines, zoomorphic and anthropomorphic vessels, offering and libation vessels, incense-burners, and miniature votive vessels. In this last chapter we shall only touch upon three of these categories. The analysis of each category can be approached from a number of aspects. Technically, the vessels illustrated here certainly are more complex and more difficult to manufacture than ordinary household wares. Artistically, ability, imagination, and inventiveness were required to produce these vessels. As for the interpretation of these vessels, their functions, and the meaning of their decorations, these are inextricably bound up with problems of cult and religion in ancient civilizations.

The drawings and photographs assembled here show a number of types ranging from the Chalcolithic period to the Iron Age. A certain conservatism in cult customs is indicated by the persistence of several types throughout long periods. This conservatism is of particular interest when it spans the transition from period to period, and especially from one civilization to another, such as is the case between the Canaanite and the Israelite periods. However, this is not the place for discussing this or related problems of attributing vessels to any particular cult, or even for trying to trace back each type to its origin. All of these belong in the sphere of cultural rather than of ceramic history.

We shall briefly survey the types illustrated here according to the functions tentatively assigned to them, which are partly borne out by the evidence of wall reliefs and paintings of various cultures of the ancient Near East, and partly by logical inferences. Many ordinary household vessels were also used for cult purposes in temples and sanctuaries, to judge from the abundance of such common pottery found among the furniture, for example, of the Early Bronze III Sanctuary at Ai,[1] or in the Late Bronze Temple at Lachish,[2] or in the Iron II A (the Solomonic Stratum) house-shrine at Megiddo.[3] These domestic vessels, when found in temples, appear also to have had a cult function. Such pottery, however, has not been included in this chapter.

a) *Incense-burners, sometimes called incense-stands:* The main characteristic of this class is the fenestrated wall of the body of the vessel. We include here the two main types: 1) A high, mostly fenestrated cylindrical stand

---

1. Judith Marquet-Krause, *Les fouilles de 'Ay (Et-Tell)* 1933–1935, Paris, 1949, Rls LII–LIII, Nos. 1506–1507.
2. Lachish, II.
3. Megiddo, II, p. 44, figs. 100–102.

302

Photo 331. Incense-burner, fenestrated-pedestalled bowl, Beer-sheba, Chalcolithic

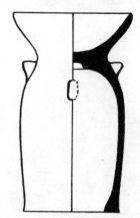

Photo 332. Incense-burner, pedestalled-bowl, Beth-shan, EBII, *MJ* (BS), Pl. IV.

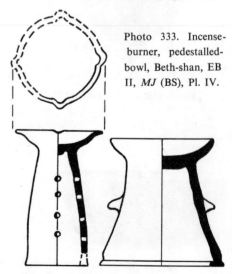

Photo 333. Incense-burner, pedestalled-bowl, Beth-shan, EB II, *MJ* (BS), Pl. IV.

Photo 334. Incense-burner, pedestalled-bowl, Beth-shan, EB III, *MJ* (BS), Pl. IX.

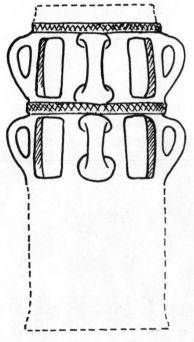

Photo 338. Carinated chalice with inner cup, joined by two holes, Megiddo, MB IIB, IDA 37.869.

Photo 335. Incense-burner, house-shaped, Ai, EB III, IDA 36.595.

Photo 336. Incense-burner, cylindrical, Nahariya, MB II A–B, *QDAP*, XIV, p. 17:10.

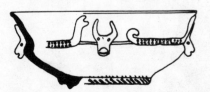

Photo 337. Incense-burner, pedestalled-bowl (pedestal missing), Megiddo, MB II B, *Meg.* II, Pl. 22.

topped by a bowl, the two made in one piece, Photos 331, 334, 341 and 348. 2) Stands of a similar form, but with the two parts made separately and therefore very rarely found together. Photo 342 shows such a composite vessel, where the two parts have been recovered.

Photos 336, 339, 343, 344, 345, and 349 show cylindrical fenestrated stands (one is perforated), decorated with human figures in high relief, animal paws, snakes, and painting. Making the two components separately may be connected with a given cult, but may also have been technically easier.

3) The house-shaped incense-burner, as illustrated by that from Ai, Photo 335, and a much later example from Beth Shan (Photo 346), and that from Megiddo (Photo 347). The relationship between the early and the late examples remains an open question.

b) *Libation vessels:* Ordinary jugs must have been used in performing libation rites, to judge from the scene on a stele from Ugarit,[4] where the worshipper is carrying such a jug in his hands while offering to the god El. In addition, some vessels of special character may be interpreted as suitable for libation, pouring, anointing, or mixing of liquids, like the beautiful carinated bowl with a tall cup built into it (Photo 338), and the well-known, but not fully understood, vessel designated as 'cup-and saucer' (Photo 340).

c) *Offering vessels:* A vessel of special character, the Kernos (Photo 350), originates in the Mycenaean-Minoan world, and is assumed to have been used in offering the first fruits. It consists of a hollow ring, upon which hollow miniature vessels, animal figures, and birds are perched.

Even this brief and fragmentary survey of cult vessels shows that Man used clay to express many of his spiritual, aesthetic, and religious needs and aspirations.

4. *ANEP*, fig. 493.

Photo 341. Incense-burner, pedestalled-bowl, Hazor, Iron I, *Hazor*, III-IV, Pl. CCCXLV.

Photo 339. Incense-burner, cylindrical high pedestal with a bowl, Lachish, LB I, IDA 34.7722/23.

Photo 343. Cylindrical fenestrated incense-burner, Megiddo, Iron I, IDA 36.1997.

Photo 344 Cylindrical fenestrated incense-burner, Ai, Iron I, IDA 36.575.

Photo 342. Cylindrical fenestrated pedestal with a bowl, Megiddo, Iron I, *Meg. Cult*, Pl. XX, The Oriental Institute, Chicago, No. A 20830.

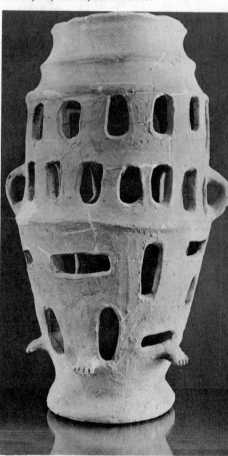

Photo 347. House-shaped incense-burner,
Megiddo, Iron I, IDA I.4447/1.

Photo 345. Cylindrical fenestrated incense-
burner, Beth-shan, Iron I, IDA P. 1803.

Photo 346. House-shaped incense-burner,
Beth-shan, Iron I, IDA P. 1804.

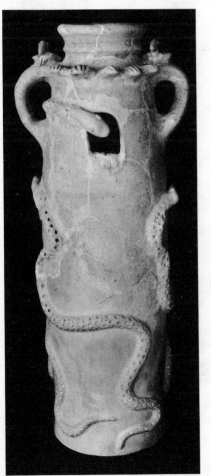

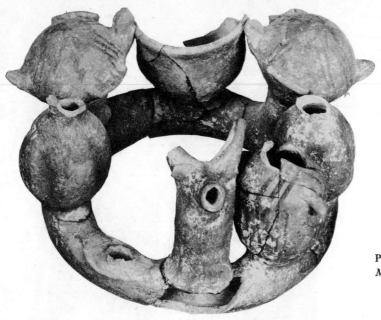

Photo 350. Kernos, Megiddo, Iron I, *Meg. Cult*, Pl. XVI.

Photo 340. Two Cup-and-saucer, Lachish, LB II, IDA 34.3071, 34.3066.

Photo 348. Incense-burner, fenestrated-pedestal with cup-and-saucer, Megiddo, Iron I, IDA I.3555.

Photo 349. Cylindrical incense-burner, Megiddo, Iron I, IDA 36.1925.

[Alacha-Hüyük]

Hattusa

[Alishar-Hüyük]

HATTI

Kanish

Troy

A R Z A W A

Mycenae

Tiryns

Miletus

Pylos

Terez
[Mersin]

Har-
Zank

Ugarit

CYPRUS Enkomi

Knossos

CRETE

Arvad
Arkhath

Ullaza

Gebal (Byblos)

Beeroth
Sidon

Tyre

Acco H.

Dor Megidd Be

M E D I T E R R A N E A N   S E A

Jaffa Sheche
Jerusalem

Ashkelon
Gaza

Baal-zephon

Beer-sheba

L I B Y A

Zoan-Ramses Migdol
Sile
Pithom Succoth

Kadesh-bar

[Tell al-Yahūdiyya]

Wilderness
of Paran

Memphis On [Heliopolis]

E D O M

[Sẽrabit
al-Khādim] Elath

[Jabal
Musa] [Dhahab]

[Beni Ḥasan]

[Tell el-Amarna]

0   100   200
|_____|_____|

km

Nile

RED SEA

Thebes